vulGar
modErnism

In the series
Culture and the Moving Image
edited by Robert Sklar

J. HOBERMAN

vulGar modErnism

Writing on Movies and Other Media

Temple University Press

Philadelphia

Temple University Press, Philadelphia
Copyright © 1991 by J. Hoberman. All rights reserved
Published 1991
Printed in the United States of America

The paper used in this publication meets the minimum requirements
of American National Standard for Information Sciences—Permanence
of Paper for Printed Library Materials, ANSI Z39.48–1984

Library of Congress Cataloging-in-Publication Data
Hoberman, J.
   Vulgar modernism : writing on movies and other media / J.
Hoberman.
      p.   cm. — (Culture and the moving image)
   Includes index.
   ISBN 0–87722–864–7 (cl.). — ISBN 0–87722–866–3 (pb.)
   1. Motion pictures.   2. Motion pictures—Reviews.   3. United
States—Popular culture.   I. Title.   II. Series.
PN1994.H58   1991
791.43—dc20   91–9287

PHOTO CREDITS
Part One: Maria Montez, courtesy Museum of Modern Art; Part Two: Robert De Niro in *The King of Comedy* (1982), courtesy Twentieth Century–Fox Film Corp.; Part Three: From Jean-Luc Godard's *Soft and Hard*; photo by Robin Holland, used with permission of the photographer; Part Four: Cinqué Lee and Youki Kudoh in Jim Jarmusch's *Mystery Train,* an Orion Classics release; photo by Sukita, copyright 1989 Mystery Train Inc.; Part Five: New Delhi, 1980; photo by J. Hoberman

Contents

Introduction
Facing the nineties

The regime of the movies is nearly one hundred years old. Centennial flurries are in the air: The motion picture camera was perfected in 1892; the first studio, Edison's notorious "Black Maria," opened in 1893; the projector that made possible the world's premiere motion picture, *Workers Leaving the Lumiere Factory,* was successfully demonstrated in 1895. The original special effect—typically a mistake (if we believe the perpetrator's no-doubt mythologized account)—was created in 1896 when Georges Méliès's camera jammed in the course of documenting a street scene and thus transformed an omnibus into a hearse. Méliès was making multi-scene "reconstructed" newsreels, the form we now call "docu-dramas," by 1899; his *Trip to the Moon,* the first international blockbuster, the *Star Wars* of the nickelodeon, was released in early 1902.

The movies are a youthful art but an elderly mass medium. As a means of expression, cinema is the protégé of theater, painting, and the novel; as an institution, it is the prototype for such subsequent mass-culture megaliths as the music industry, radio and television (which is also a form of cinema), comic books, mass-market paperbacks, theme parks, video games, popular journalism, and professional athletics. Beyond that, the movies have influenced virtually every human activity, from politics and warfare to sexual behavior and dreaming. The movies have defined "glamour." They have created new human types—stars, fans, celebrities, gossip-columnists—and blown them up to Brobdingnagian proportions.

Film may be the last modernist mode or the first postmodern one, but it has notoriously contaminated every other art form with which it has come in contact—most spectacularly the early twentieth-century novel. Commercial movies, frequently made in America, enchanted Futurists, Dadaists, and Surrealists, as did, to varying degrees, such other American mass-cultural modes as jazz, comic strips, and the tabloid press. The movies may or may not be a religion but, at least as emotionally primitive as they are technologically advanced, they are far closer than painting or drama to the cult origins of art. Cinema may or may not be a language, but it is certainly a literature: The movies are a body of interrelated, cross-referenced texts and these texts are not just individual films, but also stars, directors, genres, national industries, and more.

The movies are history. They are their own, of course—an increasingly self-conscious saga that (ever since the trickle of remakes that began innocently enough with *Farewell, My Lovely* in 1975 became a flood of recycled Jazz

Singing Scarfaced King Kong "landmarks," Roman numeral'd replays of old and recent mega-hits, and retired mixed-media figures pressed back into service) has flashed before our eyes like the life of a drowning swimmer. But they are also the century's, and even the individual's, history as well. The movies have insinuated themselves into people's memories, twined around the collective past and, in some ways, replaced it.

No art form was ever so ferociously popular yet, at the same time, so avant-garde—casually undermining the social mores and political institutions of the nineteenth century. Do movies know what they are doing? For the pioneer photographer Fox Talbot, one of the "charms" of his chosen medium was the potential for each picture to include things unknown to its maker, things that he or she might discover only later. This fortuitous quality, together with the immediate appeal of photographs as souvenirs, suggests that, mechanical though they may be, the camera-based arts are not without an unconscious—or a life of their own. Indeed, as Siegfried Kracauer has pointed out, as time goes by, the documentary aspect of a photographic object inevitably overshadows that object's original function: "Leafing through the family album, the grandmother will reexperience her honeymoon, while the children will curiously study bizarre gondolas, obsolete fashions, and the old young faces they never saw . . . pointing to odd bagatelles which the grandmother failed to notice in her day."

If the invention of photography compelled a new definition of art, the movies re-invented culture—in part by making the transitory material (pickling history and storing it in cans), in part by establishing an international mass audience and hence, an elaborate feedback system. ("When a film achieves a certain success, it becomes a sociological event and the question of its quality becomes secondary," observed Francois Truffaut.) Taken as a collective enterprise, the movies are America's pyramids, our ultimate time capsules, the closest thing we have to a universal mythology, the vessels of our second life.

Entertainment is serious business. American-ness and Americanization can virtually be defined by one's familiarity with that particular nexus of movies, pop music, television programs, sports events, and weekly newsmagazines we popularly term "the media." Umberto Eco cites the Halloween scene in *E.T.*, when the extraterrestrial is spontaneously drawn to an earth child costumed as a cuddly Yoda of *Star Wars,* as a joke which requires not just intercinematic but intermedia expertise to appreciate: "The addressee must know not only other movies but all the mass media gossip about movies." Eco calls this a "*Casablanca* universe" in which cult has become the normal way of enjoying movies. This particular casbah is our home.

There is a seamless quality to the *Casablanca* universe and yet it is the cinema, not the happening that (*pace* Susan Sontag) is the art of "radical juxtaposition." One's understanding of each individual shot is a factor of those shots which precede and follow it, and the image one sees is continually altered by its relation to the sound that accompanies it. The moviegoer habitually yokes together disparate elements in the service of a greater meaning and, in this sense, cinema hypostatizes that aspect of modernity most deeply ingrained in our daily lives—the violent montage of city streets, the absurd arrangements of news magazines and broadcast TV where reports on famine are sandwiched between advertisements for McDonald's and accounts of ozone depletion may be sponsored by GM.

Given the primacy of the image, one might expect that a science of movieology or film-analysis would be the central pursuit of the age. Why then does this imperial medium dwell in an intellectual ghetto (and "intellectual" movies in a back alley hidden deep within that ghetto)? The problem is not just the ignorance or snobbery of the literary intelligentsia—although that is a problem, manifested in the defensive elevation of selected middlebrow critics, as well as the reviews in *The New York Times* and *New York Review of Books*, which favor vapid star bios and rehashed popular history over original works of theory and scholarship. There is still something suspect in taking the movies too seriously—except, of course, as a business. (A reviewer for the *Frankfurter Zeitung* in the 1920s, Siegfried Kracauer considered his mission to unveil hidden ideological formations, to historicize movies, to break their influence. Today's movies have not been demystified by critics, but by the lawyers, accountants, publicists, and agents who run the industry.)

As the movies erupted from below, so did their intelligentsia. Where art critics are the descendents of patrons and connoisseurs, movie reviewers evolved out of fans. Andrew Sarris even titled his first collection *Confessions of a Cultist*. I'll never forget a particularly distinguished (and, equally, underappreciated) film intellectual's appalled response to an unpretentious underground filmmaker's encyclopedic knowledge of 1930s and 1940s Hollywood movies: "Don't tell me you're a *buff*." Movie buff—the term reeks of afternoons wasted in shabby theaters, midnights spent watching *The Late Late Show*. The problem, ultimately, may be that the world the movies present is so compelling, it shuts everything else out.

Movies are at once the most subjective of individual experiences, as well as the most public of public arts. The timing that elevates a routine thriller into a monumental blockbuster, the pressures that keep a Soviet movie under wraps for 20 years, are no less complex and mysterious than the drives that cathect people to a midnight cult movie or as potent and deep-rooted as those that inspire your fascinated loathing of a particular actor or actress.

Not for nothing was the first motion picture artist a professional magician nor Hollywood fondly known as the Dream Factory. Now, as in 1895, that movement on the screen is an illusion, made possible by a defect of the human eye known as "persistence of vision." The only true motion in motion pictures occurs behind our backs, up in the projection booth where thousands of individual images are beamed out at the rate of 24 per second. The problem is that—however many millions of dollars they cost to produce and market— movies exist, quite literally, in the heads of the people who watch them.

The movies, which developed in tandem with psychoanalysis, have always suggested a model for conscious and unconscious thought processes, a new form of industrialized day-dreams and individual nightmares, the vehicle for wish fulfillment and fantasy-projection on a mass scale. At the same time, however, the movies are a way of thinking.

TV IS THE quintessential postmodern form and its effect remains unpredictable. (What can one foresee for a medium whose prophets are the network comedian Ernie Kovacs, the Korean avant-garde composer Nam June Paik, and the Canadian Joyce-scholar Marshall McLuhan?) We may thank television that movies became juxtaposed with themselves—at least for the general public. Emerging from the French Cinematheque in the late 1950s, Jean-Luc Godard was among the first to understand that the period of classic cinema was over, or—put another way—to read film history as a text. This view was commonplace by the early 1960s, particularly in large American cities, where television provided a frame, placing a miniature cinematheque in every living room.

The revival, recirculation, and canonization of old movies was but one event in the construction of a new American cultural identity. (Others include the success of Pop Art, the discovery of the "media," the appreciation of the commercial roadside landscape, the worldwide triumph of rock'n'roll.) Thanks to television, the linear development by which one movie succeeded another, rolling off the Hollywood assemblyline, had been disrupted. Old movies were again new and, as in the earliest days of the media, new ideas came from outside (foreign films) and beneath (the so-called underground).

The film culture of the 1960s had the "all-over" energy of a Pollock canvas. The legendary Winter 1962/63 issue of *Film Culture* includes Andrew Sarris's "Notes on the Auteur Theory," Pauline Kael's appreciation of *Shoot the Piano Player,* Jack Smith's paean to Maria Montez, and Manny Farber's manifesto "White Elephant Art vs Termite Art," amid all manner of obscure enthusiasms, auto-interviews, reports, and historical documentations. In this sense, Farber was the decade's model critic (and mine, if I may wax confessional). Playing both ends off against the middlebrow, his pieces—published in periodicals ranging from *Commentary* to *Film Culture* to the second-string strokebook *Cavalier* to *Artforum*—were thick with inside references to painting, photography, and comic strips. Open to everything from action directors Sam Fuller and Don Siegal to underground figures such as the Kuchar brothers and Michael Snow to European synthesizers Chantal Akerman and R.W. Fassbinder (about whom Farber and his wife Patricia Patterson were the first American critics to write), Farber would claim in 1968 that "now people who take films seriously study skin flicks, TV commercials, scopitone."

This was the period of the so-called "film generation" and, for all the pretense such a term inspired, the mid-1960s was an ideal time to come to movie consciousness. There were no traditional authorities: If Hollywood was no longer hegemonic, "cinema studies" was not yet an academic discipline. I was 15 in 1964 when I started seriously going to the movies (16 when I began saving to buy an 8mm camera) and the field seemed rich and fertile and wide open. As a TV child, for whom 1930s pop was an integral part of 1950s *kinderkultur,* I already had a nascent film sense of everything-is-now; as a movie-struck adolescent, I encountered *Dr. Caligari* and *Dr. Strangelove* in the same year. Griffith and Eisenstein were as contemporary as Godard and Truffaut. The public libraries had only a handful of books on the history of film but for one fortunate enough to live in New York City, that history was remarkably available. In addition to the daily screenings at the Museum of Modern Art, there were *nouvelle vague* doublebills at the Bleecker Street Cinema, Hollywood revivals at the New Yorker, and—most exciting—the unpredictable nuttiness of the Film-makers' Cinematheque.

Movies seemed capable of being about anything—I can still remember my astonishment reading a *Village Voice* ad that described Stan Brakhage's *Dog Star Man* as a film about "the birth of the universe," my amazement at discovering *Touch of Evil* (on TV, of course) as a movie I'd never heard of rather than a masterpiece. Film artists seemed an endlessly variegated breed. A few years later, after Sarris published *The American Cinema*, it was remarkable to learn that, for example, *Invasion of the Body Snatchers* and *Baby Face Nelson* had been directed by the same person and that that person was something called an "auteur."

The 1960s was the period of radical innovators and extreme film practices: Brakhage's stream of consciousness, Warhol's outrageous identification with the camera, and, above all, Godard's meta-cinematic montage that spliced detective movies and Picasso, melodrama and vérité, film and video. Individual movies were public events: The provocations of *L'avventura, Last Year at Marienbad,* and *Flaming Creatures* may have been restricted to a coterie audience but, as the decade reached its climax, *Blow Up, Bonnie and Clyde,* and *2001* involved the country at large. Shaken on its pedestal, Hollywood was scarcely immune to the ecstatic breakdown. By 1969, five major studios were in the red. The movie industry suffered its own identity crisis—testing new limits and developing new formulae, scrambling to keep up with current attitudes, groping in the dark for the huge youth market, contributing to (even as it reflected) the prevailing delirium.

As in the early 1930s, but even more extremely, movies celebrated outsiders. The quintessential 1960s protagonists were criminals, crazies, draft dodgers, dope dealers, hustlers, and Indians—often played by recognizably "ethnic" stars and opposed by equally extreme law-and-order types. The old vérités had crumbled, anything was possible—at least until the rebirth, reconsecration, and reconsolidation of the industry that began in the mid-1970s, when the maverick revisionists (Robert Altman, Arthur Penn, Sam Peckinpah) and radical individuals (Stanley Kubrick, John Cassavetes, Dennis Hopper) who had flourished, after a fashion, were succeeded by a generation of television-bred, film school–educated directors known as the "movie brats."

If the 1960s brought a film culture of unprecedented plurality, however, the post-Vietnam period was characterized by an imperial self-absorption, a profound ignorance of world cinema and a corresponding disinterest—among American critics, even more than American audiences—in other people's movies. Where a dozen years earlier, Fellini and Bergman, Antonioni and

Godard were all known figures, their logical successors—Andrei Tarkovsky and Alexei Gherman, Hans-Jurgen Syberberg and Jean-Marie Straub, Marguerite Duras and Raul Ruiz, Chantal Akerman and Yvonne Rainer, Manoel De Oliviera and Werner Schroeter—were specialized tastes at best.

As studios were swallowed by conglomerates, the post 1960s consolidation was paralleled in other ways. A nostalgic new cinema of consensus had been anticipated by George Lucas's 1973 *American Graffiti*, the first Hollywood movie to periodicize the 1960s. Ironically, the possibility of making such small pictures diminished as costs dramatically escalated. In 1975, the average American movie cost a bit more than $3 million to make and market; in 1990, the cost was approaching $20 million. Although the number of studio releases declined steadily throughout the 1970s, the audience share of the ten top-grossing films tripled the growth rate of the film audience as a whole. The late 1970s brought a handful of movies—*Rocky* and *Close Encounters, Star Wars* and *Superman, Animal House* and *Grease*—that represented something like the genetic material for the next decade and a half, cloned and recombined. The new Hollywood could afford only one "real" artist—the Martin Scorsese of *Taxi Driver, Raging Bull,* and *The King of Comedy*. American critics could comprehend only one new national cinema—the West German "new wave" (itself hypostatized in the person of Fassbinder).

For Hollywood, June 1975 brought a vision of things to come, with two key movies—each in its way a brilliant modification of the multi-star, mounting-doom, intersecting plot format of *Earthquake* and *The Towering Inferno*. But, where Robert Altman's *Nashville* exploded the "disaster film," Steven Spielberg's *Jaws* imploded it. The 28-year-old Spielberg stripped down the genre and turned it into a pure mechanism. *Jaws* signaled the arrival of "high concept," a term Spielberg defined in a 1978 interview: "If a person can tell me the idea in 25 words or less, it's going to make a pretty good movie."

Nashville offered a critique, however flawed, of mass culture and demographic packaging; *Jaws* demonstrated its power. Opening simultaneously at 500 theaters on a wave of saturation television advertising, it became the top-grossing movie ever—for two years, that is, until the release of George Lucas's *Star Wars* (that "subliminal history of the movies, wrapped in a riveting tale of suspense and adventure," per *Time*). If, as Robert Evans, then Paramount's head of production, had announced in 1974, "the making of a blockbuster is the newest art form of the 20th century," Lucas and Spielberg were budding Michelangelos.

With Francis Coppola as their avatar and *Jaws* as proof of their manifest destiny, Spielberg, Lucas, and their epigones elevated drive-in monster movies, Abbott and Costello–style slapstick, rock'n'roll musicals, Saturday-morning science fiction—the most vital and disreputable genres of their youth—to cosmic heights. In a certain sense, these so-called movie brats were Hollywood's delayed *nouvelle vague*. As ambitious, self-confident, and steeped in American cinema as the French boys who haunted the French Cinematheque during the 1950s, they brought an unprecedented degree of celluloid erudition to their creations. The *Casablanca* universe came into its own: Films swarmed with allusions to *Psycho* and *The Searchers*, not to mention *Rebel Without a Cause*, *Forbidden Planet*, and *The Wizard of Oz*.

Unlike Godard, however, the young American directors did not see this sort of intertextuality as part of a larger cultural critique. The movies seemed lost in a hall of mirrors. Thus, the medium was enlisted in that particular aspect of postmodernism in which, as Frederic Jameson wrote, the past becomes "a vast collection of images," a photographic simulacrum "in which the history of aesthetic styles displaces 'real' history." In this light, we can only express our amazement and gratitude for a work like Claude Lanzmann's *Shoah*, which uses the resources of cinema not to recreate the past, but to give it presence.

Rather than deconstruct the Hollywood system, movie brats strove to resurrect its greatest triumphs. Where *Alphaville* disassembled the religion of pulp against a relentlessly contemporary backdrop, *Star Wars* and *Indiana Jones* carefully put it all back together in a "timeless" realm of pure entertainment. Where Altman's *The Long Goodbye* exposed the contradictions in the myth of the saintly private eye through a canny juxtaposition of the 1940s and the 1970s, Lawrence Kasdan's *Body Heat*, another contemporary thriller, used the plot devices, lighting, and compositional cliches of 1940s noir, as well as nostalgic 1940s costumes, to fabricate a museum waxwork of a passé Hollywood style—a remake without an original. (The fetishization of this lost Hollywood stimulated a hot market in movie memorabilia with Spielberg and Lucas among the major collectors, and *Casablanca*, *Gone With the Wind*, *Citizen Kane*, and *The Wizard of Oz* the top four collectable properties.) What seemed jarring or radical in Godard was here harmonious—a form of Trivial Pursuit, used to connote the past or provide a sense of pseudo-historical depth. As Marx did to Hegel, the movie brats stood Godard on his head.

But, of course, it is Walt Disney (rather than Godard) who is the spiritual father of the New Hollywood—not the Depression-era Disney of Mickey Mouse and *Fantasia*, the man whom Sergei Eisenstein called the American people's "greatest contribution to art," so much as the Uncle Walt of the 1950s, the Disney of TV and theme park. Disney was the first to saturate America systematically with cultural trademarks, to fabricate a world that was better than nature (even as he denatured one childhood "classic" after another), to use television to create a system of self-perpetuating hype. It's one of those wondrous historical coincidences that Ronald Reagan was included in the troika of TV personalities to host the grand opening of Disneyland in 1955 and that, 30 years later, the theme park presented the most compelling metaphor for his vision of America.

Following Disney, the successful Hollywood movie is an increasingly uninteresting bridge between the multi-media barrage of pre-release promotion and a potential package of spin-offs, career moves, and ancillary products. Indeed, because most critics can only write about films before people see them—thumbs up or down like parody Roman emperors—they are only another part of the vast publicity machine devoted to inculcating the urge-to-see.

MASS CULTURE RIVALS military hardware as the leading American export; the movie industry boasts of contributing a three-billion-dollar surplus to the balance of trade. And yet there are days when the movies seem like a brief interlude between the invention of photography and the perfection of television; the once-imperial medium stands on the brink of obsolescence and will have to be protected like the bald eagle or grand opera. The last bastions of popular cinemas—India and East Asia—will not long hold out against the onslaught of TV. The demise of state-subsidized cinema in Eastern Europe bids to remove another stronghold of film culture.

In the United States, moviegoing has long since ceased to be a national habit for just about everyone but teenagers and professionals. Still, the movies themselves remain a privileged instrument in the symphony orchestra of American mass culture. Unlike TV, they are larger than life. Entertainment aside, the movies function as social metaphors, showcase utopian possibilities, present new personality types, and provide socially cohesive cocktail-party conversation.

The making of the blockbuster was not only the century's newest art form. The Hollywood blockbuster is something like the r&d of American politics and vice versa—they are parallel activities. (In putting adultery on the public agenda, presidential candidate Gary Hart paved the way for *Fatal Attraction*— the most popular movie of 1987, the sound of the other shoe dropping.) Both politicians and producers seek to generate consensus by inventing images and fabricating scenarios that appeal to the greatest number of spectator/consumers.

"The good film critic is only conceivable as a critic of society," wrote Siegfried Kracauer in 1932, after a decade of reviewing movies. Now the reverse is also true. Our popular culture and electoral politics are symbiotic—together they constitute our social spectacle, an imperfect but not altogether unresponsive, mass-mediated feedback system. We live in a world of symbols and signs, governed by sound-bite and photo-opportunity. The electorate is an audience; the fan magazine has become the model for popular journalism.

This development is scarcely restricted to America: Several Indian states have been governed by star-politicians since the 1970s; movie demiurges have established power bases in Brazil and the Philippines. The actor-director Yilmaz Güney became a powerful political symbol in Turkey; Hans-Jürgen Syberberg's *Hitler, a Film from Germany* explicated the staying power of a dead star even more potent than Elvis. (Our continuing fascination with the Nazis is not only that they represent an absolute evil, but that they pioneered spectacular politics—mass rallies, orchestrated media campaigns, and pseudo-documentaries meant to glorify a star-leader.)

It is in America, however, that the politics of the spectacle have reached their peak of development. Ronald Reagan's peers were not Jimmy Carter and Richard Nixon, but *Dirty Harry, Rambo,* and Bruce "The Boss" Springsteen. No one is really surprised that, three months after taking office, President George Bush was reported in *The New York Times* to have "taken an adjustment"—an acting term for slipping into character. Our public life not only includes elections, trials, and congressional hearings, but events created to be viewed. How does one distinguish between the Conquest of Grenada and the D-Day celebration, between Liberty Weekend and the Bombing of Libya, between the Invasion of Panama and "We Are the World"? (Still, the spectacle is not altogether monolithic. Mass culture now has its own dialectic. The rise of Rambo was necessary to the success of *Platoon*—the beginning of the working through of what Time-Life, Inc. called "the Vietnam experience" in spectacular form.)

For a half dozen years we were enchanted by the Reagan movie—a saga that began with a near-successful assassination by a deranged moviegoer who had taken a popular film as his text and hoped to impress a movie star with his act and culminated with the 1984 presidential campaign, an election dominated by TV slogans and movie imagery. In its most virulent form, the mass Reaganism of 1984—a true pop phenomenon like Beatlemania or the Davy Crockett craze—was a combination of yearning and denial, puritanism and greed, all tied up in one jumbo family-sized package of all-natural space-aged old-fashioned new-improved jingoistic hooplah.

The image held America—and even the outside world—spellbound. Jean Baudrillard, the poet laureate of the 1980s, saw "the unintelligible rise of the dollar," "the fabulous apotheosis of New York," "the international success of *Dallas*" (all unstable phenomena to be sure) as proof that America had retained its political and cultural power. And yet, unlike the 1950s ("when power held power"), this was "power as a special effect," a political decline masked by public relations ascendancy. America, as Baudrillard put it, pondering the aggressive, feel-good patriotism that flowed from commercials for automobiles and beer, appeared "fascinated by itself as a lost object." America seemed imaginary to itself—witness the persistent series of movies that derived their dramatic or comic punch from the spectacle of an alien/immigrant/extra-terrestrial/mermaid coming to America and finding it somehow stranger than paradise. Reagan orchestrated a last hurrah even as the sitcom bromides he espoused were being supplanted by the eternal now of MTV's blithe amnesia.

Given the vast recirculation of cultural images that characterized the era, it should hardly be surprising that—so far as the movies went—the great unifying cause was the scandal of colorization. For the film community, this reminder that movies were a commodity occasioned the sort of op-ed outrage with which neo-conservative intellectuals greeted the elevation of movies to the Western cultural canon. But, rather than a desecration, the application of drab, patently false-looking hues to the black-and-white movies of the 1940s was the poor producer's postmodernism—the attempt to turn *The Maltese Falcon* into *Body Heat* and make *Casablanca* rival *Raiders of the Lost Ark*.

Indeed, colorization seems the last decade's master metaphor. The nostalgic public life in the Reagan era resembled nothing so much as a colorized 1950s during which even the propagandist modes of the early Cold War lurched back into life. Rarely has any decade represented so discreet a historic package as the

1980s. How eerily satisfying that an era whose opening attractions—Ronald Reagan and the VCR, MTV and *E.T.*—might be considered the apotheosis of American mass culture should end with collapse of the Cold War order, the end of European communism, and the decline of American economic hegemony. Two utopias bite the dust.

ALL OF THE pieces in this book—reviews, review-essays, and overviews—were written and published during the 1980s and, save for the elimination of superfluous topical references, typographical errors, and some blatant infelicities, I have let them stand as they first appeared—a report on the decade from the inside, rather than a revisionist view. I have resisted the temptation to soften my polemics, even when they now seem tinged by that occupational hazard of media criticism, technological determinism. If "The Super-80s," "Vini, Vidi, Video . . ." and "What's Art Got to Do with It?" now appear to me naively optimistic views of super-8, video, and music videos, "Fear and Loathing at the Whitney" is an overly pessimistic assessment of what is called avant-garde film.

My aim, in every case, was to intervene as well as report. (I backed into film criticism after an abortive career as a purveyor of mixed media spectacles and found-footage assemblages and I suppose that I am still finding footage and remaking it in my head.) These pieces, most of which were written under deadline pressure and appeared in *The Village Voice,* were part of the spectacle and cannot be detached from their specific moment. I thank my editors for their support, their patience, and their ideas—Karen Durbin, M. Mark, and Howard Feinstein at the *Voice;* Ingrid Sischy at *Artforum*; Richard Corliss and Harlan Jacobson at *Film Comment*—as well as the John Simon Guggenheim Foundation, which, in granting me a fellowship, permitted me a respite from weekly film criticism and the luxury to assess just what I had been doing for the past dozen years.

J. Hoberman
New York City
January 1991

Mapping a Position, 1980–1982

OnE

Bad movies

Originally published in *Film Comment*, July 1980.

THERE ARE A number of reasons to consider bad movies. The most obvious is that tastes change; that many, if not most, of the films we admire were once dismissed as inconsequential trash; and that trash itself is not without certain socio-aesthetic charms. Then too, bad movies have a pedagogic use value—the evolution of film form has largely been based upon mistakes. A third reason is that movies, to a certain degree, have a life of their own. They mix the documentary with the fictional, and the worst inadvertancies of one can easily overwhelm the best intentions of the other. That is, it is possible for a movie to succeed *because* it has failed.

With their perverse, pioneering affection for the detritus of industrial civilization, the Surrealists were the first to cultivate an appreciation for bad movies. "The best and most exciting films [are] the films shown in local fleapits, films which seem to have no place in the history of cinema," advises Ado Kyrou in *Le Surréalisme au Cinéma*. "Learn to go see the 'worst' films; they are sometimes sublime." This taste for Elixir of Potboiler—junky spectacles, cheap horror flicks, anonymous pornography, juvenile swashbucklers, movies "scorned by critics, charged with cretinism or infantilism by the old defenders of rationality"—was based on the innate capacity of such films to produce (if only in random moments) that "crux of Surrealism," *le merveilleux*.

The Surrealists courted disorientation: A film had a dreamlike latent content—and this could be precipitated by deranging or bypassing the manifest content of its storyline. During World War I, the young André Breton used to wander from movie-house to movie-house, entering mid-film, leaving for the next once the plot became apparent. By the time Breton became Surrealism's Black Pope, this practice had been elevated and refined into the principle of synthetic criticism. The ideal Surrealist spectator habitually broke open a film's continuity to liberate individual images from the prison of the narrative. Thus the American para-Surrealist Joseph Cornell created his 1936 masterpiece *Rose Hobart* by distilling a studio adventure film, *East of Borneo* (Columbia, 1931), into twenty-four non-linear minutes and projecting it at silent speed through a piece of blue glass to the accompaniment of the song "Holiday in Brazil."

For all their admiration for the "worst" films, and despite their propensity for deconstructing movies inside their heads, the Surrealists developed no canon of films so incoherent that *they unmade themselves*—films that transcend taste and might be termed *objectively bad*. Surrealist bad movies are lurid, oneiric, delirious. An objectively bad movie is all this and more.

"A BAD ACTOR," wrote the underground cinéaste Jack Smith, "is rich, unique, idiosyncratic, revealing." The same may be said for the objectively bad film, and for similar reasons. Smith, who began experimenting with bad acting in *Flaming Creatures* (1962), was undoubtedly thinking of his favorite star, the paradigmatic Camp icon Maria Montez. In part, his appreciation for her vehicles is a Surrealist taste. Infantile fantasies like *White Savage, Ali Baba and the Forty Thieves,* and *Sudan* are founts of inane, voluptuously exotic imagery. Smith was moved by their poetry.

But there is another aspect as well. It was precisely because Montez was so unconvincing an actress that Smith valued her performances: "One of her atrocious acting sighs suffused a thousand tons of dead plaster with imaginative life and a truth." The truth is that Montez is always herself. Montez vehicles are unintended documentaries of a romantic, narcissistic young woman dressing up in pasty jewels, striking fantastic poses, queening it over an all-too-obviously make-believe world. For Smith, her inept portrayals of Scheherezade, the Cobra Woman, and the Siren of Atlantis hyperbolized the actual situation of a Holly-wood glamour goddess. Montez's transparent role-playing, and her uncon-cealed delight at being the center of attention, were more authentic to him than the naturalism achieved by *successfully* phony actresses. The often poignant, heightened realism induced by such a failure to convince is the key to the objectively bad film.

The conventional narrative film does not demand anything so gross as a suspension of disbelief; it only asks an indulgent acceptance of its own diegetic, or fictive, space. The badly-made, unconvincing film confounds this minimal requirement by ignoring or (more often) bungling the most rudimentary pre-cepts of screen naturalism. I once saw a porn film set in Outer Space that used a suburban kitchen as the set for its rocket control room. The bluntness with which this profilmic reality disrupted the diegetic web produced a more vivid sense of science fiction than anything in *2001*.

The theoretician Noel Burch has identified a-conventional narrative films (exceptions to what he calls the "institutional mode of representation") in pre-1905 and non-Western cinema. An early Japanese talkie like *Wife! Be Like a Rose* (1935) may not fully subscribe to the institutionalized codes, but it cannot be considered badly made: the unorthodox eyeline-matches in reverse-angle sequences, odd cutaways and sound bridges, and impossible point-of-view shots are only subtly jarring. An objectively bad film, on the other hand, casually promotes perceptual havoc—as casually as the 3-D cheapster *Robot Monster* (1953) incorporated special effects lifted without modification from the two-dimensional *One Million B.C.*

Objectively bad movies are usually made against all odds in a handful of days on a breathtakingly low budget. Such extreme austerity enforces a deliri-ous pragmatism: homemade sets, no retakes, tacky special effects, heavy re-liance on stock footage. The objectively bad film attempts to reproduce the institutional mode of representation, but its failure to do so deforms the sim-plest formulae and clichés so absolutely that you barely recognize them. They must be actively decoded. In Edward D. Wood, Jr.'s *Bride of the Monster* (1956), a film that employs so many inappropriate reaction shots that it sug-gests a combined Kuleshov-Rorschach test, a secretary abruptly picks up a phone and starts talking. Did the director overlook the necessity of dialing? Did he forget to post-dub the sound of the ring? An actress in Oscar Micheaux's *God's Stepchildren* (1937) shakes her head and declares "No . . . emphatically . . . no." Belatedly, one realizes she has incorporated the script's stage direction into her lines.

Poor acting and ludicrous dialogue—though axiomatic to bad filmmaking—do not in themselves make an objectively bad movie. Neither does an absurd plot; if it did, D.W. Griffith, Josef von Sternberg, and Samuel Fuller would all be bad filmmakers. In fact to be objectively bad, a film must relentlessly draw one's attention away from its absurd plot. For Walter Benjamin (and even André Bazin), the seamless "equipment-free aspect of reality" that movies presented on screen was actually the "height of artifice." The objectively bad film acknowledges this: the lie of "chronology" is confounded by imperfect continuity; "invisible" editing is ruptured by mismatched cuts; *mise en scène* is foregrounded by cloddish bits of business. A good bad movie is a philosopher's stone that converts the incompetent mistakes of naïve dross into modernist gold. Such movies are unstable objects. They ping-pong back and forth from diegetic intent to profilmic event (or to their own jerry-built construction) the way a Cezanne oscillates between a representational landscape and a paint-gopped canvas.

Objectively bad films are almost always targeted at the most exploitable or *lumpen* sections of the movie audience (ethnic minorities, teen-agers, sub-literates, 42nd Street derelicts). Like every other sort of movie, however, the best bad films are personal, even obsessive works. Some guy had a story to tell and he was going to punch it across by whatever impoverished means were at hand. "For the budget, and for the time, I felt I had achieved greatness," said Phil Tucker of his $16,000 *Robot Monster*. The best bad movies add nutty ambition and auteurist signatures to their already-heady atmosphere of free-floating *meshugas*. "There is a very short distance between high art and trash," observed Douglas Sirk. (Who would know better than he?) "And trash that contains the element of craziness is by this very quality nearer to art." A supremely bad movie—an anti-masterpiece—projects a stupidity as awesome as genius.

THESE THOUGHTS WERE prompted in part by the World's Worst Film Festival, held at the Beacon Theatre in Manhattan. The series was itself inspired by *The Fifty Worst Films of All Time* and *The Golden Turkey Awards,* a pair of humorous non-books researched by teenaged Harry Medved and written by his older brother Michael. The Medved position—if we discount its patina of *Mad* magazine masochism and resolve to stomach its facetious tone—also suggests that the best bad movies are akin to masterpieces.

"In both cases," according to the Medveds, "the viewer marvels at the range of human imagination and creativity." Another way to put it is that anti-masterpieces break the rules with such exhilaration as to expand our definition of what a movie can be. *They Saved Hitler's Brain* (1958? 1964?), the most structurally inventive film shown at the World's Worst Film Festival, surpasses the temporal complexity of *Muriel* by intercutting two radically different movies. The first is elaborately lighted and was filmed on studio sets by Stanley Cortez; the second, involving a completely distinct set of actors, was shot *vérité*-style in 16mm some six years later. These two strands are densely interwoven, sometimes even within a single scene. Watching it, your head bursts with ideas.

Peter Bogdanovich once produced a similar, if less bewildering exercise in creative geography when Roger Corman commissioned him to add shots of Mamie Van Doren and other Venusian cuties to a womanless Soviet sci-fi film whose rights A.I.P. had acquired. But whereas Bogdanovich's *Voyage to the Planet of the Prehistoric Women* is wittily schematic, *T.S.H.B.* (as its fans in the Beacon lobby were heard to refer to it) is unpredictable and irrational. The logic it entails is so unfathomable, the shifts in its action so abrupt, that you have to pinch yourself to make sure it isn't a hallucination.

The Medveds' most sincere defense of bad movies, stated in the prefaces to both their books, is that "people show greater enthusiasm in laughing together over films they despise than trying to praise films they admire." There's a self-serving aspect to this questionable observation, but its implications are not without interest. By their unintentional "success," bad movies deflate the claims of more serious works—and they are leveling in other ways. It's reassuring, the Medveds suggest, to discover that the "larger-than-life demigods" of Hollywood are also fallible, even clumsy. Beneath the Medveds' glibness is an inchoate protest against the colonization of the imagination by ready-made, seamless dreams.

Obviously, the Medveds' appreciation of badness differs from that of the Surrealists, or of Jack Smith. While the former valorized bad movies for their "beauty," and the latter prized bad acting for its "truth," the Medved aesthetic is an affirmation of the American Way: "Absolutely anyone can recognize a lousy film when he sees one."

This democratic assertion raises hopes that the Medved books will be treasuries of objectively bad films. But although many of their "Fifty Worst" are bad to the degree that they are laughable, few are bad enough to be pleasurable, let alone radical. The book—from which aspiring screenwriter Michael prudently withheld his name—is mainly a collection of ponderous mediocrities (*Valley of the Dolls, Northwest Mounted Police*), famous flops (Ross Hunter's *Lost Horizon, Myra Breckinridge*), and lame performances by well-known stars (John Wayne as The Conqueror, Clark Gable as Parnell).

The Medveds are alive to the qualities of a *Robot Monster,* but they haven't the imagination to distinguish between purely conceptual (hence, unwatchable) absurdities like the all-midget *Terror of Tiny Town* or the Ronald Reagan–Shirley Temple match-up in *That Hagen Girl* and *films maudit* like *Bring Me the Head of Alfredo Garcia* or *Exorcist II: The Heretic.* This is not so much a factor of their petulant philistinism (they include *Last Year at Marienbad* and *Ivan the Terrible* among the Fifty Worst) as it is of the ingrained literary bias which has them habitually judging films by their bad dialogue and humorously negative reviews.

The Golden Turkey Awards, The Fifty Worst Films's more sleekly packaged sequel (it gives prizes in thirty categories from "The Worst Two-Headed Transplant Movie Ever Made" to "The Most Inane and Unwelcome 'Technical Advance' in Hollywood History"), is something of a corrective. Having solicited suggestions from readers of the first book, the Medveds shift the emphasis of their second away from punishing star vehicles to horror and sci-fi cheapsters—films which labor under the double burden of having to make the supernatural, as well as their own fictive space, appear convincing. Indicative of this reorientation is the canonization of the previously unmentioned *Plan Nine from Outer Space* (1959) and its director Edward D. Wood, Jr. as, respectively, "The Worst Film of All Time" and "The Worst Director of All Time."

NOT SURPRISINGLY, THE Worst Director of All Time was well represented at the World's Worst Film Festival with *Plan Nine, Bride of the Monster,* and the 1952 *I Changed My Sex* (also known as *Glen or Glenda?*). Writer-director-editor Wood featured Bela Lugosi in all three: and the presence of this broken-down star (in some respects a tragic male counterpart to Maria Montez) contributes to their atmosphere of rancid glitz. A sense of Hollywood Boulevard Babylon pervades Wood's universe. It's not surprising to learn that he ended up directing hard-core porn, and that his last opus was an 8mm "home study" segment of *The Encyclopedia of Sex*.

Wood evidently played Svengali to an entourage of *Day of the Locust* weirdos. His movies are less the products of Hollywood's Poverty Row than the fantasies of a parallel Skid Row populated by show biz oddities (Criswell, the TV prophet; Tor Johnson, the 400-pound Swedish wrestler; Vampira, the beatnik ghoul-girl), haggard has-beens (Lugosi, Lyle Bettger), and the talentless progeny of the money-men who bankrolled him. The pitifully emaciated Lugosi gives a particularly painful performance in *Bride of the Monster,* playing a mad scientist with a spare lightstand as the centerpiece to his art *povera* laboratory. Against all odds, Lugosi clings to shreds of his professionalism. One watches in horrified admiration as he shifts gears from enraged ranting to bathetic wimpering to insane cackling in a single, brutally endless take, or when he gamely pretends to struggle in the outstretched tentacles of an unmoving rubber octopus.

A casual *mise en scène* of half-dressed sets and visible Klieg lights is Wood's hallmark, and everywhere in his oeuvre one finds a naive faith in the power of montage. Wood was left with only two minutes of Lugosi footage when the star died early in the production of what became *Plan Nine from Outer Space*. His solution was to hire a stand-in, have him wrap his face in a cape, and use the Lugosi material anyway. Wood's action montages are so perfunctory as to be a slap in the face of public taste. *Plan Nine* features a shamelessly lackadaisical battle sequence fashioned out of scratchy World War II newsreels, inserts of wobbly tinfoil space ships, and a uniformed actor peering through fieldglasses, a white backdrop behind him. The "monster" in *Bride of the Monster* is a squid filmed through the glass of an aquarium tank; the bargain basement apocalypse (and utter non-sequitur) that ends the movie is a single shot of an atomic mushroom cloud. With a similar economy of means, every significant moment—and there are many—in *I Changed My Sex* is punctuated with the identical flash of stock-footage lightning. Wood's fondness for dramatic inserts is balanced by a startling refusal to use cross-cutting to create tension. Characters chase each other around the frame instead.

Plan Nine begins with the psychic Criswell shrilly wondering if our nerves can stand the "idea of grave-robbers from outer space," and ends with his declaration that what we have just seen was based on sworn testimony. ("Can you prove it didn't happen?" he asks in a phrase that might have served Wood as his motto.) Sandwiched between Criswell's two appearances are sequences of people knocked out of their lawn chairs by the "death-ray" of an off-screen flashlight; Vampira haunting a cardboard cemetery that, no matter the time of day in contiguous shots, exists as a zone of perpetual night; extras grinning at the camera and pointing overhead to where a flotilla of flying saucers is supposedly strafing their car.

Plan Nine is Wood's most enjoyable movie; but it is the didactic, exploitational *I Changed My Sex* that offers the key to his work. The structure and thesis of this remarkable film are far too convoluted to summarize briefly. Suffice to say that its parallel "case histories" (one a screwball explanation of transvestism; the other a ponderous depiction of a transsexual operation) are set within a thicket of multiple narratives and framed by cutaways to an omniscient Bela Lugosi surrounded by human skeletons and shrieking, "The story must be told."

The story must be told indeed. *I Changed My Sex* is a possible psychodrama and, at least, a partial autobiography. According to the Medveds, the mustachioed Wood affected women's pantsuits, pantyhose, and angora sweaters, and bragged he had worn a brassiere beneath his World War II combat fatigues. Low budgets and heavy drinking may account for the spectacular lapses of Wood's *mise en scène,* but his artistic personality (a subject surely for further research) was obviously bound up in this most primitive form of make-believe. The unconvincing magic, crackpot logic, and decomposing glamour of Wood's films are in fact a mirror of his own life. Dressed like a tacky transvestite out of *Flaming Creatures,* he played at being a megaphone-brandishing director with the demented conviction of Maria Montez impersonating a movie star. His films, like hers, intimate the full lunacy and pathos of Southern California. He deserves the title of World's Worst Director.

And yet, there is another filmmaker whose anti-masterpieces are so profoundly troubling and whose *weltanschauung* is so devastating that neither the Medveds nor the World's Worst Film Festival are equipped to deal with him. In fact, five decades after their release, his films still have no place in the history of cinema. I refer to the work of Oscar Micheaux.

I think of Micheaux as the Black Pioneer of American film—not just because he was a black man, or because in his youth he pioneered the West, or because he was the greatest figure in "race" movies and an unjustly ignored force in early American cinema. Micheaux is America's Black Pioneer in the way that André Breton was Surrealism's Black Pope. His movies throw our history and movies into an alien and startling disarray.

Micheaux's last film, aptly titled *The Betrayal,* opened in New York in 1948. "There is simply no point in trying to apply normal critical standards . . . or in trying to describe its monumental incompetence as movie-making," wrote *PM,* while the *Times* reported that it contained "sequences so gauche as to provoke embarrassed laughter." The *Herald-Tribune* was bluntest: "A preposterous, inept bore . . . Acting that is worse than amateurish but this is not even its worst flaw. Micheaux's dialogue is even worse, with senseless and unmouthable lines; his concept of human beings is absurd and his direction somewhat less artful than one would expect of home-movies. The fact that Micheaux expects one to watch this [trash] for more than three hours is a monstrous piece of miscalculation." Were the above reviews to greet a film opening tomorrow, one might rush to see it on the assumption that only a powerful originality could goad the jaded reviewers of the daily press to such fury. Edward Wood may be the Worst, but Oscar Micheaux (1884–1951) is the Baddest—with all that that implies.

Only the barest facts of Micheaux's life are in the record. He was a native of Illinois who, after several years of work as a Pullman porter, purchased a homestead for himself on the sparsely settled South Dakota plains. Inspired by Booker T. Washington, he began writing a series of thinly novelized auto-biographical tracts, which he published and distributed himself. In 1919 his third novel, *The Homesteader,* attracted the attention of one of the several black-owned movie studios that had sprung up in response to the segregated policies of American movie theaters (as well as to counter *The Birth of a Nation*). Micheaux stipulated in the sale of the screen rights that he would direct the film. When the deal fell through, he raised capital among his public and made *The Homesteader* himself.

After this audacious start, Micheaux went on to be one of the most tenacious filmmakers who ever lived. Against all odds, over the next twenty-one years (with *The Betrayal* in 1948), he wrote, directed, and produced some thirty features. His method of distribution was an elaboration of the set-up he'd used to sell his novels. He would drive across the country, stop at each ghetto theater, show the owner his new script, hype his performers ("the Black Valentino," "the Sepia Mae West"), and ask for an advance against the gate. When he had accumulated sufficient capital, he returned to New York and shot the film. Micheaux's silent pictures were more topical, more lurid, and more critical than those of other black filmmakers.

The painful ambivalence of Micheaux's racial attitudes is one reason why his films are rarely screened and less frequently written about. There seems to be a tacit agreement among scholars of black cinema to avoid discussing this aspect of his work—particularly as he is sometimes offered as a role-model for black directors and his name has been appropriated for the award given those artists inducted into the Black Filmmakers Hall of Fame. Donald Bogle, the only black critic to my knowledge who discusses Micheaux's talkies at length, describes them as depicting "a fantasy world where blacks were just as affluent, just as educated, just as 'cultured,' just as well-mannered—in short, just as white—as white America."

But Micheaux's never-never land is underscored with an almost unbearable bitterness. Despite their fantasy overlay, his films are frought with fury and despair. When the madam of a Chicago brothel in *The Exile* (1931) is reproached by her Abyssinian lover for vamping him away from his studies, she contemptuously replies that "there are enough Negro doctors and lawyers already" and that he'd only end up as a shyster or abortionist. "Colored men will sell out anyone for fifty cents" is a typically blunt comment made in the suggestively titled *Lyin' Lips* (1939); and the Harlem chapter of the Communist Party succeeded in temporarily driving *God's Stepchildren* (1937) off the screen, in part because of its hero's contention that "only one Negro in a thousand tries to think."

ONE SUSPECTS THAT Micheaux never reconciled himself to the ugly fact that, in a segregated white society, his options were severely limited. After all, in his cultivation of the West and in his success as a self-made entrepreneur, he was as American as anyone—if not more so. Trapped in a ghetto, but unwilling or unable to directly confront America's racism, Micheaux displaced his rage on his own people. In other words, part of the price that he paid for his Americanness was the internalization of American racial attitudes. Hence his horrified fascination with miscegenation and "passing," his heedless blaming of the victim, his cruel baiting of fellow blacks. *God's Stepchildren,* the imitation *Imitation of Life* which epitomizes Micheaux's complex, contradictory mixture of self-hatred and remorse, forms an essential triptych with *The Birth of a Nation* and *The Searchers.* They are the three richest, most harrowing delineations of American social psychology to be found on celluloid.

Micheaux's films were willed into existence with such strenuous singlemindedness, with so massive a determination to make them tell a story no matter what that, both in form and content, they open up a chasm between intent and actualization almost unprecedented in the history of film. Intricate narratives were based around two or three reshuffled sets (usually the homes of friends), and entire—often violent—scenes were shot in a single take.

Micheaux's films define objective badness. His camera ground relentlessly on while the key light wandered, traffic noise obliterated the dialogue, or a soundman's arm intruded upon the frame. Actors blew their cues, recovered, and continued. Wasting nothing, he re-used footage with impunity, carried the post-dubbing of his soundtracks to the outer limits of possibility, saved up his out-takes and fashioned them into second films. Micheaux films seize every opportunity to announce themselves as constructs. They are embellished with gratuitous cheesecake, tricked out with "red herring" mystery music, padded with obscurely dangling parallel action, and rife with lengthy cabaret sequences which cut his costs by providing the performers he recruited with "free advertising" in lieu of pay.

As Micheaux's distanciation evokes Brecht, his continuity surpasses Resnais. Time stops short in an avalanche of unnecessary titles and reaction shots, accelerates suddenly through the elliptical omission of an expected action, doubles back on itself in an unannounced flashback prompted by the use of earlier footage in a new context. Scenes climax in a cubist explosion of herky-jerky jump cuts wherein an actor delivering his lines appears in a succession of slightly askew angles. Micheaux's sense of timing recalls Thelonious Monk or Earl Monroe, and his narrative strategies beggar one's imagination. Actors play multiple roles, some characters seem blessed with precognitive abilities while others get marooned in alternate universes. The extensively post-dubbed *Ten Minutes to Live* (1932) makes elaborate use of telegrams and deaf-mutes to narrate the two separate stories that intermittently supercede the lava flow of entertainment erupting out of the single set called "Club Libya." *The Notorious Elinor Lee* (1939) reveals a surprise murder in a courtroom denouement that calls a parrot to testify on the witness stand.

"Every picture he made was mortgaged up to the nose," a Micheaux associate remembered. It's as though Micheaux directed his films while looking over his shoulder. His actors, their heads precipitously low in the frame, converge breathlessly at the center of the screen as a shot begins. Lines are delivered in unison, there are awkwardly failed attempts at overlapping dialogue, some actors appear to be reciting their parts by rote or reading cue cards. In *The Girl from Chicago* (1932) an off-camera voice prompts an actor to "give it to her," and his response is to mechanically repeat the phrase.

That Micheaux lacked either the time or the proclivity to invent any but the most obvious bits of business heightens the Kabuki-like quality of the performances. The non-speaking actor in a two-shot is frequently restricted to a single exaggerated tic. Thirty years before Warhol, Micheaux approached *mise en scène* Degree Zero. Left stranded in scenes that are grossly overextended, his performers strike fantastic poses, stare affectingly into space, or gaze casually off-camera.

EDWARD WOOD WAS a toadstool at the edge of Hollywood, nourished by the movie industry's compost; Micheaux constructed an anti-Hollywood out of rags and bones on some barely-imaginable psychic tundra. The spectacles he fashioned of blacks playing whites (which they sometimes did literally, in white-face) constitute a ruthless burlesque of the dominant culture. The collapse of bourgeois "niceness" that Luis Buñuel's *The Exterminating Angel* or Eugene Ionesco's plays depict, Micheaux's films actually are. Micheaux took the "institutional mode of representation," up-ended it, and turned it inside out. He demystified movies as no one has ever done and performed this negative magic for an audience that, infinitely more than the Medved boys, was victimized by Hollywood's mechanical dreams. The key to Micheaux's originality is that the social criticism that appears with such painful ambivalence in his scripts was triumphantly sublimated onto the level of form. Regardless of his intentions, Micheaux's films are so devastatingly bad that he can only be considered alongside Georges Méliès, D.W. Griffith, Dziga Vertov, Stan Brakhage, and Jean-Luc Godard as one of the medium's major formal innovators.

Three more things: 1) In *The Exile,* Micheaux uses titan of industry Charles Schwab's Riverside Drive mansion to represent the exterior of a Chicago whore-house; 2) It's been said that Micheaux deliberately left mistakes in his finished films "to give the audience a laugh"; 3) The longer Micheaux made films, the badder they got. I'm haunted by these facts because they suggest that Micheaux knew what he was doing. And if Oscar Micheaux was a fully conscious artist, he was the greatest genius the cinema ever produced.

Three American abstract sensationalists

Originally published as "American Abstract Sensationalism" in *Artforum* (January 1981).

The noiseless din that we have long known in dreams, booms at us in waking hours from newspaper headlines.

–T.W. Adorno, *Minima Moralia,* 1951

THERE ARE SENSIBILITIES so keyed to the routine textures of urban life that they hardly seem to be sensibilities at all. But, if they are invisible, it is only in the sense of sewer mains coursing beneath the Park Avenue of bourgeois critical awareness. I'm thinking of those (largely) self-taught, (mainly) prole-tarian expressionists—"primitives" who personalized yellow journalism and made abstract sensation into something as complicated as art.

The term "primitive" has, according to John Berger, three art-historical uses, all dating from the late 19th century "when the confidence of the European ruling class was at its height." The first "primitive" designates painting pro-duced before Raphael, on the cusp of the Medieval and Renaissance traditions. The second labels the "trophies and curiosities" carried home to Europe from the colonies. The last, says Berger, is meant "to put in its place the art of men and women from the working classes—proletarian, peasant, petit-bourgeois—who did not leave their class by becoming *professional* artists."

Begging the question as to whether professional artists like Jan Steen or William Blake or Eugene Atget can really be considered to have left their class, it is clear that the industrial folk-culture of the 20th century has amended Berger's formulation: The "primitive" is also that professional artist who (usually) originates from the working class and addresses a mass audience. The vehicles for such a professional have included vaudeville, movies, TV sitcoms, rhythm and blues, comic books, pulp novels, and—most polemically—the tabloid newspaper. For, ever since its inception in the years following World War I, the American tabloid has aggressively identified itself with the concerns, world-view, and vernacular—if not necessarily the interests—of the "common people."

During the period between the wars, the tabloid constituted a major arena of working class culture (and was part of the process that transformed the 19th century newspaper from a journal of record into a form of democratic litera-ture). The sociologist Robert E. Park once observed that the newspaper for the reporter was analogous to art for the artist, "less a career than a form of excitement and a way of life," and it would not be too much to say that in the American popular imagination, the yellow journalist took on the aura of a proletarian artist who used the metropolis itself as raw material. Throughout the movies of the 1930s (particularly in those of the urban prole-oriented Warner Brothers and Columbia studios), the newshound appears as a brash, even bohemian, picaro. Slangy, cynical, knowing—with a consummate capacity to function on and unmask all levels of urban society—this figure strongly suggests the fantasy projection of the city's lower orders (rural migrants, recent immigrants and their street-bred children). The mere existence of such a crea-ture was a slap in the face of polite society. "I'll tell you briefly what I think of newspapermen," says the irate millionaire in William Wellman's 1937 *Nothing Sacred*. "The hand of God reaching down into the mire couldn't elevate one of them to the depths of degradation—not by a million miles."

The tabloid—named (after the trademark of a 19th century medicinal tablet) for its compact form, appropriate to rush-hour reading—developed an esthetic of shock, raw sensation and immediate impact, a prole expressionism of violent contrasts and blunt, "vulgar" stylization. At once cynical and sentimen-tal, this mode fed on incongruity, mordant humor and the iconography of the street. The work of the tabloid school is brutal in both form and content, as assaulting as the cities which gave it sustenance and the subways where it was digested. Literary fellow travellers might have once included pulp writers like Dashiell Hammett or Horace McCoy. But the tabloid has always been half devoted to images, and the purist exponents of Abstract Sensationalism worked in visual media: B-movie director Samuel Fuller, *Dick Tracy*'s cartoonist Ches-ter Gould, the press photographer Weegee.

Weegee and Gould were exemplary newsmen; Fuller apprenticed with the tabloids, before going on to make Hollywood films. The son of an immigrant factory worker, Fuller was born in Worcester, Massachusetts, in 1911. His father died when he was 11, and his mother then moved the family to New York. Fuller went to work as a newsboy and within six years rose to crime reporter on the notorious *New York Daily Graphic*. "I'm still basically a journalist," he told an interviewer after 14 years as a director, writing else-where, "Every newsman is a potential filmmaker." *Park Row*—a feature Fuller made with his own money in 1952—is dedicated to American journalism; under the credits is a rolling title listing 2000 American daily newspapers. His other films which he called "scoops," "great copy," or "front-page material," told topical stories of war and corruption with a hyped-up, tabloid-like structure that invented filmic equivalents for shock headlines and sensational leads.

A product of the frontier, Gould was born in 1900 in Pawnee, Oklahoma, where his father was a printer and later the owner of a weekly newspaper. Gould demonstrated an aptitude for editorial cartooning as a child, and after studying commercial art moved to Chicago where he freelanced cartoons. After a decade he attracted the attention of Joseph Patterson, publisher of the *Chicago Tribune* and the *New York Daily News,* with an ur-version of *Dick Tracy*. The strip made its debut in October, 1931, and every day thereafter for the next 46 years several hundred American newspapers printed Gould's daily update of his police detective making his rounds. (Although *Dick Tracy* still survives, Gould retired in 1977.)

The first reproduction of a photograph to appear in an American newspaper was an image of a New York City slum: Weegee, perhaps the prototypical tabloidist, might well have been playing in that gutter. He was born Asher Fellig in the Hapsburg town of Zloczew in 1899 and immigrated to New York's Lower East Side in 1910. Dropping out of school to help support his family, he worked (like Fuller) as a newsboy, sold candy in burlesque houses, cleared tables at the automat, bought a camera and roamed the streets posing children on a horse. From working as a passport photographer he landed a job developing pictures for Acme Newsphoto and, in 1935, after a dozen years contemplating what a front-page photo was, lit out on his own as a freelance practitioner. Renting a room across the street from Police Headquarters, Weegee slept during the day and patrolled the city at night: "Around five in the morning was the best time for the action. That's when people kill themselves or somebody else."

With his crushed fedora, slept-in suit, and omnipresent stogie, Weegee played reporter to the hilt, boasting of photographing 5000 corpses, maintaining that "no racketeer on the FBI's list of the top ten public enemies made the grade until he had been photographed by Weegee." He flaunted his callousness: "That ax murder saved my life. I guess that some must die that others may live." In the same spirit, as a teen-age newshound, Fuller accumulated a collection of suicide notes the way other kids his age might've saved stamps. Included in Weegee's celebrated 1945 collection, *Naked City,* is a photographed receipt from Time, Inc., marked "Two murders $35" ("That's five dollars a bullet," he liked to say.) A posed photo of the artist having his shoes shined is captioned "Covering murders gets messy."

This hard-boiled attitude is the inevitable hallmark of abstract sensationalism. The tabloid sensibility not only needs to insulate itself from the horrors of the night, but requires an active appreciation of the mayhem to be formally orchestrated. It was "a beaut," wrote Weegee of one prospective photograph. "A shiny new car in a head-on collision, banged up like an accordion, with the driver's head sticking out of the windshield." Compare this to Fuller's remarks on the subway fight scene between Richard Widmark and Richard Kiley in his 1953 *Pickup on South Street*: "I liked the idea of Widmark pulling Kiley down by the ankles, and that the heavy's chin hits every step. Dat-dat-dat-dat-dat: It's musical." In *Dick Tracy,* Gould also took an evident pleasure in violence, devising baroque ends for his villains, and infused the entire strip with a grim gallows humor. From December, 1973, through the following March, the recovered skull of a long-dead bookie became a running gag. Covered with a wig, tossed from a speeding car, this memento mori was successively employed as a paperweight, a Christmas tree decoration, a hot-rod accessory, a basketball and a bookend.

Gould imagined violence far more than he ever experienced it, but for ten years, Weegee actually practiced a form of urban combat photography. Always ready, he was even permitted to keep a police radio in his car, the only journalist save Walter Winchell then accorded such a privilege. The startling immediacy of Weegee's flash froze his subjects like animals blinded in the glare of oncoming brights. But, rather than deer, Weegee's most celebrated photographs captured a raunchy menagerie of killers, crazies, and victims.

In his essay on Weegee's newsphotos, John Coplans suggests that for Weegee photojournalism legitimized an innate voyeuristic will-to-power: "Sleep, self-absorption, and unawareness were his prime stimuli, and people convulsed with pain, shocked, in terror, or blown out of their minds were his special target. . . . There is a recognizable level at which Weegee is not a detached reportorial professional."

The reporter's working assumption is fundamentally apocalyptic: every public figure—which is to say, potentially every citizen—is subject to the Judgment Day glare of remorseless publicity. ("We have shifted the responsibility for making the world interesting from God to the newspaperman," grumbles Daniel Boorstin in *The Image.*) Thus, it would be more accurate to see Weegee as a consummate professional who brought to his acknowledged social function as voyeur a heightened degree of personal expression and artistic self-awareness. The 1940 photograph *After the Season, Coney Island* makes Weegee's situation absolutely explicit. Three sleeping people huddle together on the beach oblivious to the shadow of the photographer that covers their sprawl like a tatty blanket. Occasionally, his camera's Heisenberg effect was bluntly acknowledged: the female companion to the eponymous victim of *Drowned Man, Coney Island* (ca. 1940) forces a smile and arches her back, lifted out of anonymity as Weegee clicks his shutter.

Weegee specialized in urban crucifixions, attributing his success to a universal *Schadenfreude,* but the most sensational aspect of an oeuvre can divert attention from its essential dialectic. Just as Diane Arbus has been glibly typed as a photographer of freaks (nearly two-thirds of the subjects in her 1972 Aperture monograph are more or less "normal" men, women and children). Weegee can be too quickly pigeonholed as the stormy petrel of urban catastrophe. He was, rather, a connoisseur of the vicarious. Along with numerous pictures of ordinary people having a "good time" in bars or on the beach, he did an extensive photographic series of audience reactions at concerts, nightclubs and movies, often using hidden cameras and infrared film.

The images that Weegee made in shabby midtown bars or at Sammy's

Bowery Follies—pictures perhaps of *slow* disasters—are marked by an easy, ironic familiarity (and possibly a degree of *épater le petit-bourgeois*). Their insider's celebration of this sleazy milieu is similar to the more picturesque skid-row lyricism of Fuller. *Pickup on South Street,* a 1953 film whose major characters are all unregenerate low-lifes—a pickpocket, a professional stool pigeon, and a prostitute—confines itself completely to moody reconstructions of the crime reporter's beat. (Half the movie takes place in the subway or under the Brooklyn Bridge, the rest in police stations, Bowery flop-houses, and greasy chop-suey joints. That none of it was actually shot in New York gives the film an additional hallucinated poignance.)

Weegee's favorite photographer was Lewis Hine (a sentimental choice, for Weegee's work is surely closer to that of Jacob Riis, another immigrant news-hound who prowled the sleeping city) and his oeuvre is well-salted with portraits of his fellow night-workers—peddlers, delivery men and meat-packers, as well as cops and smoke-eaters. The subjects of these photographs are often grinning, as though caught by Weegee a split second past surprise, photographed with a head-on directness that precludes Hine-style idealization. The tone is one of friendly solidarity. Illuminated by the intensity of Weegee's flash, these subjects are like featured players in the ongoing metropolitan drama that then constituted the photographer's life.

While Fuller re-created lower Manhattan out of bits and pieces of Los Angeles and a Hollywood soundstage, Weegee's 20-minute 16mm movie, *Weegee's New York,* 1948, uses trick lenses and prisms to turn midtown Manhattan into a tacky Emerald City of Oz. The film, subtitled "The Documentary with a Heart," is a half-maudlin, half-mocking expression of Weegee's identification with New York, that only comes to life in the Coney Island sequences where he juxtaposes crowd vignettes with a pop score ranging from Jerome Kern to "Bingo, Bango, Bongo (I Don't Want to Leave the Congo)." Generally speaking, Weegee's work exhibits a fascination with the urban crowd which was, after all, his audience. In pictures like the 1944 *Murder Victim* or the undated arrest photo included in John Szarkowski's *From the Picture Press,* the spectators who gather around corpses and car crashes are an integral part of the composition. It is this inscription of the spectator into the spectacle that lends a profoundly reflexive irony to Weegee's enterprise, while authenticating his assertion—the oft-proclaimed credo of tabloid journalism—that "I always considered myself the Boswell of the people."

The flashbulb had been on the market for only five years when Weegee turned freelancer, and it defined the essence of the tabloid image—scooping a searing, shallow foreground out of the night, giving bits of sidewalk or stair-wells the unreal quality of stage sets against a black backdrop. Weegee accentuated this startling effect in his prints, using the enlarger to simplify his images further by cropping extraneous details or burning them out of the background. This woodcut-like starkness, meant to arrest the eye of a rushing pedestrian at a dozen paces, finds its graphic correlative in Chester Gould's *Dick Tracy.* Like Weegee's, Gould's style was perfectly adapted to the vicissitudes of newsprint.

He played massive forms off against details, eschewed modeling and tonal gradations. Each high-contrast panel was bluntly diagrammatic. (Indeed, he showed a fondness for working blueprints and inserts into his narratives.) Gould's figures are stiff, angular and boldly outlined. Spotting fields of black throughout his panels, he employed a crude, dramatically malleable perspective, unleavened by shadows or benday dot patterns. His backgrounds were minimal and, in later years, virtually blank.

If Gould's panels look as though they were drawn in the lurid glare of the flash, the influence of the newsphoto can also be seen in Fuller's films. Shot mainly in high-contrast black and white, they favor tight, dramatic compositions, and harsh lighting. Fuller's frames, as well as Weegee's images and Gould's panels, are characterized by an iconic baldness and the deliberate suppression of detail. "The painter constructs, the photographer discloses," writes Susan Sontag. The filmmaker, of course, does both, and in a sense, Fuller's films effect a synthesis of Gould and Weegee. There is an unmistakable cartoon quality to his movies—in his use of slogans for dialogue, in his bluntly designed, two-dimensional characters (many of whom take their names—Lucky Legs, Short Round, Baldy—from exaggerated physical attributes). Fuller has a propensity (anticipated by Gould) for posting signs or otherwise inserting messages into the frame. In fact, Fuller's brother Victor was an editorial cartoonist, and one of his drawings was splashed across the front pages of a newspaper in *Park Row.* In the context of the film, this innovation is treated like a manifesto.

Dealing as they do with stylized violent action, Fuller and Gould share a number of formal traits. Fuller's movies mix lengthy choreographed takes with jolting montage. (Of his 1960 *Underworld U.S.A.,* V.F. Perkins wrote, "Every shot is a smack in the eye. Every cut is a shock cut.") Fuller is notoriously fond of close-ups. It has been estimated that they constitute over half the shots in his first film, *I Shot Jesse James* (note the Sunday-supplement title), made in 1949; in *Pickup on South Street,* he frequently starts a shot in close-up and then dollies in even tighter on his subject. Gould's narrative techniques are highly cinematic—*Dick Tracy* employed cross-cutting far more (and written sound effects far less) than other strips—and resemble Fuller's in their hyperbolic frenzy. Gould had a marked predilection for the comic-strip equivalent of the long take, being perfectly willing to devote several consecutive four-panel daily strips (or half a Sunday page) to a single gunfight. His use of extreme close-ups (cited by Alan Resnais as an influence on his own work) is even more percussive than Fuller's, and like him, Gould organized his panels with an eye to the disjunction caused by jarring shifts in angle or perspective.

Although Harold Grey's *Little Orphan Annie* (which began in the *New York Daily News* in 1924) is considered the original non-comic comic strip, *Dick Tracy* was the first to mirror the mayhem and death purveyed on the front page, and is probably the most violent non-war "funny" in the history of American newspapers. Gould's taste for raging fires and smashed automobiles rivals that of Weegee's, but unlike the latter, he would never have admitted that murders and fires were his "bread and butter" and crime his "oyster." Almost as a cover, Gould subscribed to various journals of criminology and police science, and studied detection at Northwestern University. He spent a considerable amount of time fraternizing with the Chicago police (who registered one of his cars as an official sheriff's vehicle) and kept a retired policeman on his payroll as a consultant. His admiration for, and public friendship with, J. Edgar Hoover led to popular speculation that he was in some way connected with the FBI.

Perhaps Gould's frontier childhood left him with a deep-rooted sense of the newspaper as the enforcer of community standards. There is an absolute moral quality to Tracy's five-decade war against crime. Although Gould rarely, if ever, resorted to using specific minorities—Italians, blacks, hippies—as scapegoats, during the late '60s and early '70s he made abundantly clear his contempt for liberal attempts to "handcuff" the police. Like Weegee, Gould occasionally parodied the idle rich (mainly during the 1940s), but he was basically a propagandist for the status quo. If Weegee and Fuller were ostentatiously hard-boiled, a more accurate description of Gould would be hard-assed.

Despite Gould's apparent concern with factual crime detection, what's immediately apparent about *Dick Tracy* is how utterly fanciful it is. Almost from its inception, the strip complemented its sensational violence with a measure of farce, continually approaching—without ever succumbing to—self-parody. Among *Tracy*'s more reflexive elements were the fantastically reductivist strips-within-the-strip that began to appear in the mid-60s. One of these, "Sawdust," is no more than panels, dots and corny gags; another, "The Invisible Tribe," dispenses even with the dots. Gould's fascination with police hardware, epitomized by Tracy's famous two-way wrist radio (later TV) turned speculative during the 1960s, when the strip took on a number of science-fiction elements, including one-passenger "magnetic" space coupes and a race of moon people. Even after this tendency subsided with the actual 1969 lunar landing, *Tracy* remained off-handedly sprinkled with such futuristic gadgets as a television set built into a stove.

Of course, the most obvious fantasy element in *Dick Tracy*—and the strip's trademark—was the parade of freakish villains who began to populate the strip during the early '40s with their grotesque physical characteristics apparent from their names—Pruneface, Ugly Christine, the Mole, et al. One suspects that *Tracy*'s insistence on the primacy of law and order was a psychological necessity, to keep the most disturbing elements of Gould's imagination in check. Given Weegee's education in chaos, or an environment analogous to that of post-World War I Berlin (a city that in some respects was the Chicago of Europe), Gould might well have produced work as unremittingly savage as that of George Grosz or Otto Dix.

This taste for the grotesque is another hallmark of the tabloid style. Whereas Fuller uses deformity mainly for its shock value (the most celebrated instance being the pre-credit sequence of his 1964 *The Naked Kiss*, where a pimp is beaten by a prostitute who's been shaven bald), Weegee's late career offers a freak show comparable to Gould's—portraits of politicians and celebrities that employ various trick lenses to effect brutal Minamata-like distortions upon their subjects.

Throughout Gould's tenure, *Dick Tracy* came under intermittent attack for its excessive carnage. Gould bolstered the strip's respectability with occasional exercises in pathos (generally occurring in time for Christmas), but his major diversionary strategem was *Tracy*'s consistent "educational" facade. Each Sunday page featured a helpful hint in the form of the *Crimestoppers Textbook*, subsidiary panels (suitable for clipping) which urged readers to install alarm systems in their campers or fingerprint their domestics, sometimes directing tips specifically at rookie policeman. Far more eccentric were the polemical asides— "The nation that controls magnetism will control the universe" was a favorite—that Gould incorporated into the strip itself. This sort of didacticism, deriving from the newspaper's implicit function to instruct as well as entertain, received far more complex play within the films of Samuel Fuller.

Superficially, Fuller would seem to share Gould's conservative attitude towards law and order. Early in his career he was pegged as a rightwing ideologue but, whereas the universe of *Dick Tracy* is static and Manichaean, the 17 low-budget, high-velocity films that Fuller wrote, directed and in many cases produced between 1949 and 1964 thrive on social contradictions, using neurotic loners or loudmouthed members of the lumpen proletariat to test society's official pieties.

In his admirable 1972 essay on *Dick Tracy* (published in *Prose No. 4*), Donald Phelps speaks of "the Jacobean fierceness of [Gould's] imagination." It is a quality that Fuller shares, albeit with a far more anarchic backbeat. Fuller's heroes are frequently abrasive sociopaths; America (his constant preoccupation) is invariably protected by its outcasts, who act from some emotional necessity that is pointedly a-patriotic. "Are you waving the flag at me?" snarls pickpocket Richard Widmark in response to an FBI agent's platitudinous speech in *Pickup on South Street*. This film, which appeared at the end of Hollywood's six-year-long "red menace" cycle, pushes McCarthy-style anti-Communism to the far side of self-parody. The U.S. is saved when Fuller's scum-of-Baghdad principals inadvertently connect with and thwart a Communist atomic spy ring. Thelma Ritter, the film's lovable professional informer (sic), articulates the essence of knee-jerk anti-Communism when she exclaims, "Commies! Wadda I know about commies? Nuthin', I only know that I don't like 'em!"

By the 1960s, when Gould was flirting with science fiction, Fuller's view of America had grown markedly pessimistic. *Underworld U.S.A.*, structurally close enough to *Pickup on South Street* to seem an oblique remake, presents the crime syndicate as a giant corporation, protected by dishonest elected officials and skillful public relations. (In one Gould-like touch, Fuller locates the gangster board room by the edge of a vast indoor swimming pool, a vista so bleakly disinfected that you can almost smell the chlorine.) Instead of the Communist "other," the threat to American democracy is this hot house flower of late capitalism, wherein a junior gunsel can tell his boss, "I'd like a future with your organization, a bit of security." Here, unlike *Dick Tracy,* which maintained its 1930s view of individualized crime for over 40 years, there seems to be no essential difference between the criminals and the FBI. Operating out of parallel skyscraper offices, both operations are ruthless, efficient, cold and equally anxious to exploit the rage of Fuller's safecracking anti-hero, played by Cliff Robertson. The epitome of Fuller's sense of low-life integrity is a virtual reversal of Gould's schemata. *The Naked Kiss*—a film that effectively suspended Fuller's Hollywood career for nearly 15 years—pivots on a reformed prostitute's discovery that her philanthropist-fiancé (the namesake of the idyllic New England town in which she has taken refuge) is actually a child-molester. Catching him *in flagrante,* she bludgeons him to death and then, disgusted by the corruption and hypocrisy of the straight world, returns to turning tricks.

No filmmaker has ever been more devoted to the idea of journalism, or lavished more care on his use of newspaper headlines within his films than has Fuller. However, the optimism of his early *Park Row* palled considerably a decade later. Both *Underworld U.S.A.* and *The Naked Kiss* use the newspaper front page with a great deal of ambivalence. In the former, a sequence of a child being intentionally run over by a car is followed by its alienated reification in the picture press. The headline EX-CALL GIRL KILLS MILLIONAIRE FIANCE, used in *The Naked Kiss,* at once summarizes the film in five words and strips it of its moral complexities.

Fuller's bleakest film, *Shock Corridor* (1963), deals with an ambitious journalist who feigns madness to enter a mental hospital and report on an unsolved murder that has occurred there. Shot without exteriors, the film maintains a tone of caged hysteria for most of its 101 minutes. The inmates in the hospital add up to a tabloid vision of America: an ex-GI who has been brainwashed by the North Koreans and believes himself to be Jeb Stuart, a nuclear physicist who has regressed to the age of five, and the first black student to integrate a southern university, now suffering under the delusion that he is the Grand Dragon of the Ku Klux Klan. The reporter solves the murder but goes mad himself as a result. Fuller's last shot has his hero crouched in the hospital corridor, one arm outstretched like the Statue of Liberty at half-mast. "It's tragic," a doctor remarks, "this year's winner of the Pulitzer Prize has become a catatonic mute."

Shock Corridor is the terminal manifestation of the tabloid school. When it was first released, *Variety's* reviewer found the film "so grotesque, so grueling, so shallow and shoddily sensational that [its] message is devastated." But that, of course, was Fuller's point—not the message but the messenger is devastated. A news report is not final and Fuller's method has always been to throw the ball into the audience's lap. *The Steel Helmet* (1951)—a Korean War film that suggests *Waiting for Godot* rewritten by Mickey Spillane—ends, "There is no end to this story." *Run of the Arrow* (1957)—a didactic Western on race and regional hatred—concludes with the title "The end of this story will be written by you."

Ultimately, what has elevated Abstract Sensationalism to "primitive art" has had less to do with the degree to which it is successful on its own terms than the way it has been used as a source, by more "sophisticated" artists, or seen as an analogue for their work. Thus, Fuller is frequently cited as raw material for Jean-Luc Godard (who wrote of Fuller's 1957 *Forty Guns* that it was "so bursting with daring conceptions that it reminds one of the extravagances of Abel Gance and Stroheim"). Fuller's "kino-fist" esthetic has been likened to Eisenstein's, his "vulgar" political didacticism compared to that of Brecht.

Gould, on the other hand, has never enjoyed even a minimal amount of serious critical attention. Despite the enthusiasm of an occasional artist (Resnais, Jim Nutt) his work has been taken mainly as industrial folklore. Andy Warhol employed Tracy's razor-jawed profile, softened with mock-gestural drips, in his 1960 series of comic-strip characters. A more complex use of *Tracy* as a found object were the seven "Tricky Cad" collages produced by San Francisco artist Jess Collins between 1953 and 1959, which reworked Gould panels into a pulp version of the Victorian engravings collaged by Max Ernst in the 1930s. But Gould's impact has been mainly felt on other comic strips, including "underground cartoonists," Art Spiegelman and Kim Deitch.

Weegee owes not a little of his current reputation to the fact that he is generally perceived as a primitive precursor of photographers Diane Arbus, Lee Friedlander, and Garry Winogrand. Just as Weegee's candid photographs in Sammy's Bowery Follies anticipate Friedlander's party pictures, and his street images suggest Winogrand's, so his use of odd, off-putting reaction shots presages Arbus' portraits. Weegee's photographs are filled with the jarring perspectives, arbitrary framing, and bizarrely frozen gestures that his successors have turned into formal tropes. "If people laugh in the background of a murder shot, well—that's life," he once said, a statement echoed after a fashion by a wall label at the 1967 Museum of Modern Art "New Documents" show that simultaneously introduced Arbus, Friedlander, and Winogrand: "These three photographers would prefer that their pictures be regarded not as art, but as life."

Ironically, Weegee's own work of the 1960s reversed this art/life conundrum. Indeed, the story of his success and subsequent failure is a melancholy parable of the tabloidist divorced from his milieu. By 1940, Weegee was sufficiently well-known within his profession to have landed a regular berth on the liberal tabloid *PM*. The next year he had his first gallery show, "Murder Is My Business," at the (left-oriented) Photo League. The Museum of Modern Art purchased four of his prints, and soon after invited him to lecture. He was adopted by the art world as an outstanding photographer in the documentary-journalist mode. When *Naked City* was published in the summer of 1945, Weegee was written up in *Time, Newsweek,* and *The Saturday Review,* hailed as a sort of dese-dems-and-dose Daumier-in-the-rough. When he began working for *Vogue,* he took slumming socialites along with him on assignment.

After Universal purchased the title *Naked City,* Weegee left for Hollywood. There, in a weird, denatured recapitulation of his youth, he made a minor career playing bit parts and walk-ons (always as a species of urban low-life) in a number of films including Robert Wise's *The Set-Up* (1949), *The Yellow Cab*

Man (1949), Joseph Losey's remake of *M* (1951), and *Skid Row* (1951). By the time he returned to New York, he was, in effect, a professional caricature. Having failed to make it in Hollywood's hog heaven, he strove for a comeback in the art world with the gimmickry of trick lenses. Instead of his association with gangsters, he now bragged that he had "rubbed shoulders with Picasso, Dali, the lot." Rather than demonstrate his callousness, he told interviewers, "I'm very primitive; in fact, I'm the Grandma Moses of photography."

It is tempting to see much of Weegee's late output as an ambivalent, voodoo-doll attack on the indifferent citadel of art. "I got peeved at Picasso," he exclaims in his autobiography. "That guy was imitating me . . . some nerve of him! I straightened out his abstractions and brought them back to normal." Weegee's last book, *Creative Photography* (1964), includes "an impressionist study of a circus ring," a picture with "all the qualities of contemporary 'hard edge' abstractions," another "truly striking abstract image—one even Picasso would be proud of," as well as grotesque distortions of the *Mona Lisa* and *Aristotle Contemplating the Bust of Homer.*

Talent, Adorno once speculated, "is perhaps nothing other than successfully sublimated rage." In Weegee's case, after 1945, rage was all there was.

Vulgar modernism

Originally published in *Artforum* (January 1982).

IN ITS TIRELESS attempt to mean everything to everyone and empirical willingness to try anything once, the American culture industry intermittently generates its own precursors, parallels, and analogues to local or European avant-gardism. I am not thinking so much of Pablo Picasso's interest in *The Katzenjammer Kids,* Francis Picabia's affinity with Rube Goldberg, Antonin Artaud's praise of the Marx Brothers, Samuel Beckett's fondness for Laurel and Hardy, André Breton's championing of Henry Hathaway's *Peter Ibbetson* (Paramount, 1935) as a Surrealist work on a par with Luis Buñuel's *L'Age d'or,* the inexhaustible treasure trove of jazz, or the *Learning from Las Vegas* school of architecture; rather, I am thinking of Spike Jones' primitive brand of *musique concret* and disco's version of drone-seriality, the *Channel 11 Yule Log*'s anticipation of Jan Dibbets' *TV as Fireplace,* 1969, and the way that media coverage of the Kennedy assassination—from its historic instant replay of Lee Harvey Oswald's death to its later, microscopic analysis of the Zapruder footage— inexorably points toward Ken Jacobs' *Tom, Tom the Piper's Son* and the films of Ernie Gehr.

Cinema is rife with examples of such para-art. Recent scholarship has linked the pre-Griffith film language of 1905 to the "structural films" of the 1970s, while any historian knows that the montage jokes in Buster Keaton's *Sherlock Junior* (Metro, 1924) predate those in Sergei Eisenstein's *October*

(Sovkino, 1928). Still, analogies have yet to be produced for the abstract dance numbers of Busby Berkeley, the wipe transitions of Lynn Dunn, or even the Olson and Johnson comedy, *Hellzapoppin'* (Universal, 1940). The latter, which in an alternative universe might have been scripted by Victor Shklovsky under the influence of mescaline, anticipates something of the world view (if not the actual films) of George Landow and Morgan Fisher, two structuralists who have a sense of humor. The movie opens in a projection booth out of which beams a film set in Hell—subsequently revealed as a studio back lot when the principals quit the production to stage their own "live" show. This piece of theater (within-the-film-within-the-film-within-the-film, all named *Hellzapoppin'*) is continually disrupted by antics that intersect all five layers of the reality sandwich: characters manage to throw the film in reverse, enter stills from later sequences, rescue each other when the frame goes out of alignment; there is confusion in the projection booth and simulated agitation in the actual auditorium (mock shadows thrown on the screen, etc.).[1]

But besides these random examples there is a particular sensibility that is the vulgar equivalent of modernism itself. By this I mean a popular, ironic, somewhat dehumanized mode reflexively concerned with the specific properties of its medium or the conditions of its making. Conscious of its position in the history of (mass) culture, the sensibility to which I refer developed between 1940 and 1960 in such peripheral corners of the "culture industry" as animated cartoons, comic books, early morning TV, and certain Dean Martin/Jerry Lewis comedies.

The Manet of vulgar modernism is the animation director Tex Avery (1908–80), who was instrumental in creating the distinctive Warner Brothers cartoon style of the 1940s. Avery invented Daffy Duck, perfected the Bugs Bunny/Elmer Fudd symbiosis, heightened the tempo of the Warners product, boosted its sex-violence-noise quotient, and generally spearheaded the studio's wise-guy subversion of the sentimental naturalism that then passed for the state of the art. Opposing Disney-style character-identification, Avery anticipated the distancing formalism of *Hellzapoppin'*, as well as some of its gags. A year after he joined Warners in 1936, he supervised *Daffy Duck and Egghead,* in which Egghead "shoots" a member of the audience whose shadow promptly keels over across the screen. *Thugs with Dirty Mugs* (Warner Bros., 1939) elaborates the motif. At the cartoon's climax, a silhouetted theater patron rises from his seat to finger the villain: "I know he did it—I sat through this picture twice!"

Deploying direct address and the Brechtian device of interpolated placards, Avery's cartoons were designed to comment on the screen action as it unfolds; *Who Killed Who* (MGM, 1943) blatantly announces its "victim" well before his demise by affixing a label (reading "victim") to the back of his chair. Avery's characters were as prone to violate the conventions of the iris-out or split screen as to intervene in the film credits or shoot holes through the "painted sets" behind them. In calling attention to his films as artifice, Avery used a strategy of exaggerated cartoon-ness. *The Heckling Hare* (Warner Bros., 1941) hyperbolizes the medium's relative freedom from physical constraint by extending a cliché free-fall into a minute-long descent that ends with his characters braking to a halt. The same year's *Porky's Preview* (Warner Bros.) features an audaciously primitive (if not totally infantile) cartoon-within-the-cartoon: crudely drawn or crossed-out stick figures parade against a blank background while being rained on by scribble-scrabble clouds. *The Magical Maestro* (MGM, 1952) foregrounds the filmic apparatus in an even more literal sense: a hair appears to flutter in the projector gate for several minutes and is ultimately removed by one of the cartoon's characters.

Avery's work demands to be seen in opposition to that of Disney. *The Peachy Cobbler* (MGM, 1950) parodies the latter's cozy fairytale cottages and cutely bathetic wildlife, while the eponymous antihero of his *Screwball Squirrel* (MGM, 1944) begins his career by mugging the cartoon's erstwhile narrator—an eye-batting Bambi-oid who coyly announces that "this cartoon is about me and all my friends in the forest: Charlie Chipmunk, Wallace Woodchuck, Barney Bear. . . ." In due course, the squirrel's irrepressible will-to-power leads him to wrest control of the cartoon's time-space continuum. Establishing himself as the film's prime mover, he manufactures a double, reads the future by lifting the corner of the screen to peek ahead, and—when an opponent is trapped in a barrel and sent rolling down a hill—is shown, through a tracking shot to a wider angle, to be scoring the raucous sound effects accompanying the action on a variety of whistles, cymbals, and drums. Although clearly Avery's supreme creation, this shrill, megalomaniacal rodent would obviously never emblazon a child's cocoa-mug, and, after five appearances, Avery had him killed off—affectionately crushed to death by the big dumb bear who gives his name to *Lonesome Lenny* (MGM, 1946), a take-off on *Of Mice and Men*. Typically, Screwy's last, indeed posthumous act is to brandish pathetically a sign reading "Sad ending, isn't it?"

While Avery's formalism influenced the whole Warner Brothers unit—the most celebrated example being Chuck Jones' 1953 encyclopedia of distanciation jokes, *Duck Amok*—his most important disciple was Frank Tashlin (1913–72), an animator whose apprenticeship in 20th-century sight gags was as full and varied as Kasimir Malevich's course in Post-Impressionism. Breaking into show business as Max Fleischer's office boy, Tashlin worked for several other New York animation studios before migrating west to Warners in 1933. For the next dozen years, he bounced back and forth among Warners, Disney, and Columbia Screen Gems, as an animator, script writer, director, and producer. In between and on the side, he drew a syndicated comic strip, concocted bits of business for Hal Roach's *Our Gang* comedies, wrote and illustrated several children's books, and provided material for Harpo Marx. Given this background, it's not surprising that the Tashlin oeuvre should be an elaborately cross-referenced Bartlett's of mass-culture quotations. However, this systematic approach was his from the onset. Tashlin's earliest animations included parodies of well-known films by John Ford and Lewis Milestone, as well as a newsstand extravaganza which anthropomorphized various popular magazines.

By the late 1940s, Tashlin was bored with cartoons and was concentrating mainly on radio and movie scripts. In 1950, he directed the first of his 23 features. (Surprisingly, only one other American animator ever made the leap to live direction: Gregory LaCava, best known for his screwball comedies of the 1930s, began his career as an editorial cartoonist and later headed up William Randolph Hearst's short-lived animation studio.) While Tashlin's cartoons had experimented with movie techniques, his features were steeped in Looneytunes hyperbole and packaged with bizarre framing devices: *The First Time* (Columbia, 1951) is narrated by a year-old baby, *Susan Slept Here* (RKO, 1954) by an Oscar statuette. Implacably antinatural, Tashlin's films are filled with visual distortions and iconic characters playing themselves. An actual and metaphorical flatness heightens the sense of artifice. The protagonist of *The Girl Can't Help It* (20th Century-Fox, 1956) is made to hallucinate singer Julie London in triplicate every time he hears one of her records on a jukebox; he and the film's heroine are named Tom and Jerri, after the famous cartoon cat-and-mouse combo of the 1940s. With his "advertising slogans in the form of lettrist poems,"[2] Tashlin is the original pop pop artist. His is a landscape of raucous chrome jukeboxes, vast supermarkets, newfangled credit cards, and hot pink Cadillacs, all depicted with the fetishized surface sheen—at once seductive and repellent—of a Tom Wesselmann still life. This cool visual stridence is more than matched by the elaborate, often cruel, mechanisms of his gags and the grotesque two-dimensionality of his protagonists.

Son of Paleface (Paramount, 1952) isn't one of Tashlin's masterpieces—he needed flesh and blood caricatures like Jerry Lewis and Jayne Mansfield and the supreme garishness of mid-'50s consumer culture for those—but it has a Warners cartoon's gaudy primary colors, stylized costumes, and breakneck callousness. The laws of physics are flouted with impunity; at one point, Bob Hope drives a car across an abyss. In general, Hope absorbs a tremendous amount of pain-free physical punishment, while co-star Roy Rogers is hilariously played for a stiff, mainly because he is "Roy Rogers." If humans are locked into their trademarks, animals are blatantly anthropomorphic. Trigger appears as a full-fledged reasoning character. While crossing the desert, Hope is bedeviled by a pair of phony-looking buzzards. "Beat it," he says, "or you're going to make the whole thing seem ridiculous." Hope's delayed response to Jane Russell's charms is typical of Tashlin's modus operandi: Ski-nose nonchalantly lights his pipe, it unfurls like a paper party whistle, smoke pours out of his ears, his body spins like a top but his face remains fixed front, drooling over Russell's bodice. There is a sense in which Tashlin's best gags aren't really funny. But neither is a pas de deux.

Whereas Avery's modernism focuses on the specifics of his medium, Tashlin's opens onto the larger media system (an interest paralleled by that of such artists as Hans Haacke and Les Levine, whose subjects are often the art context itself). No Hollywood director has ever been so obsessed with the ramifications of movies, TV, and advertising. Virtually all of Tashlin's key films revolve around some aspect of the culture industry. *Artists and Models* (Paramount,

1955) concerns horror comics; *Hollywood or Bust* (Paramount, 1956), the movies; *The Girl Can't Help It* (20th Century Fox, 1956), rock'n'roll; *Will Success Spoil Rock Hunter?* (20th Century-Fox, 1957), advertising. Dick Powell plays a screen writer in *Susan Slept Here,* and Tom Ewell a TV writer in *The Lieutenant Wore Skirts* (20th Century-Fox, 1956). The films, however, have less to do with the production of cultural forms than with their packaging and consumption. Tashlin's America is a nation of robotic image junkies whose minds have been colonized by the media. Jerry Lewis' landlady in *Rock-a-Bye Your Baby* (Paramount, 1958) does exactly what TV commercials tell her to do, even to the point of dying her hair vermilion; the movie fans in *Hollywood or Bust* and *Rock Hunter* are little more than popcorn and fan-mag consuming zombies. After Jerry Lewis, Jean-Luc Godard was Tashlin's aptest pupil. *Made in U.S.A.* is Godard's hymn to vulgar modernism, but *Alphaville* is his most Tashlinesque film—not only for its comic strip characters and bits like the slot machine whose only payoff is a card reading "thanks," but because, more than those of any other director, Tashlin's films seem ready-made for the somnambulistic, media-crazed *Alphaville* citizenry.

A project similar to Tashlin's, albeit located on an even less reputable cultural plane, was carried out by *Mad* magazine during the first few years of its existence. Edited by Harvey Kurtzman and published by E.C.—the same firm whose grisly horror comics (*The Vault of Horror, The Crypt of Terror,* etc.) became the target of a national crusade complete with congressional investigation—the original *Mad* was a comic book that parodied other comic books. (With the demise of E.C.'s horror line in 1954, *Mad* became a magazine and its comic strip parodies were superceded by meticulous burlesques of current advertisements.) *Mad* drew on the same talent pool as did the horror comics, but its humorous pretext allowed greater freedom. Violence reached ludicrous levels in the service of formal playfulness. *Mad* pushed certain aspects of the medium to their limits: Wallace Wood's (1927–1981) "Sound Effects" (*Mad* #20), for example, is a hard-boiled detective story told, without dialogue, over a succession of ear-splitting graphics. The Avery techniques of direct address and interpolated messages were totally integrated into the *Mad* house-style, which was itself deconstructed in Wood's "Julius Caesar" (*Mad* #17).

What distinguished *Mad*'s parodies from those of various college humor magazines, or of the pornographic "eight-pagers" which first appeared during the 1930s, was the highly developed self-consciousness of their characters. The *Mad* versions of Mickey Mouse, Superman, Dick Tracy, et al., were acutely aware of the conventions of the comics in which they appeared, as well as the language of comics in general, and the struggle against these limitations was, by and large, the subject of *Mad*'s parodies. Bill Elder's "Mickey Rodent" (*Mad* #19) devotes itself to ridiculing the irrational fetishes of the Disney cosmos— that all characters wear three-fingered white gloves, that only Donald Duck and family go without pants, that Pluto is the sole animal deprived of speech. A measure of realism enters this hermetic world in the form of "Mickey Rodent"'s jealousy over "Darnold Duck"'s popularity, while much is made of "Walt

Dizzy" 's personal control, and his trademark signature is even treated as a natural aspect of the comic's landscape. Elder's "Starchie" (*Mad* #12) is a merciless send-up of the teen-oriented *Archie* comics that not only focuses on the physical peculiarities of the characters but undermines Archie's innocence by introducing a variety of unpleasant, adolescent realities ranging from acne to juvenile delinquency. John Goldwater, the creator of Archie, was instrumental in developing the Comics Code Authority which eventually drove the E.C. horror comics out of business, and so it is with a certain grim purposefulness that "Starchie" 's splash panel flaunts a grimacing, encephalitic head as the seal of "Disapproved Reading."

For early *Mad,* even more than for Tashlin, the media constituted a single system: Little Orphan Annie and Edward G. Robinson make cameo appearances in "Starchie"; Blondie's husband is cured of a nervous breakdown by a transfer from the confines of his domestic strip to a panel from the exotic *Terry and the Pirates*; and Dick Tracy is revealed to moonlight as his parody, Fearless Fosdick. Wallace Wood, who specialized in pygmy cretins, overstacked dolls, and frames with the visual consistency of an exploding spittoon, represented *Mad* at its most aggressively tasteless, but Elder's neutral detachment and uncanny capacity for mimicking other drawing styles made him the comic book's quintessential artist. His best pieces are collagelike arrangements of advertising trademarks, media icons, banal slogans, visual puns, and assorted non-sequiturs. The splash panel for "Shermlock Shomes" (*Mad* #7), for example, has a deep-sea diver, a man wearing a refrigerator, the Mobil Flying Horse, a puzzled Saint Bernard dog, the Statue of Liberty, and the seven dwarves from Disney's *Snow White* (among other creatures) wandering through the London fog.

Elder's cartoons embalm hysteria: the opening image of "Ping Pong" (*Mad* #6) shows a giant slobbering ape towering above the mass of screaming humanity that flees before it on vehicles ranging from flying carpets to pogo sticks. Although the overall effect is monumentally static, the image yields a dozen miniature emblems of exaggerated panic: one man is running with a bathtub clutched around his middle, another's eyes have just popped from his sockets, someone else appears to have plunged his hand through the back of the head in front of him so that it emerges, flailing, through its mouth. Meanwhile, Ping— brushing off the scaffolding that has suspended itself from his underarm in an attempt to plaster a "Post No Bills" sign across his torso—is being attacked by a cannon firing puffed rice, a parachutist with a peashooter, a machine-gunner suspended in a diaper that is carried by a stork, and an army helicopter whose rear propeller has unobtrusively pulverized a portion of the frame line. (As *Mad*'s leading formalist, Elder allows internal objects to tamper with the boundaries of a panel, breaks continuous vistas into consecutive frames, offers visually identical panels with wildly fluctuating details, and otherwise emphasizes the essential serial nature of his medium.)

The premise of Elder's "Outer Sanctum" (*Mad* #5), ostensibly a burlesque of a once-popular radio show but equally a parody of *Mad*'s sister publications, is that a mass of fetid garbage is given life by a mad scientist. This "heap" is virtually a metaphor for *Mad*'s sense of Western civilization as a clutter of cultural detritus (a commonplace shared by such disparate modernists as T.S. Eliot and Kurt Schwitters). The *Mad* esthetic was the subject of a 1959 essay by critic Donald Phelps who, under the rubric "The Muck School," identified a "strain of gritty, unhousebroken, garbage-happy burlesque [which] probably owes its existence to the inert layer of disgust or passive resentment which lies like a pool of candle-wax in nearly every city dweller's soul." For Phelps, *Mad*'s originality stems from its acceptance of "the awfulness of modern life as something that isn't worth attempting to control, or submit to reason, but can only be wallowed in, for whatever laughs can be scavenged from the garbage heap." Although this characterization strikes me as accurate, it should be noted that Phelps' analysis is based on a later incarnation of *Mad*, when the edge of the publication's dadalike travesty and devaluation of American secular mythology had been somewhat blunted.

Mad aside, the other key members of Phelps' Muck School are Lenny Bruce (whose self-consciousness as a stand-up comic and subversive use of pop cultural shticks bring him close to vulgar modernism) and the TV comedian and one-time *Mad* contributor Ernie Kovacs (1919–62). Kovacs began his TV career in 1950; his forte, as Phelps put it, "was demonstrating to his public the immeasurable crumbiness of so-called professional television." (The same could be said for *You Bet Your Life*, the TV quiz show hosted by veteran vulgar surrealist Groucho Marx.) Given Kovacs' fondness for tacky special effects— snow represented by falling mattress innards, dimestore gorilla masks, catastrophes staged with toys, dolls, or imbecilic hand puppets—and his enthusiastic shilling for products like chocolate-covered spinach, Phelps suggests that early Kovacs shows were so aggressively squalid that they could have been stocked from the Broadway novelty shops that sell plastic vomit and toilet-bowl shaped pipes. The sets for *Three to Get Ready* (WPTZ, 1950–52), a wake-up show on an independent Philadelphia station, or *Ernie in Kovacsland* (NBC, 1951), a summer replacement for the popular puppet show *Kukla, Fran, and Ollie*, were literally ankle-deep with cruddy props and cheap stuffed animals, which Kovacs would deploy in an almost free-associational manner.

Some of Kovacs' gags—misprompting or inflicting off-screen pranks upon the show's news-reader, yanking the cameraman in front of the lens, taking an ax and destroying the set of a cancelled program—were founded on the improvisational quality of live television. (Hence the double joke of his blandly delivered sign-off, "It's been real.") A typical edition of *Three to Get Ready* begins with several false starts and is punctuated throughout by apparently genuine, slyly overamplified off-screen directions: the cameraman or producer is heard to complain, "Ernie, you're off the set!" or "This isn't the way we rehearsed it!" As late as 1961, Kovacs was capable of starting one of his ABC specials with several precredit minutes of tele-chaos—ghosts, bar-rolls, static— before cutting away to himself in the studio control room.

This accentuation of his medium's essential tawdriness, a strategy Kovacs shares with Avery, Tashlin, Wood, and Elder, is only one aspect of his modernity. Like Tashlin and Avery, Kovacs was a formalist; in fact, Tashlin and Kovacs seem to me the two most inventively filmic comics on the American scene since Keaton. Many Kovacs gags play upon the (a)synchronization of sound and image. In *Kovacs on Music* (NBC, 1959), he staged a scene from *Swan Lake* without any travesty save for the remarkable alienation effect of dressing the "swans" as gorillas. One of his last programs, *The Ernie Kovacs Special* (ABC, 1961), featured a performance of the song "Jealousy" played on synchronized, autonomously moving office furniture (file cabinets, water coolers, typewriters, switchboards), each piece of which functioned as a separate instrument. Kovacs' "mickey-mousing" could be astonishingly crude—a matter of blatantly tilting or jerking the camera in response to the music. Another *Ernie Kovacs Special* (ABC, 1961) includes a five-minute sequence of percussive kaleidoscopic images (mainly close-ups of fluttering fingers) scored to a bombastic piece of symphonic music. The effect is funny not because it satirizes nonobjective art (if, indeed, it does, being so visually potent itself) but because Kovacs' brand of formalism is totally blunt. Test patterns aside, it would be difficult to imagine a more abstract use of network TV.

As early as *Three to Get Ready*, Kovacs was regularly tinkering with the mechanics and perception of the televised image, using distorting lenses and disjunctive sound. Some quasi-ontological routines were more elaborate. In one Kovacs interpolated a pane of glass between himself and the camera so that he could splatter the screen with eggs; in another he used a tilted set whose angle was matched, and thus concealed, by that of the camera (Kovacs' definitive use of the latter trope was on NBC's *Saturday Color Carnival* [1957], where oranges appeared to spontaneously roll along a lunch table and Kovacs' attempt to pour himself a drink from his thermos sent a liquid jet of coffee half a foot away from the cup directly beneath it on the table.) From his Philadelphia period on, Kovacs experimented with a host of what can be seen in hindsight as pure video techniques. A dozen years before Nam June Paik invented his video synthesizer, Kovacs was keying, matting, and miniaturizing (the better to trap himself inside a milk bottle or an old horror film), as well as using split screens, double exposures, and negative images; hence his posthumous reputation as the precursor of video art. Kovacs' accomplishment is all the more impressive for its being done (initially, at least) on live—rather than taped—television, for an audience of millions.

INEVITABLY, WHAT WAS once oppositional in vulgar modernism has largely been coopted by the culture industry. Virtually all current television satire (to take only the paradigmatic example) depends on the viewer's familiarity with the full range of broadcast fare. But the hidden agenda here is less the conscious devaluation practiced by Tashlin, Kovacs, or early *Mad* than a flattering of the TV community into smug pseudo-dissociation from the banalities it otherwise accepts.

However, subversive phenomena like Norman Lear's *Mary Hartman, Mary*

Hartman (1976–77) or his *Fernwood 2-Night* (1978), the recent films of Brian De Palma, and—in their pristine state—bands like the Ramones or the B-52s have calculated their cold-eyed enthusiasm to a degree that it renders such *Saturday Night Live* dissociation problematic. These popular artists have learned from previous example that it is possible to eat one's cake and have it, too, to please the public while addressing the intelligentsia, revel in formula to the degree that formula is intermittently radicalized. The Ramones' *Rocket to Russia* is "classic" rock'n'roll that redeems rock's mindless energy; De Palma's *Dressed to Kill* (Filmways, 1980) is a "classic" thriller that deliberately flaunts its own manipulations; *Mary Hartman* is a "classic" soap opera that simultaneously uses and deconstructs soap opera appeal. Having grasped that nothing is beyond cooption, these artists proclaim their own usable past. After all, Alfred Hitchcock and the Beach Boys have long since been critically canonized. With no ambivalence concerning success, punks like De Palma and the Ramones recycle their models as brashly as Roy Lichtenstein re-presents Franz Kline's gestural brushstroke. If current developments in art stem from the recognition of modernism as a series of period styles resulting in reified closure, the attitude of such artists points toward the creation of an authentic vulgar *post*-modernism.

1. According to its director H.C. Potter, *Hellzapoppin'* was scripted to include scenes in which screen characters would address the film's actual projectionist. This was perceived as being too radical by the studio, hence the substitution of the projection booth scenes.

2. Roger Tailleur, "Anything Goes," *Positif #29*, 1958. A French film journal with a strong surrealist orientation, *Positif* championed Avery as well as Tashlin. Tashlin was also a favorite of the *Cahiers du Cinema* group. The cocktail party sequence in the first reel of Jean-Luc Godard's *Pierrot le Fou*, in which characters speak to each other in commercial catch phrases, is only one of Godard's many Tashlinisms.

Veni, vidi, video . . .

Originally published in *Film Comment* (May–June 1982).

●●● **O**R SO DISPIRITED movie purists and militant videologues would have us believe. The aphoristic comparison, *"Caïn et Abel = Cinéma et Vidéo,"* scrawled on a blackboard in Jean-Luc Godard's *Sauve Qui Peut,* perversely reverses this apocalyptic vision. But if video kills its older brother, it will be slowly—and with kindness.

The great movie-video polarity is pretty much a red herring. (The real polarity, as we shall see, is Cinema-Television.) In a recent *Village Voice* essay, Carrie Rickey posited the essential movie-video dichotomy as one of scale: "Movies microscope; television telescopes." Sure, unless you're looking at an 8mm porno loop or watching a prizefight simulcast on a wall-sized screen. Another commonly made distinction concerns the nature of the image. When we watch a TV monitor we're staring directly into the light source; when we watch a movie we're catching the light reflected off a flat surface. Fine, but where does this leave projected video?

In essence, movies and video are the same thing: a two-dimensional recording of moving light, with optional synchronous sound. This isn't to ignore the fact that certain video artists (Bill Viola and Barbara Buckner come immediately to mind) are extraordinarily sensitive to the specific qualities of the video image—just as it might be noted that Josef von Sternberg was extraordinarily sensitive to the specific qualities of studio lighting and black-and-white film. Movies and video are two kinds of Cinema. The only ontological difference between them is that movies have a chemical-mechanical basis, while video has an electronic basis. What this means is that the video image is immediately retrievable as information; it can produce instant feedback.

Video is not necessarily Television. For one thing, the latter is continuous. A TV set is a household appliance; turn on the faucet and out comes "television." If we define Cinema as the gathering together of an audience to attend a particular recorded sound-image event, then a videotape played in an art gallery is as much Cinema as the unspooling of Abel Gance's *Napoleon* at the Radio City Music Hall. Television, on the other hand, is predicated on an atomized, far-flung public. As a cinematic delivery system, Television creates a simultaneous and metaphysical "there." Its purest form would be something like transmitting sunshine to stay-at-homes. (In this sense, the soaps are pure Television.)

The communality of the TV public is of a totally different order than that of the movie audience. As a child, I remember watching the Wednesday night telecast of *Disneyland* and taking enormous pleasure in the knowledge that right then sets were blasting on all over America—every kid in the country was watching the same thing I was and we were all doing it at the exact same moment. In other words, Television (including cable, satellite, and low-power TV) is that cinematic event which everyone talks about the next morning at work. Considering the monolithic nature of network TV, the invention of the Sony PortaPak was a far more epochal event than, say, the development of the 16mm camera. Television before half-inch tape was comparable to the situation in Poland after the December coup: radio, but no telephone. (Or, to be somewhat recherché: TV before video = *langue* without *parôle*.)

THE KOREAN-BORN Nam June Paik is both the inventor and "first name in entertainment" of video art, its Vladimir Zworykin and Milton Berle combined. Paik's 1963 exhibit of doctored TV sets announced the birth of video art.

It was part of Paik's genius to see the TV as an object, as well as to discover video as a medium. Most of the artists who followed him have opted for either object "installations" or else videotapes. A rare exception is Joan Jonas's 1972 *Vertical Roll*—a tape that not only isolates a specific quality of the video image but which also, given time, creates a visual force field that totally deforms the space around the TV monitor.

Paik was seldom so stringent. With sock-a-delic insouciance, his 1973 *Global Groove* scores African rituals, Navajo rain dances, Korean ballet, and leggy tap dancers to Mitch Ryder screaming "Devil with a Blue Dress." The half-hour tape, whose images are laced with stroboscopic hot pink and cobalt blue scribble-scrabble, was originally shown as *Video Sea*—an installation of seventeen monitors, face-up on the floor, blaring and zooming in unison. The most ontologically slippery form of artist's video makes use of the technology to create closed-circuit feedback systems. When presented on tape, as with Richard Serra's 1974 *Boomerang*, these systems are clearly video; when created "live," as in the installations of Peter Campus and others, they are a form of avant-garde Television.

EVER SINCE THE mid-Sixties, Television has also availed itself of video technology. This is paradigmatic in its sports coverage—most impressively, NFL Football during the reign of Richard Nixon and ABC's treatment of the 1976 Olympics. Sports allow the greatest occasion for video feedback or "instant replay"—created, according to broadcast historian Eric Barnouw, in order to endlessly repeat Jack Ruby's assassination of Lee Harvey Oswald. The combination of multiple point-of-view and slow motion in "instant replay" (or "instant analysis" as it is known in TV news jargon) can be considered Television's greatest pure-video contribution.

It is by no means Television's only intervention into Cinema. That the proliferation of TV sets during the Fifties produced a nation of home-installed revival theaters may have done more than any other phenomena to foster a sense of American film culture. But although the cartoons, weepies, and horror flicks of the Thirties and Forties were available to students all day long, it wasn't until 1961—when NBC floated *How to Marry a Millionaire* as the first *Saturday Night at the Movies*—that the networks realized the audience-grabbing potential of the prime-time feature. In 1963, MCA-Universal invented the made-for-TV feature with Don Seigel's remake of *The Killers* (too violent, and so first released to theaters); ABC pioneered a regular series of made-for-TV movies in 1969. By the end of the Seventies, TV movies had become both Hollywood's bread and butter and a European means of avant-garde patronage: A substantial proportion of the most innovative film narrative and experimental documentaries of the last decade were produced under the auspices of West German TV.

Although the made-for-TV mode includes a few aesthetic triumphs (Steven Spielberg's *Duel,* Roberto Rossellini's *Blaise Pascal,* Hans-Jürgen Syberberg's *Ludwig*), it mainly created a recognizable and much-maligned visual style based on over-determined dramatic climaxes, shallow-spaced interiors, extended volleys of reverse-angle close-ups, the narrative use of automobiles and telephones, and frequent zooms. Although not specifically invented for Television, the zoom was one TV device which had a major impact on Hollywood production values.

The connotations of a made-for-TV movie are of a topical, low-budget, fact-blurring, consensus-oriented, disposable film, working on an intimate rather than an epic scale. Although the results can be superb (e.g., ABC's 1977 serial, *Washington: Behind Closed Doors*), the formal innovations are minor. But the development of videotape in the mid-Sixties created the possibility for new kinds of hybrid Cinema. Scott Bartlett and Tom DeWitt's 1967 *OFFON* was the first of these, transferring film images to video, exploiting video's capacity for colorizing and feedback, then transferring the result back to film. The use of video for titles or special effects in Hollywood movies also dates from the late Sixties. Nevertheless, it was only marginally explored. It is symptomatic of Hollywood's conservatism that the first American feature to make extensive use of video transferred to film, Frank Zappa's *200 Motels* (1971), came from the most self-consciously "freaky" segment of the culture industry.

Not surprisingly, Zappa's effort had considerably less cultural cachet than Michelangelo Antonioni's more recent experiment along the same lines, *Il Mistero di Oberwald*. Here, the overwhelming sensation is of looking over the maestro's shoulder while he fiddles with the knobs on the video synthesizer. Only once does Antonioni pull out all the stops, with a splendid helicopter swoop over Monica Vitti galloping through pink fields on a blue horse, her punk crimson hair limned against a canary sky. As Vitti earlier exclaimed upon discovering an assassin stumbling into her boudoir: "At last something is happening at Oberwald!"

Undoubtedly, the most brilliant hybrid has been Jean-Luc Godard and Anne-Marie Miéville's 1975 masterpiece, *Numéro Deux*. Like some American sitcoms, the film deals with the effect of modern capitalism on the sex lives of a young working-class couple, except that it's set entirely inside Godard's Grenoble studio and played out on two TV monitors. Despite the superficial minimalism, *Numéro Deux* is among the most visually compelling films that Godard has ever made, using the video monitors to develop a dozen new ways of splitting the screen or layering the image (effects which are far more easily achieved with a video synthesizer than an optical printer).

With much fanfare, Godard's sometimes patron, Francis Coppola, has moved into video as well. Coppola's original intention for *One From the Heart*, as he explained to Jonathan Cott in their *Rolling Stone* interview, was "taking theater and actually putting it on a street in Las Vegas . . . and shooting it, not like a movie, but like a baseball game." The end result—which, given its aspect ratio, color schemes, and *I Love Lucy* narrative, may actually gain in the transfer to home video cassette—made a more practical, if hidden, use of video technology.

Thomas Brown, the recent supervisor of Zoetrope's Electronic Cinema Division, designed an editing system that could construct a video "story-board" out of artists' sketches, the recorded script, and musical accompaniment. Once the actors began rehearsing, their scenes were taped and used to replace the sketches; during the actual shooting, the rushes were transferred to tape, coded, and used to produce an "instant" rough-cut. "At every point in the filmmaking process, you have a complete film at your fingertips," Brown told *American Film*. In short, Coppola used video technology to gain the same freedom of continuous revision enjoyed by more traditional artists at their easels or type-writers.

AT PRESENT, VIDEO is bestowing this power on the image consumer. Home videocassette recorders (VCRs) complicate the Cinema-Television duality. On a strictly phenomenological level, *The Tonight Show* is no longer Television once you have removed it from the Television flow and are looking at it two weeks later. If Home Box Office is a technology for transforming first-run movies into Television events, the VCR is a machine that turns Television into something for which I know no better term than "Film." (Almost alone among current video artists, Dara Birnbaum has created an aesthetic based on the premise of the VCR: She constructs her own tapes and movies out of bits of *Laverne and Shirley* or *The Hollywood Squares*.)

Television gave every American home its own personal rep house; the VCR has the potential to equip every viewer with the equivalent of a Movieola or Steenbeck. The appreciation thus engendered for fragmented (or fetishized) bits of "Film" will likely have as profound an effect on the film culture of the Eighties as TV had on that of the Fifties and Sixties.

Love & death in the American supermarketplace

A review of *What Was Literature?* by Leslie Fiedler; *The Sociology of Culture*, by Raymond Williams; *The Sociology of Art*, by Arnold Hauser; and *Media and the American Mind*, by Daniel J. Czitrom. Originally published in *The Village Voice Literary Supplement* (November 1982).

H ISTORY HAS A natural sense of rhythm and the tide of the '60s is at low ebb. We can recognize what beachheads remain by the rat-a-tat-tat of reactionary fire.

In the realm of culture, the reaction proceeds on several fronts with one goal. The Reagan administration attack on public arts funding (specifically the "expansion arts" programs designed to support minority, blue-collar, and rural culture), the Moral Majority censorship of local school and library books, the polemics of neo-Conservative ideologues are all designed to restore a lost absolute of cultural propriety.

Never mind that this imagined Golden Age is about as meaningful a notion as nostalgia for the gold standard. Scarcely was Reagan elected when Barbara Tuchman sounded the opening volley in a *New York Times Magazine* cover story, "The Decline of Quality." Embracing the shibboleth of artistic intent (all art is intended to be "timeless, universal, noble"), Tuchman argued that the mysterious ingredient "Q" was an inherent, rather than socially determined, property of specific works: "Any kind of illiterate will recognize a difference in quality between, let us say, Matisse's exhilarating interiors and hotel art of little waifs with big black eyes." Apparently unaware that the noble Matisse had once been tagged a "wild beast" by bourgeois critics, Tuchman went on to compare proponents of "non-Q" to noisy drunks.

In the maiden issue of his journal, *The New Criterion*—note the timeless, universal, and totalitarian use of the singular noun—Hilton Kramer scans the rubble of critical standards and diagnoses the low level of current intellectual discourse. "A very large part of the reason for this sad state of affairs is, frankly, political," his manifesto reads. "We are still living in the aftermath of the insidious assault on mind that was one of the most repulsive features of the Sixties. The cultural consequences of this leftwing turn in our political life have been far graver than is commonly supposed. In everything from the writing of textbooks to the reviewing of trade books; from the introduction of kitsch into the museums to the decline of literacy in the schools to the corruption of scholarly research, the effect on the life of culture has been ongoing and catastrophic"—a veritable eve of destruction.

Among other things, what happened in the '60s was something for everyone—namely the displacement of America's never-secure high culture by a rude surge of energy from below. Movies and popular music, mass forms once beneath contempt or critical awareness, achieved a sudden aesthetic (or "camp") prestige. Silk-screened Brillo boxes were trafficked in the booming art market, while minimalism (Brillo boxes without the logo), concept art, and earthworks further undermined the sanctity of the traditional art object. In the universities, dissident academics and, more often, students agitated for the creation of entire disciplines devoted to the cultural production of hitherto marginal groups (racial minorities, women, working and non-Western peoples). The censorship laws of major cities were challenged and overthrown in court, creating the possibility for unimagined pornographies.

What is more, the country had just been wired for simultaneity. By 1960, television had fully saturated America's homes, bars, and motel rooms, thus establishing itself as the culture's dominant mode of information and entertainment. Less a medium than an environment, TV was the great equalizer, a ubiquitous spectacle offering everybody everything in the whole gaudy marketplace, including something to blame.

The distaste for so dynamic a cultural moment is by no means restricted to Uncle Hilty's reactionary bellowing. In a recent *Nation* piece, Princeton lit prof Louis Menand pondered the post-'60s leveling of standards that either compelled or legitimized (his reading is ambiguous) serious aesthetic response to mass culture on its own terms. Now, Menand observes, "intellectuals are not merely tolerant of but responsive to the very characteristics of the popular work that make it evanescent, the shameless desire to engage our feelings . . . the penchant for capitalizing upon the fad or news item of the moment . . . its formulaic predictability . . . its glitziness—the sheer monumentality of its excesses; and not least, its frequent contempt for the solemn formalism of high culture." Of course, any number of works in the high canon could be similarly analyzed; the taste for *Macbeth,* Cubism, haiku, Wagner, and *Huckleberry Finn* hasn't always been universal. But this is to miss Menand's point. What he fears is the perversely self-willed regression of an entire caste, namely his own.

With the bourgeois revolutions of the 17th and 18th centuries, professional critics assumed the function—hitherto controlled by church or state—of setting standards, providing the social signification and cultural seal of approval, Art, the big Q. But "once all cultural objects [are] seen in the same light," as Menand complains, critics are forced "to treat all culture as commodity, or treat all culture as art." For Menand, such leveling inevitably creates monsters: the academic structuralists ready to diagram any piece of literature into a semiotic formula, the ga-ga American Studies scholars who fill *The Journal of Popular Culture* with appreciations of Johnny Carson, free-lance intellectuals who write books on pop that compare Elvis Presley and Herman Melville, and the critical journalism of *The Village Voice,* "where every cultural experience is rendered in the same hyperbolic prose."

Yet it was not simply the "repulsive" tumult of the '60s that yanked down the temple of critical standards. The crisis Menand identifies as "the collapse of a cultural hierarchy" and the resultant "demystification of all art" is implicit in the very development of mechanical means of reproduction. The printing press is likely the first of these but the camera is a better example: the sudden appearance of a machine by which any idiot could create a perfect representational likeness threw professional painters and their critics into a fertile confusion which has lasted over a century and continues to this day. It is called modern art.

Menand naively locates such "camera" democracy—upending of aesthetic criteria by some primitive form of industrial expression—in Susan Sontag's 1965 *Against Interpretation,* where she suggests that "the feeling (or sensation) given off by a Rauschenberg painting might be like that of a song by the Supremes." What's telling here is that this instance involves the bracketing of high art and rock 'n' roll. Menand could have made the point with a linking of Charles Dickens and D. W. Griffith or Arnold Schönberg and Ornette Coleman. But the natural constituency for rock 'n' roll is even more barbaric than the great unwashed immigrant hordes who popularized the nickelodeon or the colored races who spawned ragtime. Movies and jazz have academic beachheads; rock, on the other hand, is the tribal music of adolescent students. It's supposedly meant to be outgrown (as you can't naturally "outgrow" your race or social status). There's even a country song about some guy "pushing 40 and still wearing jeans," and what can be more evanescent (not to mention topical, shameless, formulaic, or glitzy) than a three-minute ditty over AM radio.

Who in 1956 would have predicted that 25 years after Elvis arrived on *The Ed Sullivan Show,* the music would still be listened to, let alone inspire a rock intelligentsia sufficiently literate to juxtapose "Hound Dog" and *Moby Dick*? If nothing else, rock 'n' roll has demonstrated considerable staying power in the American supermarketplace. Consequently it has a history, formal and ideological development to the point of Punk—a self-conscious vanguard analogous to

Dada and other modernist art movements in its attempt to demystify, devalue, and otherwise short-circuit the process by which the expressive work becomes a commodity. To admit this, however, is to admit the possibility that similar epidemics of modernist art practice—conscious or otherwise—might be found in such disreputable mass culture barrios as animated cartoons (Tex Avery), comic books (Harvey Kurtzman's *Mad*), Jerry Lewis–Dean Martin vehicles (Frank Tashlin), or network TV (Ernie Kovacs).

At least Menand realizes, as Kramer apparently does not, that under capitalism all culture has become commodity. It's a rude shock for the humanities to be competing with Elvis Presley for attention in the shrinking supermarketplace, but that's America. When newspapers report that video games are not only outgrossing the movie industry but the record industry as well, it's obviously the tremors of a new mass cultural volcano. The grungy 12 year old in that storefront arcade feeding quarters to Donkey Kong is perhaps the Robert Christgau of the future.

Life is evanescent but, by accident and design, materially (as well as ideally), art is what lasts. No more, no less. "The attempt to distinguish 'art' from other, often closely related, practices is a quite extraordinarily important historical and social process," writes British Marxist Raymond Williams in *The Sociology of Culture*. But nothing arises from nothing. "The attempt to distinguish 'aesthetic' from other kinds of attention and response is, as a historical and social process, perhaps even more important." The fact of aesthetic attention transcends the art object at hand and while, in the final analysis, "art" is not necessarily made by artists, it is always made by aesthetes. This is what Robert Smithson meant when he observed that "a great artist can make art by simply casting a glance."

Marcel Duchamp—who flung down the gauntlet when he chose to exhibit a urinal at a Paris art gallery and who encouraged the myth that he abandoned art for chess, a primitive form of Pac Man—put this most succinctly, remarking that "the artist may shout from all the rooftops that he is a genius; he will have to wait the verdict of the spectators in order that his declarations take on a social value and that, finally, posterity includes him in the primers of Art History."

MORALISTS BELIEVE IT is art's responsibility to uplift and instruct, as well as to delight and to last. For them, the superficial hedonism of pop is nothing less than cultural desecration. Leslie Fiedler—who violates academic decorum when he boasts of his TV exploits or professes to weep over *Gone with the Wind*, and who reveals his '60s roots by the very title his new book, *What Was Literature?*—attributes the hatred of pop culture to Plato's ancient quarrel with poetry. The stuff is dangerous and its opponents are characterized by the (not unjustified) "fear of fantasy," the "distrust of myth," and hence the "unacknowledged hostility to all emotion and art itself."

Fiedler, of course, achieved prominence in the early '60s with *Love and Death in the American Novel*—an enormously controversial book which, among other things, first proposed the now commonplace notion that classic American literature was rife with fantasies of misogyny and interracial male bonding. Clearly, Professor Fiedler is not a man to shy away from art's "unpleasant" realities. To plumb the emotional economy of pop, he suggests we face up to its four most disturbing genres—sentimental tearjerkers, tales of horror and spectacles of violence, comedies of "hilarious desecration," and pornography. (Put them all together and you have a recipe for the epic travesties perpetuated by the old Playhouse of the Ridiculous or the recent films of Brian De Palma.) Fiedler goes even further in suggesting that all four genres are fundamentally porn. Pop is blatantly sensational. It titillates through the transgression of basic taboos and strives to effect some gross physical catharsis—weeping, screaming, laughing, coming, and God help us if we mix our genres.

By the same logic, jazz and rock 'n' roll are forms of pornographic music. They inspire us to shake our booties or at least beat rhythmic time on the dashboards of our cars. In other words this crypto-porn is everywhere, and one contributor to *The New Criterion* celebrates his blinders by hypostatizing the decline of the *Partisan Review* in its mid-'60s publication of an essay on pornography (naughty Sontag again), among other subjects unworthy of serious attention.

A more serious charge leveled against pop is its alleged power of mystification. In this view, most cogently expressed by the critics of the Frankfurt School (Theodor Adorno, Max Horkheimer, Herbert Marcuse) and fellow travelers like Arnold Hauser, mass culture—like advertising—is ultimately a form of social propaganda for the status quo. "Can one really distinguish between the mass media as instruments of information and entertainment, and as agents of manipulation and indoctrination?" asked Herbert Marcuse. Or, as his colleague Leo Lowenthal once put it, "mass culture is psychoanalysis in reverse." High art, on the other hand, is critical—a "negation" of the modern capitalist world, the supermarketplace. "It creates the images of conditions which are irreconcilable with the established Reality Principle" (Marcuse).

What's more, mass art routinely traffics in collective release, a far more dangerous phenomenon than individual appreciation. Thus, given their experience of German history, it is hardly surprising that the Frankfurt School was obsessed to the point of brilliance and irrationality with the relationship between mass culture and fascism. Evacuated to an America mobilized for war, Adorno and Horkheimer lost sight of the dialectic and interpreted America's more democratic mass culture as a monolithic industry dedicated to hypnotizing the masses with tawdry circuses. "Pleasure hardens into boredom because, if it is to remain pleasure, it must not demand any effort and therefore moves rigorously in the worn grooves of association. No independent thinking must be expected from the audience; the product prescribes every reaction: not by its natural structure (which collapses under reflection), but signals."

Implicit in this left-wing horror of the modern world is a nostalgia for preindustrial folk art. (For right-wingers, it's a nostalgia for church or courtly art.) In distinguishing between folk culture and mass culture, the late Arnold Hauser offers a class analysis that supports the Frankfurter notion of mass culture as social control. The producers and consumers of folk art, Hauser writes, are "hardly distinguishable from each other," whereas the " 'hits,' trashy novels, melodramas" of mass culture "come from the pens of professional upperclass writers who remained linked to their class." Hauser is more oblivious than hostile to the possibility of culture erupting from below. But, as the camera demonstrated, even monkeys or juvenile delinquents can make coherent images. And such 20th century forms as hot music, vaudeville, pulp novels, and peep shows were (initially at least) produced by members of the urban proletariat for members of the urban proletariat.

The characterization of popular art as evanescent is used to minimize its claims to either serious attention or a piece of the cultural canon. What it more fruitfully suggests is the profound connection between popular art and performance. In this sense, the now obsolete—but formerly all inclusive—mode of vaudeville is a useful paradigm. Once a largely oral tradition, popular culture has just recently gained access to writing. "It is only in the last hundred and fifty years, in any culture," Williams observes, "that a majority of the people have had even minimal access to this technique which already, over two millennia, had been carrying a major part of human culture. (Moralists may consider this injustice as analogous to living in a future where the use of television is restricted to Ronald Reagan and his friends.)

Perhaps because universal literacy is so recent, writing has proved a lesser mass cultural form than certain types of performance. And before the development of mechanical means of reproduction, all performances were evanescent. Paganini is a legend, but within a few years of the nickelodeon, Charlie Chaplin became the first denizen of the aesthetic lower depths to impinge upon elite (not to mention global) consciousness.

It can be argued that, even when mass produced, all popular art is a performance designed for evanescence. Take, for example, the tabloid newspaper—meant to be devoured and discarded in the course of a single rush-hour subway ride. During the period between the two world wars, the American tabloid aggressively identified itself with the concerns and vernacular (if not necessarily the class interests) of the "common man." Accordingly, the picture press developed an aesthetic of shock, raw sensation, and immediate impact, a form of packaged graffiti intended to arrest the eye of a rushing commuter at 100 paces.

A Marxist might dismiss the violent discontinuity and blunt stylization of this proletariat expressionism on the grounds that the workers who created it did not themselves control the means of production. But this is to ignore the artlike task that these reporters, photographers, and cartoonists performed for an audience of their peers. No less than hash-slingers or cabdrivers, modern artists have been part of this audience. The urban sensationalism developed by press photographers like Weegee, pulp novelists like Horace McCoy, cartoonists like Chester Gould, or journalist-filmmakers like Samuel Fuller has noticeably altered the perceptions of "higher" artists, toiling in the vineyards of Western

Civilization (e.g., Garry Winogrand, Diane Arbus, Albert Camus, Alain Resnais, Jean-Luc Godard). More often than not, the discoveries of this tabloid school have—like blue jeans—returned to us with French designer labels.

In *The Sociology of Culture,* Raymond Williams offers a social explanation for the growth of modernism in the immigrant cities of Paris and New York that suggests equally the appeal of the nickelodeon or ragtime. "Certain factors in avant-garde culture, and especially the conscious breaks from 'traditional' styles have to be analyzed not only in formal terms but within the sociology of the metropolis."

The turn-of-the-century metropolis created encounters between recent immigrants, lumpen or otherwise, who shared no common language (save that of the melting pot) and whose "received sign systems"—including visual ones—had become obsolete. Hence cubism; hence the tabloid. Because industrialization and mechanical reproduction are the bane of traditional values, the Scylla and Charybdis of modern life, mass culture and the avant-garde arrived at the same historic moment in response to the same historical processes and equally in opposition to bourgeois culture. Neither was conceivable before the industrial revolution—they represent the two poles of modern art.

Even Hilton Kramer realizes as much. In an essay called "Postmodern" (a buzz word which, to put it mildly, has no fixed meaning), he attacks the modernist taste for camp—Sontag, yet again—that is basically the reclamation of obsolete mass cultural forms (old movies, old songs, old postcards, etc.) as aesthetic objects. Of course, the unholy alliance between avant-garde and mass culture has taken an impressive number of forms over the past 120 years. Novelists from James Joyce to Thomas Pynchon, composers from Charles Ives to Don Cherry, painters from Edgar Degas (or on the other side, Douanier Rousseau) to Julian Schnabel, and poets from Charles Baudelaire to that anti-hero of '60s term papers, Bob Dylan, not to mention every photographer and filmmaker who ever lived, have set up aesthetic shop in the space between the two.

Of course, nostalgia for the 19th century is by no means the monopoly of cultural reactionaries. Georg Lukacs, the preeminent Marxist critic of our time, built an aesthetic around the novels of Sir Walter Scott, and Fiedler—as conservative as he is radical—wistfully invokes the names of Dickens, Balzac, Dostoevsky, Fenimore Cooper, and Twain. But, for the left, it is not the certifiable literary quality of *Bleak House* or *Huckleberry Finn* that gives them their aura so much as the universality (hence, implied democracy) of the audience they originally addressed. A second-generation American like Fiedler, no less than a Marxist like Lukacs, experiences this vision of universal access to culture with particular piquance.

Nevertheless, excepting the brief intellectual vogue for Mickey Mouse in the 1930s and an even briefer one for the Beatles in the late 1960s, there has not been much in the way of universal cultural acceptance since the discovery of Charlie Chaplin after World War I. Needless to say, this has not been for want of a universal culture whose movies, comic books, pop songs, and TV soap operas have been decried with ambivalent regularity by culture critics on both the right and left for the past hundred years.

Fiedler, Menand, Kramer, and Tuchman might equally shudder at Raymond Williams's command of jargon—although Williams, author of the invaluable etymological dictionary *Key Words,* makes wonderfully precise use of his terms—but they all concur with his statement that "increasingly, this 'popular' sector is the major area of bourgeois and ruling class cultural production, moving towards an offered 'universality' in the modern communications institutions, with a 'minority' culture"—namely, high culture—"increasingly seen as residual and formally 'preserved' in those terms." And does anyone dispute that the mother lode, the prime gusher, the veritable Saudi Arabia of "this 'popular' culture" is—love it or leave it—the United States of America?

The fact is that for NeoCon, NeoLib, and bourgeois critics in general, the universal democracy of the American supermarketplace has become something of a nightmare. ("A question that puzzles me," Tuchman whines, "is why inexpensive things must be ugly; why walking through the aisles in a discount chain store causes acute discomfort in the esthetic nerve cells.") It is at this point that the Kleenex-thin objections of NeoCon aesthetes, who double as "realistic" advocates of marketplace rule and American hegemony, dissolve into hopeless contradiction and the circular file of history.

FOR LESLIE FIEDLER, the dream of social equality is embodied in "two particularly American institutions, the supermarket and the landgrant college, where all are permitted access and everything is made available." This vision is typically the immigrant's fantasy of America—a fantasy given its most heartbreaking literary expression in the final "Nature Theater of Oklahoma" chapter of Franz Kafka's *Amerika.* But where Kafka (who, of course, never came to America) imagines the end of history, Fiedler imagines "a slow, inexorable evolution toward an egalitarian community in which everyone, rich and poor (the native tradition can conceive of equalizing everything but wealth), will speak the same classless dialect of their native tongue, hear the same music, read the same books and periodicals, see the same movies and television programs, as well as drive the same cars, eat the same food and wear the same clothes."

Less than democracy, what Fiedler describes is the "benign" plutocracy celebrated in Mario Puzo's homage to the magic kingdom of Las Vegas. In Vegas—unlike, say, Monte Carlo—"opulence is available to everyone regardless of race, class, appearance, religion, etc. All you need is a small bankroll."

It is precisely the inequality that Fiedler reduces to a parenthetical aside, and Puzo pushes right to the fore, which gives us the sham democracry of the supermarketplace where, as Andy Warhol once observed: "The president drinks Cola-cola, Liz Taylor drinks Coca-cola, and just think, you can drink Coke too. A Coke is a Coke and no amount of money can get you a better Coke than the one that the bum on the corner is drinking." Warhol's contemporary Herbert Marcuse called this commodity democracy "repressive desublimation." But Marcuse was an immigrant socialist, whereas Warhol is an ethnic entrepreneur.

The cultural paradigm of such reified democracy, as you have doubtless guessed, is that universal cornucopia and cretin King Midas—the television set, where entertainment, culture, news, politics, religion, and commercials coexist at their lowest common denominator, commodity. Marcuse's countryman, Arnold Hauser, has but one paragraph on television in his 761-page *Sociology of Art* and it's not bad. For the television audience, Hauser suggests, TV is "the triumph of technology over nature, the view of the *theatrum mundi* from their armchair, the participation of everyone in everything. The world in miniature, however naive that may sound, is not an idea which is alien to art: every work of art attempts to achieve it. The chief charm of art consists in the reduction or the regression of artistic creation to this infantile wish fulfillment, which at the same time represents *the substitute satisfaction pure and simple for everything which is denied us*" (italics mine).

So television, if not precisely a "negation" of the supermarketplace, at least addresses the same negative psychic need. Could even television be art? Fiedler reports that cultivated Europeans consider the "incursion into their midst of rock music, country-and-western, comic books, schlocky TV sitcoms and cop shows" (for stuffy Brits, he adds, "Ernest Hemingway")—the glitziest items in the supermarketplace—as "creeping Americanism." But this is foolishly monolithic. The corollary to this "creeping Americanism" (which patriotic NeoCons call the "leveling of standards") is, as students of modernism know, the not-so-creeping "Americanitis"—the avid love of slapstick movies, newspaper funnies, and hot jazz which infected the French and Russian avant-gardes of the 1920s.

If nothing else, the radical differences between a universal narrative/performance artist like Charles Dickens and a universal narrative/performance artist like Charles Chaplin should alert us to the mutable nature of this thing called "art." As Bertolt Brecht argued against Georg Lukacs, it is fruitless to search for 19th century masterpieces in the 20th century.

But it *is* useful to examine the history of American cultural production. Fiedler suggests as much when he observes that "American culture came of age at the very moment when old aristocratic sponsors of the arts were being replaced by the mass audience," noting that his privileged form, the novel, is "the first successful form of popular art to have entered culture." The novel is "related not to such forms as the epic on the one hand or the folk ballad on the other—in fact, to nothing which precedes it, but to much that follows: the comic strip, the comic book, cinema, TV."

Because Fiedler is more a critic of culture than literature, he tends to read works for their underlying myths and archetypes (not so different from the structuralists he deplores). Having discovered that "archetypes are not eternal but socially determined" and concluded that "mythopoeic power [is] independent of formal excellence," he spends the second half of *What Was Literature?* making a persuasive case that such "sub-literary" efforts as *Uncle Tom's Cabin* (and the melodramas it engendered), *The Klansman* (and *The Birth of a Nation*), *Gone with the Wind* (book and movie) and *Roots* (book, miniseries, phenomenon) are a single "inadvertent epic"—a story America told to itself.

Still, the braving of the supermarketplace does not in itself make Fiedler a modernist critic. For that you need to risk received standards by examining experience, no matter how evanescent. It was Gertrude Stein who discovered (as recounted in her aptly titled *The Geographical History of America*) "that any kind of a book if you read with glasses and somebody is cutting your hair and so you cannot keep the glasses on and you use your glasses as a magnifying glass and so read word by word makes the writing that is not anything be something. Very regrettable but very true."

A more radical attempt to harpoon the inadvertent epic was made by another college lit prof, Marshall McLuhan. However, unlike Fiedler, McLuhan was a professional modernist—a student of Yeats, Eliot, Pound, and above all, Joyce. And like Roland Barthes, McLuhan was extraordinarily interested in signs—the nuts and bolts of how meaning is expressed. Thus, McLuhan made one of the essential discoveries of *What Was Literature?* back in 1951, when he published *The Mechanical Bride*. As paraphrased by Daniel J. Czitrom in *Media and the American Mind*, McLuhan "argued that formal education of any type could not hope to compete with the unofficial education people received from the new media." For McLuhan, the inadvertent epic was first advertising, comic strips, and newspapers—"the folklore of industrial man." Ultimately, it was television.

Suppose, instead of a urinal, I exhibited a videotape of a complete programming day of a single network TV station—everything from the wake-up news and early morning game shows through the reruns of *The Love Boat* and afternoon soaps through the evening news, primetime attractions, and late-night movies—and declared this 20-hour effusion a single work of art. Suppose you were a working anthropologist from the year 2525 and discovered such an artifact. The rhythms might be static but the system of signs and allusion would beggar *Finnegans Wake*. Now suppose Nam June Paik took this material and shuffled it around.

Among students of media, Czitrom has a refreshing lucidity. "It is possible," he writes, "to criticize the worst tendencies of modern media—banalization, encouragement of the commodity fetish, the urge towards global hegemony—but at the same time to hold out real hope for future promise." Head firmly planted in the sand, Tuchman decries using school time to teach television awareness as hopelessly non-Q. ("A high-school student of my acquaintance in affluent suburbia was recently assigned by his English teacher, no less, to watch television for a week and keep a record on 3-by-5 index cards. This in the literature of Shakespeare to Mark Twain, Jane Austen to J. D. Salinger!") The social importance of Fiedler's *What Was Literature?* is its refusal to surrender the '60s notion that the university is capable of such work, that it might and should be a place of living culture or what Ishmael Reed—with respect to its irrepressible eruption from below—calls "Jes Grew," and what I'm terming modern art.

The cultural reaction promoted by Kramer's "new (new? *nu?*) criterion" is, in its heart of darkness, the fear and loathing of the modern world and its terrors (mechanization, urbanization, democratization). Anyone of parents born can empathize with the pathetic yearning for the "eternal" verities of the old criterion. But, *hypocrite lecteur,* it's a brand new ballgame. Has been for some time now.

No critic conjured "Jes Grew" into existence and no amount of *Times Magazine* thinkpieces will wish it away. And that is why, however destructive the current reaction has proved on an economic level, however cruel its assault on social equality, however close the mutant Stone Age its *realpolitik* threatens, this reaction can never be more than sterile in the production of culture.

Personalities and Oeuvres

tWo

The star who fell to earth

Originally published as "That Reagan Boy: The Education of an All-American" in *The Village Voice* (September 10–16, 1980).

HE MAY HAVE the beady eyes, leathery hide, and social conscience of a stegosaurus, but as an American politician Ronald Reagan is right on time—and not just because he pioneered the use of pancake on the stump. Reagan made a successful career out of establishing the "likeability" of his two-dimensional image. He spent three decades practicing a form of hoodoo—the Dr. Strange-like projection of his ectoplasmic form—over radio, in the movies, and on TV. The package may be a bit shopworn, but the historian must stand in awe of its prophetic vision. In the sine qua non of American telepolitics, Reagan is the best-trained candidate who ever lived.

There have, of course, been other movie stars who made the transition to gov biz. John Davis Lodge was elected Senator from Connecticut and appointed Ambassador to Spain, but then his movie career was itself a kind of vacation from the family firm. Helen Gahagan Douglas, another middling star of the '30s, became a California congresswoman, only to be smeared off the map when she ran for the Senate against the young Richard Nixon. If song-and-dance man George Murphy was more successful, it may be because his opponent, JFK press-secretary Pierre Salinger, was a paradigm of ineptitude. The fact is, no previous star-pol has ever had an iota of Reagan's ambition, staying power, and versatility.

The story of Ronald Reagan is the story of his image—how he developed it, refined it, layered it, solved its problems. The key to his behavior as president is not to be found in his eight years as governor of California. That was, after all, just another role. Reagan presented himself to the American public in successive phases: Good Joe, Patriot, Cowboy, and Corporate Logo. The sum of these is Reagan the Politician.

Reagan, it's been noted, has been a professional purveyor of "simplistic fantasy" nearly all of his working life. When did he realize that he could equate this with what passes for American political dialogue? In 1936, the San Antonio chapter of the Gary Cooper Fan Club, inflamed by Coop's portrayal of a millionaire do-gooder in *Mr. Deeds Goes to Town,* launched a national campaign to elect their idol president of the United States. Is it possible that the full implications of this bizarre human interest bit were grasped only by a 25-year-old sportscaster out of Des Moines named Ronald "Dutch" Reagan?

Very often a performer "finds himself" by using cues from audience responses and making himself into what people want.
—Orrin E. Klapp, *Symbolic Leaders* (1964)

Well, an actor has to please people and so does a senator.
—Shirley Temple Black, campaigning for former costar George Murphy (1964)

REAGAN HAS ALWAYS made the most out of what he had. Breaking into show business as a radio announcer, his forte was fabricating Chicago Cubs games out of telegraphed dispatches while a sound-effects man backed him up with the crack of the bat and the roar of the crowd. After five years he followed the Cubs to spring training and landed a Hollywood contract. The studio that signed him was Warner Bros., the major that specialized in "ordinary" (even proletariat) stars like Cagney and Bogie and Joan Blondell. Despite the fact that it was the most pro-Roosevelt studio in Hollywood, Warners was run like an assembly line. Movie stardom was less a condition than a job. Reagan turned out to be a good worker.

In his first three years as a Warners factory-hand, he appeared in over 20 pictures. He played news hounds, radio announcers, and Tugboat Annie's son. He was part of gossip columnist Louella Parson's entourage in *Hollywood Hotel* (1937) and the next year shared billing with a horse in *Sergeant Murphy*. The year after that, in *Hell's Kitchen* and *Angels Wash Their Faces,* he was a straight-man for the Bowery Boys. They chewed up the scenery; he courted "Oomph Girl" Ann Sheridan and crusaded for slum clearance or reform of the reform schools. In 1939, Reagan was rewarded with his own kiddie series, the four *Secret Service of the Air* flicks, in which he got to rush around like a sexless Errol Flynn protecting top-secret "inertia projectors" from nefarious enemy agents. His attitude was impeccable. "Believe what you are doing is important," he would advise the youth of America in a ghost-written movie magazine article, "even if it is only grubbing for worms in the backyard."

The ambitious starlet bought the Hollywood myth in toto, marrying co-Warners contractee Jane Wyman in a burst of studio-manufactured publicity. Brokered by Louella Parsons, their match was consecrated at the Wee Kirk o' the Heather chapel of fashionable Forest Lawn cemetery. It was a storybook union—eight solid years of *Photoplay* fodder. Ronnie and Janie played it the company way. They invited press photographers and fan-mag scribes to document each new acquisition (home, first baby, second baby). Off camera and on, Reagan played the Good Joe. "I'm no Flynn or Boyer," he told the world. "Mr. Norm is my alias." Once pressed to name his hobbies, he replied, "I like to swim, hike, and sleep."

In 1940, the 29-year-old but still fresh-faced Reagan landed a plum part in *Knute Rockne, All American.* As the Christ-like Gipper, he played a Notre Dame football star who died two weeks after his last game. The *Brian's Song* of its day, it was a film to make Richard Nixon weep. (Nixon even incorporated the movie's tag-line, "Let's win this one for the Gipper," in his 1968 RepCon acceptance speech. For "Gipper" he substituted "Ike," then conveniently on his death-bed.) Perhaps seeking to probe Ronnie's potential as a tragic ingenue, Warners cast him as the young George Custer in the big-budget *Santa Fe Trail* in 1940; he elicited further sympathy in *King's Row,* playing a small town Lothario whose legs are gratuitously amputated.

The success of the latter led the studio to consider pairing him with Sheridan in *Casablanca,* but when Ingrid Bergman became available they shunted the couple over to *Juke Girl* instead. This saga of a "nickel-hungry broad" was just a bargain basement *Grapes of Wrath* in 1942, but it became a Telegraph Avenue cult film 25 years later for casting California's governor in the unlikely role of a militant migrant fruit-picker. *Juke Girl* epitomizes the flaming liberal past Reagan is wont to evoke with the relish of a dried-out alkie describing his last binge. Playing at Cesar Chavez left him with a paucity of sympathy for a real Chavez—hell, if he could marry the eponymous heroine of *Million Dollar Baby* (1941), didn't that show that America worked? Through Reagan's adminis-tration he sided with the big growers and corporate plantations against the farm workers. But then, the two Bowery Boys films notwithstanding, a sense of fair play for the underdog was never to be Ronnie's strong suit. He jettisoned Warners' New Deal ideology, although he did retain the studio's flare for wisecracking dialogue: "It's too bad we can't have an epidemic of botulism," he quipped in 1974, during the Symbionese Liberation Army's chaotic free food distribution program.

On the eve of Pearl Harbor, Reagan was a rising star—a useful but not yet valuable commodity. The disruption of the war consigned him permanently to Hollywood's second rank. Reagan spent most of it stationed on a Culver City soundstage but he managed to make almost as much publicity out of this military service as he had with his marriage: "Mr. Average Guy on the bright side is now in the Army with your brother Joe" (*Photoplay,* 1943). Even so, Mr. Average Guy remained defensive about his contribution to the war effort and would later complain that "some people can't respect a uniform unless it's on a dead soldier." (Could he have meant a dead gipper?) Reagan's major military assignment was an appearance in the lavish propaganda musical, *This Is the Army.* Conspiracy buffs should note that Screen Actors Guild activist George Murphy, the man who would test the political waters for Reagan 20 years later, co-starred as his doughboy dad. Reagan credits Murphy with giving him his anti-Communist basic training.

Politics is just like show business. You need a big opening. Then you coast for a while. Then you need a big finish.

                                                                    –Ronald Reagan, 1966

AFTER THE WAR, Ronnie was ready to resume his career playing what *Silver Screen* called "the typical young American," but nobody was sure that was what they wanted to see. As an actor he had always been a bit limited. His stock in trade—then as now—was a bashful, boyish innocence. His best emotion was "dismay"—a state of mind he would telegraph by raising one eyebrow and compressing his lips. (This is still how Reagan signals his disapproval of SALT II, the ERA, or Darwin's theory of Evolution.) Wondering how to repackage their overage juvenile, Warners put his development on hold. In 1947, to celebrate his return to civilian life, they cast him as the veterinarian hero of *Stallion Road,* an innocuous yawner that the star described as his "favorite picture of all time."

It is a measure of Reagan's good-natured lack of focus that he was designated to play opposite 18-year-old Shirley Temple in her first "adult" film, *That Hagen Girl* (1947). Ronnie was cast as a heroic veteran (decorated for his contribution to the "successful launching of atomic warfare") with Shirley as a winsome orphan girl, rumored to be his illegitimate daughter. The issue is resolved when they elope together to Chicago. One of Reagan's most ludicrous films, *That Hagen Girl,* has apparently been suppressed. (The authors of *The Fifty Worst Films of All Time* reported that when attempting to obtain a print from its erstwhile distributors they encountered a wall of "embarrassment" and "frightened silence.") At the time of its release, *New York Times* reviewer Bosley Crowther considered the film so perverse as to be "downright un-American." He sure knew how to hurt a guy: That same year, Reagan flew to Washington with Gary Cooper, Robert Taylor, George Murphy, and Robert Montgomery (later to be Ike's TV coach). Solemnly they had told the House Un-American Activities Committee how they had carefully scanned all prospective scripts for "communistic" propaganda, while monitoring Hollywood in general for any "subversive" activities.

As his postwar career faltered, Reagan increasingly immersed himself in the muddy waters of movieland politics. "It was no secret in Hollywood that Reagan had political ambitions," *Time*'s L.A. correspondent Joseph Lewis recalled, "But the cosmopolitans of the movie industry never considered him more than an overgrown Boy Scout constantly crusading for something or other." He was really a kind of a bore—forever quoting from the *Reader's Digest,* holding forth at cocktail parties on the horror of the graduated income tax, or earnestly speculating how the proper deployment of mounted cavalry would've hastened the end of World War II. Smitten by Ayn Rand, he publicly offered to dye his hair red to get the lead role in *The Fountainhead.*

As president of Screen Actors Guild, Reagan had reason to take himself seriously. During one strike (which he opposed) he began packing a gun—just like they do in the movies. His actual role in the Hollywood witch hunts was marginal, but by 1965, when he published his autobiography (remarkably titled *Where's the Rest of Me?*) he retroactively cast himself as the anti-Communist messiah. Fancifully he boasted that when "testifying under oath on the Communist Maneuvers to take over Hollywood, Sterling Hayden was asked what tripped him up. His reply: 'We ran into a one-man battalion named Ronald Reagan.'"

As the Red Scare gained momentum, Reagan's Warners contract expired and left him a free agent. Then Janie left him too. "I'm weary of being dreary, of being the good, the sweet, the dull, colorless charm boy . . . I'd make a good louse and I hope they're not out of style before I get a chance to find out," he complained to *Silver Screen* in 1950, the same year that *Modern Screen* ranked him among "Hollywood's 10 Loneliest Stars." It was a while before Reagan would get to play the louse of his dreams but he did manage to shed his juvenile image and pull together a string of films wherein he embodied low-keyed, affable authority figures. The most notorious of these is the 1951 Universal production of *Bedtime for Bonzo,* a movie ostensibly inspired by the success of *Francis the Talking Mule.* Without quite knowing how it happened, Reagan found himself cast as a pointy-headed college prof attempting to prove the primacy of environment over heredity by raising a chimpanzee as his own child. Publicity stills posed him standing on his head alongside the grinning simian and welcoming the creature into his bed.

Speaking about the film from the vantage point of 15 years, Reagan put up a game front: "Like all really good comedy, this one was based on a solid, believable foundation." (The film has continued to dog him. While visiting New York last April, he again defended its comic "credibility.") One can only imagine the extent of his paranoia, however, when after *Bonzo*'s release, its scenarist Val Burton was named as a Communist and banned from the movie industry. Under President Reagan, S.A.G. had already capitulated to the blacklist, but it was clear that Ronnie would have to toughen his own image as well.

He instantly went into training. In 1951, when Paramount cast him in a low-budget western called *The Last Outpost,* he waxed ecstatic: "I've been itching to sling a sixgun ever since I put on greasepaint. . . . Now at long last I've made the grade and I'd like to keep on making horse operas as long as they'll let me." His next two, even chintzier films gave him an education in foreign policy he's remembered to this day. *Hong Kong* (1952) sent him to a studio-built Orient to save school-marm Rhonda Fleming from the lascivious Chinese Reds. Then it was off to the *Tropic Zone,* where he again teamed with Rhonda to protect a Central American banana republic from an "outlaw" takeover. By the time Reagan had introduced compulsory loyalty oaths and non-Communist affidavits into S.A.G. and turned up as an ersatz Wyatt Earp in *Law and Order* he was approached to run for the Senate. But in 1953 such a move would've been premature. "I'm a ham—always was and always will be," he stoutly told reporters.

Building his persona as a third-string John Wayne, Reagan took roles in films you practically had to pay people to sit through. In M-G-M's cheap and lugubrious *Prisoner of War* (1954), he played a counterspy pretending to be brainwashed so that he could investigate a North Korean POW camp. The film was made with government assistance, although the Department of Defense ultimately withdrew support, reportedly because they wanted a harder line. Reagan's role—deprogramming hapless traitors—paralleled his activities as a member of the Motion Picture Industry Council committee for the "rehabilitation" of repentent movieland commies. *Prisoner of War*'s fade-out saw him teaching his men an inspirational mantra: "Here's a little thought that will get you on the go / Your old Uncle Sam is a better man than their old Uncle Joe."

With this kind of routine, anyone could see that Reagan's screen days were numbered. He must have known it himself. It was around this time that he married his second wife, Nancy Davis; he couldn't have done better if he'd called central casting. Perhaps he did. Davis was a post-debutante with an M-G-M contract whose specialty was playing demure, dutiful, usually pregnant, wives. She was the perfect postwar American woman. Her greatest role had been in *The Next Voice You Hear* (1950), a deliriously turgid exercise in political apocalypse wherein the voice of God commandeers the airwaves for six successive nights to endorse the American way of life.

Who has written his speeches? Who—or what board of ghost-writing strategists—has fashioned the phrases, molded the thoughts, designed the delivery, authored the image, staged the presentation, put the political show on the road to win the larger number of votes? Who is the actor reading the script?
   —Ad taken out in *Life* by John Wayne to coincide with JFK's nomination in 1960

TOGETHER WITH NANCY, Reagan built a second career out of the ruins of his first. The shift was a bit rocky. Surviving from guest spot to guest spot on the tube, he hit bottom in 1954. That was the year he had to take a two-week gig at the Last Frontier lounge in Las Vegas fronting for a comedy dance team with a shtick that reflexively parodied his appearance as a high-class no-talent m.c. But if things looked dark, there was an electric light bulb at the end of the tunnel. Casting around for a respectable Name (rather than a flashy talent), General Electric signed Reagan to host their new TV show.

   For eight years he served as a corporate trademark, the Speedy Alka-Seltzer of the all-electric kitchen. He was, in fact, a glorified front man whose stint as a GE flack coincided with a period of rampant electrical industry price-fixing. Meanwhile, Reagan achieved the bland ubiquity of a television personality. *TV Guide* tagged him "the ambassador of the convenience of things mechanical." His work was not only confined to the tube. As GE super-salesman he toured the country speaking at factory outings and pitching what's-good-for-General-Electric-is-good-for-the-U.S.A. to Rotarians and Knights of Columbus. The emotional core of Reagan's speech was always his evocation of his Midwestern boyhood. Its dramatic highpoint was the story of how he beat the Kremlin plot to take over Hollywood.

   Then the trademark went out of control (or perhaps found another sponsor) and began to introduce new material into his act. In 1962, Reagan's persistent criticism of the Tennessee Valley Authority, a major GE customer, prompted the corporation he liked to call "as human as the corner grocer" to cancel his program. The sponsor's official explanation was that *Bonanza* was pulverizing *The General Electric Theatre* in the ratings. In any case, Reagan was prepared. Donning a Barry Goldwater-style stetson, he signed on for two years as the host of *Death Valley Days*. A nationally televised election-eve speech for Goldwater—the supreme distillation of a decade spieling on the rubber chicken circuit, complete with inspirational *Mr. Smith Goes to Washington* ending—left him heir apparent to Goldwater's minions and paved the way for his governorship.

   Out of the blue, Reagan made one last move, Don Siegel's *The Killers* (1964). When critic Manny Farber described the quintessential Siegel opus as "a raunchy, dirty-minded film with a definite feeling of middle-aged, middle-class sordidness," he most likely had *The Killers* in mind. Made for TV shortly after the Kennedy assassination, but released to theatres because it was too violent for the tube, it is a key film of the '60s—one of the first to depict the robotic hitman as a space-age American anti-hero. To the delight of every audience I've ever watched the film with, its cynical arch-criminal, the brains and money behind Lee Marvin's implacable assassin, turns out to be a squinty-eyed, orange-conked Ronald Reagan. Why a man who was already planning his gubernatorial run should have taken this role is a mystery. Nancy claims it was a favor to his agent. Perhaps Reagan needed the money, perhaps he relished the opportunity the script gave him to smack New Frontier sweetheart Angie Dickinson across the mouth. Or perhaps, in a Nixon-like blunder of inadvertent disclosure—he couldn't resist a bit of last minute practice playing at what he hoped to become.

I'll probably be the only fellow who will get an Oscar posthumously.
—Ronald Reagan, 1965

ONE DAY IN 1966 Ronnie changed out of his working duds, freshened his makeup, and marched onto another set on the *Death Valley Days* lot. It was fixed up like the den from *Father Knows Best* with a phony fireplace, dummy bookcases, and an easy-to-read TelePrompTer. There he told the TV audience that he was a candidate for governor of California. Conventional wisdom held that Reagan's glamourous past would act against him. The reverse, of course, was true. As one campaign strategist explained it, "People say, 'Look at this character, he could be smooching Doris Day and he's worried about the budget.' They're impressed."

"America," observed a denizen of Saul Bellow's *Mr. Sammler's Planet,* "is the world's greatest dispenser of science-fiction entertainments." For years we were primed to land men on the moon. When it finally happened what was really interesting was that the event was telecast "live" (complete with Nixon phone-call) into every bar and motel-room in the Free World. Intermittently since Elvis Presley, we've been titillated by the vision of a demagogic pop star running for president. When it finally does happen—albeit in the form of a 69-year-old Hollywood has-been with a cast-iron pompadour—the interesting thing is the media's blasé attitude. But why shouldn't they take Reagan for granted? Isn't the nightly news one more kind of entertainment? And aren't polls just another form of ratings?

What I mean is this: All the hip pols went Hollywood long ago. The persona of Calvin Coolidge—the first modern president and the one whom Reagan most closely resembles—was designed by Bruce Barton, the promotional genius who invented Betty Crocker and wrote a best-selling depiction of Jesus as a go-getter whose success was achieved through a visionary grasp of sound advertising techniques. "The president shouldn't do too much and shouldn't know too much," Coolidge once told his PR man—or was it vice versa? Silent Cal passed the five years of his administration posing for pictures, acting out manufactured pastimes (his real hobby, he once admitted, was "holding public office") and making speeches over the radio. I imagine this is approximately what Ronald Reagan had in mind.

In a totalitarian state, entertainment is an obvious function of politics. But in the American mediacracy, where TV has hopelessly blurred the distinction between art and life, private and public, great and petty, it would seem that the reverse is closer to the truth.

The show biz messiah

Originally published as "Deracinatin' Rhythm: Is *The Jazz Singer* Good for the Jews?" in *The Village Voice* (January 7–13, 1981).

THE CURRENT REMAKE of *The Jazz Singer* is a mediocre film but a compelling one. Anachronistic from its title on, it updates the 1927 Al Jolson vehicle that is not only remembered as the first "talkie," but is also the bluntest and most resonant movie Hollywood ever produced on the not irrelevant subject of American Jews. For *The Jazz Singer* is a metaphoric account of Jewish modernization—it deals with the secularizing of religious impulses and the ensuing crisis of Jewish identity. The archetypal American, it's been suggested, rebels against the father's rule; the archetypal Jew accepts it. This is the precis for *The Jazz Singer*: A cantor's son breaks with a thousand years of tradition to reinvent himself as an American superstar, disguised in blackface and singing about his "mammy from Alabammy" on the vaudeville stage.

A once-popular Yiddish tragedy, *Der Vilner Balebesl,* deriving from oral legend and written in Poland a few years after the turn of the century, tells a similar tale. A gifted cantor is consumed by his desire to experience life in the secular, Gentile world. Abandoning family and position he leaves for Warsaw, becomes a great opera star, is feted by Polish society, consorts with a countess. But at the height of his success it all turns to ashes. The ex-cantor returns to Vilna on Yom Kippur, the Day of Atonement, to find his wife out of her mind and his child dead. In Europe, the fruits of assimilation were seen as madness, ruin, and death. In America, of course, it was a different story.

Samson Raphaelson, who wrote the original *Jazz Singer,* was at one point the Yiddish theatre critic for *The New York Times,* but his work does not derive from *Der Vilner Balebesl.* It was inspired by Al Jolson, the greatest of the immigrant Jewish entertainers who burst with astonishing force upon the American scene in the early decades of the 20th century. The second son of a Russian cantor, Jolson assimilated the oldest conventions of New World show business (the blackface makeup that was the central characterization of America's first indigenous theatrical form; the "mother song" that had given sentimental comfort to three generations of pioneers) and imbued them with a ferocious vitality. His introduction of ragtime syncopation into the dying world of the minstrel show had the same explosive effect on audiences that Elvis Presley's infusion of black and white rural idioms would have nearly a half-century later. Jolson was the first modern American superstar, and he reigned supreme for more than 20 years.

As a student, Raphaelson had been inspired by one of Jolson's performances to write a short story about a cantor's son who reinvents himself as a ragtime singer and yet, in the end, cannot break free of the Jewish tradition which simultaneously forced his rebellion and fueled his art. In the mid '20s, Raphaelson recast his story as a play which ran on Broadway for several seasons with George Jessel in the lead, before Warners purchased it as a vehicle for Jolson. The first talkie was thus a psychodramatic reenactment of Jolson's youth, and it is due primarily to his performance that moments—and even entire scenes—remain immediate and moving. Within this often inert film are fossilized deposits of passion and melancholy.

The original *Jazz Singer* reaches critical mass on the afternoon of its hero's long-awaited Broadway debut which is, with a cosmic inevitability equaled by its comic improbability, *erev* Yom Kippur, the most sacred event of the Jewish year. The singer has broken with his family but in the midst of his final rehearsal, his mother detonates a cobalt bomb of tribal guilt by arriving backstage to inform him that only by taking his father's place in *shul* that night can he make peace with the dying man (and by extension, the Jewish community). His producer flatly warns him that if he walks out on the show now, he will never get another chance to play Broadway. Caught between the single commandment of show biz and several of God's 10, the tormented Jazz Singer returns to the Lower East Side and sings for his father's congregation.

It is with the chanting of the prayer *Kol Nidre* that the play ends: The repentant son replaces his dying father as cantor, who had in turn replaced his father, who had in turn . . . a ritual, albeit sentimentalized, affirmation of the pain, burden, and eternal nature of the Jewish covenant. In the film, however, the Warner brothers opted for a more upbeat ending. In a dreamlike reversal, Jolson appears once more in blackface and back on Broadway (his career magically undisrupted), down on one knee to sing "Mammy" as his mother sits *kvelling* in the audience, a fatuously proud stand-in for the Jewish community beside her, and his intolerant, demanding father conveniently gone from the picture. "It had to be like that," wrote one Jolson biographer. "No audience would really expect to see Al Jolson give up show business—even in a film."

AMERICA OFFERED THE Jews of Eastern Europe unprecedented opportunities for assimilation or mutation, and its relative freedom liberated a tremendous, long-suppressed collective longing among them to transcend their ghetto isolation and express their potential typicality. Yet among these immigrants, sustained and defined as they had been for centuries by both the hostility of their environment and the religious inwardness of their daily lives, this great awakening produced a deep ambivalence. As Harold Rosenberg once observed: "Freeing oneself from the collective 'I' has always been presented to the individual Jew as the ultimate horror." Thus, threatened by the loss of tribal identity, emancipated Jews rushed to embrace new secular religions (socialism, art, Americanism, show biz). For Jolson, as for innumerable others of his generation, the vaudeville stage promised a psychic unity with the American masses, sweetened by the possibility of unimaginable success.

In his streetwise apprehension of American popular culture, his fantastic vitality, and his gangsterish monomania to get ahead, Jolson was cut from the same cloth as the so-called movie moguls—the itinerant peddlers, junk-dealers, and sweatshop entrepreneurs who had parlayed their slum-located storefront peepshows into America's fourth largest industry. Indeed, one cannot but be struck by the concern for authenticity with which the Warner brothers invested the project they would advertise as their "Supreme Triumph." That they felt it necessary to reconstruct the Orchard Street Synagogue on a Hollywood back-lot, or use the Winter Garden theatre (Jolson's "personal kingdom") for the final number, that they shot the Lower East Side scenes on location and included a performance by Cantor Joseph Rosenblatt—touches to which the vast majority of filmgoers would be oblivious—all indicate that on some level the Warners strove to realize a myth.

Included in *The Jazz Singer*'s souvenir program is the terse declaration that "The faithful portrayal of Jewish homelife is largely due to the unobtrusive assistance of Mr. Benjamin Warner, father of the producers and ardent admirer of *The Jazz Singer*." This statement, which attempts through paternal approval to legitimize the overthrow of Jewish traditionalism depicted in the film, suggests the Warners were uneasily aware that the story of *The Jazz Singer* was not only that of Jolson or many of their employees, but of themselves as well.

As the foremost Jewish American celebrity of his day, Jolson had a special significance for Jewish audiences and performers. If he seemed to the patrician pop culture critic Gilbert Seldes to possess a "daemonic" fury, to his disciple George Jessel, he was something else again. "In 1910," eulogized Jessel at Jolson's funeral, "the Jewish people who emigrated from Europe were a sad lot. Their humor came out of their troubles. Men of 35 seemed to take on the attitudes of their fathers, they walked with stooped shoulders. When they sang, they sang with lament in their hearts. . . . And then there came on the scene a young man, vibrantly pulsating with life and courage, who marched on the stage, head held high with the authority of a Roman emperor, with a gaiety that was militant, uninhibited and unafraid. . . . *Jolson was the happiest portrait that can ever be painted about an American of the Jewish faith*." (My emphasis.)

For Jessel, Jolson was a secular savior who redeemed the Jews from their unhappy (hence, un-American) traditions. This is the role Neil Diamond has taken upon himself in his current incarnation of *The Jazz Singer*. The opening credits identify his upflung arm with that of the Statue of Liberty, and the film's climax is equally explicit. Appearing at last on nationwide TV, Diamond struts the stage in a red, white, and blue spangled shirt, a scarf around his neck like a vestigial prayer shawl, singing an ode to America that even includes the solemnly intoned lyrics to "My Country 'Tis of Thee." Meanwhile, in the audience, his cantor father is dazzled by the power of Diamond's delivery. Having seen the light at last, he claps his hands over his head with disco abandon.

It could be argued that the 1980 *Jazz Singer* was made for no other reason than to turn a profit, but I think it's more complicated than that. Diamond, who is something of a pop religioso (he wrote the score to *Jonathan Livingston Seagull*), does not appear to take himself lightly. In two separate interviews he has said, "I don't dream of being George Gershwin. I dream of being Beethoven and Tchaikovsky and Robert Frost." The star, who had total script approval written into his contract and who is reported to have made major changes in the film all the way through its production, obviously identifies with his role. "I wanted to do *The Jazz Singer* as far back as 1975," he told the *Daily News*. "It seemed a wonderful vehicle for me, and in a sense it really was my story."

Now, one can take this literally and assume that what the Brooklyn-born Diamond means is that (presumably against parental wishes) he dropped out of the pre-med program at NYU to try his luck on Tin Pan Alley, then divorced his first wife and married a Gentile. Or one could take it metaphorically, and see *The Jazz Singer* as Diamond's attempt to celebrate his cultural roots, a not uncommon phenomenon among third-generation Americans. Explaining to the *News* that *The Jazz Singer* was not a critic's movie, he did allow that he would prefer reading reviews "saying it was the greatest Jewish epic of all time."

The original *Jazz Singer* depicted, in essence, a religious struggle—"My songs mean as much to my audience as yours do to your congregation," Jolson tells his astonished father in perhaps the pithiest summation of mass culture before John Lennon's observation that the Beatles were more popular than Christ. The 1980 *Jazz Singer* lowers these stakes considerably. Whereas Jolson's father (stolidly played by Warner Oland in preparation for a lifetime career of exotic oriental roles) is an enormously potent figure, Diamond's father (played by Sir Laurence Olivier in a hapless attempt to give the production a touch of class) is less a patriarch than a wind-up guilt machine. (By tastefully minimizing a subplot which makes the cantor a Holocaust survivor—a fact which would have given him a tragic dimension and immeasurably complicated his emotional ties to his son—the film deprives itself of the emotional excess it needs to work as melodrama.) Set in a Lower East Side immigrant-Orthodox Jewish milieu that now barely exists, the remake takes no account of the fact that the battle it depicts was won long ago. Which is not to say that conflicts in the American-Jewish identity no longer exist.

Unlike the original *Jazz Singer,* in which Jolson takes his Americanness for granted, the remake is haunted by Diamond's longing to be seen as truly—indeed, quintessentially—American. After he is declared "dead" by his hysterical father, there is a lengthy sequence in which the already successful Jazz Singer reinvents himself again as a barroom country-and-western songster. In the end, Diamond does return to the Lower East Side to sing *Kol Nidre* (his game but smirkingly self-satisfied rendition is carefully set up by having him replace a cantor whose light tenor would give him problems getting a job at a synagogue in Laredo). However, what ultimately reconciles him to his father is not this act of cost-free loyalty but rather the presentation of a grandson whose mother is an Italian Catholic and whose name is Charlie Parker Rabinovitch. Still doubting that he's touched all bases, Diamond then goes on stage and wraps himself in the American flag for the climax of "the greatest Jewish epic of all time."

In its aggressive patriotism, the 1980 film outdoes even the 1953 remake of *The Jazz Singer,* which starred Danny Thomas and is salvageable as entertainment only for Peggy Lee's rendition of "Just One of Those Things." The location is shifted to Philadelphia, Thomas is a returning GI, his father is cantor of a temple that was founded by his ancestors in 1790, *Kol Nidre* segues into a ditty called "This Is a Very Special Day," the mother—eliminated in the 1980 version—speaks in the Main Line cadences of Katharine Hepburn. Released the year of the Rosenberg execution, it would seem as though the hidden agenda of the Thomas version would be to establish Jews as a priori Americans (if not latent Protestants).

Since Diamond isn't a communist, why should he doubt that he's an American? The answer, I think, is negatively imbedded in his remake. The 1980 *Jazz Singer*'s most significant omission is not the role of the mother who intercedes between father and son. (The only Jewish woman in the film, Diamond's first wife, is a four-star kvetch who assumes only the mother's unpleasant characteristics.) What the film never acknowledges is that the Jewish diaspora is over. The significant absence here is Israel.

The establishment of a Jewish homeland has changed the equation that balanced the original myth. In its crudest form, the dilemma for American Jews amounts to a choice between repatriating to Israel or reconciling themselves (as Olivier ultimately does) to a slow assimilation into American culture. But there is a corollary to this, of course, that's no less obvious for its being largely passed over in silence. The existence of Israel has the potential to confront diasporic Jews with a traumatic division in national loyalties.

For all its evasion, the Diamond film expresses an anxiety that is real and profound. There is a sense in which Jews are still caught between two worlds. Perhaps this in itself is the Jewish condition. In the final analysis, what's anachronistic about the 1980 *Jazz Singer* is not its central conflict but the displacement of that conflict back 50 years onto the "world of our fathers."

The good, the bad, and the ugly king

Originally published as "Güney's *Yol*: Listen, Turkey" in *The Village Voice* (November 23, 1982).

NAIVE REVIEWS, UNLIKELY venue, and gorgeous photography notwithstanding, Yilmaz Güney's *Yol* is one of the most ferocious political films to arrive here in years. The movies *Yol* suggests are populist hunk-of-history epics like *Man of Marble* or *Reds,* although it's more agonized than it is elegiac. For *Yol* comes neither from the crucible of class struggle nor the cocaine kingdom of Hollywood; it comes to us from a Turkish jail.

The Turks called Güney *Cirkin Kiral,* the "Ugly King." From the mid-'60s until he was imprisoned for the third time in 1974, Yilmaz Güney was the most popular movie star in the country. Even after his 1974 conviction for killing a judge—indeed, until the army swept aside the government in 1980 and banned his movies—Güney's posters were hawked from kiosks across Istanbul. Face weathered by pain, martyr's eyes smoldering with revolt, the image of the Ugly King hung beside icons of Kemal Ataturk, founder of modern Turkey, in bazaar stalls, cafes, and hovels from the Bosporus to Mount Ararat.

Like Raj Kapoor and Bruce Lee (or, it can be argued, Ayatolla Khomeini and Muammer el-Qaddafi), Güney was a third world superstar. His type was the outcast. He played the dispossessed, the insulted, and the injured, the wretched of the earth—men from the lower depths pushed past the limits of human endurance until they exploded into solitary, pyrrhic violence. For the Turkish audience, Güney films were rituals. "Güney has been transformed into a popular myth," one critic wrote. "His films are viewed with as much attention and 'respect' as would be a religious ceremony. You are humiliated when he is, you suffer when he suffers, and when, at last, he decides to take it no more, the public joins in with applause and cries of joy."

As a star, the Ugly King was something like Clint Eastwood, James Dean, and Che Guevara combined. As a man, he's harder to pull into focus. A British newspaper describes him as a flamboyant playboy dressed like Zorro with a silk scarf around his neck, a gun in one pocket and a woman in the other; Elia Kazan visits him in prison in 1978 and finds a sober Marxist, as pedantic and "untroubled by doubt" as the instructors at the Workers School in the 1930s. The friend of a friend of a friend who once met Güney says he's "crazy." But, last month, he sounded as lucid as could reasonably be expected talking to me through a translator over the phone, while some rhythmic force vibrated the Atlantic cable in an interview that had to be held to 45 minutes because Interpol was on his trail.

When Güney turned director, he put Turkish cinema on the international film festival map and became a culture hero for the European left as well as the Turkish masses. "His career has been one long crisis and struggle," wrote *Positif* in 1980. It is "reflected in the titles of his films—*Hope, Elegy, Anxiety, Sufferers.*" *Yol* (literally, "The Way"), which Güney escaped from Turkey to complete, premiered last May at Cannes and split the Palme d'Or with Costa-Gavras's *Missing.* "It's one of the films that has touched me so deeply—like barely anything else in the last 10 years. It's just a masterpiece," another Cannes laureate, Werner Herzog, told *Rolling Stone.* Herzog's empathy is understandable; the making of *Yol* was no less a logistical triumph than the making of his jungle epic *Fitzcarraldo,* albeit in a less perversely self-willed Amazon.

Remarkably, Güney had continued to make films as a convict, writing elaborate scripts for his assistants to direct, supervising the production and editing from his cell. Although *Yol* contains only a few brief scenes inside stir, it grows directly out of Güney's prison experience. "Apart from maybe one or two details, all the events depicted in this film are taken from life, and the characters in it are actual friends of mine," Güney says. "Before writing the screenplay I solicited the help of nearly a hundred inmates. I listened to the story of their paroles. I asked some of them to write them up themselves. I recorded some of the others. And I took the rest down on paper."

As exotic as any travelogue and filled with searing set pieces, *Yol* is the story of five Turkish prisoners, furloughed for a week to visit their families. One convict loses his identification papers and is held at the first checkpoint, another is murdered, another kills his wife. One seeks drunken solace in a seedy brothel, another joins the Kurdish resistance, but no one escapes—even for a moment. The prisoners carry their prison with them. Or rather, they are merely paroled into the larger prison of present day Turkey, policed by a ubiquitous army and the brutal social codes of patriarchy run amok.

The view from a Turkish prison

Every respectable intellectual in Turkey has served a sentence in jail," Elia Kazan reported after his 1978 visit. In 1961, Yilmaz Güney, then a young scriptwriter and production assistant, did his first stretch—serving 18 months for writing a novel that the 1960–61 military regime deemed "Communist propaganda." Upon his release, the 26-year-old Güney became an actor. You might say he took it up with a vengeance, appearing in more than 20 films a year. By the mid-'60s he had become Turkey's greatest star—the tough, unglamorous, victimized Ugly King.

In Turkey as elsewhere, the late '60s were a period of political tumult sparked by left-wing student movements. Reradicalized by 1968, Güney set up his own production company and began to direct his vehicles himself. His third film, *Umut* ("Hope"), made him the spiritual leader of the so-called Revolutionary Cinema Group. A mixture of neorealist grit and blunt surrealism, *Umut* illustrated the pathetic illusions and religious false consciousness of a marginalized horse cab driver (Güney). Compared to *The Bicycle Thief* and *The Treasure of Sierra Madre*, hailed as a model for future production by left-wing cineastes, and as popular as the Ugly King's other movies, *Umut* soon became a cause célèbre when it was banned by the Turkish government in 1970.

The same year saw the beginning of Marxist armed struggle in Turkey. Whatever his actual political associations, Güney was certainly a revolutionary sympathizer. In 1971, the Turkish army staged another coup, jailing thousands of students and trade unionists while launching a military assault on the various Maoists cadres who had taken to the hills. The following year, Güney was arrested for "aiding and harboring" terrorists from a group alleged to have assassinated the Israeli ambassador and three American army personnel. At the official Turkish film festival that year, Güney's *Father* won first prize and he was named best actor. According to *Variety*, the festival jury was sequestered 24 hours later and asked to reconsider. By unanimous vote, the new best film was a "run of the mill romance" and the new best actor "a heart throb thespian without apparent political ties."

Rather than mobilize Turkish society against the left, the repressive military regime of the early '70s only managed to create greater political polarization, including the spread of the native fascist Action Party. As *New Left Review* observed, when civilian government was restored in 1974, "The militants found themselves released into a situation where the mass youth following of the left had grown enormously, despite the debacle of its actions." Barely had democracy returned when a series of events, precipitated by the Greek junta's attempt to annex Cyprus and Turkey's subsequent occupation of the island's Turkish areas, brought down Bülent Ecevit's parliamentary socialist government in favor of a right-wing coalition that included the fascists. Güney had been released from prison in Ecevit's 1974 general amnesty; given the prevailing climate, his freedom lasted precisely three months.

In the midst of making his next movie, Güney was returned to jail for an 18-year sentence. The charge was murdering a local magistrate in a cafe brawl. Güney denies the charge, and there is no way for us to know what actually happened, but, by all accounts, the structural formula of the incident resembles the ritual of the Ugly King. Güney—who was either drunkenly firing bullets into the sea or else peacefully eating dinner with his wife—was accosted by an irate, drunken, fanatically anti-Communist judge who persisted in harassing him so violently (cursing him, insulting his wife, slapping his face) that the shamed Ugly King finally pulled out a gun and shot him dead. Although Güney's associate Serif Gören was reportedly wounded during the fracas, and a number of individuals (including Güney's cousin) came forth to take the rap, no one other than Güney was convicted.

Back in prison, Güney continued to script and oversee new films—including *The Herd* and *The Enemy*—directed by Serif Gören and other sympathizers. He is said to have divided his movie royalties among his fellow prisoners, written several books, published a monthly bulletin called *Güney*, occasionally visited Istanbul, and been readily accessible by phone. When Kazan visited Güney in 1978, he was surprised to find the man himself ushering him into the prison. (Kazan's description of the event was published in *The New York Times Magazine*, shortly after Alan Parker's *Midnight Express* created a Western world scandal by depicting an Istanbul prison as a den of squalor and sadism where children were tortured and convicts beaten to death.)

Güney told Kazan he was free to escape any time he wished—the government actually wanted him to—but he felt safer inside the prison. Outside was an Argentina-like situation with thousands of political killings by both right-wing death-squads and left-wing terrorists. In Istanbul, 16 people died when a cinema showing a Güney film was bombed. Nor was this an isolated act. By the late '70s, Turkey was dotted with "liberated zones," controlled by fascists or revolutionary Marxists. However, while the Turkish left was typically balkanized into competing splinter groups, the fascist right was included in the government coalition and poised to seize power. When Ecevit was reelected in 1978 he placed two-thirds of the country under martial law. A 1980 military coup took care of the rest.

Characterized variously as a socialist, a Maoist, a "Sovietic," and a follower of Enver Hoxha, the Albanian isolationist-Stalinoid diehard, Güney became increasingly identified with Kurdish nationalism after 1975. In one sense this was a coming out—although the child of Kurdish peasants, the Ugly King was not immediately recognizable as a Kurd—but his shifting position also followed the general drift of the Turkish left. The largest liberation front abandoned Maoism (as did the Chinese) in the mid-'70s and began following the anti-Moscow, newly anti-Beijing Hoxha line. Meanwhile, guerrilla warfare had broken out in the eastern third of Turkey, illegally known as "Kurdistan."

A people oppressed by the oppressed

The successor state to a once formidable empire, Turkey occupies a singular position in the third world, located at the intersection of Europe, Asia, the Soviet Union, and the Middle East. (Güney feels there can be no Turkish democracy as long as the rivalry between the superpowers exists.) Never colonized, Turkey has, in fact, an internal colony of its own—namely, Kurdistan.

The dissolution of the Ottoman Empire was scarcely less convulsive than the near-simultaneous collapse of the Hapsburg and Romanov empires, and equally replete with instances of colliding national aspirations. (Consider the recent history of the former Ottoman territory, Palestine.) The creation of modern Turkey involved the repulsion of a Greek invasion plus the massacres of a million Armenians and some 700,000 Kurds. At the 1920 Sèvres Conference, the European "great powers" paid lip service to Armenian and Kurdish autonomy and wound up dividing mountainous, backward Kurdistan among the newly established nations of Turkey, Syria, and Iraq, with a chunk going to Persia (Iran).

The subjugation of the Kurds by such once and future "progressive" states explains why—despite their being variously used and discarded over the past 60 years by British, French, Turkish, Iraqi Ba'athist, imperial Iranian, American, and, more than once, Soviet interests—left-wing opinion has denied the Kurds the support automatically given most national causes. The Kurds, as French professor Maxime Rodinson put it, are "a people oppressed by the oppressed."

Turkish Kurds rebelled in 1925 and again in 1930. In 1937—the year Yilmaz Güney was born in a village near Adana, a south-central Turkish city with a large population of migrant Kurdish workers—the Ankara government began a systematic policy of Kurdish pacification. The army occupied Turkey's eastern provinces and triggered one last Turkish-Kurdish war. Using mass deportations and aerial bombardment, poison gas, organized terror, and the destruction of at least one city, the army crushed the guerrilla resistance. The Turkish Communist Party—which regards Kurdish nationalists as "bourgeois chauvinists"—once estimated that, between 1925 and 1938, more than a million and a half Kurds were deported and massacred. Turkish Kurdistan suffered a permanent state of siege through 1950; it remained a military area from which foreigners were restricted for another 15 years.

Figures vary, but it is generally agreed that there are some 10 million ethnic Kurds in Turkey, representing more than 20 per cent of the total population. It is difficult, however, to be certain: the words "Kurd" and "Kurdistan" are banned from Turkish history books and dictionaries; the Kurds are officially termed "Mountain Turks," who speak Kurdish—itself illegal—because they have forgotten their mother tongue.

Torture and imprisonment were widespread in Turkey before the 1980 coup and became more so afterward. According to Amnesty International, the new regime took 122,609 prisoners into custody during its first seven months. Thousands of these were Kurds who, even before the coup, had been under military rule. In March 1980, Mehdi Zana, the mayor of Diyarbakir—the largest city in Turkish Kurdistan—was tried by a military court for making "separatist propaganda." (Last August, Amnesty reported that Zana was "physically broken" by torture and now "unrecognizable.") Two months after the September 1980 coup—and five months after a *New York Times* story attributed Kurdish unrest to widespread unemployment—the military regime staged what has been termed the largest mass trial in Turkish history, prosecuting over 400 Kurdish activists on charges ranging from "secessionism" to "participation in Kurdish cultural events." Last March, a non-Kurdish sociologist, Ismail Besikci, was sentenced to 10 years in prison for describing the Kurds as a separate ethnic group.

Identity grows existential when the statement "I am a Kurd" brings a mandatory two-and-a-half-year stretch in a Turkish can.

Before the revolution

Some filmmakers, most famously Bernardo Bertolucci, are nostalgic for life "before the revolution." In the third world, this may be a bit much to expect.

Three of *Yol*'s five protagonists are Kurds. This in itself makes the film powerfully political. The most obvious Kurdish character returns to his village on the Syrian border to find its cluster of adobe houses under assault by the Turkish army. Another is a city Kurd who panicked and left his brother-in-law to die in an abortive robbery. Tracking down his wife and children to her family in a Diyarbakir shantytown, he is publicly humiliated by his unforgiving in-laws. Still, he prevails upon his wife to leave with him for parts unknown. In one of the film's most stunning sequences, the long sundered couple submit to a paroxysm of human desire and attempt to make love standing up in a railroad train toilet. Discovered *in flagrante*, they're nearly torn to pieces in front of their children by a howling mob of fellow passengers. The authorities grudgingly protect them, but they're shot dead by the wife's 12-year-old brother—who stowed away intending to punish the convict's cowardice—before the next stop.

The most tormented and taciturn of the convicts is the mountain Kurd,

Seyit Ali, who receives word while in prison that his wife has abandoned their son and become a prostitute in the city. Recaptured by her family and returned to their village, the "she devil" has been half-starved and chained in a stable for eight months. Seyit Ali is expected to expunge the collective shame by killing her. If he doesn't do his duty, her brothers surely will.

His thoughts a cipher, Seyit Ali takes her—and their son—on a forced march through the snow country, expecting the weakened woman to die of exposure. When she collapses midway, his composure snaps; he beats her in a rage that is also a futile attempt to bring her back to life. Watched by the boy, Seyit Ali hoists the comatose woman onto his shoulders and carries her to the next village where she dies in a hospital without regaining consciousness. Her relatives praise Allah and congratulate the widower.

When Güney submitted a 24-page precis called *The Feast* to the Turkish censor, it appeared to be a script for a film about the prison practice of permitting deserving inmates to visit their homes to celebrate the three-day Feast of the Sacrifice. The treatment was approved, not only because it was incomplete (or seemed to offer a partial rebuttal to *Midnight Express*), but because it was also relatively unimportant. "When the junta took over the government, they had many other tasks at hand before grappling with art in general and filmmaking in particular," Güney says. Moreover, *The Feast* was shot in so many different parts of Turkey that local authorities never had a clear idea of what was going on.

Güney rejects the notion that he "directed" *Yol* from prison as at once insufficient and politically incorrect. Serif Goren is credited as director; as for Güney, "Not only did he write the script," his translator told me, "he resolved practical problems in the shooting as a consultant, drawing on his long experience." But, just as the narrative drew on the collective experiences of Güney's fellow inmates, so the production depended on the kindness of the masses. "Whatever regime exists in Turkey," the translator explained, "Güney can count on support from all kinds of people—honest bureaucrats and army officers as well as simple people and politicals." In other words, with Güney as catalytic medium, *Yol* is a story Turkey told and gave to itself.

The main difficulty in making the film, Güney says, was in its timing. *Yol* took longer than anticipated to shoot, and he'd already set plans for his escape. There is reason to believe Güney expected to be pardoned in 1982, for the 60th anniversary of the Turkish state. The military coup not only dashed this hope but threatened him with fresh trials for making "Communist propaganda" and espousing "Kurdish separatism" while in jail. "In point of fact, I wanted to spend the last remaining bits of freedom in my own country," Güney explained in a lightning appearance at Cannes. "But since the coup d'etat, nothing's possible, nothing's reasonable anymore. They bombed the cinemas where my films were being shown. The date of my new trial was approaching, and they continued to slander me. My book, *Story of My Child*, was banned from the bookstores. And so I decided to escape."

Sometime into the production of *Yol* (if not before), Güney must have realized that this film—perhaps the last he would ever make in Turkey—would never be shown in Turkey under the military regime. Seizing this negative moment—as Andrzej Wajda had seized a correspondingly positive one and inscribed Lech Walesa into *Man of Iron* (thus guaranteeing that, in a nation where history has been regularly rewritten, his film could never be separated from Poland's political life)—Güney produced a movie so explosive that were it shown in his homeland it would signal the prelude to revolution. *Yol* is about the essential, unspeakable Kurdishness of Turkey. Not only does the film depict a full range of Kurdish life (with the *verboten* Kurdish language dubbed into some sequences as "background music"), but it bluntly asserts that, under military rule, all Turks are now Kurds—the oppressed of the oppressed.

But the chain of oppression does not end there. A few American critics were startled to observe *Yol*'s blunt insistence on sexual politics, the fact that Güney located the oppression of what he or his translator unfailingly calls the "fascist-military-regime" in hyperbolic instances of patriarchal revenge and antierotic hysteria. For Güney, the political situation of Turkey is not simply a matter of state terror but also arises from below, from "the moral debris left behind by feudalism and patriarchy." "It seems at first sight that [the stories in *Yol*] are stories about men," he says. "In fact, they are about the women—their pain, their misery, their waiting, and the semifeudal relations which bind them to the men."

There is a key sequence in *Yol* set inside a brothel. One convict has gone to visit his fiancée in the city of Gaziantep. ("You'll obey my every command," he announces. "You're so good with words," she demurely replies. "Did you learn that in jail?") The girl's fanatically overprotective brothers won't even let the engaged couple take a walk together without the company of two black-shrouded female relatives. Drunkenly railing against these outmoded traditions, the convict goes off to assert his manhood among the local whores. In their relations with men, the prostitutes are the freest women in the film—they mock them, tease them, reject them as they please. At the same time, they're nothing more than merchandise. I asked Güney if prostitution was legal in Turkey. He told me that it was not only licensed but operated by the state. "One town decided to raise money by selling their brothel to private interests. They sold them their 'capital'—do you know what that means?"

To be a Turk is to be a Kurd, to be a Turkish woman is to be a Kurd's slave—such is life before the revolution. Virtually the only other recent political film I know that constructs so vivid and devastating a model of prerevolutionary consciousness is Vivienne Dick's super-8 *Beauty Becomes the Beast*. As in *Beauty Becomes the Beast* (whose subject is sexual, rather than political, repression), *Yol* offers no individual solution. On the contrary: the film's final image has Seyit Ali, alone and uncertain, on the train going nowhere. The absence of solidarity is particularly striking in that, early in the film, Seyit Ali has established himself as the most empathetic character of all—dispensing his few remaining cigarettes (the prisoner's coin of the realm) with bemused resignation to a group of fellow travellers.

Yol ends with Seyit Ali a convict, a Kurd, a wife-killer, a victim, the Ugly King of a pestilent land. The film's epilogue can only be written by the Turkish people. "And when at last, he decides to take it no more, the public [will] join in with applause and cries of joy."

Martin Scorsese and the comedy of public life

Originally published as "King of Outsiders" in *The Village Voice* (February 15, 1983).

IT'S LATE IN the final day of shooting on *The King of Comedy,* and the press has been invited to a studio so far west it's practically in New Jersey to watch Martin Scorsese film inserts. Technicians have begun dismantling the set, tables are being pushed together for a modest champagne celebration, members of the crew are gravitating toward the refreshments. The star, Jerry Lewis, has long since returned to Las Vegas, but Scorsese is still working—he's perched on a ladder having close-up after close-up taken of Robert De Niro handing him a business card.

On most sets, this routine chore would be a matter of stand-in and second-unit crew. Scorsese, however, is doing double duty, directing the scene while wearing Lewis's sports jacket. In France, where Scorsese is an auteur and Lewis a superstar—America personified—their teaming is regarded as a cultural event. (*The King of Comedy* has already been announced as opening the Cannes Film Festival in May.) Here, it's considered a tough sell and 20th Century-Fox is nervous. "They know Lewis fans will hate the movie," one industry savant explains. "And they're afraid that the people who hate Lewis won't go near it."

As talk-show host Jerry Langford, Lewis has given Scorsese his first dramatic performance. Actually, Lewis is not so much De Niro's co-star as his straight man; it is De Niro who plays the self-appointed "king of comedy." Dressed in garish polyester, he's grown a pencil-thin mustache and slicked his hair into a razor-sharp pompadour for the role of aspiring comic Rupert Pupkin, a 34-year-old messenger and autograph hound, still living in his mother's Union City basement, who constructs an obsessional fantasy around Jerry Langford. "I find comedians fascinating," says Scorsese. "There's so much pain and fear that goes into the trade."

PAIN AND FEAR—and the convulsive desire for public recognition—are Martin Scorsese's meat. Not even Woody Allen has chosen to dramatize his neuroses more flagrantly. Unlike Allen, however, Scorsese offers no apologies. Racism, misogyny, selfishness, paranoid fury are right up front. More than any other studio director, he resembles an avant-garde filmmaker like Yvonne Rainer, who unpacks her mind and fissures her persona with each feature, then figures it out later. Except, of course, Scorsese's subject is macho.

With De Niro as his alter ego, Scorsese has created a memorable gallery of jittery, psyched-up loners: Johnny Boy, Travis Bickle, Jimmy Doyle, Jake La Motta. As embodied by De Niro, *homo scorsesian* is a frustrated outsider fueled by a highly combustible combination of guilt, jealousy, and delusions of grandeur. Ellen Burstyn plays a female, suburban variant of the type in *Alice Doesn't Live Here Anymore,* but Scorseseville is mainly a man's world. Women are unknowable Others, children the promise of destruction. The family is at once a sacred value and something to flee like the plague.

The bruisingly kinetic, starkly lyrical *Raging Bull*—Scorsese's masterpiece and the one possibly great Hollywood movie of the past five years—goes so far into professional aggression and sexual anxiety that it becomes a critique, a lament for stone age maleness in which blood drips from the boxing ring ropes like tears down the cheeks of the Virgin of Guadalupe.

Rupert Pupkin may be less violent than Travis Bickle or Jake La Motta, but he's no less possessed. Although he has never performed for an audience, Pupkin demands the TV show watched by half of America each night as the launching pad for his career. "To have drive is what counts!" Scorsese exclaimed in an early interview. "Anything to meet people to generate events towards your goal." Pupkin personifies precisely this crazed pragmatism: rejected by Langford's aides and thrown out of Langford's weekend house, he ultimately gets himself on *The Jerry Langford Show* by kidnapping the star.

"*The King of Comedy* is a film about the desperate need to exist publicly which is so American," says Paul Zimmerman, the 44-year-old former *Newsweek* critic who wrote the screenplay. "It's the ultimate outgrowth of the question 'What do you do?'" Hirsute, talkative, and the author of unproduced scripts for Sidney Pollack, Alan Pakula, Milos Foreman, and Stanley Donen ("I'm unproduced at the highest levels"), Zimmerman explains Pupkin's complaint. "The problem Rupert faces is, will he ever count? And for him, it's a matter of life or death."

Zimmerman labored over *The King of Comedy* script for the better part of a decade before Scorsese ever became involved with the project, but the screenwriter sees the finished movie as essentially Scorsese's. "There is much more conflict in *The King of Comedy* than what I wrote. The film is darker than the script. Marty takes everything and makes it his own," reports Zimmerman, unperturbed. During production, he recalls asking Scorsese what the director thought their film was about. "Marty looked at me, smiled, and said 'me.' For *me, King of Comedy* is a fable. For Marty, it's true. . . ."

The interpolated home movies in *Mean Streets* and *Raging Bull,* the memorabilia Scorsese characters fondle in *New York, New York* are scarcely the only evidence of the director's emotional investment in his work. Like Samuel Fuller, Scorsese fills his movies with personal talismans; like Werner Herzog, he riddles them with documentary subtexts. The single chair in Rupert Pupkin's basement, for example, is the actual chair of one of the authentic autograph hounds Scorsese and De Niro interviewed for the film. A key scene in *The King of Comedy* is played entirely with nonactors. Scorsese used a real FBI agent, a real

TV producer, a real lawyer, and a real agent (his own). "And they really fought," he remembers. "When I yelled cut, they kept on going."

Scorsese rounds out his casts with nonactor buddies, regularly gives himself cameos, even provides bit parts for his parents in each of his films. (A scholarly paper—if not a case study—could be written on the roles Charles and Catherine Scorsese have played in their son's oeuvre.) The only character Scorsese introduced into Zimmerman's script was Rupert's mother—heard, but never seen, and played by Mrs. Scorsese. "Each film is like a family," Scorsese says; for Sicilians, he explains, "family" is a value more transcendent than religion.

In fact, Scorsese's associates are highly protective, resembling nothing so much as an extended family indulging the tyranny of an adored, precocious child. No less impressive than the director's actual films is his ability to create this situation in the world.

ON THE SET, Scorsese doesn't seem to direct so much as conduct, communicating with co-workers in private asides and precise gestures. He doesn't exactly fit the stereotype of the Hollywood artiste—Josef von Sternberg directing in boots, jodhpurs, and carrying a riding crop—but it's an autocratic scene, full of its own subtle codes. When some minor mishap occurs, Scorsese barks goodnaturedly for Tylenol the way a less highstrung maestro might call for tempo.

Short, bearded, and mercurial, Scorsese could have been animated by Bill Tytla, the Disney artist who designed Pinocchio's nemesis Stromboli and half the Seven Dwarfs. At 40, the director is said to have mellowed. There are no recent reports of telephones sent hurtling around hotel rooms, but Scorsese remains a tightly wound spring—courteous, controlled, and wary as a fox.

"Marty used anything he could to get where he is, and once he got there he calmed down," says editor Thelma Schoonmaker, who won an Oscar for *Raging Bull* and labored for 11 months cutting *The King of Comedy*. Schoonmaker has known Scorsese since both were students at NYU film school, 17 years ago, and she mainly remembers, "Marty's incredible ambition. . . . He was manipulative, too," she adds, "but I admired that." Scorsese's apparent modesty is as deceptive as it is disarming. Critic Roger Ebert saw an early version of Scorsese's grad-school opus *Who's That Knocking on My Door?* at the Chicago Film Festival in 1965 and ventured a guess that in 10 years its director could be "the American Fellini." " 'Gee,' " he remembers Scorsese saying, " 'do you think it will take that long?' "

Schoonmaker is not the only Scorsese associate who goes back to the '60s. Indeed, much of the director's success derives from his capacity to form extraordinarily close bonds with his collaborators; his professional relationships are virtually the most stable in his life. Publicist Marion Billings has handled every Scorsese film since *Who's That Knocking?* ("This fat little NYU professor came to me in 1967 and said he wanted the same kind of coverage I got for *The Shop on Main Street*. I looked at *Who's That Knocking?* and thought, 'He's so talented, he'll never work again.' ") Harry Ufland has been the director's agent since he first saw Scorsese's student films in 1965. Harvey Keitel starred in

Who's That Knocking? and has appeared in three Scorsese films since. Mardik Martin, another NYU graduate, has worked on the scripts of five Scorsese films, from *Mean Streets* to *Raging Bull*; Paul Schrader wrote *Taxi Driver,* worked on *Raging Bull,* and has just completed an adaptation of Nikos Kazantzakis's *The Last Temptation of Christ*—the capper to their trilogy—which Scorsese plans to film in the fall.

Meanwhile, the Scorsese-De Niro collaboration has been one of the richest director-actor alliances in Hollywood history, comparable in its mingled identities to the teaming of von Sternberg and Marlene Dietrich. It was De Niro who brought Zimmerman's script to Scorsese's attention (as he had La Motta's autobiography) after Michael Cimino, originally tapped to direct, got bogged down with *Heaven's Gate.*

De Niro is notoriously press shy, and Scorsese shares his working habits. "If there are too many people on the set I don't like it," he has said. "I like to be out of the limelight as much as possible when directing so that nobody knows, nobody can see what I'm doing." Scorsese describes the direction of *New York, New York,* his most logistically complex film, as though it were a business deal in *The Godfather*: "All the actual directing was done in whispers and in the dressing rooms, and nobody would see."

Rehearsing actors individually, Scorsese shapes and refines their improvisations on the script. The situation calls for considerable mutual trust. "I essentially wrote 50 per cent of my part," says Sandra Bernhard, who gives a chilling, comic performance as Rupert's accomplice and Langford's most ardent fan. Scorsese doesn't deny her claim. "That's why we take so long with casting," he says.

Associates assert that it's painful for the director to audition performers, yet Scorsese estimates that some 500 actresses read for the part before Bernhard, a 27-year-old Los Angeles-based stand-up comedienne with limited screen experience and an act Scorsese describes as based on "sexual menace," got the role. For Bernhard, the part provided her with something akin to psychodrama. "If anyone can understand needing and wanting the attention of famous people, it's me," she grins. "I was a manicurist for seven years in Beverly Hills."

Originally, Scorsese wanted Johnny Carson for the role of Jerry Langford. When Carson demurred he approached Jerry Lewis. "Jerry has done nearly everything in show business. He had a lot to draw on and he was eager to play the part," the director recalls. Lewis's career was then at low ebb and his personal life was strained by several financial and marital woes. "I had two meetings with Jerry over the course of a year and a half," Scorsese says. "I could see the man was *ripe* for it."

Scorsese once called *Raging Bull* "a documentary with actors," and he has used Lewis as a kind of found object, pure celebrity: "The less Jerry docs, the better he is." According to Scorsese, Lewis is "almost playing himself. He's wearing his clothes, his glasses. That's his dog in the apartment." Scorsese maintains that Lewis improvised a sustained invocation of the burdens of success—delivered by a desperate Langford to his captors—while the cameras were rolling. Others recall Scorsese inducing the hostage Langford's barely controlled fury through endless retakes of a scene which begins with the star bound like a mummy with adhesive tape.

"Directing is lousy. It's not an enviable position," Scorsese complains without much conviction. "You have to be tough. It's like a screwdriver going through your stomach," he elaborates with morose intensity. "Especially if you *like* the person." Scorsese himself is immediately likable—quick, funny, and unpretentious—but his closest associates regard him with more than a touch of fear. No one denies the director can be demanding and compulsive, restless and paranoid. "There's nothing he wouldn't do when it comes to making the film," says Bernhard. "He's everywhere he doesn't need to be. He's a fanatic, a perfectionist."

Scorsese's projects habitually run over schedule because of his painstaking attention to detail. It took a grueling 16 weeks to finish the 40-track sound mix for *Raging Bull*. Schoonmaker says it was assembled "inch by inch." When he's on, Scorsese drives himself to the point of exhaustion—at one juncture in 1977 he was editing *New York, New York, The Last Waltz,* and the documentary, *An American Boy,* simultaneously—and he expects his colleagues to do the same. When he's off, suffering nerves or from the asthma that has afflicted him since childhood, a project may stall. "A noise in the corridor can distract him," says Schoonmaker. "I'm glad I don't have to live with Marty, although when we're working, I practically do."

"*His* needs are top priority—and he has a lot of them," another associate says. To hear Scorsese describe it, each film takes on the nature of an ordeal, a psychodrama, a working through. Not that it necessarily resolves anything. "When the film is finished you go into a mourning period," Scorsese says gloomily. "Then you realize, my God, it isn't enough just to put it on screen. To put something on film doesn't mean you're rid of it." "I was crazier when I finished *Taxi Driver* than when I began," he told Paul Schrader in a conversation published by *Cahiers du Cinéma* last spring. Scorsese acknowledged his shrink in the credits for *Mean Streets* and has recently reentered psychoanalysis. ("It helped me the first time," he says hopefully.)

SCORSESE'S SENSE OF himself is rooted in a childhood formed by illness, fantasy, and the Catholic church. The second son of first-generation Sicilian garment-workers, Scorsese was set apart from other children when he developed asthma at age four following a traumatic tonsillectomy. He was eight when his family moved from a house shared with relatives in Corona, Queens, back to their old neighborhood on the crumbling Lower East Side. Small and sickly, Scorsese did not fit easily into the tough Little Italy street life he would ambivalently celebrate in *Who's That Knocking?* and *Mean Streets*.

"I couldn't mix in," the director says with pained diffidence. "I mean, I did mix in, but for comic relief. If you weren't able to give a beating, you had to take one." Scorsese may have felt powerless but he wasn't passive: "He was always the littlest guy, the weakest, but he fought," one schoolmate has remembered. "He would work himself into a frenzy."

Unable or unwilling to participate in athletics—"I developed this great hatred of sports when I was a boy, a hatred I have to this day"—Scorsese applied himself to Catholic school and found himself at the movies. "My father used to take me to see all sorts of films. From three, four, five years old, I was watching film after film, a complete range." Scorsese was a child of unusual devotion. He readily holds forth on the B-westerns and biblical spectacles that impressed him as a child, conjuring up specific scenes as though they were epiphanies. With ingenuous total recall, he cites the movie theaters—tawdry roads to Damascus—where he witnessed each vision, taking care to acknowledge the disciples who accompanied him. "Even as a kid I couldn't give up movies for Lent," Scorsese remembers. "I'm still guilty about that."

Not content merely to consume, the young Scorsese was inspired—or compelled—to reexperience and master each film. From the age of eight on, he drew elaborate pencil versions of the films he'd seen, sketching shot-by-shot breakdowns in the manner of the *Classics Illustrated* comic books his father bought him. (Precociously, the future director invented the storyboard, a standard tool for cinematic exposition, years before he would attend film school and learn that such things existed.) Scorsese meticulously reproduced each film's standard or Cinemascope frame ratio; when Hollywood flirted with 3-D in the early '50s, he followed suit with cutout paper constructions.

These early attempts to articulate his fantasies were not unconflicted. Scorsese showed his projects only to a chosen few, and after his parents discovered his "3-D movies," he destroyed his handiwork. "They must have thought I was cutting out paper dolls or something," he later explained. "My mother went along, but I don't think my father liked it. Not that he *didn't* like it; he just didn't know what I was doing. I felt embarrassed, so I threw them away."

In effect, Scorsese spent much of his childhood giving himself a second education, supplementing the Catholic schooling supplied by the Old St. Patrick's School on Mulberry Street with an intensive course in American mass culture, its glories and its detritus. Devouring movies, TV shows, and comic books, the strong-willed, often bedridden boy recycled them in his own terms and according to his own interests: "Jealousy was a big theme even then." Scorsese's taste for widescreen epics of the ancient world—*Quo Vadis, The Silver Chalice, Samson and Delilah, Land of the Pharaohs*—complemented his fascination with Catholic ritual, and, encouraged by his parents, in his early teens he gave up on becoming an artist and spent an unhappy year attending a junior seminary in preparation for the priesthood.

In her 1980 monograph on Scorsese, former nun Mary Pat Kelly compares the filmmaker's abortive religious vocation to that of James Joyce and calls his films quests for "redemption in a fallen world where evil is real and violence can erupt at any moment." Asked if he still considers himself a Catholic, the director laughs ruefully, "I'm afraid so." It has been many years since he went to confession or took communion, but Scorsese acknowledges the sexual guilt with which his upbringing left him and which torments many of his characters. "If I could resolve it, it might be resolved for them." Since leaving the church in his early twenties, Scorsese has been married and divorced three times, most recently from model Isabella Rossellini, the daughter of Ingrid Bergman and Roberto Rossellini. Their three-year-old marriage broke up during the shooting of *The King of Comedy*. "I think it is very hard to be with a person who is completely dedicated to his work," Isabella told *People* magazine. "When the horrible stuff was about to start—neurosis and insecurity—we just split." "It's impossible for me to talk about," Scorsese says tersely. "You find all sorts of ways to punish yourself."

Observance fades, wives come and go, but the love of movies is eternal. Scorsese's lower Manhattan triplex—a 10-minute jog from the mean streets of his youth—is not unlike an affluent version of Rupert Pupkin's fetish-crammed shrinelike basement. The loft will never make *The New York Times Magazine*, but it offers eloquent testimony to the totality of its inhabitant's obsession.

Shelves are crammed to the ceiling with dog-eared film books and leather-bound scripts. Copies of *Video Review* and *TV Guide* litter the coffee tables. At least one of Scorsese's numerous TV sets is always on. An entire floor is given over to editing consoles. Scorsese and Thelma Schoonmaker labored over *The King of Comedy* here, working mainly at night. Omnivorous in his consumption of electronic images, Scorsese habitually projects movies silently on a huge Advent screen while editing. Along with lists of the movies he's seen since childhood, he has hundreds of videotapes of his favorite films catalogued in cardboard boxes and an impressive collection of vintage movie posters; his staff includes a full-time archivist. In 1980, Scorsese organized a petition intended to pressure Eastman Kodak to recognize its "responsibility to the people it services" and develop longer-lasting color film stock. (The crusade appears to have fizzled and Scorsese dismisses it: "I was rash to lash out at Kodak," he now says, disingenuously adding, "The problem is not so much with the film stock as care of original negatives.") Still, his psychic investment in the preservation of filmed ephemera is beyond question. Cinema totems surround him, and each has associations all its own.

An enlarged still from *Duel in the Sun*—Gregory Peck facing down Jennifer Jones in the shadows of the old corral—dominates one wall: "My mother took me to see it even though it was condemned from the pulpit. . . . To this day I love the picture." A triptych composed of the credits from *The Searchers* is framed by the window: "Made by old men, but seeing it is like going to the Fountain of Youth." A garish French poster for George Stevens' *Giant* hangs across the room: "An inspiring film. I don't mean morally, but visually. It's all visual."

REDOLENT AS IT is of squandered afternoons and adolescent daydreams—and darker satisfactions than those—the passion for movies lacks the cachet of more elevated aesthetic concerns: *Film Comment,* the most self-consciously literate of American movie magazines, regularly asks directors or critics to reveal their "guilty pleasures," the unredeemable movies they unaccountably love. Most restrict their choices to 10 or a dozen. When Scorsese published his confessions he could barely stop—describing 28 movies and listing another 103 "random pleasures" from *The Agony and the Ecstasy* and *Al Capone* to *The Vampire Circus* and *Where's Poppa?* One suspects that for a child of the Church and the Loews Commodore, all movies are guilty pleasures. "Yeah," laughs Scorsese, "and Schrader would consider the 'guilty' redundant."

Scorsese has directed a glossy Liza Minnelli musical, a nostalgic rock-doc, the prototype for a long-running sitcom, and even a public TV documentary portrait of his parents, but he's typecast as a purveyor of cinematic mayhem. *Taxi Driver,* his greatest success, only avoided an X-rating for violence after the director agreed to tone down the gore of its climactic massacre. The 10th highest grossing Hollywood release of 1976, the film made headlines five years later when John Hinckley Jr. claimed it as the source of his obsession with teenage actress Jodie Foster and the inspiration for his attempted assassination of veteran personality Ronald Reagan. (According to one of the mental health experts who testified in Hinckley's defense, the would-be assassin "felt like he was acting in a movie.")

In 1980, months before the Hinckley shooting, Scorsese had already been singled out by *The Saturday Review* as the "exemplar" of a new school of Hollywood "brutalists," including Brian De Palma, Walter Hill, and Paul Schrader. "At the very least," wrote Robert F. Moss, "brutalist films are glorifying and encouraging the immense potential for savagery that already exists in America, attracting groups who seek any match that will ignite their seething aggressions."

Scorsese keeps a stock answer for this sort of charge: "*Taxi Driver* is about a man racked by dark feelings. I think everybody has them. It's unfortunate that some people act them out." Anyway, *The King of Comedy* was already in preproduction when the ultimate fan opened fire. Still, nobody will deny that Rupert Pupkin bears an uncanny generic resemblance to John Hinckley. Zimmerman traces his script's genesis to a 1970 *David Susskind Show* on autograph hunters: "I realized that autograph hounds are just like assassins except that one carries a pen instead of a gun."

Not surprisingly, Scorsese is loath to describe the guilty pleasure he may have felt when he discovered that the president of the United States had only narrowly escaped death at the hands of a man who reportedly saw *Taxi Driver* 15 times, fell pathetically in love with one of the film's stars, and told *Newsweek,* "I bought so many handguns because Travis bought so many handguns. Ask him, not me."

Scorsese refused to comment on the case for more than six months. "For a while I didn't feel like making any more films," he says, although production on *The King of Comedy* was not delayed. Last May, when Hinckley went on trial, *Taxi Driver* actually became the cornerstone of his defense. Three psychiatrists and a psychologist testified that Hinckley identified so strongly with the film that he sometimes "almost thought he was Travis Bickle" and suffered the delusion that he had to commit a violent act to effect a "magical union" with Jodie Foster. Dr. Thomas C. Goldman testified that when Hinckley first saw the film in 1976, "he felt as if this was the story of his life. . . . He identified with Travis Bickle's sense of loneliness and isolation." The defense rested its case by screening *Taxi Driver* for the jury. Hinckley was acquitted on grounds of insanity.

"It's like a purging," Scorsese once said of his filmmaking. "It's got to be done, and you just have to be honest with yourself." Although he evinces only casual interest in the remarkable fact that one of his films has been judged capable of driving a man mad, an even more disturbing suggestion is that Hinckley might be his distorted doppelgänger. "The dividing line between Life and Art can be invisible," the would-be assassin wrote from prison while awaiting trial. "After seeing enough hypnotizing movies and reading enough magical books, a fantasy life develops, which can be harmless or quite dangerous."

Hinckley's obsession doesn't even strike Scorsese as particularly bizarre. "I don't mean to seem glib," he says prescriptively, "but you *must* have a varied viewing pattern. You can't see *Taxi Driver* and *Mean Streets* together on a double bill. You must see *Taxi Driver* and . . . *His Girl Friday*." Pressed further on his feelings about the Hinckley case, Scorsese grows agitated, then serious. "What should we do?" he wants to know. "Should we ban the film?"

I attended one screening of *The King of Comedy* with a cadre of editors from *The New York Times Magazine*; after the film the big question was, would this new Scorsese vision inspire some lunatic to abduct Johnny Carson? "The thought has crossed my mind," Scorsese allows, his staccato delivery picking up speed. "But I don't see how that can happen. I mean, guys on that level have already dealt with this sort of thing. Show business personalities can handle themselves. They have to." Pausing, he adds, "At first I thought you were asking if I thought someone might try to kidnap *me*. Or Bob. . . ."

Scorsese has had other cause to ponder the effect of "hypnotizing movies." Last March, while he and Schoonmaker were editing *The King of Comedy*, Theresa Saldana, a 27-year-old actress who had a bit part in *Raging Bull*, as well as roles in other films, was stabbed four times in front of her West Hollywood apartment by a British-born drifter, Arthur Richard Jackson. Evidently Jackson only knew Saldana from her films; police found a diary in which he invoked her name more than 50 times. Scorsese doesn't seem surprised that such an attack occurred; after all, evil is real and violence can happen at any moment. But, "I was totally shocked because she was just *starting*," he says. "I immediately got very protective about the people around me. I'm just now starting to go out again."

There is a scene in which Rupert Pupkin's pathology hyperbolizes the profoundly ambivalent relationship Americans have with the aristocracy of winners who, presented on TV or paraded through the pages of *People* magazine, live their lives as public drama. Among other things, the mild gossip purveyed by the news and entertainment media promotes the socially cohesive illusion of an intimate America where everyone knows (and even cares) about each other. Part of Rupert's motivation is a simple hunger for intimacy with Langford, the celebrity he idolizes, impinges upon, violates, and ultimately supplants.

"*The King of Comedy* is about people falling in love with idealized images of each other and how misleading and selfish that can be," says Scorsese. Rupert imagines he "knows" Langford personally just from years of watching him on television and nights spent waiting for his autograph. Moreover, he comes to feel that Langford actually owes him something for this "unselfish" loyalty.

In *The Fall of Public Man,* Richard Sennett suggests it is "the complete repression of audience response by the electronic media" that produces "a magnified interest in persons or personalities who are not similarly denied." *The King of Comedy* takes the rage and wounded narcissism implicit in such denial as the fulcrum for an Oedipal drama. Splitting its sympathies between the "have" Langford and the "have-not" Pupkin, the film offers a both-sides-now dialectic of American celebrity.

"MARTY'S NOT AN intellectual," says Schrader. "When he finally realizes something, he also feels it." Scorsese has called *The King of Comedy* "a reappraisal of my first 15 years of making films, what it's been like." "Rupert becomes a star," he says, "but for what?"

Scorsese also speaks of his identification with Langford. "Jerry walks into his empty apartment, and he does exactly what I do, he turns on the TV." Scorsese ponders the loneliness of his alter egos: "I've lost a lot." The director maintains that he identifies with both protagonists in *The King of Comedy.* Which one more? "At this point, I think it's Jerry," he says without hesitation, adding, "There are kids who will do anything, *anything,* to get into movies."

The King of Comedy is Scorsese's view of celebrity—a situation he experiences as almost more perilous than the absence of celebrity. "*The King of Comedy* is a very funny film," he cautions, "but it's not a comedy. The end is full of despair." Is it dangerous? Scorsese hems and haws, then answers like a filmmaker: "How can you be afraid to show something that already exists?"

His *Parsifal*: Following the Syberbergenlied

Originally published in *The Village Voice* (February 22, 1982).

BUOYED BY THE insinuating leitmotifs of Richard Wagner's heady score, *Parsifal* is the most fluid and enjoyable of Hans-Jürgen Syberberg's films since *Ludwig.* This, more than any change in the Syberberg world view, accounts for the favorable press the movie has received—at least compared to his outrageous *Our Hitler.*

To paraphrase Susan Sontag on *Flaming Creatures,* the problem with *Our*

Hitler (or *Hitler, a Film from Germany* as it's known in Europe) is that it's hard to simply talk about the film: one has to continually defend it. Or rather, to forever explain Syberberg's *meshugas*, which is nothing less than salvaging the ghastly wreck of the German Romantic tradition so we can have a look at it in all its decomposed irrationality.

While Syberberg acknowledges Hitler as the bitter flower of German "irrationalism," he argues that the blanket repression of this tradition—"mysticism, *Sturm und Drang*, large portions of classicism, the romantic period, Nietzsche, Wagner, and expressionism"—amounts to a cultural lobotomy. Syberberg refuses to cede the German ideology to Marxist (or bourgeois) materialism; he not only sees himself as Wagner's heir but very likely as the greatest vocational German since Thomas Mann, if not Hitler himself.

Because he views art as ultimately therapeutic—Syberberg's aesthetic credo is articulated in *Parsifal*'s third act: "The wound heals by that lance alone that made it"—he attempts to minister to the German audience by exhuming its traumatically repressed myths. Not surprisingly, many of his countrymen find this disorientingly tasteless, and, in this sense, Syberberg is a useful political lightning rod. He hasn't caught on in Germany as Fritz Lang did in the '20s. *Au contraire*. Of course, one can't help but be relieved that his work is more highly regarded in France, England, the U.S. and, according to Syberberg, even Israel than at home.

Characteristically, Syberberg sees his *Parsifal* as a slap in Germany's face, bracing perhaps, but still an affront. "I made a provocation on plastic society, mass democracy," he explains. "I tried something impossible today, a classic style of what Kleist or Goethe would call *das Erhebenselbst*—full of sincerity, uplifting. This is the first time you can see the footwashing in act three without laughing." Although tolerantly attentive to his reviews, Syberberg is blithely self-absorbed, aristocratically disdainful of official culture and counterculture alike. Asked about his position on the West German political spectrum, he says, "As a contrast to the ruling system, the Green people are interesting to me. But they are not my audience, I think. They are against art. They want something anarchistic, and I am the contrary of that."

Sometimes pegged as a right-wing Brechtian, Syberberg is actually an antimodern modernist. (One is tempted to say "antimodern postmodernist" if only because modern Germany went down in flames in 1945.) Wagner's *Parsifal* is a meretricious vision of future redemption; Syberberg's *Parsifal*, like *Our Hitler*, is a *Trauerspiel*—a "sorrow play"—that mourns the pseudo-redemption's cataclysmic failure. *Parsifal*'s prelude is set to a ceremonial camera crawl over picture postcards of destroyed German cities floating in a stream of fetid water. "We start from the end of the world, and all that follows is memory," Syberberg explains. Later settings suggest a blasted nursery with puppets of Marx, Wagner, Nietzsche, and Ludwig propped against the inexplicable contraptions that dot the set like abandoned toys.

Syberberg's *Parsifal* is set in ruins and played against a Mount Rushmore representation of Wagner's deathmask. (The composer's colossal nostrils dominate most of the third act before Parsifal and his followers ascend to heaven through the starry lining of Wagner's smoking jacket.) When the landscape fissures—as it does in act two to reveal a misty chasm full of grotesquely erotic *Blumenmädchen,* topless and painted blue, leaning against the rock like Place Pigalle hookers—the action seems to be taking place inside Wagner's head. "Yes, the girls are fixed in the wall—a piece of thinking in the brain of Wagner," says Syberberg dreamily. "As Wagner has chosen Christianity as the frame of the story, I use the head of Wagner."

Like most reasonable commentators, Syberberg dismisses *Parsifal*'s super-ficial Christianity to locate Wagner's myth in the more archaic context of the German *volk*. The Grail is guarded by Teutonic knights and decomposing war dead; with shocking matter-of-factness, the heraldic banners that signal its approach include Hitler's swastika. "Out of *Parsifal* I make a religion," Hitler declared during a visit paid the Wagner heirs in 1923, the year his Munich putsch flopped; when the Führer came to power a decade later he turned his annual pilgrimage to Bayreuth into a national ritual of Superbowl proportions.

"More than the *Ring, Parsifal* was the gospel of National Socialism," writes Robert W. Gutman in a study of Wagner that draws heavily on the composer's anti-Semitic political rantings. As Gutman sees it, *Parsifal* is something like Wagner's *Birth of a Nation*: "With the help of church bells, snippets of the Mass, and the vocabulary and paraphernalia of the Passion, Wagner set forth a religion of racism under the cover of Christian legend." Amfortas—the wounded Grail King—"contrasts the divine blood of Christ in the Grail with his own sinful blood, corrupted by sexual contact with Kundry, a racial inferior," which is to say, a Jew. (Klingsor, the jealous necromancer who puts Kundry up to her tricks, is also Jewish.)

If anything, *Parsifal* demonstrates the essential fragility of German Chris-tianity. Carl Jung, not immune himself from the blandishments of National Socialism ideology, had *Parsifal* in mind when he observed that, in Wagner, "Germanic prehistory comes surging up, thunderous and stupefying, to fill the gaping breach in the Church."

"WAGNER IS A neurosis," wrote Nietzsche of the onetime guru he had come to see as a decadent, dangerous P. T. Barnum. Wagner's art, Nietzsche warned, is "brutal, artificial, and idiotically 'innocent' at the same time." In his treatment of Wagner's last opera and the one the composer termed the "holiest" of his works, Syberberg appears to have taken Nietzsche at his word. The movie is simultaneous travesty and celebration—a sumptuous, tawdry mixture of the ridiculous and the sublime, the young and the damned, the bad and the beauti-ful, art as religion and religion as kitsch.

Syberberg's mise-en-scène is blatantly theatrical, full of miniature props and rear screen projections, with performers ankle deep in his trademark dry ice vapors. ("The crew likes the fog effect more than me," he insists.) The opposite of a straight recording, *Parsifal* is entirely postdubbed; only one principal—the garrulous Gurnemanz—is sung by the actor who plays the part. Syberberg revels in this artifice by audaciously loading the film with lengthy close-ups, some nearly 10 minutes in duration. "The faces are masks that reveal the music," he says. The director stresses that the opera's key moment is the kiss Kundry and Parsifal exchange. "That can *never* work on stage—it was made for film!"

Although Reiner Goldberg sings the role of Parsifal throughout, Syberberg splits Wagner's holy fool into teenage male and female personae. The former is a cow-eyed hippie (Michael Kutter), whose callow, seductive gestures continually derange Goldberg's mature tenor; the latter (Karen Krick)—replacing Kutter after he rejects the temptress Kundry at the climax of act two—is a dour Modigliani, whose solemn "innocence" is rendered palpably absurd by the undersized helmet perched on her head.

Syberberg refuses to give a rational explanation for his two Parsifals or any of his permutations on Wagner. His faith in art amounts to total faith in his own unconscious. "I read a lot, forget a lot, and I have a certain concept worked out. Then we go into the studio, and suddenly I think things can't happen. The moment I realize that, I change." Syberberg ultimately composes his movie by playing with his set. "I never go out of the studio when I work," he insists. "Normally, directors go out to have coffee or to make jokes. I always sit there and look, and I see new possibilities."

Still, by displacing Wagner's campiness onto the "hero," Syberberg frees Kundry to be something more than a Theda Bara magdalene. "The attempt of Kundry, the succubus, to ruin the hero by luring him to carnal intercourse forms the drama's crisis," writes Gutman. And Parsifal's "resistance" calls to mind "Huysman's conclusion that the chaste alone can be truly obscene. For all its greatness, the second act of *Parsifal* must be protected by its stage director from resembling a series of satirical drawings by Beardsley or Lautrec."

This Syberberg achieves through the performances of Edith Clever. Embodying the nuances of Yvonne Minton's voice with every muscle of her face, neck, and torso, Clever gives a performance of absolute genius—comparable to, and perhaps better than, Falconetti's interpretation of Jeanne d'Arc. Alternately wild and submissive, and, in the end, tragic, Clever turns the latter half of act two into one of the most electrifying pleas for physical love ever put on film. ("After *The Left-Handed Woman,* Clever seemed maybe the best movie actress in the world," I wrote dizzily from Cannes following *Parsifal*'s midnight premiere. "After *Parsifal,* she seems something like divine.") "Edith Clever, there is only one . . ." says Syberberg of this extraordinary performer. "She comes in the studio and she is trembling—like a very sensitive, noble horse. To this day she has nightmares of Minton pursuing her, menacingly."

Wagner's *Parsifal* is founded on a queasy oscillation between sexuality and asceticism. (The opera's "alliance of beauty and sickness goes so far," wrote Nietzsche, that "it casts a shadow over Wagner's earlier art—which now seems too bright, too healthy.") Syberberg makes Wagner's sexual paranoia—pure boys, devil Jews, seductive Liliths, tainted blood—everywhere apparent. Images of castration are ubiquitous: a broken lance is visualized as a shattered stone lingam, Amfortas's wound is carried around on a velvet cushion, detached from his body and dribbling blood, a portable gash that's the very image of vagina as castrated phallus.

In a strictly Syberberg touch, Kundry carries the shield of Medusa, a symbol Freud analyzed as "a representation of the female genitals [that] isolates their horrifying effects from the pleasure-giving ones . . . a representation of woman as a being who frightens and repels because she is castrated." And, of course, Syberberg's two Parsifals not only serve to foreground his bravura postdubbing but transfer the burden of perversion from Kundry to Parsifal. Once the knight refuses her love he becomes, in the film's libidinal scheme of things, a castrati more monstrous than the self-mutilated Klingsor.

Parsifal may be the most blatantly Freudian movie since *Un Chien Andalou.* Asked if he thought of the film in psychoanalytic terms, Syberberg blandly agrees: "Yes, but what does it mean? Freud invented a science for this century. I'm not educated in that science, but I'm sure everyone of us knows a lot about it. It's in the air."

Still, Syberberg is more comfortable with Nietzsche. "We have a German word, *Versöhnnung,* that means a reconciliation of father and son. This is what I want for Wagner and Nietzsche." But that isn't *Parsifal*'s only reconciliation. Syberberg calls the wound a symbol of lost paradise and notes that in *his* version, Kundry herself takes its place in the end, lying down beside the dead Amfortas in an image that suggests the *Versöhnnung* of lance and wound, male and female, Aryan and Jew in an impossible, lost, alternate universe. Syberberg has managed to stand Wagner on his head, and it is with a certain ironic indulgence that he explains, "Wagner made gold out of the shit of his private ideas."

SYBERBERG'S STANDING OVATION, the night of *Parsifal*'s Lincoln Center premiere, was laced with a hearty chorus of boos. But the next day, when the filmmaker addressed the New York chapter of the Wagner Society, his audience accorded him more respect than, say, a conclave of Tolkien freaks might grant Ralph Bakshi: after all, Syberberg's desecration was but one of the multitude of eccentric readings the master inspired. In fact, Syberberg did almost as much listening as he did explaining. "Yes," he reassured the faithful at one point. "My film is Wagner, still Wagner, but more. . . ."

Tarkovsky arrives

Originally published in The Village Voice as "The East is Read" (October 26, 1982); "Tarkovsky's Planet" (August 23, 1983); "The Condition His Condition Was In" (January 10, 1984); "Cold Comfort" (January 17, 1984); "This Island Earth" (September 30, 1986); and "Andrei Tarkovsky, 1932–1986" (January 13, 1987).

A S RUSSIAN IN its tormented vision as *E.T.* is buoyantly American, Andrei Tarkovsky's *Stalker* deserves the same recognition as a cultural event. It's a foregone conclusion that *Stalker* won't appeal to every taste. The film is deliberate in its pacing, enigmatic in its implications, brutal in its poetry. Yet no one interested in world cinema or the Soviet Union should miss it. The 50-year-old

Tarkovsky, who in two decades has completed only five features—*My Name Is Ivan, Andrei Rublev, Solaris, The Mirror,* and *Stalker*—makes movies with an ambition and intensity that, save for the work of Serge Paradjanov, has been absent from Soviet film for 40 years.

Loosely adapted from *Roadside Picnic,* a 1973 novel by the Soviet science-fiction writers Arkady and Boris Strugatsky, *Stalker* is a perverse replay of *Solaris*'s cosmic voyage, a remake of *Rublev* in a secular world of postapocalyptic misery. Tarkovsky jettisons the novel's unconvincing North American setting and virtually everything else except its premise and protagonist. The former is the existence of a mysterious, government-restricted "Zone," where the laws of nature have apparently been altered by a meteor shower or an extraterrestrial visitation. The latter is a "stalker" (the English word is used), who lives on the periphery of the Zone and will, for a price, illegally guide seekers through its treacherous terrain. With his shaven head and dirty, shapeless clothing, the stalker resembles a zek (political prisoner), and, indeed, his first words to his slatternly wife are, "I'm imprisoned everywhere." The Zone's risks are enormous: many who go never return, those who do face prison terms and the possibility that their children will be genetically deformed. Nevertheless, the story circulates that the Zone contains a Room that can reveal and even realize one's deepest desire.

The world outside the Zone—ostensibly universal but recognized by Russians as specifically Soviet—is weirdly reminiscent of David Lynch's *Eraserhead.* The stalker, his wife, and their legless mutant daughter share a heatless hovel by a vast, polluted lake in some industrial wasteland. Bleak as the gulag, it's a desolate landscape of smoke, water, and debris rendered hauntingly beautiful by Tarkovsky's sepia-tinted film stock and exaggerated Rembrandt lighting. The stalker, who has just been released after a lengthy jail term, is engaged to escort two disillusioned intellectuals—one a cowardly, careerist scientist, the other a cynical, self-pitying writer, and both in search of psychic renewal—through the Zone to the Room. Once the trio elude the armed patrols who guard the Zone and slip into it, the film turns color. But, unexpectedly, the supposed wonderland proves closer to Kansas than Oz. The Zone, too, is a junkyard—albeit a deserted one—where houses lie in ruins and the streams are clogged with rusting artifacts.

Stalker is preeminently a film of landscape and atmosphere. Tarkovsky's evocation of the Zone is so concrete that it precludes the use of special effects. Yet, waiting to see the alleged marvels of the region, one shares his characters' frustration. The stalker warns his charges that they are faced with a maze of deadly constantly shifting traps, but they often disregard his instructions and seemingly never come to grief. The journey toward the Room—located in an abandoned farmhouse less than a football field away from their point of entry into the Zone—is less hazardous than it is inexplicably roundabout and physically uncomfortable. (The images of the men crawling through subterranean tunnels or fording cisterns chest-high with oil-slicked water are reminiscent of the ordeal suffered by the partisans in Andrzej Wajda's *Kanal.*) The visuals are visceral and unforgettable; *Stalker*'s weakest elements are the arguments between the writer and the scientist about their respective disciplines and, especially, the philosophical debate that flares up on the threshold of the Room. (In a rare comic touch, the scientist abruptly pulls a 20-kiloton bomb out of his knapsack and threatens to destroy the Zone.) Inevitably, the trip ends in failure. The miserable stalker returns to his hovel (which bears no small resemblance to the Room), complaining of intellectuals who have lost their sense of hope.

If the stalker is a tormented holy fool—it should come as no surprise that Tarkovsky is currently working on an adaptation of *The Idiot*, a novel he calls "the tragedy of the loss of spirituality"—what is the Zone? The director, of course, resists any allegorical reading of the film. When in London in 1980 for *Stalker*'s premiere, he told an interviewer that the images meant no more than they showed and complained that children understood his work better than critics. Nevertheless, *Stalker* begs for exegesis, and the illusory freedom of the Zone has been variously interpreted as a metaphor for religious redemption, for the West, or for the privileged status of an Eastern elite. In his intelligent *Sight and Sound* review, Gilbert Adair suggests that the Zone has actually been sanctioned, if not designed, by the authorities: "The legendary difficulty of access to the Zone [seems] almost a contrivance, a pretence of barring entry (when in reality a select few were being 'permitted' it) by which the state could perhaps foster the useful illusion of limited but just attainable freedom." At a press conference at the 1981 New Delhi Film Festival (where I first saw *Stalker*), a Marxist student suggested to a leading Soviet film critic that the Zone represented the October Revolution. Smiling indulgently, the critic—who had previously defended *Stalker* as a movie that could never have been produced in a marketplace economy (he's right)—countered that he had no idea what the Zone was and didn't care for the film much anyway.

Truly, *Stalker* is a devious movie. The only certain thing is its blatant anti-technological, antirational, antimaterialist bias—no small dissent in Soviet society. The presence of an iconic zek, two disaffected intellectuals, and a landscape ravaged by haphazard industrialization gives the film immediate political resonance, but, ultimately, the issues the Zone raises have less to do with freedom than with faith. (Accordingly, *Stalker* cruelly tests our naive faith that, once inside the Zone, something miraculous will happen.) Tarkovsky calls the Zone "a diseased area" and allows his scientist ample time to polemicize that the mere existence of such a place creates false hopes and festering discontent. However, neither the scientist nor the writer are affected by the Zone. Only the pitiful stalker—who calls the place his home and who believes that only the most wretched and hopeless will be permitted to pass through the Zone unharmed—finds some shred of solace there. And even the stalker's faith is shaken by the failure of the Room.

Throughout the Zone, the stalker insists there is no going back—all motion is forward. The Room then suggests some Hegelian fulfillment of history. *Stalker,* it seems, mourns the impossibility of religious (political, technocratic) faith even as it acknowledges the damage this faith inflicts. It's a vision of despair illuminated by only the faintest ray of hope. Near the end of the movie, the stalker's wife addresses the camera directly: "I'd rather have bitter happiness than a gray, dull life." And in a final scene capable of raising the short hairs on the back of your neck, Tarkovsky suggests that—for good or for evil— something of the Zone's power is internalized in the unformed psyche of the stalker's mutant daughter.

TARKOVSKY FILMS are rarely graspable on a single viewing and *The Mirror* is his most notoriously difficult piece. But it's close to being an essential film, an extraordinarily beautiful movie whose enigmas, paradoxically, provide a key to his other work.

Solaris, adapted from the novel by Polish sci-fi writer Stanislaw Lem, invited some to peg Tarkovsky as a manufacturer of grandiose, intellectually gaudy entertainments—a russki Stanley Kubrick. That image has persisted although, if nothing else, *The Mirror* makes it clear that he's closer to being a socialist Stan Brakhage. "It's not that I don't want to be understood," Tarkovsky told a British journalist last year. "But I can't, like Spielberg, say, make a film for the general public—I'd be mortified if I discovered I could." On the other hand, as he put it in a statement for *Variety*: "It will take [state] intervention to protect and defend film art against commercialization. Film art is as worthy of protective laws as legislation to protect the environment." (Indeed, after spending two years in Italy making *Nostalghia,* Tarkovsky maintained that the western film world is in worse shape than the western environment.) More than anything else, *The Mirror*—released in Moscow in 1974, three years after *Solaris* and three before *Stalker,* resembles a million dollar version of Brakhage's autobiographical *Sincerity* produced with a grant from the Jerome Foundation under the auspices of the New York State Council on the Arts.

Less a narrative than an assemblage, *The Mirror* mixes apparently personal anecdotes—a child's wartime exile, a mother's experience of political terror, a divorcing couple's quarrel—with slow-mo dream sequences and poetic chunks of stark newsreels (the bombing of Barcelona, the Chinese cultural revolution, a boy being cured of his stutter through hypnosis). Tarkovsky's psychodramatic-bricolage-big-budget aesthetic is underscored by his fanatically precise manipulation of film stocks and recorded sound and encapsulated in his trademark camera move—an overhead tortoise crawl, preferably telephoto, across some piece of soggy terrain, a river bed or forest floor covered with lichen, bottles, rusty tools, toadstools, and assorted moldy detritus.

On Comrade Tarkovsky's planet, there's a continual backbeat of earth, wind, fire, and mainly water. Like *The Mirror*'s obsessive image of fire in the rain, past and present, private and public are completed commingled. The film's two-tiered time frame blends memories of Tarkovsky's childhood with fragments of his adult life. The same actress (haunting Margarita Terekhova) plays both the abandoned mother and abandoned wife, the same towhead kids play the protagonist as a boy as well as his son.

The Mirror flows, but it's a flow of concentrated jolts. Tarkovsky's fragments and "details," the Hungarian film theorist Yvette Bíró once observed, "do not behave like events, but—in conformity with Eisenstein's prophesy—like theses and propositions." Tarkovsky is a master of form but he's hardly a formalist. *The Mirror* is steeped in the battle of the sexes and the yearnings of what one character calls Russia's "primeval, Asiatic kind of bourgeoisie."

From the perspective of progressive politics—and particularly antipatriarchal politics—*The Mirror*, like *Sincerity*, is not unproblematic. (But, then, from the perspective of progressive politics what isn't problematic?) In this case, you either accept stream of consciousness, which is to say poetry, as a valid aesthetic strategy or, like Plato, you nix it.

Given its national origins and the circumstances of its making, *The Mirror* is a fascinating, challengingly complex ideological artifact. More than that, and despite the title, it's really a window. We look into Tarkovsky's *Mirror* and encounter a vision, a mind, the invigorating intensity of the filmmaker's gaze.

IF NOTHING ELSE, Tarkovsky's *Nostalghia* is the most extraordinary film by a Soviet citizen working abroad in the 50 years since Sergei Eisenstein's *Que Viva Mexico*. The bombshelter mentality of 1984 notwithstanding, that's reason enough to catch the movie while the print is still fresh. But go prepared to jettison the narrative, the angst, the mid-life crisis, the spiritual confusion and simply watch the screen.

Even more than *Stalker, Nostalghia* is not so much a movie as a place to inhabit for two hours. "Look at it as if it were the window in a train travelling through your life," is Tarkovsky's advice. Made in Italy (and scripted by Tonino Guerra who co-wrote every Antonioni from *L'avventura* through *Blow Up* as well as *Amarcord, The Night of the Shooting Stars, Lucky Luciano*, and *The Tenth Victim*), *Nostalghia* is scarcely less exotic than *Que Viva Mexico*. But where the Eisenstein trip is an exuberant camp frenzy, solemn Tarkovsky orchestrates a glacier-stately tour through a world of fantastic textures, sumptuously muted colors, and terrarium-like humidity. This is a film which turns the spectacle of an ancient, leaky cellar—slow droplets bombarding a futile cluster of green or brown bottles—into an image as memorable as any this century.

Sure, *Nostalghia* has a plot. But what strikes you first (and ultimately, too, I suspect) about this loopy, majestic film are the subtle shifts in light and color, the voluptuous deliberation of the pacing, the fanatical attention given to each noise on the soundtrack, the portable Russia this visionary carries around with him every waking moment. Having explored Italy and set up shop on the exact spot that reminded him most of the Moscow countryside, Tarkovsky and cinematographer Guiseppe Lanci photograph a moldering 16th century Tuscan spa as though it were a calcified, detritus-clogged backwater of the Zone or a misty figment of Prince Myshkin's imagination. Even *Nostalghia*'s final movement transforms the Eternal City into a sunbaked hallucination of Moscow, the Third Rome after the Third World War.

Basically, *Nostalghia* has something to do with the morose, mystical East meeting the crazy, mystical West; it's a film about the circumstances of its own making. The Russian term *nostalghia,* Tarkovsky explained, "mixes the love for your homeland and the melancholy that arises from being far away"—which he had, first in Italy and now in London, for the better part of four years. "It is an illness, a moral suffering which tortures the soul. It can be fatal if one is not able to overcome it, but it can be contracted only in a foreign country." During the lengthy *Nostalghia* shoot, Tarkovsky told an Italian journalist that the film was precisely about "my own condition at the moment."

As befits a movie made by a tourist—if not a cosmonaut—*Nostalghia* broods on the impossibility of ever knowing the Other. The problem is conceptualized in sexual-national terms as an extremely bleak comedy of misinterpreted signals. For maybe an hour, an ascetic Russian intellectual (Oleg Yankovsky, Tarkovsky's alter-ego in *The Mirror,* here as well called "Andrei")—ostensibly in Italy to research the life of an 18th century Russian expatriate composer—and his lushly carnal translator-guide (tawny-maned Domiziana Giordano in her first movie role) drive each other nuts on the brink of an unconsummated affair.

For Andrei, it's apparently all or nothing. Realizing that he can never truly know, for example, Piero della Francesca's pregnant Madonna del Parto, he refuses to even enter the church of Monterchi to see the altarpiece. Domiziana goes in anyway (the clickclackclick of her fashionable shoes over the babble of praying peasant women) and—ah, the degeneracy of the modern world—gets dressed down by the sacristan for looking at rather than praying to the fertility fetish.

Although less conventional in his dogma, Andrei hardly gives Domiziana an easier time. Swaddled in his fantasies of Mother Russia, he can as little help himself from scorning her earnest attempt to read Russian poetry in Italian translation (the verses, incidentally, of Tarkovsky's father Arseni) than he can from blatantly appreciating her Junoesque aura: "Stop, you're prettier in this light." Of course, his aesthetic offends her as much as hers offends the sacristan. "You dress badly and you're boring" is her exasperated response to his final sexual rejection. "You're the kind I'd sleep with rather than explaining why I don't feel like it."

Midway through, *Nostalghia* takes a leap into the void which, if one doesn't share Tarkovsky's religious faith, can only seem a kind of theater of gibberish. Days before he is scheduled to depart Italy, Andrei does encounter a kindred soul in the bearish local madman, played by Erland Josephson. A former mathematician who locked his family in the house for seven years waiting for Armageddon, Josephson is ejected from the spa while attempting the redemption of mankind by carrying a lit candle from one end of the ancient mineral bath to the other. Josephson is even less interested in Andrei than Andrei is in Domiziana. In fact, for her, the Russian's sudden fascination with this lunatic is virtually the last straw. She petulantly returns to Rome and her well-heeled older lover as Andrei drifts into alcoholic reveries: "There are too many shoes in Italy," he proclaims.

The film's final movement begins in Rome. Domiziana phones Andrei's hotel with a message from Josephson who has moved his act to the city. Andrei is scheduled to fly back to Moscow but, instead, returns to the Tuscan hills to complete Josephson's interrupted ritual. In Rome, Josephson climbs Michelangelo's statue of Marcus Aurelius and, standing on the emperor's horse, advocates the integration of the mad and the sane. Placing the "Ode to Joy" on a portable phonograph, Josephson douses himself with kerosene and sets himself ablaze—the fire warping the record and torturing Beethoven out of recognition. Meanwhile, out in Tuscany and chest deep in the baths, Andrei manages to get a candle lit on his third cosmic attempt. Upon crossing over he apparently suffers a heart attack and, perhaps dying, has an astounding final vision of the snowy Russian countryside enclosed within a Romanesque cathedral, itself within the Russian countryside.

Showier than the mystical images that end *The Mirror* or *Stalker,* this synthesis of East and West brings the full weight of Tarkovskian grandeur to bear on the theme at hand. It's his equivalent of C.B. DeMille's parting of the Red Sea and it's an undeniably forceful way to push a point home. *Nostalghia* may not be Tarkovsky's greatest film (what could top *Andrei Rublev* except maybe *The Mirror?*), but it's certainly his least compromised.

TARKOVSKY PASSED THROUGH New York in the autumn of 1983, en route from a retrospective at the Telluride Film Festival in Colorado to London, where he was preparing a production of *Boris Godunov* at Covent Garden. Thin and intense with strikingly pale green eyes, he seems a man of imperial nervousness. You're delighted (but not taken aback) when he traces his Tartar origins directly to the prophet Mohammad. Still, he knows his Russian folklore wisdom. "If you're going to live with the wolves you have to howl like a wolf," he advises me at one point through a translator. The greatest pleasure he seems to get from the interview is when I describe the official explanation of *Stalker* delivered by the head of the Soviet delegation to an Indian Marxist at the 1981 New Delhi Film Festival and ask if the film's tormented protagonist is meant to suggest a Gulag zek. "That is sitting on the porcupine without getting quills in your bottom," he and his wife chuckle.

On the other hand, as the *New York Post* was that day reminding us, Tarkovsky's countrymen had recently blasted a South Korean passenger liner out of the sky. Dressed in chinos and sporting a gold chain, Tarkovsky is gnawing his thumb cuticle raw. Who knows what he's really thinking? The only other time he ever visited America he says was during the 1962 Cuban Missile Crisis and his estimation of the U.S. is pithily p.c. "It's extraordinary what Americans have achieved in the short time they've been on the continent."

In addition to Telluride, Tarkovsky visited Monument Valley and Las Vegas. He rhapsodizes over the former as "an overwhelming experience" even—according to his translator—"the most fantastic thing that ever happened to him." As for Las Vegas, our national id, Tarkovsky is dismissive. "Oh everybody has the same impression. It's a tasteless place. Apparently there's a statue of Marcus Aurelius there"—does he mean Caesars Palace?—"if I had seen it, I wouldn't have believed it." To my naive surprise, Tarkovsky does not seem particularly anxious to get back home. What he proposes to do next is film *Hamlet,* in English, maybe even in Monument Valley.

Forgetting for the time his notions of cultural exclusivity, Tarkovsky pronounced *Walden* his favorite book. "I am on principle hostile to technology and progress." Why? Because "technology turns us into its slaves," he replies in a rather less dialectical formulation than one would expect from the author of *Solaris.*

The truth is that, like Stan Brakhage or Hans-Jürgen Syberberg, Tarkovsky is an antimodern modernist, a natural surrealist seemingly innocent of official surrealism's radical program. Brakhage, Syberberg, and Tarkovsky are all would-be national shamans who see their art as a quasi-religious calling. Tending towards the solipsistic, all three see themselves as essentially unique and have more or less reinvented film language to suit their visions. Brakhage, the most generous soul of the three, introduced Tarkovsky at Telluride with lavish appreciation as a virtual comrade in arms: "To me, the three most difficult and necessary things for film to accomplish are (1) the epic work, to tell the tales of the tribes of the world; (2) to keep it personal, to work only out of what one loves the most, because that's where each of us know most about truth; and (3) to do the dream-work, that is, to illuminate the borders of the unconscious. The only filmmaker that I know that is equally great in all three of these accomplishments in every film is Andrei Tarkovsky."

It's a melancholy fact of life that, for too many people (including, I suspect, Tarkovsky himself), the praise of Stan Brakhage is something like the kiss of death. *Stalker* and even *The Mirror* have done surprisingly well in limited runs downtown at the Film Forum but, dog knows what sort of audience exists for Tarkovsky in the foreign film ghetto of Lincoln Center and environs. Something tells me he's an unwelcome guest, one more orphan of the storm toting a shopping-bag full of junk across upper Broadway. Like, who invited this long-winded Russian prophet into the world? I mean, who needs this guy whose movies pretty much demand to be seen twice or not at all?

Who indeed? You can loath Tarkovsky or you can adore him. What's mindless is to pretend that his particular genius doesn't exist.

WHEN I INTERVIEWED Tarkovsky last autumn, I gathered that he had been negatively impressed by the Stan Brakhage films he had seen the previous week at the Telluride Film Festival. In fact, my distinct impression was that Tarkovsky—who became even more nervous than usual when the subject of Brakhage came up—regarded the American filmmaker as something of a certifiable lunatic.

Now, I understand. Too late to include in last week's piece on Tarkovsky and *Nostalghia,* a colleague has provided me with a truly hilarious account by Brakhage of his Telluride meeting with his Soviet counterpart. The piece is published in the journal *Rolling Stock* and comes complete with a sidebar in which Brakhage talks about the other films he saw at the festival. (His favorite seems to have been *Danton*.)

After offering a naive explanation of Tarkovsky's position in the Soviet film industry, Brakhage describes his presentation of a medallion to Tarkovsky and gives a description of his response to *Nostalghia*. ("I was absolutely enchanted, even though I have a prejudice against long, structural scenes. . . . When I stumbled out, it was like a religious conversion, but unlike a religious convert, I was absolutely free.") The piece then continues with a digression on Brakhage's previous confrontations at past Telluride festivals where "Hollywood moviemakers [have compared] themselves to giants of literature and music. The most extreme example of that was the maker of Bugs Bunny one year. I said to him, 'If you're a great artist, then what in the world is Van Gogh?'"

The heart of the article, however, has Brakhage, Tarkovsky, their wives, Krzysztof Zanussi, Zbigniew Rybczynski (the irrepressible maker of *Tango*), Tarkovsky's assistant Olga ("a plump, sweet, charming girl"), and an unidentified Russian film student squeezed into a sweltering Boulder hotel room for an impromptu screening of Brakhage's work (including *Window Water Baby Moving*, the last part of *Dog Star Man*, *Made Manifest*, and *Murder Psalm*) on the wall. Brakhage's description of the scene is at once wonderfully comic and utterly self-serving. Tarkovsky screams throughout in a nonstop rage, claiming the films are hurting his eyes; the wives giggle and hold hands; Zanussi vainly tries to translate for everyone.

In the end Brakhage has the charming Olga confiding to him that she has never seen anything like his films. "There have been three books written on you in Russian but nobody has ever seen any of your films. When I get back to Russia and tell them that I have seen your films, they won't let me talk about anything else for months, maybe years!"

THE SACRIFICE, Andrei Tarkovsky's second feature since his defection to the West, is a film that demands its own time and creates its own night. The film is a story of death and resurrection, in which the horror of personal mortality blazes into a vision of universal destruction, then subsides, no less affectingly, back into itself.

Produced under the auspices of the Swedish Film Institute, *The Sacrifice* may be solemn and uneven, but it's not boring. There's an urgency that belies the stately pace: In the space of 24 hours, Tarkovsky's protagonist, Alexander (Erland Josephson), destroys his worldly possessions, takes a vow of silence, has sex with a witch, lives through the outbreak of World War III, and celebrates his birthday (not exactly in that order).

Still *The Sacrifice* has at least as much talk as action, and no director is more vulnerable than Tarkovsky to the clumsy derision of middlebrow critics. What saves him from white elephantiasis is his fantastic degree of formal control, his profound immersion in the image (and the sound track), his obsessive working out of his own particular destiny. Virtually every one of *The Sacrifice*'s themes is introduced in the film's discreetly showy opening shot, a 10-minute take in which Tarkovsky's detached, implacable camera follows, in reserved middle-shot, Alexander, his young son, and a garrulous postman (Allan Edwall) as they meander along a marshy, green shore.

It's a setting to evoke the edge of the world. The air is full of disembodied voices, but Alexander can't stop talking. A former actor, he was once renowned for his interpretations of Prince Myshkin and Richard III (the two poles of human nature?), until a crisis of authenticity compelled him to quit: "For some reason I began feeling ashamed on stage." For me, this suggests Tarkovsky's own role-playing and self-imposed exile—his jump from the frying pan of the Soviet film world into the fire of the West. Although less flamboyantly so than *Nostalghia, The Sacrifice* seems equally the vision of a stranger in a strange land.

What's falsest about the film is its Scandinavian domesticity. Alexander's birthday—celebrated by his high-strung English wife (Susan Fleetwood), their moody daughter (Valérie Mairesse), the supercilious doctor (Sven Wollter) both women appear to love, and the irrepressible postman—is an excruciating mix-ture of Strindberg and Yves Saint Laurent. The women are ridiculously tricked out in brocade costumes—even the maid is chic—while the house is the essence of bourgeois elegance, if not a veritable *New York* magazine photo spread (bare wood floor, marble fireplace, candelabras, burnished oak furniture, wicker chairs). Nor is Alexander the only noisy ghost. The house is haunted. Lace curtains billow, cabinets creak open by themselves.

Since *The Mirror,* Tarkovsky's films have involved a serious flirtation with the absurd. His is the realm of the holy fool. Clumsy and ponderous, Alexander is a middle-aged Myshkin. Indeed, *The Idiot,* the first of Dostoyevsky's major novels to be written abroad, offers a number of suggestive parallels to *The Sacrifice*—not the least in Tarkovsky's apprehension of both as dealing with the loss of the spiritual. Both works seem intended as interventions—designed to revitalize Christianity and even produce political results. *The Sacrifice* is a film that means to change the world. A form of magical thinking underscores the continual emphasis on models, mirrors, and miniatures. On a second viewing it becomes obvious that even the credit sequence proposes the alchemical leap from art to life.

That Tarkovsky suffered from cancer was scarcely a secret—at one point it was reported that he might be too ill to finish editing *The Sacrifice,* while, writing from Cannes, Andrew Sarris bluntly called the film "the last testament of a dying director." Made palpable as distant thunder, the sense of impending annihilation hovers over *The Sacrifice*—45 minutes into the film, Tarkovsky dramatizes the universal nightmare of the late 20th century. It's a measure of his audacity that Armageddon breaks out in the second act and a tribute to his imagination that he can redeem its clichés—the abortive TV broadcast, the idiotic standing around, the expression of pure hysteria (a long, purposely unpleasant scene that ultimately reflects as severely on the pretensions of doc-tors as it does on the helplessness of patients). There's a shocking literalization of the adage that it's no use crying over spilled milk and a shock of recognition when Josephson realizes that he's waited for this moment all his life, that his life has been, in fact, "one long wait for this."

This is it—but, as anyone who has seen *Stalker* knows, Tarkovsky can be withholdingly antidramatic. Thus, the shameful beauty of catastrophe is displaced back onto the personal; anticipating the end of the world, you get instead the end of Alexander's world. And even that is deferred until the film's virtuoso final movement—again a long, intricately choreographed exterior shot (*The Sacrifice* is nothing if not symmetrical), at once detached and full of existential pressure, as well as the kind of giddy gallows comedy one is more apt to associate with the Jean-Luc Godard of *Weekend*. (Tarkovsky's sense of humor—his jokes at his own expense, his use of a rumpled heavenly messenger who finds Leonardo "sinister" and prefers Piero della Francesca—deserves more attention than it's received.)

Although *The Sacrifice* is peppered with chronological ellipses, and events often come in disorienting clusters, it's by far Tarkovsky's most accessible film. Given the film's language, setting, casting, and overall heaviness—not to mention Sven Nykvist's impeccable cinematography—audiences unfamiliar with *Andrei Rublev* or *Stalker* may see *The Sacrifice* as ersatz Bergman, in much the same way that Andrzej Wajda's mediocre *A Love in Germany* succeeded as pseudo-Fassbinder. It's ironic that this spurious familiarity may hasten Tarkovsky's acceptance by mainstream reviewers—in this case, the New York audience has been leagues ahead of the critics. Tarkovsky's films are steady revival fare; his retrospective last spring drew turnaway crowds at the Museum of Modern Art.

The Sacrifice is less visually spectacular than early Tarkovskys. It lacks the savage splendor of his Russian films or even *Nostalghia*. The dolly shots have a plush, overstuffed feel; the images are as dainty as porcelain miniatures; the muted color, imperceptively fading in and out, seems overrefined and depressed. Yet the film's cumulative effect is undeniable. Tarkovsky makes "this deadly, sickening animal fear" tangible. By the time two and a half hours have elapsed, and Alexander has struck his hopeless bargain with God, the final image—a dead tree splayed out against the blinding sea—may seem the only crucifix appropriate to this blasted age.

THE SACRIFICE was far from Andrei Tarkovsky's finest work, but the knowledge that it was made by a dying man gave its evocation of universal annihilation and vain bargaining with God a piercing grandeur. Characterized, like Tarkovsky's previous six features, by a voluptuous degree of formal control, an almost unbearable seriousness, and a near fanatical belief in the power of art, this film was made to change the world.

A true visionary, Tarkovsky was one of the giants of current cinema. His reputation rests on the strength of five films—*My Name Is Ivan, Andrei Rublev, Solaris, The Mirror,* and *Stalker*—which are marked by an ambition, an intensity, and a virtuosity that, save for the work of Serge Paradjanov and a handful of others, is virtually absent from postwar Soviet film. Tarkovsky's genius is no less evident in *Nostalghia* and *The Sacrifice,* films made in Italy and Sweden, but something is clearly missing. That missing something is, indeed, one of *Nostalghia*'s themes.

In a Marxist theocracy, Tarkovsky performed the illuminating function of obsessing in public over contradictions between the spiritual and the material, the natural and the social, the historical and the individual—variously addressing himself to the Great Patriotic War and the birth of Muscovy, the power of memory and national identity, the nature of art and the impoverishment of modern life. In the Soviet Union, Tarkovsky was a conscience and an inspiration—but what did he mean to the godless West?

Once the director left Mosfilm for Western Europe, it was inevitable that he would become a chip in Cold War II. The first sentence of Walter Goodman's shameless *New York Times* obituary identifies Tarkovsky as a "Russian director who won acclaim in the West for films that were criticized and banned in his homeland." The errors and assumptions in this smugly simpleminded formulation would take a page to explicate. Save for *Andrei Rublev,* shelved for five years, all of Tarkovsky's films were released in Russia soon after completion. Does Goodman actually believe that the two-week Film Forum runs and grotesquely dismissive *New York Times* reviews accorded *Stalker* and *The Mirror* were superior to the reception these films received in Moscow? Thanks to Tarkovsky's intransigence, *Andrei Rublev* was ultimately shown to Soviet audiences in his version; it was in the U.S. that *Rublev,* like *Solaris,* was re-edited by its distributor.

The Mirror, which rivals *Rublev* as Tarkovsky's masterpiece, resembles nothing so much as a Stan Brakhage film with a million-dollar budget. Can Walter Goodman actually believe that a filmmaker as uncompromising and original as Tarkovsky would have had an easier time of it in the West, let alone Hollywood? One mark of Tarkovsky's integrity as an artist was the fear and incomprehension he inspired in apparatchiks of all denominations.

Ritwik Ghatak: A cloud-capped star

Originally published as "A Walk with Love and Death" in *The Village Voice* (November 19, 1985).

HOW PLEASANT TO discover a first-rate director who is young or French, who can electrify the New York Film Festival, galvanize publicists, and excite distributors, whose prints are minty fresh and destined for a long life in some uptown theater. How inconvenient to come upon a first-rate director whose work will be studiously ignored, whose prints will come 'round with the frequency of Halley's Comet (deteriorated a bit more on each return), who has been dead for nearly a decade and is Bengali besides. Such is the case with Ritwik Ghatak.

Ghatak makes few concessions to a non-Indian viewer. ("Ritwik was a

Bengali director in heart and soul, a Bengali artist—much more of a Bengali than myself," said Satyajit Ray after Ghatak's death.) An intellectual who used popular forms with mixed success, Ghatak made films that are almost all veiled autobiography. He came of age during the convulsions of the '40s—World War II, the terrible "man-made famine" of 1944, the communal violence that came with independence—and the partition of Bengal obsessed him all his life. His subjects are almost invariably the uprooted and the dispossessed: parentless children, homeless families, disoriented refugees. He focused mainly on the petit bourgeoisie, economically broken by their exile, living in DP camps or lost in Calcutta, clinging to the memories of their villages and the illusions of their class.

Trafficking in themes that Ray would scarcely touch until *The Middleman* (and then never again), Ghatak combines Ray's emotional depth and passionate lyricism with the left politics and adventurous stylization of Mrinal Sen. At their best, Ghatak's films exhibit a visual style comparable in its visceral pow to that of Sam Fuller—although, according to him, his major influence was Sergei Eisenstein, "the primeval Adam of the cinema, the first man." He does not appear to have been influenced by Hollywood.

BORN IN DACCA (now the capital of Bangladesh) in 1925, the youngest of nine children of an affluent, Europeanized family, Ghatak—like Sen—was deeply involved in the itinerant, communist-oriented Indian People's Theater Association (IPTA) where he wrote, directed, acted, and translated Brecht. In 1950, he entered the film industry as an assistant director, initiating his first project two years later. *Nagarik* ("The Citizen") was a cooperative venture, produced for a pittance with a cast that had never acted before a camera. "Nobody took any money for working on it, not even the laboratory or the studio," Ghatak recalled. "I even got the raw film stock for free." But the co-op had less luck organizing a distribution deal, and, as it turned out, the film was never released. (Existing prints were struck from a moldering negative discovered, 25 years later, in a Calcutta lab.)

A naturalistic slum drama with a generic relation to Clifford Odets (scarcely foreign to the People's Theater aesthetic), relentlessly focusing on its protagonist's inability to find a job, *Nagarik* is static, stagy, and earnest—punctuated with street montages of Calcutta and the sounds of the "Internationale." Still, however plodding, the film is characterized by a burning conviction, as well as a nascent style founded on expressive angles, sensitive use of music, deep focus, and jarring mismatches.

It was not until 1958 (after a brief stint in Bombay) that Ghatak got another chance to direct. In the interim, the international success of *Pather Panchali*, begun by Ray the same year *Nagarik* was completed, improved the prospects for independent productions within the Bengali film industry. Ghatak's second film could be said, like Ray's first, to address the 20th century disruption of traditional Bengal. But, with its graphic invention and gutbucket pantheism, the picaresque *Ajantrik* ("Pathetic Fallacy") is a movie unlike any other. Ghatak orchestrates the rapid-fire jive of a working class Warners comedy within a neorealist, distinctively Indian milieu—dusty stacks of worn tires, crazy beggars, a hierarchy of gofers hanging around a rural cabstand.

Opening with a cackle of hysterical laughter, *Ajantrik* takes its drama from a back country cab driver's lunatic, all-consuming belief that his decrepit Model A has a soul. Although often read as an image of traditional man coping with the Machine Age, the relationship between the driver, Bimal, and the jalopy he calls "Jagaddal" ("special friend") can be seen as a metaphor for tradition as well as modernization—suggesting everything from the man with the movie camera to the Hindu reverence for cows. Just as Bimal is more civilized than the Oraon "tribals" who populate the film (and were the subject of a short documentary Ghatak made a few years before), so is his Jagaddal more primitive than the svelte autos of his fellow cabbies.

The unsentimental pathos of this hectic, gritty parable is heightened in that neither man nor car is particularly lovable. The shambling, obsessed Bimal is suspicious and volatile, while Jagaddal is jealous, sulky, and thin-skinned. Ghatak has enormous fun anthropomorphizing Jagaddal (who in the course of the film is variously referred to as a "skeleton," a "python," a "tiger cub," a "jaguar," and Bimal's "wife," with Bimal observing at one point that Jagaddal is human but *he* is a machine). Yet, as the Indian filmmaker Kumar Shahani has pointed out, "the transference of human pathos to nature" takes place only in the minds of the characters; Ghatak "counterpoints it with his distinctive 180-degree panoramics on empty landscapes. Nature, in the end, is grandly indifferent to human joy or sorrow."

Peppered with popeyed clowning, employing a marvelously dense soundtrack, and conjuring compositions as startlingly beautiful as any in cinema, *Ajantrik* itself would warrant Ghatak an international reputation. Albeit in a lighter vein, Ghatak carried *Ajantrik*'s bold compositions, twangy sound effects, and cartoon exaggerations into the following year's *Bari Theke Paliye* ("The Runaway"). Here, an impressionable 10-year-old runs away from his strict father, the village schoolmaster (one of the numerous teachers found in Ghatak's films), to seek his fortune in El Dorado. Based on a well-known children's story, the film is a sort of Bengali *Wizard of Oz,* with Calcutta (full of eccentric types and unexpected encounters) standing in for the Emerald City. Good and evil are not so clearly defined, however, nor is human suffering far from the surface. Beneath Ghatak's sunny tone, the film is a dark allegory of displaced peasants, humiliated job seekers, and broken families.

After a false start in 1959, Ghatak produced a second masterpiece, one wholly different in mood and pacing from *Ajantrik* but just as stylistically assured. The protagonists of his 1960 *Meghe Dhaka Tara* ("The Cloud Capped Star") are a refugee family living on the outskirts of Calcutta. Although there are two grown sons, for most of the film the family's sole means of support is the scholarship money and then the salary contributed by Nita, the older of the two daughters.

As "the only earning member," Nita initially embraces her fate with a kind of voluptuous self-abnegation. She even contributes to the support of an erst-while suitor. (The title comes from a compliment he pays her, and it's fully justified by Supriya Choudhury's luminous performance. The film rises and falls on her private, inward smile, sudden turns toward or away from the camera.) It gradually becomes clear, however, that the clouds which conceal Nita's radiance also prevent her from seeing the world. By the time she recognizes the futility of her sacrifice, she no longer has the strength to reorient her life—she has literally been consumed. In the end, *Meghe Dhaka Tara* has the ferocitiy of a middle-class *Los Olvidados*. With implacable logic, Ghatak allows Nita to become utterly obliterated, then, in a devastating coda, he elevates her plight to a universal principal.

At once restrained and melodramatic, a film of broad characterizations and Chekhovian nuance, *Meghe Dhaka Tara* makes stunning use of traditional Indian music. (Nita's beloved eldest brother is a self-absorbed, aspiring singer.) The movie is as formally exciting as it is emotionally absorbing. Here, as in *Ajantrik*, Ghatak plays with scale and composition, pushing things smack at the camera, staging action deep within the frame. He's not afraid to rack-focus to catch a reaction, use a jarring near-mismatch, or lay the crack of a whip on the soundtrack to emphasize Nita's pain. Taking a sentimental story from a popular magazine, Ghatak designs this limpid pool of sorrow with such exquisite control, the surface tension doesn't break until the penultimate scene where, with brutal directness and in the lap of "indifferent" nature, the dying Nita sobs out her desire to live.

Meghe Dhaka Tara was not only the summit of Ghatak's art but also evidently his last box office hit. His 1961 follow-up, *Komal Gandhar* ("E Flat") was a spectacular failure. Quasi-autobiographical, the film portrays the People's Theater Movement of the late '40s—agonizing over its jealousies and schisms. The title comes from a Tagore poem comparing a girl with a particular melody and the melody with Bengal, and the script has an equally elaborate structure, with the divided mind of the film's heroine, Anasuya (Supriya Choudhury), mirroring the divided leadership of the People's Theater and, ultimately, divided Bengal.

Throughout, Ghatak makes iconic use of inserts and montages, as well as doing weird and interesting things with the proscenium. The film's centerpiece is an opening night fiasco in which, although the audience is never seen, the camera obsessively dwells upon the sets, backstage machinery, and dressing rooms. Still, despite a surprisingly upbeat ending, *Komal Gandhar* never soars—this dense, subdued film is made tolerable mainly by the presence of Supriya Choudhury as the conflicted Anasuya.

According to Kumar Shahani, it was the failure of *Komal Gandhar*, "partly engineered by people who were exposed by it," that drove Ghatak to despair and increasingly heavy drinking. *Subarnarekha*, named for a Bengali river, is probably his grimmest film. Although completed in 1962, it could only be released three years later. Here, he employs a quieter style in the service of an outrageously contrived melodrama which, far more clumsily than *Meghe*

Dhaka Tara, recounts the tragedy of yet another petit bourgeois refugee family. It's a tribute to Ghatak's raw talent that his blatantly lurid ending, which includes the ironic transposition of *La Dolce Vita* to Calcutta, is affecting in spite of itself.

Subarnarekha seems to have spelled Ghatak's doom in the Bengali film industry. In 1965, he was appointed vice-principal at the Film Institute in Pune, where, although he only served for a year, he is said to have decisively influenced Kumar Shahani, Mani Kaul, Ketan Mehta, and Adoor Gopalakrishnan, students who have come to form the nucleus of the Indian art film. His failing health notwithstanding, Ghatak was able to realize two more features. In 1973 he was invited to make a film in Bangladesh, *Titash Ekti Nadir Naam* ("A River Named Titash"); around the same time, he directed himself in the autobiographical, indeed psychodramatic, *Jukti Takko Ar Gappo* ("Reason, Debate and a Tale"). Here, in what is scarcely the least of his films, the emaciated Ghatak—a grizzled, rubberfaced imp—gives an astonishing performance as a burnt-out Bengali intellectual, abandoned by his long-suffering wife and dangling at the end of his tether. Two years later, he died at age 51 of tuberculosis complicated by chronic alcoholism.

Although Indian critics have written persuasively of his other films (while underrating *Jukti Takko Ar Gappo*) for me the three features Ghatak made between 1958 and 1960—*Ajantrik, Bari Theke Paliye,* and *Meghe Dhaka Tara*—are the essential ones. All are characterized by their thematic resonance, visual invention, and intellectual verve; if *Bari Theke Paliye* is the least of the three, that's partly because the other two are so good and partly because its child hero pales before the protagonists of the two other films.

By all accounts, Ghatak was a complicated, volatile personality, and it seems fitting that his two greatest films should be centered on characters so psychologically rich and so clearly the battlefield of social forces. Bimal the paradoxical modernist and Nita the self-sacrificing nurturer are haunting in a way that suggests archetypes rather than roles—and it would be a mistake as well to see them as exotics. Few films have ever mapped an obsession more convincingly than *Ajantrik* or delved more deeply into the cruelty of family life than *Meghe Dhaka Tara.* They belong to world cinema, and it would be satisfying indeed if some enlightened distributor or determined curator were inspired to snare them before they vanish down the memory hole.

Hou Hsiao-hsien: The edge of the world

Originally published in *The Village Voice* (July 14, 1987).

IF RECENT WARS are any indication, Eastern Asia looms as large in America's consciousness as Western Europe—even if the products of its still vital movie industries do not. New French or German directors are taken as a matter of course; one almost has to apologize for introducing a major talent from a backwater like Taiwan. Hou Hsiao-hsien is frequently compared to Yasujiro Ozu. But in his own context he's virtually sui generis. "Before two years ago I had never seen a film by a 'big master,'" Hou told one interviewer. "During school it was all sword fights and westerns."

The use of landscape shots as punctuation in Hou's most recent film suggest that he's now seen some Ozu, but he also has affinities to Satyajit Ray and Ermanno Olmi (a dry but cozy lyricism), to Mikio Naruse (the odd mixture of turbulence and restraint), and even to the George Lucas of *American Graffiti.* His films are characterized by a fluid, low-key naturalism, a fascination with the details of ordinary life, and extraordinary ensemble acting by mainly non-professional casts—although the oblique quality of Hou's work may also have something to do with Taiwan's tough censorship laws. Distance is built into the spectacle; Hou often films his most dramatic scenes in long shot, and he's prone to framing the action with grills, doorways, and courtyards. (Taiwan appears to enjoy a tropical, semi-outdoor way of life.)

Although Hou uses the entire frame as a compositional field (it's a kind of nest of worn objects), his narratives are characteristically indirect. A story gradually coalesces out of anecdotes, character sketches, and apparent non sequiturs. "The events seem random and pointless," David Edelstein wrote of *A Summer at Grandpa's* when it was shown at the 1985 edition of "New Directors/New Films." And of *A Time To Live and a Time To Die,* which had its local premiere at a New York Film Festival, he observed, "The events in the film aren't prepared for with music or structural gimmicks; they just happen. The secret of [Hou's] movies is that the pattern becomes clear only after they've ended."

There's an underlying romanticism to some of Hou's incidents, but his basic attitude is wistful and rapt. It's as though the camera is transfixed. Hou employs long takes and static setups, muted colors, and a deliberate use of sound. If the gravity of his films seems an intentional corrective to the tinny hysteria of most commercial Hong Kong and Taiwanese cinema, their severity is mitigated by a taste for ordinary human activity (meals are frequent) and an appreciation for the lush and varied Taiwanese landscape. Like a painting by Seurat or Monet, Hou's films are less the imitation of life than its distillation.

Dust in the Wind opens in a mining village in the mountainous interior and concerns the dislocation that's one of Hou's major themes. (His films are mainly about young people and their families, actual and surrogate.) Following a pattern common to their village, two students, a boy and a girl, quit high school and move to Taipei. She unhappily finds a job as a seamstress; he works for a printer, then quits and becomes a delivery boy. In the evening they hang around a friend's studio or have drinking parties to send off other friends as they're drafted into the army. Small incidents eddy this indolent calm: The boy's motorbike is stolen, the girl scalds her arm. Like his friends, the hero is drafted and stationed on Quemoy (where the major activity seems to be interrogating terrified fishermen who have drifted over from the mainland). When his brother writes to tell him the girl married someone else, the film suddenly comes together as an affecting saga of impossible escape, of biding time, of the iron rule of history, and of unhappy love.

These are Hou's themes; they seem intrinsic to his situation. He was born in 1947 in Mei county on the Chinese mainland. One year later his family moved to Taiwan, where they were effectively marooned after the Revolution. The director tells this story in his best known film, the 1985 *A Time To Live and a Time To Die*. An act of re-creation, using his childhood house and neighborhood, the film is a relatively straightforward chronicle of lower-middle-class family life (somewhat marred by sentimental, if spare, piano music), in which the generations inexorably drift apart—the elders still yearning for Mei county, the children trying to find their footing in provincial Taiwan.

It's appropriate that the tormented, taciturn semi-delinquent Hou shows himself to be in *A Time To Live and a Time To Die* would emerge as part of the Taiwanese "new cinema" of the early '80s. (Among other things, Hou's movies were among the first to make extensive use of Taiwanese dialects rather than official Mandarin.) His first feature, *Green, Green Grass of Home* (1982), was a hugely successful vehicle for the local pop star Kenny Bee and made Hou's less commercial films viable. "I was lucky that when I started I made a lot of money," he's said. "That's why everybody wanted me to work for them. But about three years ago things changed. I made films that did not make money . . . I discovered what film really is." (How are his movies received in Taiwan? the interviewer wanted to know. "Worse as it goes along!" Hou laughed.) In a number of Hou's films, the commercial cinema is a phantom presence. Its posters and (in one superb scene) its soundtrack are dispersed throughout *Dust in the Wind,* lurking in the background as dialectical shards of the Other.

The Boys from Fengkuei (1984) tells a story similar to *Dust in the Wind*'s: a group of street kids leave their sleepy island, an entropic world of surf-side poolhalls and old American cars, for the southern Taiwanese port of Kaohsiung. Finding work in an electronics factory, they attempt to drink from the well of big-city sophistication—buying tickets from a swindler for a nonexistent porn film, hanging out with someone's glamorous sister, befriending the young mistress of the petty thief across the courtyard. At length one of the boys gets a letter that his paralyzed father has died, and he returns to Fengkuei to find that either he or it has subtly changed. The film is a triumph of the hauntingly ordinary. Kaohsiung, too, proves empty; the thief's girl has left for Taipei.

Hou's characters are often in transition—the train station is an image in virtually all of his films. But *Summer at Grandpa's* (1984) reverses his usual trajectory. Their mother in the hospital, two small children of the urban middle class are sent to stay with their grandfather, a rural doctor. The mood is set when the boy trades his remote control toy car for another kid's turtle. (As a result, the house is besieged by children bearing turtles in hopes of making the same deal.) Filled with scenes of playing and swimming, *Summer at Grandpa's* is the most bucolic of Hou's films—as well as the one in which, from just beyond the frame, sex and death cast the darkest shadows. Hou manages the difficult task of maintaining a child's point of view without ever seeming cute or unduly nostalgic. At one point, grandfather recites a poem suggesting that the children are not simply strangers from the city, but exiles in adulthood's foreign land.

This sense of uprootedness is part of Hou's particular modernity—indeed, one could argue that it's precisely his evocation of displacement that moves him from the provincial margins of the industrial world toward its emotional center. Colonized by Japan for the first half of the century, peopled by political exiles and their children since 1949, Taiwan has been described to me as "a temporary country"; Hou makes it seem at once familiar and alien, as much to his characters as to the viewer. All but becalmed, Hou's protagonists float toward an uncertain, never articulated future; beneath them courses an undercurrent of violent upheaval. The Chinese revolution is the absence that structures Hou's work—his placid, melancholy Taiwan is the eye of history's storm.

Harold Rosenberg's magic act

Originally published as "Harold Rosenberg's Radical Cheek" in *The Village Voice Literary Supplement* (May 1986).

The most exhilarating thought of the twentieth century: "We are making History!"
                                                                    —Harold Rosenberg

L IKE A VENERABLE statue in a busy square, Harold Rosenberg occupies a curious spot—at once memorialized and ignored. As art critic for *The New Yorker* from the late '60s until his death in 1978, Rosenberg was the most visible and widely read of the old *Partisan Review* crowd. More than that, he was perhaps the most gifted intellectual promoter of modern art in America.

The University of Chicago, where Rosenberg taught, has published his collected essays in nine uniform volumes. It's the ultimate validation, yet Rosenberg's essays on postmodernism are no more apt to rate footnotes in *October* than his pieces on Marx are likely to find citations in *Social Text*. Some of Rosenberg's finest work was published in the 1970s, but in *The New York Times* obit, John Russell found these *New Yorker* reviews more notable for their "Lear-like rages" than "any insights of permanent value." This peculiar mixture of respect and avoidance recaps the contradictory logic of Rosenberg's career.

Originally a poet, he had a knack for memorable phrases—"the tradition of the new," "the herd of independent minds," "the anxious object," and, the best known of all, "action painting." He was a product of the '30s, and the specter of politics haunted him until his death. A career-long equation of modern art and radical politics (together with his Francophilia) is one reason that, unlike others of his generation, Rosenberg was not altogether immune to the events of May

1968. The following year he wrote that art must become increasingly political—that, indeed, this was its only valid direction, the only way to avoid disintegration into mere "decoration and entertainment."

Just as "tradition of the new" echoed Trotsky's "theory of permanent revolution," there were times when Rosenberg took the double meaning of vanguard literally. Aesthetic avant-gardes, he wrote, gave art "the passion and momentum of radical politics"—and it was the memory of political radicalism (not to mention rhetoric) that underscored his aesthetic fervor.

Rosenberg saw Modernism's enterprise as essentially critical—"Joyce's writing is a criticism of literature, Pound's poetry a criticism of poetry, Picasso's painting a criticism of painting"—if not always revolutionary. At the very least, modern art repudiated "the exalted sentiments of the middle class"—including of course the petit bourgeois kitsch of the Stalin-era Popular Front. That modern art might come to be the very emblem of the middle class was not something Rosenberg was prepared to concede.

We are stuck with ourselves, and the world is stuck with us at the price of making itself perfect. Perhaps when everyone has defected from the common "reality," that is, when everyone has become an intellectual, the role of the intellectual will be ended, and with it that unhappy species itself.

—"Twilight of the Intellectuals" (1958)

FOR THE SAKE of brevity, let's define the "New York intellectuals" as the gang that will always be associated with the glory days of *Partisan Review* and Abstract Expressionism, the defenders of Leon Trotsky and Henry James, the cronies of Saul Bellow and Delmore Schwartz. Reinventing themselves as a native intelligentsia—street smart, contentious, and insecure—the New York intellectuals used art and literature as an escape from their Jewish marginality. They were likely the first ethnic arbiters of taste and political theory in American history. But were they foot soldiers or generals in the modernist army?

Suspended between Brooklyn and the Ukraine, the New York intellectuals were compelled to be internationalists; excluded from power, they could afford to be radicals. Because they refused to specialize, they were experts on everything. Their greatest contribution, however, was the re-Europeanization of American culture. They wrote knowledgeably about global politics, helped make the American university curriculum safe for Kafka and Dostoevsky, introduced such a-Modernist political novelists as Silone, Orwell, Malraux, and Koestler to American audiences (just as, in the '70s and '80s, their heirs championed the dissident writers of Eastern Europe).

Yet, even more than their onetime hero Trotsky, the New York intellectuals remained "rootless cosmopolitans." Trotsky at least found a mass movement, while the failure of socialism in America left his New York cousins talking mainly to themselves. (Had their parents remained in Eastern or Central Europe, it might have been a different story.) Still, in one form or another—if only as anticommunism—Marxism remained a source of fascination and definition for the rest of their lives. In Rosenberg's case, Marx provided the underpinnings for an eccentric but all-encompassing modernist aesthetic.

Unlike others of his generation, Rosenberg wrote little about his background. Born in Brooklyn in 1906, the son of Abraham and Fanny Edelman Rosenberg, this future "matinee idol of the intellectual underground" (to lift a phrase from Seymour Krim) attended City College and took a law degree from St. Lawrence University. By the early '30s, he had abandoned law to explicate Freud and Jung for *The Symposium* and publish militantly dreadful Eliotic poetry in *New Masses*: "Take your alphabet to the drawing-rooms / To the phthisic old ladies who hobble on Fifth Avenue / With black poodles bobbing on their bosoms, / Wheeze it to the harps of the mystical individualists. / I have been seduced by the bricklayer of daylight . . ."

By his own account, Rosenberg encountered Marxism as an immigrant from the old country of Modernism: "Like everyone else, I became involved in Marxism, but from the start my Marxism was out of date." Perhaps, but it would have been difficult for an intellectual of Rosenberg's generation and background to remain a greenhorn for long. His younger brother is said to have been an active Communist, and he may not have been Harold's only close relative with a Party card.

Covering the 1935 League of American Writers Congress for *Poetry* magazine, Rosenberg was sanguine about the future of proletarian literature. He hewed to the CP line until 1937. When *Partisan Review,* originally the organ of the John Reed Club, broke with the Party during the Moscow Trials, so did he— perhaps with some relief. In a famous aside written two decades later, Clement Greenberg observed, "Some day it will have to be told how 'anti-Stalinism,' which started out more or less as 'Trotskyism,' turned into art for art's sake, and thereby cleared the way, heroically, for what followed." Actually, it was the other way around. Art for art's sake, chafing under the crude exigencies of proletariat realism and the Popular Front, identified the CP with the bourgeoisie and brilliantly reconstituted itself as Trotskyism.

Although Rosenberg started writing for *PR* in the late '30s, co-editor Philip Rahv's attitude toward him seems to have been dismissive and fearful. According to William Barrett, Rahv thought that, however dazzling his mind, Rosenberg was basically a luftmensch, an intellectual boho—that *Trance Above the Streets,* the title of his lone poetry collection, perfectly described the author's airy state.

In truth, though, Rosenberg's life was an odd mixture of public service and bohemianism. He was employed by the WPA Writers Project and, between 1938 and 1942, was art editor for the WPA's American Guide Series. He hung out with the cream of the French expatriate community (Breton and Duchamp), did French translations, co-edited a little magazine with Robert Motherwell (it lasted one issue), and wrote poetry. At the same time he served in the Office of War Information and then briefly as a consultant for the Treasury Department. (In his memoirs, Lionel Abel recalls a lunch with Rosenberg and Rahv in which the subject of support for the war—a hot Trotskyist issue—arose. "It isn't a question of whether we support the war," Rosenberg pointed out. "The war is supporting us.")

From 1946 until 1966, when he went to *The New Yorker,* Rosenberg was a program consultant for the Advertising Council of America—reviewing proposals, writing background papers, developing campaigns for voter registration or polio vaccination and then evaluating them. According to colleagues there, Rosenberg "touched every campaign the Council was involved in." When Motherwell or Saul Bellow dropped by to visit, however, he was vague about his job. Still, he must have told someone that he invented Smokey the Bear. "The sheer deliciousness of it," Irving Howe notes in his memoirs, "this cuddly artifact of commercial culture as the creature of our most unyielding modernist!" Twenty years of toiling in the vineyards of advertising may account for Rosenberg's brilliant phrase-making and abiding hostility to popular culture. "With so much bought interest in bad art," he sniffed, "there would hardly seem any need for volunteers."

In the memoirs of his peers, Rosenberg is an uncanny presence—a solitary peak looming on the intellectual landscape, at once familiar and foreboding. It's as if, on some level, he was perceived as the smartest of them all. With his massive head and pugilist's jaw, he was at least as imposing in person as in print. Howe's first impression was of a huge "pirate, complete with a game leg [and] rasping voice." For Krim, Rosenberg "shone like the Lion of Judah," his bad leg "propped up like a bayonet." Barrett recalls that when Rosenberg and Clement Greenberg publicly disagreed on some aesthetic issue, "Greenberg (who had been prone in other cases to use his fists) came away saying, 'I'm not going to tangle with that guy, he's too big.'" Indeed, Rosenberg's *Times* obit describes the elderly critic scaring off a prospective mugger by brandishing his cane.

Victor Wulpy, the aging protagonist of Saul Bellow's "What Kind of Day Did You Have?," is transparently modeled on Rosenberg: "A New York-style king . . . good-natured, approachable, but making it plain that he was a sovereign; he took no crap from anybody." Bellow was Rosenberg's colleague at the University of Chicago and his novella, first published in *Vanity Fair* in 1984, is both fond and malicious: "About how many Americans had leaders of thought like Sarte, Merleau-Ponty, and Hannah Arendt said, 'Chapeau bas! This is a man of genius!'" Of course, one could no more imagine Arendt turning that phrase than Rosenberg writing *The Origins of Totalitarianism*. Still, Merleau-Ponty published Rosenberg on Marxism and it's an open secret that Rosenberg's essay on Hamlet influenced Sartre's *Dirty Hands*. American sovereign that he was, however, Rosenberg remained aloof from certain contemporaries. Never did he acknowledge those European thinkers—Sartre, Adorno, Benjamin, Barthes—he'd obviously read and even been influenced by.

For one obsessed with the situation of the individual protagonist in a historical drama, Rosenberg didn't seem overly concerned with his own place in history. He left no system; each essay offered its own occasion. (The University of Chicago has engraved this cavalier attitude in stone by reissuing Rosenberg's books as they were originally published, rather than reorganizing them in terms of his major interests—Abstract Expressionism, Politics, Postmodernism, and so on.) King Rosenberg set his own agendas and picked his own quarrels.

Spontaneity was his blessing and his curse. "Never have I known anyone who could talk with such unflagging manic brilliance, pouring out a Niagara of epigrams," Howe recalls. "I used to think, when visiting his studio: suppose I were suddenly to drop dead, would he stop talking?" (Rosenberg could be as much wise guy as wise man. By one account, he offhandedly termed Rahv's Henry James anthology "the Henry James delicatessen"—a shtickle herring in the golden bowl!—and when the crack got back to Rahv he 86'd Rosenberg from *Partisan Review*.)

As a practitioner of the intellectual shpritz and the lethal one-liner, Rosenberg is related to Philip Roth, if not Henny Youngman. He was a master of the elegant putdown. Ellsworth Kelly was "the Grandma Moses of abstract art," the surfaces of Jules Olitski's paintings were "disagreeably insensitive, like spotted linoleum or dried milk stains," and the French proto-conceptualist Yves Klein exhibited "a gross romanticism of the order of taste that keeps an ocelot for a pet." It was as a mystifier and a sophist that Rosenberg was attacked once he became established. One should never lose sight of him, or any of the New York intellectuals, as performers. Every cafeteria (or living room) confrontation was a test of mental agility; every essay was a provocation or a tour de force, a virtuoso monologue bristling with polemic and sarcasm.

This was a highly original stance for intellectuals to take. Perhaps only in America could a thinker feel so free to showboat. Indeed, the short-lived literary magazine Rosenberg founded in 1932 was called *The New Act*.

American radicalism in art conducts its battles over issues that are formal and metaphysical rather than social.

—"What's New" (1973)

It's by now a commonplace to everyone except the diehards of *The New Criterion* that the rise of Abstract Expressionism and the ascendancy of New York as the world art capital were not simply functions of a wayward zeitgeist that might just have easily roosted in Portugal or Honduras. Rather, the triumph of American painting was something intimately bound up with America's new status after World War II.

Soon after Hiroshima, Clement Greenberg was challenging the superiority of Parisian art with reviews in *The Nation* that privileged American vitality over French polish, posing Jackson Pollock against Jean Dubuffet. America suddenly became the trustee of avant-gardism, as it was the guardian of the Free World. "Radical artists purged themselves of radical politics because serious politics would drain too much from the courage needed for their own artistic tasks," Max Kozloff wrote 10 years ago in a once-controversial piece on Abstract Expressionism and the Cold War. "They heroicized these tasks in a way suggestive of American Cold War rhetoric."

For Rosenberg, the breakthrough of the Abstract Expressionists, virtually all of whom he'd known from his stint at the WPA if not his evenings at the Cedar Tavern, must have seemed close to miraculous. "In the thirties," he later noted, "modernism was to all appearances part of the past, suppressed by force in Moscow, Berlin, Rome, silenced in Paris by the conflict between the political right and left. In that decade, a spectator in New York was looking *back* to modern art; new as they seemed, the exhibits at the Museum of Modern Art belonged to art movements that were already extinct." Suddenly, Modernism was reborn on 10th Street—the torch passed to a group of New York City painters.

This may explain Rosenberg's postwar optimism about America. Proletarian internationalism had fallen by the wayside, but History was catching up with some sort of vanguard. Just as Picasso's heirs were now living next door, the fierce anti-Stalinism of New York's literary Trotskyites had become government policy. In some respects, Rosenberg was a premature neo-con: Not only did he publish his definitive anticommunist diatribe in 1947 (the Communist is "an intellectual who need not think") but, for him, America became an absolute value. In his memoirs, Abel recalls Rosenberg's assertion that the only people who understood foreign policy were the Americans—and this during the Korean War. Abel remembers that Rosenberg had a great admiration for Dean Acheson; he even compared the secretary of state's command of rhetoric to André Breton's.

But Rosenberg's political transformation was hardly simpleminded. If anything, it was a masterpiece of applied sophistry. In a remarkable series of articles published between the elections of Harry Truman and Dwight Eisenhower, he transposed the revolution into the cultural sphere, attempting to transcend the polemics of the '30s. First, he posited the war between the mass media and the individual as the key cultural struggle of the age. "The Herd of Independent Minds" (*Commentary,* September 1948) argued that mass culture was potentially true for the mass but always false to the individual. Rosenberg didn't exclude intellectuals from this formulation; they too exhibited a grandiose tendency to generalize their theories into "formulas of common experience" as totalizing as the clichés of Hollywood or Madison Avenue.

Ten years earlier, Clement Greenberg had linked (true) socialism and Modernism in the struggle against Hitler, Stalin, and kitsch. Rosenberg was less internationalist. In "The Pathos of the Proletariat"—which appeared in the *Kenyon Review* in 1949—he cited the defeat of the working class in Germany, Italy, and (in a different way) the Soviet Union, suggesting that the proletariat had been stymied. The stage was set for a new historic actor. Rosenberg proposed the American.

This entire essay, one of the lengthiest of Rosenberg's career as well as his closest reading of Marx, can be seen as an attempt to wrest the flag of the revolutionary vanguard from the Soviet Union. "The proletariat is a barbarian in exactly the same sense that the American is, traditionally, Europe's barbarian," he maintained. But if the proletariat was the objectification of the modern as misery, the American was a far more successful "natural representative of the modern."

"From Marx to Lenin to Trotsky, American practices have been cited to illustrate qualities needed under socialism," Rosenberg argued. Indeed, almost without knowing it, the American had *already* "realized Marx's vision of communism as a society in which "the present dominates the past." The American and not the Leninist was thus the model for the proletariat: "Speaking half figuratively, to become a human being the proletarian must 'Americanize' himself, that is, overcome the void of his past by making a new self through his actions." But, obviously, not just any American would do. Rosenberg's archetypal American was a sort of perpetual pioneer, a proponent of the new, a being engaged in continuous reinvention.

After passing briefly over into patriotic anticommunism, Rosenberg recoiled. He quarreled with *Partisan Review,* where the "Orwell of *1984,* with its frigid rationality and paranoically lifeless prose, rose as the ideal author, while Sidney Hook's precautionary logic became the measure of political wisdom." *PR* emerged from the war vindicated beyond its wildest dreams; Rosenberg remained true to the ideals of the luftmensch opposition. (Eventually he aligned himself with the independent socialists at *Dissent,* even though, according to editor Irving Howe, Rosenberg felt himself to be to their left.)

Working on his own, without specific turf or even an intellectual gang, Rosenberg continued to excoriate the herd of independent minds. The younger intellectuals seemed hopeless careerists. Leslie Fiedler's vaunted "end to innocence" was just "an abusive goodbye to Karl Marx by shivering jobholders"; Norman Podhoretz was "an ideologist without an ideology," a propagandist for the "happiness" to be found in embracing middle-class notions of work, religion, the nation, and the family. ("The slogans of 'free love' and 'the liberation of women' were not invented merely to supply people of an earlier generation with 'radical values,'" Rosenberg tartly pointed out.)

The optimistic Americanism of "The Pathos of the Proletariat" paved the way for Rosenberg's most remarkable stunt. Co-opted by the Cold War and official anti-Stalinism, the onetime radicals of *Partisan Review* were half-heartedly searching for a way to maintain some sort of left opposition or vanguard militance. The journal's 1952 symposium "Our Country and Our Culture" heralded the end of bohemia and the intellectuals' alienation from the larger culture, but Rosenberg managed to find an avant-garde, right under their collective nose.

"The Herd of Independent Minds" had already proposed the artist as the only unalienated figure in American society. (Unalienated because "he works directly with the materials of his own experience and transforms them.") Hadn't Marx defined unalienated labor as work done for the sake of the worker, rather than for the sake of the product, and proposed the artist as the model for future generations? Rosenberg's most influential essay took both of these ideas literally. "The American Action Painters," published in *Art News* in late 1952, set out to transform the Abstract Expressionists from mere painters into paradigms of revolutionary action.

To embody the world-historic role Rosenberg assigned them, the Action Painter had to approach painting as an autonomous practice—an echt American "condition of open possibility," transcending the old realms of art and politics. According to Rosenberg's scenario, the Action Painter confronted the canvas with the seriousness and anxiety and commitment of a general studying a battle map or an explorer setting out upon an unknown ocean. Leaping into the Modernist void, the artist turned painting into an authentic Act: "At a certain moment the canvas began to appear to one American painter after another as an arena in which to act—rather than as a space in which to reproduce, re-design, analyze or 'express' an object, actual or imagined. What was to go on the canvas was not a picture but an event. . . . The big moment came when it was decided to paint . . . just TO PAINT. The gesture on the canvas was a gesture of liberation, from Value—political, esthetic, moral."

Although this angst-ridden representation of Abstract Expressionism has obvious parallels to the worldview of French existentialism, Rosenberg preferred to cast the Action Painter in the American pioneer tradition. (It seems hardly coincidental that the three American artists who figured most prominently in Rosenberg's pantheon—Willem de Kooning, Arshile Gorky, and Saul Steinberg—were all immigrants.) Rosenberg not only emphasized Action Painting's disdain for commercialism, careerism, and the middle class but always insisted that self-liberation was the moral imperative of contemporary art. "In the creations of the pioneer Abstract Expressionists, a principle was manifest— the avant-garde principle of transforming the self and society."

This was heady stuff—as late as 1978, Rosenberg was musing on the "danger" of Action Painting. And yet the "gesture of liberation" he cited did not free the Abstract Expressionists from aesthetic value. *Au contraire.* What made the American Action Painter so gutsy was precisely his insistence on himself as Modern Artist, the American heir to Picasso and Mondrian.

In the early '50s—when abstract art was still subject to periodic attacks from right-wing congressmen like Michigan's George A. Dondero—Rosenberg posited Abstract Expressionism as a third force, establishing its credibility by drawing the hostility of both the American and Soviet establishments. (This corresponded to his political line at the time as well—Howe recalls Rosenberg insisting that to maintain one's integrity in the Cold War one had to attack both sides.) But it was naive for Rosenberg to think that Action Painting would forever remain outside the official sphere.

Another 1952 article, written by Alfred Barr for *The New York Times Magazine,* proved even more influential than "The American Action Painters"—at least in terms of providing the U.S. with an authentic, exportable high culture. "Is Modern Art Communistic?" Barr asked. Answering his formulation with a resounding "no," the director of the Museum of Modern Art attacked the retrograde "social realism" of Nazi Germany and the Soviet Union alike. By linking totalitarianism to academic realism, Barr recuperated abstract artists as heroic individuals while relieving Modernism of its "revolutionary" pretensions.

This Rosenberg refused to do. In an off-handed swipe, he noted that although *The New York Times* hesitated "to see things hanging in respectable American homes and museums given the embarrassing label of revolutionary," it was obvious that "in the twentieth century the world of art and world of revolutionary politics, both of the Right and of the Left, have been thoroughly mixed together. The same Words are at their center."

Having invented the notion of Action Painting and inescapably if undeniably profited by collecting it, Rosenberg remained forever faithful. He praised artists like Klee or Miró as Action Painting forebears and pointed out that Action Painting anticipated Conceptual Art in being "communicated through documents." At times he seemed to fancy himself an Action Critic: "The unity of this book is self-generated, rather than imposed through pursuing a preconceived theme," he wrote in the introduction to *Act and the Actor.*

For Rosenberg, Action Painting was "the last 'moment' in art on the plane of dramatic and intellectual seriousness." Of the 1946–52 period, he would write that "no period since has come close to equalling it." The '60s lacked "avant-garde élan," painters were now only concerned with securing a place in art history and attacking their predecessors. "If one had to choose the single outstanding feature of the art of the nineteen-sixties," Rosenberg wrote in the mid-'70s, "it would be the attitude, varying from indifference to soured ideological hostility, taken toward the metaphysical feelings and exalted psychological states of the Abstract Expressionist generation."

Unlike the formalist Greenberg, who linked Abstract Expressionism to cubism, Rosenberg looked for parallels with Dada and Surrealism—movements "to liquidate art as a classification of objects and to redefine it in terms of the intellectual acts of artists." Although Rosenberg had written far less than Greenberg on contemporary art, "The American Action Painters" offered so catchy a brand name (and dramatic a scenario) that he soon became Greenberg's rival. But as the '60s began, Greenberg saw a new tendency. His influential "Modernist Painting" was a sophisticated, Hegelian reformation of art for art's sake, providing an aesthetic rationale and historical justification for the cool, reductive painting of color fields and stripes.

Greenberg's essay occasioned Rosenberg's left oppositional call for painting to recognize the totalitarian threat and "purge itself of all systems that place so-called interests of art above the interests of the artist's mind." One ex-Trot to another, Rosenberg taunted Greenberg in quasi-Marxist terms: "Action painting does not escape the law of fetishism of commodities, by which Pollocks, for example, have carried on all kinds of magical shenanigans—such as becoming the parents of Nolands and Olitskis long after the artist himself was hurled into his violent grave."

Thinking of Greenberg and his disciples, Rosenberg observed that art criticism had reversed its traditional function: "Instead of deriving principles from what it sees, it teaches the eye to 'see' principles." He described contemporary painting and sculpture as "a species of centaur—half art materials, half words." Criticism creates the context in which a particular work is to be seen, Rosenberg argued, and this is what locates a Barnett Newman, for example, in the tradition of Abstract Expressionism rather than that of the Bauhaus. (Incredibly, linking Newman to the Abstract Expressionists was something Rosenberg had done himself.) Thus language interposes "a mist of interpretation" between the work and the eye and it is from this "quasi-mirage" that the work's prestige arises.

One can only imagine Rosenberg's sense of irritation and disgust when several years after his essay was published in *The New Yorker,* Tom Wolfe picked up this observation and made it the centerpiece of *The Painted Word,* a satire of the artworld with Rosenberg one of the main targets.

Regardless of semantics, modern art is art of the past, a period style, with its masterpieces, heroes, and legends.

—"Art on the Edge"

UNDOUBTEDLY THE GREATEST trauma of Rosenberg's professional life was the displacement of Abstract Expressionism by Pop Art. This was something more than just the arrival of a new generation of artists—it was an intimation of Paradise Lost. Modernism, which had miraculously transplanted itself from Paris to New York, was again under assault—not by fascists or Stalinoid kitschmongers, but by the American landscape itself. For Rosenberg, the triumph of Pop—which functioned simultaneously on the planes of mass communication and art history—and the eclipse of Action Painting raised the possibility that art itself might be superseded by "newer forms of expression, emotional stimulation and communication."

Rosenberg's identification with Abstract Expressionism and his estrangement from the movements which consolidated New York's aesthetic hegemony inspired an analysis far more widespread today than it was when he first formulated it in the mid-'60s. His bitterness led him to declare that the cultural revolution of the last century had finally played itself out, that Modernism was over and the avant-garde no longer existed. This insight was supported by the unexpected growth of art consumption, the assimilation of high culture by the middle class: "The utilization of masterpieces as cultural spectaculars—as in the instance of the Mona Lisa in New York—deprives them of their inner substance and incorporates them into the mass media." Although seldom credited for this, Rosenberg was one of the first American art critics to articulate a sense of the postmodern.

In such essays as "Art and Its Double" (published in France in 1968), "Set Out for Clayton!" (1971), his mid-'70s pieces on Duchamp and Warhol, and "The Mona Lisa Without a Mustache: Art in the Media Age" (1976), Rosenberg meditated on the demise of Modernism. "The essential connotation of 'post-modern,'" he wrote the year of his death, is "a period without vanguards." The corollary of this, for Rosenberg, was the end of art as we knew it.

For, by his lights, the only force that kept art from merging with the media was "the pressure of new creations *against* art" and the one thing that had maintained this "pressure of de-definition" was the presence of aesthetic avant-gardes. Of course, none of the post-Action Painting movements were true vanguards. By allying themselves with fashion (a world where "freshness and shock do not represent the emergence of the new but are mere artifices for refurbishing the familiar"), these avant-garde movements found themselves in a trap of planned obsolescence.

Rosenberg viewed the postmodern art world as a new sort of wasteland, littered with the remains of dead and recycled movements: "The revivalist nature of current art is confessed in names that bear the prefix 'new' or 'neo' or 'abstract' appended to earlier movements." He eventually coined the term "déjàvunik" to describe such modernist revivals. The postmodern vanguard had to do a complicated shuffle—justifying itself with the art historical authority of its precursors, then dancing away to establish its own originality.

The only new developments, Rosenberg thought, were the shift in historical context—"The background of neo-Dada is the new affluence, not war and revolution"—and art's changed relationship to its audience. What distinguished neo-Dada from historical Dada was solicitude for the spectator. "Instead of goading him into indignation at the desecration of art, the new Dada converts him into an aesthete." The oxymoronic tradition of the new had truly become a tradition. "Today," Rosenberg wrote two decades after the *PR* symposium, "both the alienation of the artist and the antagonism of public opinion to art have been successfully liquidated."

Under the circumstances, Rosenberg executed a surprising judo move and decided to go with the flow. Without exactly extolling them, he acknowledged the significance of Marshall McLuhan and Andy Warhol as the major ideologues of postmodernism. It was McLuhan, he wrote in an influential *New Yorker* piece, who raised to the level of philosophy "the refusal to see any difference except as a means of presentation between works of art and the products of the media." And Warhol, "by demonstrating that art today is a commodity of the art market," succeeded in effacing "the century-old tension between the serious artist and the majority culture."

Rosenberg's detachment produced a new interest in Marcel Duchamp (anathema to orthodox Greenbergians). Duchamp, he realized, was the "great critic of the changed status of art" brought about by the substitution of the marketplace for the patron. Rosenberg's 1976 essay on Duchamp terms him a "permanent borderline case" whose great theme is "the power of the machine to duplicate human activity." In the ultimate act of acceptance, Rosenberg even reads Duchamp's "Great Glass" as a precursor of Action Painting.

By 1976, Rosenberg would observe that "art in its old form"—what could be *objectively* classified as art—was over, "swallowed up in a sea of image-making without boundaries." In this primordial postmodern chaos, "all images are mingled together in one indefinable agglomeration, and . . . there are only one-person cultures, which each of us pieces together as best we can." Citing the precedent of Freud, tacitly aligning himself with semiotics, Rosenberg suggested that "in the age of reproductions, interpretation takes precedence over direct response."

Rosenberg's late essays even allow for a measure of cultural relativity ("the fact that the taste of any one social group no longer has power over art, and that all tastes are compelled to co-exist with rival tastes and with tastelessness, need not be a cause for regret by American painting and sculpture"). The acceptance of Duchamp signaled Rosenberg's mellowness: "History has decreed that what was once anthropology shall now be art. . . . By a process seemingly irreversible, onetime cultural outsiders and undersiders are being lifted into visibility. *This movement may well turn out to be the most radical art accomplishment of the twentieth century.*" The collapse of class culture signaled by "the immersion of all strata of society in the same mass media" reinforced Rosenberg's notion that the cultural revolution had preceded the political-economic one. His sense of postmodern politics, however, was considerably less indulgent. For without the heroic American Action Painter, where was American heroism?

"Criticism-Action," published in *Dissent* 30 years ago, anticipates both the New Left critique of late capitalism and the Reaganite recuperation of the American dream. Describing the spread of proletarianization ("the processes of depersonalization and passivity through one's vocation"), Rosenberg argued that the expanding social organization of production and the ensuing dependence and isolation of the individual have made "the psychic condition of the nineteenth-century factory worker" the universal condition of 20th century society.

In advance of Marcuse's *One-Dimensional Man,* Rosenberg asserted: "Demoralized by their strangeness to themselves and by their lack of control over their relations with others, members of every class surrender themselves to artificially constructed mass egos that promise to restore their links with the past and the future." Only a new historical protagonist could resolve the crisis. But where briefly Rosenberg saw the American (and then the Action Painter), now he saw no one. "Instead of the self-creating revolt of nothings at the base of society, history appears to hold out a horror Utopia of universal de-individualization headed by leaders who *are* their masks."

Politics haunts the art of our time as Nature haunted the paintings of the nineteenth-century and myths and sacred episodes those of earlier epochs.

—"Art of Bad Conscience" (1969)

ROSENBERG CAME TO politics as an aesthete but remained closer to his particular form of Marxism than did most New York intellectuals of his generation. The arguments of the '30s underscored his art criticism; Rosenberg's writing percolates with brilliant, superficial analogies. He compared Ad Reinhardt's absolutism to Lenin's, Mondrian's anticipation of "the end of the tragedy of history" to Marx's classless utopia, a de Kooning canvas to the freewheeling rhetoric of Union Square.

These juxtapositions could cut both ways: In his memoirs, Lionel Abel recalls a 10-member communist splinter group so militant that when he first heard them condemn the "compromises" of a rival sect, he thought they were excoriating Republicans rather than Trotskyites. Rosenberg was enchanted by such quixotic, tough-minded purity: "They are our political cubists," he told Abel. In the '50s, Rosenberg maintained that what he first saw in Lenin was "a new kind of hero, a sort of political M. Teste." Perhaps the equation of the century's supreme revolutionary tactician and Valéry's archetypal solitary genius seems outrageous—but then, as Rosenberg also wrote, the phrase "I Like Ike" was the "esthetic self-assertion of the common man." American politics, he mused, is "determined by esthetic preferences—and such an esthetic!"

Never anti-Marx, Rosenberg called Marx's writings a "grand scaffold on which current political, social and cultural phenomena appear to interact in a significant way." But Rosenberg's Marxism was hardly orthodox. For him, the triumph of the proletariat ("a non-existent collective actor") was an illusion. Marx's mistake, he boldly wrote, lay in "assuming that the alienation of individuals and the ancient drama of self-recognition would be resolved through revolutionizing the social conditions of work." The unhappy result could be found in Soviet-style societies where individuals were nothing more than their social roles, the articulation of their inner doubts and turmoils proscribed.

Unlike Marx, Rosenberg saw history as fundamentally disorderly. Weren't German and Italian proletarians seduced by fascist madness and "the politics of illusion"? For him, the great Marxist text was *The 18th Brumaire of Louis Bonaparte*. (In "What Kind of Day Did You Have?" it's the subject of Victor Wulpy's lecture.) Because *The 18th Brumaire* analyzes a pseudoevent, Rosenberg wrote, it is central to "our epoch of false appearances and aimless adventures." This sterile repetition of archaic roles demonstrated the power of the past exerted upon the collective psyche. Here Marx can be seen to brush by Freud: "In history, as in dream, past actions come to life again in current happenings, and these residues keep the living present at a distance." Typically, Rosenberg compares the Bonapartist putsch to "nonplot theater," "art by chance," and programless avant-gardism—and in this, he's following his reading of Marx. What fascinated Rosenberg about *The 18th Brumaire* was Marx's application of aesthetic categories to political situations.

Underlying all of Rosenberg's criticism is a magical equation of art and politics, both sites where fact and illusion meet and entangle. His late writing in particular reveals a wistful desire for art to enter the political realm. By training as well as temperament, artists had the capacity to engage history. Art, Rosenberg insisted, could be action: "The aesthetic avant-garde is potentially the cultural nervous system of the political avant-garde." But alongside this hope was the pessimistic realization that aestheticized politics had long since triumphed over politicized art: "The older generation of political commanders—Churchill, Eisenhower, Hitler—used to paint landscapes. Artists could pat them on the head and say 'Not bad for a twelve-year-old. Keep at it.' Today, presidents, dictators, and government agencies have given up painting for theater—guerrilla theater, that is, plots enacted in real life." How Rosenberg would have enjoyed Komar and Melamid, if not Ronald Reagan.

In a 1974 letter to Alan Wald, an English professor at the University of Michigan, Rosenberg identified himself as "primarily a Luxemburgian," coyly adding, "My relationship to Trotskyism is not easy to formulate." Indeed, Rosenberg seems to have interpreted Luxemburg's dispute with Lenin as a tacit argument against party politics and Bolshevism, and her notion that the proletariat creates its own ethic in the course of the struggle as support for his belief that "action brings forth the unforeseen." (If Greenberg appropriated the Hegelian notion that [art] history has a goal, Rosenberg read Hegel as an argument that truth becomes evident only through historical events.) As Donald Kuspit once noted, Rosenberg's perception of art and, by extension, art criticism as social action led him to believe that these activities were not simply engaged in making art history, but in making real History as well.

This passionate conviction was Rosenberg's greatest conjuring trick, better even than his style. For him, painting could be a radical activity. By valuing the act of creation over the object created, Marx became the philosophical forebear of Klee and de Kooning (just de Kooning could be a model for the revolutionaries of the future). Like Marx, the Action Painters point the way to a "dynamic world" in which the tyranny of things has been overthrown by the activities of men. What remains perverse and exciting about Rosenberg's criticism is that he made painting seem that it was really about something. Which is to say, he wrote on art as if it actually mattered.

After the Gold Rush: Chaplin at one hundred

Originally published in *The Village Voice* (April 18, 1989).

HE SLEEPS IN the gutter and uses a rope to hold up his pants. He is frequently homeless and at best marginally employed. When he does work, his disorderly conduct often wrecks his employer's business, injuring innocent bystanders and bringing the police down. His world is filled with cops, to whom his instinctive response is instant flight—a madly determined, arm-flailing dash.

He is sneaky and sometimes violent. He desecrates public property. A petty thief when need be, he has no respect for authority. He is, of course, Charlie Chaplin's "Little Tramp," and if we stepped over him today on the streets of New York, we might scarcely recognize the prototype for the world's greatest film star, once the most popular man on earth, the icon of the 20th century, Jesus Christ's rival as the best-known person who ever lived.

Charlie Chaplin, born in London a century ago and the subject of a modest fete at the Museum of Modern Art, enjoyed sustained popularity on a scale that is difficult to imagine and may never be duplicated. He was not exactly a plaster saint, although if we judge him by the quality of his enemies (Hedda Hopper, Howard Hughes, HUAC, Hitler), his luster could hardly be greater. Scarcely a corporation man, Chaplin used his power to defy Hollywood mores and go his own way—ignoring the conventions of talking pictures, making highly personal political tracts, reinventing his image in a way no studio would have permitted.

Chaplin wasn't simply the first mass cultural icon, the embodiment of mass man, he *was* mass culture—vulgar, repetitive, shameless, addictive, utopian. In his disdain for language, he personified the universality of silent movies. As Charles Silver points out in his new monograph, Chaplin's two-reelers were immediately apprehendable: "No particular level of sophistication or even literacy was necessary . . . to see that he was special: you only had to *see*." As ancient as these artifacts are, children don't have to be educated to find them funny. His love of play and passion for disorder mirrors their own, although Chaplin's uncanny appeal is perhaps innate. (Is it that toddler walk and those spaniel eyes that, like Mickey Mouse's outsized, infantlike head, push the love button in our brains?)

Although Chaplin has been encrusted with sentimentality (much of it his own doing) and relegated to the realm of the timeless, he is and was a historical being. In the late '60s, when I came of age as a self-conscious moviegoer, Chaplin was being displaced by a revisionist reappreciation of Buster Keaton. Back then, Keaton's formalism and reflexiveness, his stylized cool and absence of sentiment seemed far more interesting than Chaplin's puppy dog, in-your-face humanism and crude theatricality. The icon obscured the artist: Chaplin's well-worn divinity concealed the radical nature of his enterprise, the degree to which his pre-1919 two-reelers thrive on urban chaos and visceral class awareness, the Wobbly esprit de corps that infuses his hatred of work, which he continually subverts and transforms into sport.

The subject and object of mechanical reproduction, Chaplin was the original parody automaton. In a recent issue of *Radical History,* Charles Musser contextualizes him in terms of Henry Ford's newfangled assembly line and the industrial efficiency technique known as "Taylorism." Indeed, reeking of class hostility, the baldly titled *Work* (released in 1915, four months after *The Birth of a Nation*) features Charlie as an assistant paperhanger employed by a bourgeois family called the Fords. *Modern Times* (1936), Chaplin's most elaborate production, is a virtual anthology of such slapstick two-reelers, every skit revolving around the struggle for survival at its most primal level. (Few movies have ever been more obsessed with the act of acquiring food.) "I came away stunned at the thought that such a film had been made and was being distributed," the critic for *New Masses* wrote. "*Modern Times* is not so much a fine motion picture as a historical event."

A historical event but not, relatively speaking, a hit. Today, *Modern Times* (which, among other things, allegorizes the process of studio filmmaking) seems Chaplin's definitive statement. Contrary to the five-year run of IBM commercials that have been spun off it, *Modern Times* criticizes not just industrial capitalism but work itself—as well as authority, the family, and the very nature of adult behavior.

HE KNEW HIS audience. One thing he never sentimentalized was the rich. "No comedian before or after him has spent more energy depicting people in their working lives," writes Robert Sklar in *Movie Made America* of the star whose first film—a Keystone two-reeler released in February 1914—was aptly called *Making a Living*.

Chaplin exploded out of the Keystone ensemble at a time when the movies had again become rowdy, shaking off the five or six years of defensive gentility that followed the antinickelodeon crusades of 1908. Fittingly, the revolt against the new decorum was led by Mack Sennett, who had apprenticed with order's architect, D. W. Griffith. Although Chaplin perfected his supreme creation several months after leaving Keystone, it was there that he had his first and most extensive contact with the American people, that he mastered his timing and internalized Sennett's grotesque assault on the social order.

Within a year of leaving Sennett, Chaplin was considered the essence of laughter—although not everyone was amused. After *Work* was released, Sime Silverman, the founding editor of *Variety,* complained that "the Censor Board is passing matter in the Chaplin films that could not possibly get by in other pictures. Never anything dirtier was placed on the screen than Chaplin's 'Tramp.' " The association of Chaplin with impurity—sexual, racial, political—was something that would dog him for the next 40 years.

That spring, however, Chaplinitis swept the English-speaking world. By now Chaplin was his own trademark; the tramp was totally industrialized. There were Chaplin songs, Chaplin dances, Chaplin sketches in theatrical revues, Chaplin cocktails, Chaplin dolls, Chaplin shirts, Chaplin ties, Chaplin postcards, Chaplin animated cartoons, and a Chaplin comic strip. It was as if a new religion had been born and everyone wanted a piece of the cross. Placed beneath a marquee, the cardboard image of the little man with the skimpy mustache—his silhouette rendered indelible by bowler hat, baggy pants, and outsized shoes—was sufficient in itself to fill a theater. Demand far outstripped supply. The 26-year-old actor could not produce movies quickly enough to satisfy his fans.

Imitators were legion. "Among the happy youths of the slums, or the dandies of clubdom or college, an imitation of a Chaplin flirt of the coat, or the funny waddle of the comedian, is considered the last word in humour. To be Chaplinesque is to be funny; to waddle a few steps and then look naïvely at your audience," *Motion Picture Magazine* reported in a 1915 article simply called "Chaplinitis." Soon Chaplin look-alike contests were being held in amusement parks all over the U.S. Leslie T. (later Bob) Hope won one such in Cleveland. So many comedians were impersonating Chaplin on the screen—among them, Stan Jefferson (subsequently Laurel)—that Charlie had to file suit. It was said that for a time costume balls were ruined, because 90 per cent of the men appeared dressed as the Little Tramp. (In *The Idle Class,* Chaplin attended one such ball dressed as himself.)

America definitely had Chaplin on the brain. In Cincinnati, a holdup man used a Charlie Chaplin disguise. In a mysterious occurrence on November 12, 1916, the actor was simultaneously paged in 800 hotels. Chaplinitis spread to Europe and raged throughout the Great War. According to the British film historian Kevin Brownlow, Chaplin cut-outs were kidnapped from the lobbies of British movie theaters and born off to the trenches: "These life-sized models were popular with the troops, who would stand them on the parapet during an attack. The appearance of a crudely painted tramp, with baggy trousers and a bowler hat, must have bewildered the Germans, who had no idea who he was. To add to the confusion, British officers with a sense of humor would cultivate Chaplin mustaches, and in prison camps, every hut had its Chaplin impersonator." Nor were the French immune. "Charlot was born at the Front," wrote Blaise Cendrars. "The Germans lost the war because they didn't get to know Charlot in time."

Just as the war ended, Chaplin released his own vision of the trenches, the totally apatriotic *Shoulder Arms,* a spiritual precursor of *Catch-22* whose bits include a fantasy of shelling the Germans with Limburger cheese and, an even more visceral evocation of combat, sleeping in a bunk that's virtually under water.

He was taken seriously almost immediately. The author of "Chaplinitis" called him a "genius" and boldly stated that "once in every century, a man is born who is able to color and influence his world. . . . Charles Chaplin is doing it with pantomime and personality." In May 1916, *Harper's Weekly* published "The Art of Charles Chaplin," an appreciation by a well-known stage actress that bracketed "the young English buffoon" with Aristophanes, Shakespeare, and Rabelais.

In France, Charlot was the subject of the first monograph on an individual film artist. In the Soviet Union, archformalist Viktor Shklovsky published a book on Chaplin in 1923. Chaplin was the movies' first *esque,* the only mass culture figure one could bracket with high modernists Eliot and Joyce, a fitting subject for a Cubist collage. (Later, Léger featured him in *Ballet Mécanique.*) It's easy to imagine Chaplin as a character in a Brecht play or Kafka novel, but in America, he was seen as the ultimate Horatio Alger hero. He arrived here a penniless immigrant—bona fide wretched refuse—and, within 24 months, became the highest paid actor in the world. (That Chaplin refused to consummate the myth by becoming an American citizen would be held against him later.)

As an artist, he infused the pathos of the British proletariat—Dickens and the music hall—with the jazz rhythms and streamlined optimism of the newer, American variety, absorbing by osmosis French aestheticism and Jewish soul. (Feckless *Luftmensch* that Chaplin played, he was perceived as Jewish by both Jews and anti-Semites.) In a sense, Chaplin was the mascot of Western democracy. He was mobbed in Paris and London during his 1921 European tour, but ignored in Berlin, where—although some hipster had included his photograph among the Heartfields and Picabias of the 1920 Berlin Dada Fair—his films had not yet been released. Of course, the Germans would soon get their own Little Tramp/Hero of the Trenches/Man of the Century.

In *Modern Times,* Chaplin bid his greatest creation farewell. For the first time, the tramp's voice was heard (singing a nonsense song in a routine that contains in embryo all early Fellini), while the movie's last shot showed the tramp walking off down the road—no longer alone, but hand-in-hand with Paulette Goddard. "It is an ironical thought that the mustached face of Adolf Hitler will be the only living reminder of the little clown," *The New York Times* nostalgically editorialized shortly after the film's release. The thought bothered Chaplin as well. Before Hitler took power, he had been attacked by the Nazi press as "a little Jewish acrobat, as disgusting as he is tedious." (In fact, Chaplin wasn't Jewish, but, as a matter of principle, he never contradicted such accusations.) During Hitler's rule, Chaplin's movies were banned and all mention of his name proscribed. It was inevitable that this pair would go one on one.

Like twin gods in some fertile-crescent myth, the two most compelling personalities of the 20th century were born four days apart, in April 1889. They were both raised in poverty and domestic disorder, both lived as vagabonds, both dreamed of being artists, both captivated the masses, both sought absolute control over their worlds. Many, including Chaplin, believed that Hitler even borrowed his mustache from the Little Tramp. What was the secret of the atom compared to the source of Chaplin's power? Chaplin thought he understood the origin of Hitler's. In *The Great Dictator* he once and for all broke the speech barrier with a full-fledged Hitler rant in gibberish German. Thus did the Little Tramp acknowledge the tyranny of sound.

HIS REPUTATION HAS had violent ups and downs. In 1919 *Theatre Magazine* published an article, hopefully entitled "Is the Charlie Chaplin Vogue Passing?" which scored "the appeal of every Chaplin picture to the lowest human instincts." Even when his artistic reputation was at its highest, Chaplin carried intimations of the underclass. "You have to go to squalid streets and disreputable neighborhoods if you want to see Chaplin regularly," Gilbert Seldes advised his readers on the eve of *The Gold Rush*.

No doubt Ronald Reagan would have pieties to mouth on Chaplin's birthday, but there were periods in Chaplin's career when his most passionate defenders were Surrealists or Communists, and not even the mature success of *The Gold Rush* prevented American women's clubs from organizing a boycott of his pictures because Lita Grey divorced him. As movie-phobe H. L. Mencken noted with no small satisfaction, "The very morons who worshipped Charlie Chaplin six weeks ago now prepare to dance around his stake while he is burned." A quarter of a century later, he suffered the most dramatic fall of any star. Small wonder that he would ultimately cast himself as the genteel mass murderer in *Monsieur Verdoux*.

Once a tramp, always a tramp: The subversion of public order, the potential for anarchy, was inextricably bound up in the Chaplin persona. He always found a way up authority's nose. Chaplin was attacked as a draft dodger during World War I, spuriously indicted for violating the Mann Act during World War II, threatened with deportation, and ultimately red-baited out of the United States at the height of the McCarthy period. But all that is forgotten now. On the 100th anniversary of Chaplin's birth, his progeny are everywhere and nowhere—as Garry Wills pointed out, Ronnie and Nancy mimed the last shot of *Modern Times* (embellished with an affectionately Chaplinesque kick in the butt), in *New Morning in America,* the movie shown to the world at the 1984 Republican convention.

Chaplin at 100 has become a free-floating image and an all-purpose *esque*—familiar now because he was familiar then. He is a neutral symbol of the information age, a million dollar trademark licensed to IBM to make their personal computers seem user-friendly. Leasing the Little Tramp's image from his heirs, IBM upgraded his wardrobe and occupational status: a floppy Little Yuppie for the Age of Reagan. (To approximate the full flavor of what in better days we called co-optation, one has to imagine a blue-chip corporation entrusting their $25 million advertising campaign to Richard Pryor in his "Bicentennial Nigger" heyday.)

Welcome to postmodern times: Released from the assembly line, transmuted into the pure being of empty signifier, the Little Tramp has been put back to work; he's making a living once more, earning his keep, sentenced in his afterlife to labor as a flack for the corporate order. But remember that *Modern Times* is set in Brazil and *The Kid* on Lafayette Street; that *City Lights* is a film about Donald Trump and Billie Boggs. Look at the early movies and then look around you. See if you can't find Chaplin—our contemporary—out there on the street.

tHree

The super-80s

Originally published in *Film Comment* (May–June 1981).

TO TALK ABOUT film you have to talk about money. Shortly after the Hunt brothers tried to corner the silver market, I found myself on a panel discussing the future of avant-garde film. As Kodak had just responded to the silver panic by raising its prices fifty percent, and as lab costs continued to escalate, the prognosis was grim. When I suggested that this meant not the end of avant-garde filmmaking, but a pragmatic switch to black-and-white, shorter films, and super-8, one panelist responded as though I had suggested she exchange her SoHo loft for a Lower East Side tub-in-kit: "I feel like we're being pushed out of 16mm."

The point is, though, that just as the avant garde opened up 16mm, it will open up super-8. In fact, for twenty years, 8mm and super-8 have been an underground underground—the stuff of a distinctively cheap, experimental, and democratic mode of filmmaking. As the bargain basement of film production, the narrow-gauge format is less akin to 16mm than 16mm is to 35mm. Its whole aesthetic is a series of trade-offs. Super-8 film stock is grainy, but super-8 sound reproduction is first rate. Editing is difficult, but long, hand-held takes are not. Lab services are spotty, but camera design is superb. Narrow-gauge cameras are consumer appliances and, as such, built for maximum automation. On the other hand, narrow-gauge filmmaking accentuates all that is fragile, fugitive, and ephemeral about film in general—a point underscored by the fact that many 8mm and super-8 filmmakers edit without benefit of a work print, and/or chose to screen their camera originals.

There is surely no consensus among narrow-gauge filmmakers but, no matter how disparate their work or contradictory its ambitions, every one of their home-made productions serves to criticize the prodigal values of the larger culture industry. Against this oligarchy, spaghetti-thin super-8 presents itself as a utopian alternative. Although too rarely put to overt political use, narrow-gauge filmmaking is an inherently radical practice. It is as though the format itself were stamped with Theodor Adorno's prescription that no idea or work of art "has a chance of survival unless it bears within it a repudiation of false riches and high-class production, of color films and television, millionaire's magazines, and Toscanini."

The existence of a substandard film gauge for non-professional production dates back to the dawn of cinema. The Birtac, a British camera-projector marketed in 1898, was designed for amateur use and 17.5mm (made by slicing standard 35mm down the middle). Within a year, commercial 35mm movies were being offered in substandard format for home projection, and by the turn of the century, there were half a dozen or more British, French, and German 17.5mm movie-camera projectors available. In 1923 Eastman Kodak introduced the first safety (as well as reversal) film in a new substandard gauge, 16mm. The idea was to prevent dealers from splitting and selling 35mm nitrate to unwary amateurs. It soon became apparent that 16mm could itself bifurcate, and in 1932 Kodak brought forth "double 8mm" as a cheaper amateur format. Even so, throughout the Depression, home movie-making remained largely an upper-class pursuit. (In 1930, the British cinematographer William Scull suggested that amateurs in search of a trademark consider using their family coat of arms.) After World War II, the elevation of 16mm to semi-professional status left the home-movie field to 8mm, while postwar prosperity made feasible the proliferation of narrow-gauge cameras as mass-produced consumer appliances.

To the best of my knowledge, no underground masterpieces have been excavated from the first few decades of 8mm filmmaking. I don't doubt they may exist; but, then as now, narrow-gauge filmmaking has been an elusive, almost terminally underground, practice. Although pioneer avant-gardists Curtis Harrington and Gregory Markopoulos (and possibly Kenneth Anger) produced 8mm films during the Forties, it would be another twenty years before the narrow-gauge format made itself felt as any sort of artistic force. The first recognized 8mm practitioners were themselves a scattered and variegated group. They included Bob Branaman, a master of multiple superimposition and flash-frame montage, who began shooting his improvised, edited-in-camera rolls in Wichita around 1958, and the even more hermetic Wallace Berman, a Los Angeles assemblage artist, whose painted-over home movies were never publicly exhibited during his lifetime. In 1960 the Italian poet Piero Heliczer and the English painter Jeff Keen collaborated on *The Autumn Feast,* an anarchic send-up of classic surrealism; and back in California, beatnik activist Bob Chatterton was making 8mm vehicles for Taylor Mead. A few years later, George Landow, a New York art student, began shooting his 8mm studies of TV sets and skin infections. What all these filmmakers had in common was a provocative primitivism, either studied (Landow, Berman), or authentic (Branaman).

In a class by themselves as naifs, were George and Mike Kuchar, Bronx teenagers who spent the last half of the Fifties making grotesque 8mm parodies of Hollywood movies. These violent, hyperbolic melodramas, accompanied by taped pastiches of over-wrought scores, were screened mainly for flabbergasted 8mm travelogue societies until they circuitously came to the attention of the New York underground in 1963. While early Kuchar films like *The Thief and the Stripper* (1959) and *A Town Called Tempest* (1961) took their stars and local color from the neighborhood around Jerome Avenue, the brothers responded to this new recognition by producing *The Lovers of Eternity* (1964), a burlesque of bohemian squalor set on the Lower East Side, featuring a monstrous cockroach and several avant-garde filmmakers (notably Jack Smith).

Although the dramatic clichés, expressive pantomime, perverse morality, and even the length of many Kuchar films are startlingly evocative of D.W. Griffith's two-reel Biographs, the Kuchars are not solely important for developing a form of narrow-gauge narrative. A greater contribution was their invention of one of the format's intrinsic modes: the ironic spectacle, in which the visionary ambition of the filmmaker is continually underscored by the paucity of his or her means.

The "discovery" of the Kuchars by Ken Jacobs and Jonas Mekas, together with Stan Brakhage's encounter with Branaman's work, created a small 8mm wedge with the New American Cinema. "You know what?" wrote Mekas in his April 13, 1963 column in *The Village Voice*. "It is the 8mm movie that will save us. It is coming. You may think I am crazy. But I know people, very talented people, shooting their movies on 8mm. The day is close when the 8mm home-movie footage will be collected and appreciated as beautiful folk art." A few months later, Mekas balanced a projector on a balustrade in the Gramercy Arts Theatre and held the first 8mm program ever screened in a movie house. The bill included Markopoulos's *Eldora*, Red Grooms' *The Unwelcome Guests*, Linda Talbot's *Vermont in 3½ Minutes, Films by Robert Ronnie Branaman*, and three Kuchar flicks: *I Was a Teenage Rumpot, Pussy on a Hot Tin Roof*, and *Born of the Wind*.

In 1964, 8mm entered its heroic age when two major figures of the New American Cinema, Stan Brakhage and Ken Jacobs, switched (albeit temporarily) from 16mm to narrow-gauge production. Around the same time, Piero Heliczer returned to filmmaking with a series of manic extravaganzas—*The Soap Opera, Dirt, Venus in Furs, Saint Joan*—that jumbled all previous avant garde, painter Al Leslie started work on the feature-length, sync-sound *Philosophy in the Bedroom*, which he planned to blow up to 35mm; and a number of younger filmmakers, including Saul Levine and Andrew Meyer, began to release 8mm work. Ironically, this surge of 8mm activity coincided with Kodak's introduction of their new super-8 format. Super-8's smaller sprocket holes allowed for a fifty-percent larger frame, as well as space for a magnetic stripe—and hence the possibility of sound. Nevertheless, until the latter innovation was realized in the mid-Seventies, 8mm remained the preferred format of avant-garde filmmakers.

In the case of Jacobs, the move to narrow-gauge was purely pragmatic. His 16mm camera was stolen after the shooting of *Baud'larian Capers* (1963) and, from 1964 through 1967, he worked almost exclusively in 8mm. This shift proved decisive to his development. The relative mobility and built-in zoom lens of the 8mm camera stimulated his interest in the manipulation of space, precipitating anew concern with actorless cinema. *The Winter Footage* (1964) made extensive use of calculated camera movement, while *Window* (1965)—shot in 8mm and later blown up to 16mm—was an even more highly choreographed, edited-in-camera work that Jacobs called "a true instance of cinematic action-painting." Jacobs' other narrow-gauge films—the lyrical *We Stole Away* (1964) and the assemblage *Lisa and Joey in Connecticut, January 1965: "You've Come Back!" "You're Still Here!"* (1965) used these techniques in the service of the informal home-movie mode he invented with his 16mm *Little Stabs at Happiness* (1963). Later in 1965, Jacobs began *The Sky Socialist*, one of the most ambitious narrow-gauge projects ever undertaken, an epic work addressed to the Brooklyn Bridge with a cast of characters that included Anne Frank, the Marx Brothers, and the Muse of Cinema. The three-hour film, which Jacobs worked on through 1967, remains unfinished.

Brakhage also purchased an 8mm camera after some of his 16mm equipment was stolen. It has been suggested that neither this loss, nor the economic advantage of working in a narrow-gauge, entirely determined this switch. In *Visionary Film,* P. Adams Sitney cited Brakhage's desire to depart from the monumental form of his four-and-a-half-hour *The Art of Vision* (1961–65), as well as his cognizance of 8mm's "polemical" value: "Not only would his example dignify and encourage younger filmmakers who could afford to work only in 8mm, but he would be able to realize, on a limited scale, a dream he had had for years of selling copies of his film." (The latter thought also occurred to the San Francisco-based Bruce Conner, who began making 8mm versions— sometimes quite different from the 16mm originals—of earlier films like *Cosmic Ray* and *Report.*)

Taking home-movie events (births, weddings, trips, portraits of family and friends) as his subject matter, Brakhage began a series of short 8mm films called the *Songs.* Eight were released in 1964, and twelve more the following year. By that time it was apparent that what had begun as a series of lyrical sketches devoted to aspects of daily life had become a major undertaking. The *Songs,* which Brakhage continued to make throughout the Sixties, ultimately grew into a work longer and more varied than *The Art of Vision.* Brakhage's initial formal concerns had been with the in-camera editing (and superimposition) that narrow-gauge film seemed to demand, and with the more obvious quality of 8mm film grain. Before long though he was able to scale down his previously-mastered techniques of painting, scratching, and close-editing film. The apotheosis of the *Songs*—and arguably of narrow-gauge filmmaking too—is his *23rd Psalm Branch* (1966–67), a feature-length meditation on war that cuts 8mm stock footage of World War II atrocities into images of the Colorado landscape, making painstaking use of two-frame shots and a blitz of tiny, hand-applied ink dots. Obsessive and harrowing, *23rd Psalm Branch* provided an ironic spectacle of a completely different order than that found in the Kuchar or Heliczer films.

For the ten years following the first *Songs,* Brakhage was the dominant influence upon serious narrow-gauge filmmaking. His example encouraged a host of younger filmmakers (Saul Levine, Michael Stewart, Howard Guttenplan, Marjorie Keller, Diana Barrie, Willie Varela, and many others) to produce 8mm or super-8 films that emphasized personal vision and the rhythmic orchestration of daily life. That narrow-gauge production has an affinity for "dailiness" should be obvious. Like all forms of amateur photography, amateur filmmaking is promoted and sold primarily as a technology of nostalgia—as a means of documenting one's family, or authenticating one's travels. Most 8mm or super-8 films could be characterized as either home movies or vacation films; and, following Brakhage's lead, the narrow-gauge avant garde bore out Victor Shklovsky's famous recipe for new art forms by "canonizing" these two "peripheral" modes.

IN 1972, AT a time when the anti-expressive "structural film" enjoyed its greatest ascendancy, Jonas Mekas polemically insisted that the only experimental work currently being done was confined to the narrow-gauge format: "There is something about the 8mm camera and film, they lend themselves to personal, lyrical statements." Mekas's hunch proved right: The most innovative post-structural (or anti-structural) films of the Seventies were produced in super-8. Lyricism, however, was not to be their primary attribute.

The first artist to develop a significant body of super-8 work was Vito Acconci, who released 16 short films and two features between 1969 and 1974. A post-Warhol (rather than post-Brakhage) filmmaker, Acconci's exhibition space was neither the living room nor the theater but the art gallery; and more than most narrow-gauge practitioners, he used his super-8 camera as a simple recording device. Acconci's films were not devoid of perceptual issues, but in their purely clinical aspect they surpassed Landow's 1965 study of a skin infection (*Not a Case of Lateral Displacement*) if not the dental documentary, *A Class V Gold Foil Restoration,* cited in an early issue of the magazine of the Amateur Cinema League as a particularly impressive narrow-gauge achievement.

For the most part, Acconci's films were close-up documents of his own performances: portraits of the artist stuffing his mouth with grass, plastering up his anus, trying to upstage a naked woman, plucking the hair around his navel, crushing cockroaches against his chest, and so on. (This deadpan, tawdry exhibitionism made near-subliminal reference to that most common form of narrow-gauge collectable, the pornographic film.) In his way, Acconci reinvented the psychodrama—the original genre of American avant-garde film—in which the filmmaker-protagonist acted out before the camera as though it were a looking glass. But Acconci's psychodrama is founded on the grossest possible behaviorism. In *See Through* (1970), Acconci actually punches his reflected image until the mirror is completely shattered.

Although Acconci confined nearly all of his filming to his loft, the automatic features and lightweight unobtrusiveness of the narrow-gauge camera is particularly suited to filming in public spaces. Nearly a dozen years ago, the German social critic Hans Magnus Enzensberger observed that "tape recorders, ordinary cameras, and movie cameras are already extensively owned by wage-earners. The question is why these means of production do not turn up at factories, in schools, in the offices of the bureaucracy—in short, everywhere there is social conflict." While the potential of narrow-gauge filmmaking for producing agit-prop or exposé remains relatively untapped, the format did come into its own during the Seventies as a vehicle for a kind of personalized urban vérité. Super-8 proved to be the ideal cinematic tool for the artist as either *flâneur* or voyeur.

Paula Gladstone's *The Dancing Souls of the Walking People* (1974–78), for example, is an hour-long tour de force—at once gritty and abstract, tough and poetic—that observes the play of life and shadow beneath the boardwalk at Coney Island. Dave Lee's *To a World Not Listening* documents a series of New York derelicts and street crazies. Even more aggressive are Manuel DeLanda's super-8 films, *Harmful or Fatal If Swallowed* (1975–80) and *Ismism* (1977–

79). The former shows New York City as the province of garbage eating derelicts, defecating dogs, garish parades, and assorted blind or crippled beggars. Through frenzied cutting and optical effects, DeLanda transforms this material into a city symphony of terrors. *Ismism,* by contrast, is a straightforward documentary of DeLanda's spray-painted graffiti exhortations and his grotesque revisions of subway advertising posters. Even the extremely formal films of the late Greg Sharits can be seen as a form of *flâneurism*: As much as the Gladstone or DeLanda films, these percussive, edited-in-camera compositions, superimposing the neon lights and illuminated storefronts of downtown San Francisco, could only have been shot off-the-cuff in narrow gauge. The most metaphysical example of urban vérité also comes from San Francisco. Joe Gibbons's hour-long *Spying* (1978–79) is a perverse and resonant exercise in applied scopophilia wherein the filmmaker covertly observes his neighbor's daily activities, using porno inserts (crudely shot off the screens of Market Street grind houses) to fill in the blanks.

Super-8 sound cameras went on the market in 1974. A year later, Lenny Lipton (author of the best-selling technical guide *Independent Filmmaking*), released his *Children of the Golden West.* Billed as the world's first super-8 sync-sound feature, it is an episodic home movie in which Lipton interviews a mixture of camera store salesmen, family members, and aging veterans of the Sixties. Wrote *Film Quarterly*'s Michael Shedlin: "The film could almost be considered a parody of the counterculture by anyone who was not wide open to unabashed hippieness."

The availability of cheap sync-sound effectively split the followers of Brakhage into two schools. Although the purists eschewed the new technology, Saul Levine—who was more profoundly influenced by the *Songs* than perhaps any other filmmaker—switched to super-8 sound in 1976. His first talkie, *Notes of an Early Fall,* was a characteristically raw work that parlayed the sound of microphone rumble into a formal element. Featuring a lengthy sequence devoted to the dance of an outrageously warped record, and a cameo appearance by an on-the-blink TV set, the forty-minute film suggests an entropic, melancholy *Ballet Mécanique.* Another early talkie, *Misconception* (1977), by Marjorie Keller, was marked by greater ambivalence, if not explicitness, than many of the birth films which followed Brakhage's 1959 *Window Water Baby Moving.* But Brakhage's birth films were silent, and Keller's use of sync-sound served to criticize their idealizations by grounding her visuals in a grittier, more visceral reality.

(Brakhage himself, inspired by one of his students, briefly returned to narrow-gauge filmmaking. Many of the ten silent super-8 films he released in 1976 resemble the early *Songs* in their in-camera editing, rapid camera movements, and casual or diaristic qualities. Others, notably *Airs* and *Absence,* went far beyond *Songs* in their unsettling, near-abstract consideration of the diffuse, ethereal quality of the super-8 image.)

More innovative uses of super-8 sound began to appear in the late Seventies. Ericka Beckman's idiosyncratic films—*White Man Has Clean Hands* (1977), *We*

Imitate; We Break-Up (1978), *The Broken Rule* (1979), and *Out of Hand* (1980)—used primitive but ingenious special effects to combine dream imagery with archaic movie conventions (e.g. employing a whirlpool of superimpositions as a segue into a flashback). Filled wiht images of disembodied limbs, toy-like models, and anthropomorphized furniture, scored to a combination of doo-wop mantras and abstract high school cheers, Beckman's films suggest the combination of an oneiric Max Fleischer cartoon like *Bimbo's Initiation* with Oskar Fischinger's Bauhaus-styled animation, *Composition in Blue*. Aspects of Beckman's work recall the psychodramas of the Forties and Fifties; but, with her emphasis on perceptual gameplaying and childhood cognition, they're inspired less by Freud or Jung than by Jean Piaget.

When Joe Gibbons switched to sound in 1979, he invented a new form of psychodrama which might be termed the "confessional." In *Weltschmerz* (1979), the camera sits on a tripod considering Gibbons as he hunches over his kitchen table, slugging vodka, chain-smoking, and toying aimlessly with a half-eaten potato. Morose and giggling by turns, the filmmaker launches into a broken account of his present unhappiness, which is punctuated by extended cutaways to dying plants, freeway traffic, and TV soap operas.

Some of Gibbons's performances are lighter. *Buffalo Film* (1980) opens at a screening of *La Salamandre* but soon reverts to the filmmaker's kitchen where he seeks to divert us by reading from a book entitled *How to Be an Entertainer*. He takes phone calls, scarfs down a piece of cake, mugs while a friend tells a fatuous story, smashes a drinking glass, and finally attempts to juggle. *Confidential* (1979–80), Gibbons' most powerful film and a worthy companion to his silent *Spying*, is a series of unedited three-and-a-half-minute camera rolls in which he speaks to the camera about their "relationship." The most startling aspect of the film is that Gibbons is clearly not talking to the audience—the sequences are mainly midnight *tête-à-têtes* which the viewer self-consciously overhears. Over the period of forty minutes, Gibbons confides in, coddles, apologizes to, berates ("you can't even be objective!"), and ultimately attacks the machine.

The quintessential super-8 filmmaker of the late Seventies and early Eighties has been Vivienne Dick. Her movies fuse the various traditions of urban vérité, confessional psychodrama, and home-movie dailiness into an original style that's marked by its political overtones. Dick's *Guerillere Talks* (1978) could be seen as a punk feminist correlative to Lipton's *Children of the Golden West*; *She Had Her Gun All Ready* (1978), in the words of critic Karyn Kay, "speaks the contemporary unspeakable: women's anger and hatred of women at the crucial moment of overpowering identification and obsessional thralldom"; *Beauty Becomes the Beast* (1979) depicts a world of women where mother and daughter are reciprocal roles in an ongoing chain of victimization; *Liberty's Booty* (1980) uses a matter-of-fact view of prostitution as a means to demystify sex.

All of Dick's films are jagged, sometimes fragmentary assemblages in which the camera appears to be as much participant as observer. Filled with mordant media quotations, they're shot through an ironic ashcan lyricism and an unsentimental love of rock and roll. Although Dick's favorite locations have been moldering slum tenements, subway stations, Coney Island, and Lower East Side luncheonettes, her *Visibility: Moderate* (1981) is a parody of a vacation film in which the filmmaker returns to her native Ireland in the guise of an American tourist.

Dick initially came to prominence as one of a loose group of super-8 filmmakers—including Beth B and Scott B, Eric Mitchell, James Nares, and Becky Johnston—associated with New York's "no wave" rock scene. Using members of local bands as a readymade pool of dramatic talent, Dick, the Bs, and Mitchell all made films that paralleled the music's energy, iconography, and pragmatic anyone-can-do-it aesthetic. Their films were often premiered at local rock clubs. The Bs, for example, released their punk melodrama, *The Offenders* (1978–79), as a weekly serial shown between sets at Max's Kansas City.

The dominant mode of the "no wave" film has been the ironic spectacle. James Nares' *Rome '78* (1978) is a burlesque of *I, Claudius* using thriftshop Roman costumes and present day New York locations. Becky Johnston's *Sleepless Nights* is a *film noir* so stringently minimal it makes Edgar G. Ulmer's *Detour* seem like *Ben-Hur*. Mitchell's *Kidnapped* (1978)—advertised as "a 1960s underground movie happening today" when it opened at a Lower East Side storefront theater—is an hour-long series of unedited camera rolls wherein a group of punk bohemians hang around his barren slum apartment, casually pretending to be terrorists while an elaborately aimless camera sweeps by them, chopping off torsos at the neck and knees. In this startling debut, it was not the Hollywood melodrama that was turned Kuchar-style into an ironic spectacle, but a dated mode of the avant-garde film itself.

The super-8 "no wave" infused New York's avant-garde film scene with a populist energy that had been largely absent for a decade. One needn't be a technological determinist to recognize the catalytic effect of cheap, automatic super-8 equipment. Of the most interesting young filmmakers to emerge during the late Seventies, some like Marjorie Keller and Manuel DeLanda have shuttled back and forth between narrow-gauge and 16mm production, while others (like Ericka Beckman, Vivienne Dick, Joe Gibbons, and the Bs) have worked exclusively in super-8. I don't expect all of these filmmakers to confine themselves to narrow gauge indefinitely. What I do expect is that the format will remain the cutting edge of avant-garde filmmaking for some time to come.

Paik's peak

Originally published in *The Village Voice* (May 25, 1982).

I F YOU LIKE your art dour you won't much care for Nam June Paik, the Korean-born video artist whose first American retrospective occupies the entire fourth floor of the Whitney Museum. "I come from a very poor country. I have to entertain people every second," Paik likes to say.

Not precisely an immigrant boy, Paik was born in Seoul in 1932 to "one of the most corrupted families in Korea," industrial magnates who fled the country during the Korean War. Paik studied European music at conservatories in Tokyo and Munich; his interests were Stravinsky and Schönberg. Then, in 1958, he met the American avant-Zen composer John Cage. Suddenly, Paik was tipping over pianos and pulverizing violins onstage. The startled Cage found these performances "terrifying," particularly the notorious "Étude for Pianoforte," which Paik began by playing Chopin and ended by vaulting into the audience to snip off his mentor's necktie with a scissors.

When the young "cultural terrorist" arrived in New York in 1964, he enlivened a performance of Stockhausen's "Originale" by appearing on the stage of Judson Hall with his ramshackle *Robot K-456*—a radio-controlled Saul Steinberg scarecrow that walked, talked, defecated white beans, and recited John F. Kennedy's inaugural address while rotating one of its lopsided Styrofoam breasts. The organizer of the concert was a 24-year-old cellist named Charlotte Moorman. The next year, she premiered Paik's Cello Sonata No. 1 for Adults Only at the New School. Moorman interrupted the Bach prelude she was playing every few measures to remove an article of clothing and complete the piece completely naked. In 1967, Paik and Moorman were busted at the Film-Makers' Cinematheque on 41st Street. As a result, Moorman lost her job with the American Symphony Orchestra. The pair was invited (but declined) to take the act to Vegas. As Paik would later explain, "Charlotte's renowned breast symbolizes the agony and achievement of the avant-garde for the past 10 years."

During the mid-'60s, Paik was associated with the Fluxus gang—a group of Cage-influenced New York poets, filmmakers, and musicians (including Yoko Ono) who shared a common interest in chance operations, "mono-structural" forms, and "neo-haiku events." The late George Macuinas, the group's main organizer, once defined its aesthetic as "the fusion of Spike Jones, vaudeville, gag, children's games, and Duchamp." More a fellow traveler than a card-carrying Fluxist, Paik added flashy sex and then television to the brew.

The television zeitgeist came complete with Marshall McLuhan. "Paper is dead . . . except for toilet paper," Paik proclaimed in 1968. "If Joyce lived today surely he would have written his *Finnegans Wake* on videotape." Typically, he proposed to take the notion of the Global Village literally: "If 100 top Americans have their tele-fuck-mates in USSR, we can sleep a little bit safer."

BIZARRE AS IT may seem, Paik is the D.W. Griffith of video art. (The even less likely Ernie Kovacs is the form's affably primitive Georges Méliès.) Paik's 1963 gallery exhibit of "prepared" television sets—held in Wuppertal, West Germany, under the baleful gaze of a decapitated cow's head—announced the birth of homemade video. Two years later, he purchased the first Sony PortaPak sold in America. By the end of the decade, Paik and the Japanese techno-wiz Shuya Abe had developed a video "synthesizer" that enabled him to lay on special effects as thick and spectacular as one of Dagwood Bumstead's sandwiches.

The first Paik-Abe synthesizer was built at WGBH-TV in Boston. Subsequent models were constructed for Cal Arts, WNET-TV, and the Experimental

Television Center in Binghamton, New York. The call for "public access" was resounding in the land, and, as David A. Ross notes in one of the exhibition catalogue essays, "unlike his followers (and fellow inventors)," Paik "immediately made his instrument available to the public." The florid disco solarizations that now psych fans for network sports shows are third-generation Paik.

But Paik's tapes are more rhythmically complex than this run-of-the-mill "vuzak." They cook. Like Griffith, who applied the narrative devices of Charles Dickens to five-cent peepshows, Paik brought his knowledge of a more highfalutin' art form, namely the electronic music of Stockhausen and Cage, to bear on a brand-new media. Structurally, Paik's videotapes derive from the audiotaped *musique concret* sound collages he was making in Europe before Cage deflected him toward performance. On the other hand, Paik (like Griffith) is a populist. But whereas Griffith cribbed from Victorian stock melodrama, Paik swipes from TV spots.

In an era of media overload—with the promise of "public access" still an open question—Paik is something of a radical conservative. He recycles everything: "Once on videotape you are not allowed to die." Key themes (Beethoven's "Moonlight Sonata," Saint-Saëns's "The Swan," Mitch Ryder's "Devil with a Blue Dress") and visual motifs (Allen Ginsberg chanting a mantra, Japanese Pepsi-Cola commercials, zappy go-go dancers, ubiquitous TV sets) appear in virtually every one of his tapes.

Not the content but the context keeps changing as Paik invents new ways to look at TV.

One of the most impressive pieces that was at the Whitney is a heap of 40 monitors, with the 24-inch models at the base and a gaggle of tummy TVs at the apex. They're all playing the same tape—most of it recycled from Paik's four-minute distillation of the 1980 Winter Olympics. The effect is even more compelling than the monolithic simultaneity of a shopping plaza display beaming out 40 images of *As the World Turns*. By turning sets on their heads and sides, Paik creates a sort of pyramid-shaped, matrixless mandala. The speeded-up Soviet-American hockey match becomes a crystalline blur of forces. When a close-up of a female nude appears, the effect is a kaleidoscope of limbs around her sex.

It was part of Paik's genius to use the TV set as an object, as well as to pioneer video as a medium. One of his earliest pieces is a *Participation TV* whose scribble-scrabble image alters its shape in response to ambient sound. His austere *Moon Is the Oldest TV Set* consists of a dozen monitors purchased at a hotel rummage sale and electronically recircuited to produce a series of perfect spheres ranging from slender crescent to full moon.

"There are as many sorts of TV circuits as sorts of French cheese," Paik explained after several years of rewiring old sets or deranging their images with giant magnets. A few of these relics were at the Whitney, along with Paik's TV mailbox, TV flower pot, TV fish tanks, TV sunglasses, an 18th century Buddha contemplating its telecast image, a kitsch miniature of Rodin's *The Thinker* pondering the mystery of afternoon TV, Charlotte Moorman's TV brassiere, and the *TV Cello* that Paik created for her. (Sometimes Charlotte is even there to play the instrument. It's "the first real innovation in cello design since 1600," she says.)

More diabolically perverse is the *TV Chair,* which invites you to park your carcass upon the broadcast image. The *TV Chair* made its New York debut at a 1968 Museum of Modern Art exhibit called "The Machine as Seen at the End of the Mechanical Age" (for Paik, this literally meant the tail end) and served as the essential prop in his legendary 1975 intervention into the *Tomorrow* show. Tom Snyder's program on "video art" included a live-remote from Paik's Soho loft during which the artist managed to visibly rattle his "host" by blandly sitting down upon the *TV Chair* as it beamed out a prerecorded close-up of Snyder's face. Back at the NBC studio, an embarrassed Snyder attempted to cut short their interview, while deadpan Paik took advantage of the confusion to follow talk-show protocol, introducing his wife Shigeko Kubota and plugging her video work.

Paik's TVs immodestly propose that television will supplant writing, sex, nature, and travel—not to mention the museum itself. "Mantovani was more important than Schönberg," he wrote recently in *Artforum.* "You cannot put Schönberg's music into an elevator."

The Whitney show is the museum used at its best—as the public (if not neutral) presenter of an integrated world view. It also has to do with art. The first thing that smacks your eye when the elevator doors slide open is 15 guppy-filled fishtanks, each backed by a madly strobing color TV monitor.

Two programs alternated along the wall-length installation, punching out staccato images of goldfish in the sky, New York City landmarks, streaking jet planes, color bars, and Merce Cunningham dancing. Not surprisingly, some people identify immediately with the fish. "I think it's cruel," one visitor announced to her companion. The guppies, however, seemed totally unconcerned. Have they mutated or is it their natural guppy trance? "I use technology in order to hate it more properly," Paik once said.

Deeper into the exhibit *we* become the fish. *Hanging TV (Fish Flies on Sky)* is a darkened room with 30 or so color sets of varied sizes beaming down in tilted clusters from the ceiling. The same two programs—with perhaps a bit more jet plane—are being shown, but the room is filled with the sound of pounding surf. A few (too few) mats cover the floor, inviting us to lie down, stretch out, gaze up, immerse ourselves in the radiance of distant TVs.

It is the ultimate viewing situation. The elaborate suburban rec (or hospital day) roomlike Video Lounge at Danceteria seems cramped by comparison. *Fish Flies on Sky* is fantastically relaxing, virtually hypnotic. The atmosphere reeks of alpha waves.

When *Fish Flies on Sky* was first installed in a West Broadway gallery in 1976, Gregory Battcock observed that for the first time since Michelangelo painted the ceiling of the Sistine Chapel, the traditionally upright position for looking at art had been subverted. But *Fish Flies on Sky* also epitomizes the aspirations of "advanced" 20th century painting: one necessarily relaxes one's gaze under the steady pressure of peripheral visual data. As art-psychologist Anton Ehrenzweig points out, the Cubist "weaving in and out of the picture plane was perhaps the first manifestation of a new abstract pictorial space which later became fully revealed in the painting of Jackson Pollock." The result: "Our attempt at focusing must give way to the vacant all-embracing stare . . . the conscious signal of unconscious scanning." In '60s terms, *Fish Flies on Sky* produces a heightened, drugless form of being stoned.

LIKE ALL AMBITIOUS American artists, Paik tackles the native landscape. Just by taking television as his medium, he appropriates a formidable piece of it. "Americans dream of taking home raw chunks of nature," Harold Rosenberg maintained in an early '70s essay. "Redmen to Earthworks." But what exactly is modern Nature?

TV Garden, the piece that occupies the Whitney's second-floor theater, could have been pedantically titled "The Global Village" or "The Machine in the Garden" or "The Natural Paradise." ("In the beginning, all the world was America," marveled Enlightenment philosopher John Locke.) Thirty monitors are scattered face-up at various angles amid a mini-jungle of tropical plants. So dense is the foliage that no pulsing screen in the entire habitat is visible in its entirety. Never has the unearthly quality of video illumination seemed more beautiful than flickering off these fern leaves, tiger lilies, and assorted creepers. A delicious coolness rises from the installation's depths. One's first impulse is to laugh with delight.

"Postindustrial society will be a kind of egoless society," Paik told Calvin Tomkins. Despite variations of size and hue, all the TVs are broadcasting the same program—a relatively lengthy mishmash out of *Global Groove,* conflating John Cage, a leotard-clad tap dancer, Richard Nixon, a solarized Sally Rand, traditional Asian music, the Living Theater, and Japanese commercials. Pure television.

If you're lucky enough to wander in during the corny Spanish guitar sequence or while Charlotte Moorman is playing "The Swan" soaking wet on her TV cello (the image overlaid with gobs of lurid psychedelia), the effect is a boffo combination of schlock and sublimity, as achingly elegant as Marguerite Duras's *India Song.* Indeed, like *India Song, TV Garden* essays the dialectic of East and West, and winds up giving absence a tangible form.

This *must* be the end of the rainbow: TV sets flowering in the jungle like seductive science-fiction poppies. One tears oneself away with difficulty. Does the surge of energized emptiness with which you greet the street = the Zen of TV?

Teen angel

Originally published as "Personal Best" in *The Village Voice* (May 3, 1983).

BARBARA RUBIN'S MIND-BLOWING *Christmas on Earth* is getting its first public screening in perhaps 15 years at the Collective. Shot during the summer of 1963, the film is an essential product of one of the richest periods in New York underground filmmaking. *Flaming Creatures* had not yet been busted and Jack Smith was making his Technicolor sequel *Normal Love,* Ron Rice was editing *The Queen of Sheba Meets the Atom Man,* the Film-makers' Coop had recently been established, Jonas Mekas had just discovered the Kuchars, and Andy Warhol was thinking of buying a Bolex.

Into this delirious ferment plunged Barbara Rubin, a 17-year-old schoolgirl from Queens who, borrowing Mekas's camera and—influenced by *Flaming Creatures,* Brakhage, Anger's *Inauguration of the Pleasure Dome,* everything that was in the air—produced far and away the most sexually explicit film to startle the preporn avant-garde. When Mekas described *Christmas on Earth,* he was moved to poetry: "A woman; a man; the black of the pubic hair; the cunt's moon mountains and canyons. As the film goes, image after image, the most private territories of the body are laid open for us. . . . A syllogism: Barbara Rubin has no shame; angels have no shame; Barbara Rubin is an angel."

If Barbara Rubin was an angel, she was a remarkably busy one. Embarrassingly worthy of an *Edie*-style biography, Rubin was one of the '60s key scene-makers. She led the charge when *Flaming Creatures* was shown illegally in Knokke-le-Zout and engulfed the Belgian minister of culture in a riot; she introduced Allen Ginsberg to Bob Dylan (that's her, massaging Bobby's curls on the back cover of *Bringing It All Back Home*) and Andy Warhol to the Velvet Underground; she organized New York's first light-shows and squired visiting dignitaries like Donovan or the Byrds around the city. By the early '70s she found religion, and joined an ultra-orthodox Jewish sect. Around 1979 she died giving birth to her sixth child.

Of the three major histories of '60s avant-garde film—David Curtis's out-of-print *Experimental Cinema,* P. Adams Sitney's *Visionary Film,* and Stephen Dwoskin's *Film Is*—only Dwoskin cites *Christmas on Earth* and then basically to quote Mekas. So far as I know, not one other word was written on Rubin's film until 1979 when Amy Taubin, reviewing Vivienne Dick's super-8 *Beauty Becomes the Beast* for the *SoHo News,* made apt and illuminating comparison between Dick's current transgressions and Rubin's earlier one. Of Rubin's brief film career, Taubin observed, "perhaps terrified by the enormity of what she had achieved and the pain of sustaining her work and lifestyle in a scene that was male-dominated, she opted for marriage and motherhood in a European Hasidic community."

The silence surrounding *Christmas on Earth* is at once appropriate and appalling, for the film more than delivers on the promise (and, for a Jewish sister, the poignant yearning) of its wonderful title: *Christmas on Earth* is an ethereal tangle of Day-Glo faces and dangling cocks, guys posing as Greek statues and girls painted like archaic fertility goddesses, fingers probing cunts and assholes in bleached black-and-white and mega-close-up. The camera explores bodies with a kind of ecstatic curiosity, neither clinical nor precious so much as bluntly innocent. Rubin's paint-spattered backdrop and overall harsh lighting (softened by the outdated film stock) give her mise-en-scène a primitive elegance suggesting a cross between paleolithic cave painting and Aubrey Beardsley. No one with a serious interest in the development of film culture can afford to miss the Collective's two screenings. To see *Christmas on Earth* is to watch history remade.

According to Mekas, who should be honored for preserving Rubin's film as he has other avant-garde classics, Rubin used to present the two 30-minute reels of *Christmas on Earth* in various ways—projected side by side or superimposed with one reel inverted or cut into four frame shards and respliced at random, on the silver ceiling of Warhol's old Balloon Farm. When she could, she projected one reel inside the other—literalizing the film's interest in penetration while creating a sumptuous interplay of texture and scale—and this is how the Collective will present the film. Afterwards, the reels will be shown consecutively, a necessary way to see them if only to appreciate how skillfully contrived Rubin's apparently artless spectacle is. And her teenage sexual utopia is nothing if not all-embracing. When the veils of superimposing are lifted, you can see that in the corner somebody's dog is even mounted on a cat.

Once upon a time in *Amerika*: Straub/Huillet/Kafka

Originally published in *Artforum* (September 1984).

Even the loveliest dream bears like a blemish its difference from reality, the awareness that what it grants is mere illusion. This is why precisely the loveliest dreams are as if blighted. Such an impression is captured superlatively in the description of the nature theatre of Oklahoma in Kafka's *Amerika*.

–Theodor Adorno, *Minima Moralia*

When relating an event someone sometimes says: "Words cannot describe it." . . . The Straubs have filmed a text by Kafka and they say clearly: "Film cannot describe it."

–Harun Farocki

POPULATED BY SLY vagabonds and implacable cops, immigrant proles and enigmatic plutocrats, Franz Kafka's Amerika is a land of arbitrary good fortune and sudden exploitation, at once a theater of comic cruelty—with vast cities, country estates, and imposing hotels serving as backdrops for grotesque reversals or slapstick chases—and a dream of redemption. While writing the novel Kafka thought he was producing an imitation of Charles Dickens; subsequent commentators (German as well as American) have been virtually unanimous in comparing the book to the nearly contemporaneous comedies of Charlie Chaplin.

Amerika is Kafka's most extroverted novel; it's almost picaresque. If, as Adorno has observed, many scenes in the Kafka oeuvre read as though written to describe "expressionist paintings which should have been painted but never were," *Amerika* is the adventure that Lyonel Feininger's pop-expressionist comic strip, *The Kin-der-Kids,* should have recounted but never did. Indeed, the first two paragraphs of Kafka's novel could serve as a caption for the epic, madly angular, and bustling view of New York harbor that Feininger emblazoned across the front page of the May 6, 1906, edition of the *Chicago Sunday Tribune* comic supplement—except that Feininger's Statue of Liberty is waving a handkerchief and Kafka's, like the angel assigned to police the Garden of Eden, holds aloft a sword.

Since America was a land Kafka knew only from books, the place he describes is as imaginary as Karl May's New World or the land so numbingly detailed in the *Impressions of Africa* Raymond Roussel published at his own expense in 1910. Still, it was an escape hatch he must often have pondered. Even as a child, Kafka planned a novel about two warring brothers, "one [of whom] went to America, while the other"—the good one, naturally—"remained behind in a European prison," the writer's own European prison (a castle, perhaps).

Begun in early 1912 and rewritten later that year (Kafka's imagination fueled by his epistolary wooing of Felice Bauer), with the first chapter published in May 1913 as "The Stoker" and the remainder of the novel then revised through 1914 before finally being abandoned in 1916 (a year before Chaplin made *The Immigrant*), *Amerika* is Kafka's fantasy of himself alone and free in the New World as a 16-year-old innocent named Karl Rossman. The author read the opening chapters to his friends with unbridled delight, laughing at this splendid joke. "Kafka is in ecstasy, writes whole nights through. A novel set in America," Max Brod—Kafka's friend, biographer, and executor—noted in his diary entry of September 29, 1912. It was Brod who gave Kafka's unfinished work its title; the author had planned to call it *Der Verschollene,* which can be translated as "The man who disappeared," or "was forgotten, lost without a trace, presumed dead, never heard from again." Adapting the novel for the screen, Jean-Marie Straub and Danièle Huillet take the same liberty as did Brod. They call their 1984 version of Kafka's novel *Class Relations.*

Virtually every Straub/Huillet film is an adaptation of a preexisting text. That these texts have ranged from musical scores by J.S. Bach (for Straub/Huillet's *Chronicle of Anna Magdalena Bach,* 1967) to Bertolt Brecht's novel-fragment *The Business Affairs of Mr. Julius Caesar* (*History Lessons,* 1972), Stéphane Mallarmé's poem *Un coup de dés jamais n'abolira le hasard* (*Every Revolution Is a Throw of the Dice,* 1977), a letter sent from Friedrich Engels to Karl Kautsky (*Too Early, Too Late,* 1981), a children's book by Marguerite Duras (*En Rachachant,* 1982), and even graffiti found in a German post office

(*The Bridegroom, the Comedienne and the Pimp,* 1968) suggests that every representational film is a re-presentation, that all subject matter is borrowed, that each film is to be studied for its lapses and infidelities, that nothing can ever be translated. Straub and Huillet's subject, at least in part, is precisely the disjunction between the original text and its cinematic adaptation. Far from offering a substitute for the original, their films document that disjunction, document the attempt to make a movie out of a text. Typically they are drawn to texts that have been marginalized or, like *Amerika,* abandoned before completion and which thus resist adaptation all the more.

Shot in ascetic black and white, *Class Relations* aspires to a studied neutrality. The sets have the ahistorical character of finished basements or doctors' waiting rooms. The few exteriors are mainly (but hardly explicitly) German. The costumes are of neither 1912 nor 1984 but some blandly unobtrusive mixture of the two. The mainly static camera positions and dry, emptied-out mise-en-scène make Robert Bresson seem as prodigal as Vincente Minnelli. *Class Relations* isn't even ostentatiously minimal.

The film's disorienting lack of establishing shots and characteristic eschewal of conventional reverse-angle editing is at once a political decision to refuse the viewer an invisible position within the narrative construct (and thus, presumably, an unproblematic identification with the characters and action) and a means to emphasize each particular camera setup, this reinforced by Straub and Huillet's practice of holding locations for as much as half a minute after the actors have left the frame. The frame itself is enormously emphasized by the way the filmmakers use it to isolate the performers from each other, so that most of the dialogue is addressed to characters outside the compositional field. Voices emanate from elsewhere, beyond the frame, and several key activities—a political rally, Karl's beating at the hands of the perfidious Robinson and Delamarche—are heard but not seen.

The hallmark of *Class Relations* is the impassive reaction shot. Dialogue tends toward soliloquy, the narrative flow congeals into a textual presence, Kafka's language becomes an object. A succession of characters, mainly immigrants, recite a litany of jobs lost and found in which fate is only slightly less malevolent than those capricious bosses with which *Amerika* abounds. The cast mixes professionals with amateurs, and the performances of all are perversely theatrical. Characters stand and declaim their lines in singsong recitations. "The cast is not being asked to act out a text," as André Bazin wrote of Bresson's *Diary of a Country Priest* (1950), "nor even to live it out, just to speak it. . . ."

Diary of a Country Priest is the great precursor of Straub/Huillet's method, and Bazin's comments on it (in *"Le Journal d'un curé de campagne* and the Stylistics of Robert Bresson," 1951) are readily transposed to *Class Relations*:

> The novel is a cold, hard fact, a reality to be accepted as it stands. One must not attempt to adapt it to the situation in hand, or manipulate it to fit some passing need for an explanation; on the contrary it is something to be taken absolutely as it stands. Bresson never condenses the text, he cuts it. Thus what is left over is a

part of the original. Like marble from a quarry the words of the film continue to be a part of the novel. Of course the deliberate emphasis on their literary character can be interpreted as a search after artistic stylization, which is the very opposite of realism. The fact is, however, that in this case the reality is not the descriptive content, moral or intellectual, of the text—it is the very text itself. . . . *At first sight the film seems to be somehow made up on the one hand of the abbreviated text of the novel and illustrated, on the other hand, by images that never pretend to replace it.*

As Robert Altman's *Popeye* (1980) makes strange the most familiar of Hollywood cartoons by pedantically transposing it to "live action," or as Manoel de Oliviera's *Doomed Love* (1981) defamiliarizes the 19th-century novel through the fanatically faithful transposition of its narrative conventions into film, so *Class Relations* reinvents the by now clichéd Kafka—or rather re-presents the frightening irrationality of his world in all its deadpan splendor. Eschewing the baroque bombast of Orson Welles' *The Trial* (1962)—Kafka is Art—or the lush naturalism of Rudolf Noelte's *The Castle* (1968, with Maximilian Schell as "K")—Kafka is Real—*Class Relations* is the most matter-of-fact, the most literal, the least encumbered cinematization of Kafka that one can imagine.

"We simply wanted to show kinds of behavior linked to belonging to a certain class," say Straub and Huillet; when the rich Senator Jacob tells his long-lost nephew Karl, a greenhorn just off the boat and already agitating for justice, not to "push things too far" but rather to "understand your position," the filmmakers immediately cut to a severe low-angle shot of the monstrous commercial towers of "New York."

Structurally, Kafka's *Amerika* is a triptych. The first panel is "The Stoker," the opening chapter and the only portion of the manuscript that Kafka cared to publish. The middle panel is the body of the work, during which, as Berlin filmmaker/film theorist (and *Class Relations'* Delamarche) Harun Farocki puts it, Karl "struggles for a place in life as others struggle for a place in eternity" until the narrative breaks off with the 16-year-old immigrant boy being held captive by the monstrous Brunelda and his two nemeses, Delamarche and Robinson, in a brothel-like apartment whose balcony affords them a disconnected spectacle not unlike TV's. The third panel is the final chapter which Brod titled "The Nature Theatre of Oklahoma" (despite the fact that Kafka refers only to a "Theatre of Oklahoma").

Admirably abrupt, this epilogue begins with Karl free (again) and unemployed:

At a street corner [he] saw a placard with the following announcement: The Oklahoma Theatre will engage members for its company today at Clayton racecourse from six o'clock in the morning until midnight. The great Theatre of Oklahoma calls you! Today only and never again! If you miss your chance now you miss it forever! If you think of your future you are one of us! Everyone is welcome! If you want to be an artist, join our company! Our Theatre can find employment for everyone, a place for everyone! If you decide on an engagement we congratulate you here and now! But hurry, so that you get in before midnight! At twelve o'clock the doors will be shut and never opened again. Down with all those who do not believe in us! Up, and to Clayton!

According to Max Brod, it was Kafka's plan that within this fabulous theater (whose imagery the writer seems to have derived by superimposing the dilapidated splendor of the Yiddish theater he frequented upon that of the naturopathic sanatoriums he favored) Karl should "find again a profession, freedom and standing, even his old home and his parents, as if by some celestial magic." It is as if at this point, the narrative makes a convulsive return to Europe and, with the heightened poignancy that Karl's experience of Amerika provides, re-presents his most innocent dream of the New World. For the Nature Theatre is the America of *Amerika,* the immigrant's fantasy of a place where all are allowed and one need only be one's own self to find a new identity and begin again.

This surely accounts for the fascination that this sequence of the novel has exerted. According to Walter Benjamin (who never found his way out of the Castle and consequently became an intellectual cult figure second only to Kafka), writing in his essay "Franz Kafka" (1934), "the Nature Theatre of Oklahoma . . . harks back to the Chinese theater, which is a gestic theatre. One of the most significant functions of this theatre is to dissolve happenings into their gestic components"—as, incidentally, Straub and Huillet do for *Amerika.* ("One can go even further," Benjamin continues, "and say that a good number of Kafka's shorter studies and stories are seen in their full light only when they are, so to speak, put on as acts in the 'Nature Theatre of Oklahoma.' ") With its pasteboard angels tottering on huge pedestals and blaring away on trumpets for a handful of spectators, the Nature Theatre is less a theater than a state of being. In a 1972 essay ("Set Out for Clayton!") comparing the Nature Theatre to the postart art world, Harold Rosenberg calls it the "situation beyond all cultures— a situation that offers a role to everyone, regardless of talent or training."

The Nature Theatre is that utopian democracy where, as Rosenberg puts it, "everyone not only can be an artist but is a work of art," where everyone is not only a work of art but "automatically in 'the right place.' " Seen thus, the Nature Theatre begins to suggest such other esthetic democracies as the early films of Andy Warhol, the wretched refuse of Kurt Schwitters' Cathedral of Erotic Misery, 1920–36, or the similar (but mutable) "center of unused objects and unwanted objects" proposed by Jack Smith in 1978 as a substitute for palaces of official culture. The Nature Theatre is nothing less than the millennium itself, the end of human history and even class struggle. "The metaphysical problem of identity, whose solution Marx deferred until the advent of the classless society," Rosenberg wrote, is here "dealt with directly by individuals, each acting in accordance with his inner form." Yet this is not precisely true, for in order to join the Nature Theatre Karl must surrender his name. "He felt shy of mention-ing his own name and letting it be written down. As soon as he had a place here, no matter how small, and filled it satisfactorily, they could have his name, but not now; he had concealed it too long to give it away now. So as no other name occurred to him at the moment, he gave the nickname he had had in his last post: 'Negro.'"

Negro! Without undue emphasis, Straub/Huillet turn this mysterious bit of business (and the comic repartee that follows it) into the Nature Theatre's main event. Their treatment of *Amerika*'s climax is as homogenous as their dramatization of "The Stoker" or any of Karl's subsequent adventures. Karl studies the Oklahoma Theatre poster on a graffiti-covered building (of all possible underlying slogans, Straub/Huillet have selected the bold graffito: *streik*); then, suddenly, a delayed passage of Bach bursts from the soundtrack like an intimation of paradise. Radical surgeons, Straub and Huillet delete the race course, the angels, and Karl's bureaucratic runaround, proceeding directly to Karl's interview—presented in a low-angle shot of him being interrogated (in English!) by two men in an auditorium.

> "Negro?" said the chief, turning his head and making a grimace, as if Karl had now touched the high water mark of incredibility. Even the clerk looked critically at Karl for a while, but then he said: "Negro" and wrote the name down. "But surely you haven't written down Negro?" the chief shouted at him. "Yes, 'Negro,'" said the clerk calmly, and waved his hand, as if his superior should now continue the proceedings.

For Straub and Huillet, ultimately there is no escape, no millennium, no America. There are only, as they insist, class relations. Compare their dour Karl to the giddy time-traveler played by Robert De Niro who dreams his own lethal Nature Theatre of Oklahoma in Sergio Leone's current *Once Upon a Time in America*. For Leone, America is an opium fantasy where scum can live like aristocracy, if they have the nerve to kill for the privilege. Or compare *Class Relations* to Jim Jarmusch's *Stranger Than Paradise,* another ascetic immigrant adventure (albeit one which "rewrites" Wim Wenders as Kakfa rewrote Charles Dickens) where the transcendent shabbiness of the Nature Theatre—contentless Walker Evans or Robert Frank—is all that exists. In the Jarmusch film as much as the Leone, money can still be found in the street and the spell of America is precisely its difference from Europe. But these, Straub and Huillet would say, are films about class relations as well and, as for otherness, America is that foreign country where we all live.

Class Relations bears like a blemish its difference from *Amerika*. The endings, though, are the same. Karl (or "Negro," not yet "K"), having been accepted by the Nature Theatre, rides on the train toward Oklahoma: "For two days and two nights they journeyed on. Only now did Karl understand how huge America was. Unweariedly he gazed out of the window. . . ." *Class Relations'* final image, perhaps the lengthiest shot in the film, is of an unspoiled landscape as seen from the window of a moving train.

"Film cannot describe it," this text by Kafka. The archetypal Straub/Huillet landscape is the now-bucolic site of some past political conflict—a massacre, a revolt, a strike. But there is no suggestion of a history lesson here. Dotted with trees, reflected in a lake, this landscape is empty yet imminent, still pure possibility, a slate without a trace. Unique in their oeuvre (as *Amerika* was unique in Kafka's), this vista is a text that's yet to be written.

Show time

Originally published as "Once More with Feeling" in *The Village Voice* (May 14, 1985).

COMPARABLE IN FORCE and originality to Godard or Fassbinder, 35-year-old Chantal Akerman is arguably the most important European director of her generation—and nothing says more about the state of current film culture than the time it has taken her to find an American audience.

For movies, the '70s and '80s have proven to be a period of severe aesthetic balkanization. Loved or hated, films like *L'avventura* or *Last Year at Marienbad* sparked intellectual debates. They may have been "difficult," but their audience was general. Yet Akerman, who is surely no more esoteric than Alain Resnais, has scarcely gotten beyond the specialists. Until recently, *Jeanne Dielman* was the only one of her seven features with an American distributor, and despite its formidable reputation, mainstream critics had to be tickled with cattle prods even to see it.

Les Années 80, which was shown once (at midnight) during the 1983 New York Film Festival, may not make Akerman a household word, but it demonstrates her range. Where *Dielman* is monumental and severe, *Les Annéss 80* ("The Eighties") is Akerman's most playful, purely pleasurable film. The dense, fragmentary first hour is culled from some 40 hours of rehearsal tapes for what you gradually realize is a musical comedy. Roles are auditioned, routines blocked out, songs recorded. Akerman's deft, jagged montage has a cubist logic: She'll do a scene, feeding lines first to the female principal, then to the male, then repeat it with a different actress. The film is raw but sensuous. The video transfer has its own smudged, pastel quality, while the spectacle of actors—mainly chic young women, poised and pretty as mannequins—responding to offscreen direction or slipping in and out of character is a sort of minimalist vaudeville with peppy yé-yé music and a choreographed structure.

Although the first hour of *Les Années 80* is a musical the way *Stranger Than Paradise* is a road film, the movie climaxes à la Busby Berkeley with a series of lavish production numbers. Shot in 35mm on a fairly elaborate set—the Toison d'Or, or Golden Fleece, shopping mall—*Les Années 80*'s giddy, half-ecstatic finale makes you think Akerman's actors have died and gone to heaven. Lines, scenes, dances fall into place as the members of the cast sing and cavort their way through the drugstores, beauty parlors, and boutiques of the Toison d'Or, absurdly extolling the transcendent power of love.

Akerman's all-dancing, all-singing jigsaw puzzle is typically described as a deconstructed musical, a term that's worth unpacking. It's not just that *Les Années 80* breaks down a musical into its various components, Akerman uses those elements to alter one's perception of the whole. Because the repetitions, the varied readings, and the vocal dubbings of the first hour serve to drive a wedge between performer and performance during the final 20 minutes (when the rehearsal work is subsumed in a stylized representation of "work"), *Les Années 80* is one of the few movies that can legitimately call itself realist. While a film like Ken Jacobs's *Tom, Tom, the Piper's Son* reveals the riches in the original material it refilms, *Les Années 80* shows you how it got that way. It's a modernist reworking of one of the great subjects of musical comedies, namely that of making a show.

"Between a script and a movie, one must go through a whole landscape," Akerman has written. "*Les Années 80* covers the time spent in this landscape." But *Les Années 80* is not simply a film about film, it's also a portrait of the artist. Consistently heard and intermittently popping in and out of frame throughout the first hour, Akerman turns performer near the end of the rehearsals—conducting a singer with such intensity she seems to be playing an instrument, which, of course, she is. Few films are so exuberant, let alone frank, in revealing their directorial *jouissance,* and Akerman goes even further, turning ventriloquist and singing the ballad that will be dubbed into one of the climactic numbers. Missing the beat, going flat, she stops and goes on, her limited but serviceable voice putting the song over on a mixture of enthusiasm, concentration, and desire.

According to Akerman, *Les Années 80* is a sort of pilot, made to help her get funding for a multimillion-dollar musical. Whether this was her only intention (suggested by the millennial tag line "next year in Jerusalem"), the film succeeds brilliantly on its own—as a deconstruction, a documentary, a parody of petit bourgeois sentiment (the endless banalities about love) and suffering (the shopkeepers of Toison d'Or complaining about their work). And although Akerman disclaims feminist readings of her films, it takes no great powers of imagination to see *Les Années 80* as a movie about how women learn to play their roles—as lovers, workers, "women," and movie directors. The film's subtextual concern with (de)constructing femininity gives an added piquance to Akerman's observation, "This is how through reality we arrive at fiction." No less than *Jeanne Dielman, Les Années 80* is a film about the female condition.

What's art got to do with it?

Originally published in *The Village Voice* (September 17, 1985).

THE MUSIC VIDEO is the quintessential postmodern form—this week, anyway. As the Second Annual MTV Video Music Awards were handed out at Radio City, three and a half blocks uptown the same mode (if not the same program) was exhibited at the Museum of Modern Art. That the market-place celebration promises to be less entertaining and more sanctimonious than the museum installation is a reversal inherent to the age.

"The erosion of the older distinction between high culture and so-called mass or popular culture," Frederic Jameson has suggested, is a hallmark of postmodernism. So is the acceleration of this process: It took nearly half a century and a technological upheaval for movies to become culturally respectable; it's taken music videos the relative equivalent of half a minute.

For MTV's target audience, videos are pop songs, movies, sitcoms, pulp novels, and comic books all rolled into one. At their very least, mainstream videos are the prime show biz fossils of the future—packed with incidents and privileged moments. (Bette Midler's unsuccessful "Beast of Burden" [dir: Allan Arkush, 1983] is a rich example, complete with Mick Jagger cameo.) But superior "marginal" work notwithstanding, are they ever anything more?

For the past few years, many of the hippest film buffs I know have been fascinated by videos—as well they might be. For one thing, music videos reverse the customary relationship between sound and image. For another, they challenge the tyranny of the feature-length film. (I would rather watch a great five-minute video like Cyndi Lauper's "Girls Just Want to Have Fun" or Billy Idol's "Dancing by Myself" 15 times than sit, even once, through three-quarters of the movies that open in New York.) And, although most videos are panderingly puerile, when not monotonously parasitic—lifting from *Casablanca* and Cocteau alike—the form is basically non-narrative and theoretically open to anything.

If the marriage of television and rock 'n' roll was consummated with Elvis Presley's epochal appearance on *The Ed Sullivan Show,* the offspring was slow to arrive. Only gradually building momentum from the mid-'70s on, video promos didn't truly emerge as a cultural force until Warner Amex's MTV went on line in 1981. Within two years, however, rock videos rejuvenated the moribund record industry (fending off the threat of video games) and made the leap to network television. Since then, the oft-derided MTV aesthetic inexorably has invaded prime time (from *West 57th Street* to *Miami Vice*) and inspired several Hollywood blockbusters, as well as more than a few clinkers. Music video promos are now all but de rigueur for commercial movies.

While a number of rock video's more flamboyant directing talents, notably Russell Mulcahy and Steve Barron, have gone on to make commercial features, the traffic has been thicker the other way—Brian De Palma, Tobe Hooper, Bob Rafelson, Jonathan Demme, Allan Arkush, John Sayles, Paul Schrader, and John Landis having all made videos that can be compared usefully to their other work. But as hypnotic as the spectacle of MTV-inspired movies and TV shows may be, what's really interesting about rock videos isn't their impact on Hollywood feature-making; it's the videos themselves.

PERHAPS BECAUSE ITS blatant commercialism is one more affront to the utopian rock consciousness of the counterculture, rock video seems to have come in for more analysis from film critics than the rock intelligentsia. *Film Comment, Film Quarterly,* and *Jump Cut* all have published major pieces on the form; music videos have been featured at film festivals on three continents; and papers on individual videos are beginning to crop up at academic film conferences.

As yet, there's no consensus about what makes a good, let alone a great, music video. (USA For Africa's "We Are the World," for example, seemed destined to win MTV's Best Video award for reasons that have nothing to do with the quality of the direction, performances, or original material.) Nor is there yet a critical strategy by which the form can be politically redeemed.

Last year in *Film Quarterly,* Marsha Kinder pointed out that "everything on MTV is a commercial—advertising, news, station IDs, interviews, and, of course, the music video themselves." The videos are again characteristically postmodern in that, to paraphrase Jameson, they tend to reproduce and reinforce the logic of consumer capitalism. (Indeed, another Jameson account of the postmodern condition is a virtual description of MTV: "the transformation of reality into images, the fragmentation of time into a series of perpetual presents.") Still, the left has a sorry history of rejecting mass culture out of hand—like any popular entertainment, music videos express utopian yearnings all their own.

If MTV is the most fully realized example of one-dimensional culture we have, there should be a special place accorded the videos that either address this directly, e.g. Bowie's "Let's Dance" (dir: David Mallet, 1982), in which the video subverts the positivist "message" of the song or, alternately, those that hyperbolize their commercial nature, e.g. Madonna's "Material Girl," an MTV nominee for "Best Female Video." Similarly, "Dancing in the Dark," directed with sinister cool by Brian De Palma and nominated for two MTV awards including "Best Stage Performance," presents Bruce Springsteen as the sweatless Stakhanovite of rock 'n' roll, a heroic model worker whose infinitely repeatable—and here artfully synthetic—rite climaxes with the dramatic selection of a partner out of the front row.

The perversely radical realism of this approach seems preferable, for example, to Springsteen's subsequent video—the affirmatively patriotic beer commercial montage of "Born in the U.S.A." (dir: John Sayles, 1985). As for "Dancing with Myself" (dir: Tobe Hooper, 1983), Billy Idol dramatizes his blatant narcissism, romantic solipsism, desire to obliterate the world, and love-hate relation with his fans (visualized as implacable zombies who try to consume him) with such panache it's impossible not to get the joke. The song's title even mirrors the situation of the adolescent viewer.

As FAR AS art history goes, it's telling that the first 10 videos in the MOMA show (assembled by video curator Barbara London) all were produced in the form's pre-MTV stone age, and have been inducted into Michael Shore's Rock-Video Hall of Fame. Published late last year, Shore's indispensable *Rolling Stone Book of Rock Video* is, partly for lack of anything else, the standard work on the subject. (Shore combines at least a reading acquaintance with relevant film history, a fan's enthusiasm, and an insider's knowledge of the music industry.) Taking the Hall of Fame/MOMA 10 as a basis of sorts, it's possible to establish some genres and pose a few useful juxtapositions.

Advertisements for myself: "Penny Lane"/"Strawberry Fields Forever" versus "Lick My Decals Off, Baby." At their worst (which is not infrequent), music videos are tediously literal illustrations of banal songs, with a generic resemblance to television commercials. When not straight performance documentary, they attempt to reinforce product familiarity with shtick, be it narrative mini-melodrama or the worst clichés of a denatured pop surrealism. The product they sell, however, is far more ethereal than an automobile, a credit card, or a roll of bathroom tissue. Music videos are meta-showbiz; they're entertainment about entertainment in the same sense that photorealist paintings were images of images. Thinking about them, you have to wonder just what "entertainment" is. It's as though movie trailers developed into, first, a sort of free-associative meditation on the movies they promoted and then, things unto themselves.

Because music videos are even more steeped in the cult of personality than Hollywood movies, the easiest videos to theorize about are those in which the performing artist is also the auteur. (For the highbrow aesthete, this is something akin to recognizing what Lévi-Strauss felicitously termed "the thinking of savages.") Rightly or wrongly, the first rock stars to be taken seriously by intellectuals and middlebrow pundits were the Beatles. In this sense, they resemble Charlie Chaplin—the first movie icon perceived as an artist. Canonized as meaningful pop, the Beatles were thus the most visible members of the first wave of postmodernist rock, and it's fitting that both MOMA and Shore recognize them as pioneers of video.

If the films the Beatles made with Richard Lester remain among rock video's most enduring sources, the Beatles were the first to tap them—with their 1967 promos for "Penny Lane" and "Strawberry Fields Forever" and then, the following year, *Magical Mystery Tour*. Yet, nostalgic cult value aside, "Penny Lane" and "Strawberry Fields Forever" are relatively weak, all jolly self-indulgence and cute self-satisfaction. Bigger than Jesus, freer than any pop artists had been before (or have been since), the Beatles could do little more with their image than coat it with a treacly surrealism: Like we're not morons, we have inner lives too, y'know? (The "Penny Lane"/"Strawberry Fields" tendency to mimic surrealism rather than embody it reaches a grotesque apotheosis with Paul Simon's solemnly idiotic "René and Georgette Magritte with Their Dog After the War" [dir: Joan Logue, 1984], arguably the most abusively postmodern video in the MOMA retro.)

On the other hand, Captain Beefheart's elegant, enigmatic "Lick My Decals Off, Baby" (1970) is a primitive video that's still years ahead of MTV—a severely formal, as opposed to preeningly anecdotal, piece whose most percussive element is the grossly overamplified sound of a cigarette butt repeatedly flicked against a wall in tight close-up. Flaunting its disposable nature, this video actually *is* a commercial for Beefheart's album of the same name.

The moral of this is not just that anyone can be lousy, or that performance artists necessarily should take Beefheart's radical step and submerge themselves in anonymity. Rather, it's the recognition of the invention of a self as an artist's raw material and prime concern. A year before *Sergeant Pepper,* Harold Rosenberg looked at the ascendance of Warhol, Lichtenstein, Oldenberg et al. and saw the future: "Painting"—read art—"is no longer a haven for self-defeating contemplatives, but a glamorous arena in which performers of talent may rival the celebrity of senators or TV stars."

Less is more (but not always): "Bohemian Rhapsody" versus "Land of 1000 Dances" and "Secret Agent Man"; "Frankie Teardrop" versus "Two Triple Cheese, Side Order of Fries." According to Shore, Queen's "Bohemian Rhapsody" (dir. Bruce Gowers, 1975) is not simply the first example of a video "primarily responsible for making a song a hit" but the major anticipation of rock video's prime strategy—the use of showboat special effects to "enhance an already bombastic performance." But whether or not "Bohemian Rhapsody" is the source for the video love of visual sturm und drang, its elaborate lap dissolves and prismatic mock opera pale before the sinister shenanigans of a garage tape like "Land of 1000 Dances" (dir. the Residents, 1975) and, to a lesser degree, Devo's uneven "Secret Agent Man" (dir. Chuck Statler, 1976).

As the title suggests, "Land of 1000 Dances" is far less pretentious than "Bohemian Rhapsody" (as well as far more bohemian). Dressed like derelict Kluxers in hoods fashioned from old newspapers, the Residents jump spastically up and down, banging drums and chanting the words to the mid-'60s hit (originally sung by Cannibal and the Headhunters) in what sounds like second-generation pidgin English, until, amid much doodling discord, a tinfoil Metalunan appears and shoots them down. The scene then dissolves to a candle-lit stage on which skulls, shopping carts, guitar-swaddled TVs, and outsized steaks cavort under the sign of the swastika (and ultimately a cutout of Adolf Hitler), the accompaniment to this bizarre coda shifting from "Telstar" to sour surf music to "Bongo Rock." The entire spectacle resembles a collaboration between Kenneth Anger and David Lynch; the whiff of sulfur and sense of public performance transmuted into a private rite carries over into the band's "One-Minute Movies" (dir: Graeme Whifler, 1980), also at MOMA, a video that in its compact creepiness could give lessons to Robert Wilson.

Less underground than the Residents, less sentimental than the Beatles, more ironic than weird, Devo may have been the first group to revel in the unity of music, image, and marketing. (Shore quotes the band's "head conceptualizer," Gerald Casale: "To us, it was a very quaint, obsolete, holdover-Sixties-utopian idea to keep the music and the marketing separate. This is the music business, and its business is music. You can't separate the two. . . .") In its way "Secret Agent Man" is a more brutal cultural appropriation than "Land of 1000 Dances." Taking another mid-'60s AM radio artifact, namely Johnny Rivers's trashy ode to James Bond et al., Devo turns it into a toneless dirge that dwells on the relationship between pop, labor, and alienated leisure with an obsessiveness that would do Herbert Marcuse proud (while putting rock's official working-class heroes to shame).

The Residents and Devo are obviously highly self-conscious, if not deliberately marginal, acts. On the other hand, in postmodernism's brave new world, aesthetic savvy, artistic pretensions, and avant-garde credentials don't in themselves insure a good video. Super-8 transferred to video, Alan Vega and Suicide's 10-minute-plus "Frankie Teardrop" (dir. Paul Dougherty and Walter Robinson, 1978), a sort of prismatic *Why Does Herr R Run Amok?*, is a dreary, if authentic, underground film—even financed by an NEA grant. But Commander Cody's equally primitive "Two Triple Cheese, Side Order of Fries" (dir. Joe Dea, 1979) is actually a more direct intervention into the seamless universe of MTV. In this aggressively tacky ode to bad taste, filled with threadbare special effects (flying burger saucers, dancing french fries), shameless clowning, and grossly messy imagery, the equation of junk music and junk food is so bluntly hypostatized it could turn Sid Vicious into a vegetarian Mozart freak.

Real men don't pastiche: "Rio" versus "Accidents Will Happen." Ex-Monkee Michael Nesmith's impossibly sappy "Rio" (dir: William Dear, 1977) is another early instance of a song sold by its video (at least in Europe and Australia; it flopped here). Its significance lies in its prescient use of Hollywood imagery and blatant nostalgia. Although succeeding videos would be more macho in their orientation, recycling noir and horror more often than Astaire and Rogers, "Rio" 's nonparodic pastiche anticipates the mode's major modus operandi.

The ultimate magpie form, rock videos are crammed with media allusions even more than the films of hard-core movie brats like Spielberg and Scorsese. Still, for all the Hollywood iconography they purvey, they're far closer (as cinema) to avant-garde films and animated cartoons than to commercial genres. That's one reason narrative-bound critics have a hard time dealing with them—and also why more avant-garde types find them anathema.

Writing in *Film Comment* in 1983, David Ehrenstein identified the music video's precursors: Scopitone jukebox movies, Busby Berkeley production numbers, the kicky stylistics of Richard Lester, and the avant-garde—"the final sedimental layer, the mother lode, the Ali Baba's cave of images and ideas plundered on so many occasions as to now resemble the aftermath of a department store sale in a Tashlin comedy. There's hardly a rock-vid made that doesn't owe something to either *Un Chien Andalou* or *Blood of a Poet*. . . . Kenneth Anger's *Scorpio Rising* and Bruce Conner's *A Movie* have likewise served as iceboxes raided at midnight by sensibilities far simpler than theirs."

Although there's an underlying elitism to Ehrenstein's position (it's okay for real artists like Conner or Anger to harness their sensibility to the pop energy of Ray Charles or The Crystals; it's degrading for pop to assimilate the discoveries of avant-garde), his bitterness is understandable. American avant-garde filmmakers have never received the recognition, either critical or financial, that other appropriated artists have taken as their just deserts. But Ehrenstein ignores the ambition inherent in certain music videos as well as their convergence with the avant-garde films of the '70s and '80s. Love it or hate it, Malcolm McLaren's rap-disco-spaghetti western compression of "Madame Butterfly" (1984) has an aesthetic bravado that surpasses any recent opera film this side of Syberberg's *Parsifal* (itself a sort of epic music video).

Keeping to the MOMA show, "Land of 1000 Dances," for example, is as inventive a film as any produced in post-1968 San Francisco—reminiscent of midnight hybrids like *Eraserhead* and *Forbidden Zone,* movies that have never gotten their aesthetic due. If Accept's "Midnight Mover" (dir: Zbigniew Rybczynski, 1985) uses a post-Michael Snow kineticism to satirize heavy metal pretensions, and the slick stuttering abstraction of Fishbone's "? (Modern Industry)" (dir: David Hogan, 1985) has the brash, objectlike quality of a Paul Sharits flicker, a video like Yello's "Pinball Cha-Cha" (dir. Dieter Meier, 1982) is actually less derivative of than complementary to the work of Manuel DeLanda or Tony Oursler. Talking Heads's "Road to Nowhere" (dir. David Byrne, 1985) is an attempt to extend, rather than simply emulate, the earlier avant-garde. Despite bouts of corniness (due in part to a plethora of ideas), the video's crazed last minute is sensational. "Sensoria" (dir: Peter Care, 1985), by a group whose very name—Cabaret Voltaire (after the original Dada wateringhole)—signals their artistic ambition, has a crude cinematic power that teaches you to appreciate it in the best avant-garde tradition. Another English video, "Total State Machine" (dir: Test Department, 1985), is equally uncompromising and compares most favorably to English avant-garde film production.

The fact is, a few music videos have connected intelligently with avant-garde movies almost from the beginning. Indeed, the level of video animation exceeds virtually everything else currently being done. Smooth and snappy, "Accidents Will Happen" (dir: Annabel Jankel and Rocky Morton, 1978) literalizes Elvis Costello's song, as a fragmented, venetian-blind rotoscope of the singer alternates with diagrammatically represented, mockingly high-tech mishaps ranging from household spills to the state of California taking a bath. The piece is as fast on the eye as it is eclectic; Jankel and Morton steal from the best (mainly Robert Breer), their graphics anticipate the style of *RAW* magazine, and their flickering images are rhythmically far ahead of the music. As a promo, "Accidents" makes Costello seem rather plodding; as animation, however, it's a virtuoso labor of love. The paradox is, it fails as video; it's actually stronger when shown silent—complicating the notion of performers, rather than directors, as music video auteurs.

THE MOMA SHOW is pointedly subtitled "the industry and its fringes," and, the presence of the Beatles, David Bowie, and Michael Jackson notwithstanding, its emphasis is less on the industry than on the margin. This is as it should be, but it presents a skewed image of music videos as a medium: Art aside, the two most prevalent genres are the mini-movie and the performance documentary. And, with the exception of Jackson's compelling "Beat It" (dir: Bob Giraldi, 1983)—

a rousing paean to the power of show biz, as well as the '80s equivalent of Frank Sinatra's socially responsible "The House I Live In"—and Thomas Dolby's ambitious "Field Work" (dir: Thomas Dolby, 1985), a quasi–*Taxi Driver* with Ryuichi Sakamoto playing an embittered Japanese war veteran, the MOMA show deemphasizes narrative. (Completely absent is the English director Julien Temple, whose 1983 "Come Dancing" and "Undercover"—with the Kinks and Rolling Stones, respectively—are models of dramatic compression and dream-like layering.)

Curator London is further inclined to demonstrate music video's affinities with video art rather than with film. For all the name directors who have made videos, MOMA's movie auteurs are both underground: Beth B and Andy Warhol, neither of whom is shown to spectacular advantage. (B's cheerfully kinky "The Dominatrix Sleeps Tonight" [1984] is a pale reflection of her super-8 *Black Box* while Warhol's "Hello Again," made for the Cars, is basically a factory second—not even as kicky as the Cars's "You Might Think" [dir: Jeff Stein, Alex Weil, and Charlie Levi, 1984], which MTV viewers voted their favorite video.) The MOMA show acknowledges many of the most talented video-makers but here, as much as on MTV, the strongest auteurs are the performance-artists: Laurie Anderson, Toni Basil, David Bowie, David Byrne.

From the mega-pop realm of Michael Jackson, Madonna, and Bruce Springsteen, moving (toward the front line of aesthetic self-consciousness) through the artier domains of Bowie, Byrne, and Anderson, to the far side of clubland where, for example, Michael Smith has just completed a mock video, "Go for It, Mike," the most interesting current rock stars are primarily the authors of their own image. In this sense, Bowie, particularly, is a prophetic figure.

Clearly, music video has induced the convergence of pop and performance art, crystallizing the element of psychodrama that always has been latent in rock 'n' roll. The fascination Michael Jackson exerts has as much to do with his self-presentation as show biz messiah, misunderstood elf, and werewolf-in-disguise as with his dancing, while Madonna and Cyndi Lauper are closer to Yvonne Rainer than to Little Eva. (Lauper's "Girls Just Want to Have Fun" [dir: Ken Walz, 1983] can be construed as an answer song—to Sigmund Freud, no less. "There is so much pathos and desire secreted in this piece of squeaky blippy frou-frou sexism that it calls for a redefinition of the word 'fun,' if not 'girls,' if not 'just,'" Greil Marcus observed—and he wasn't even referring to the astonishing display of anarchic energy, neither sexually nor socially sublimated, that Lauper packs into the video.)

MTV's "Best Video" category offered a further amplification of the pop star as performance artist. Besides "We Are the World," the nominees were Don Henley's "The Boys of Summer" (dir: Jean Baptiste Mondino), Tom Petty's "Don't Come Around Here No More" (dir: Jeff Stein) and—cornering the market in manic self-presentation—the two David Lee Roth items, "California Girls" and "Just a Gigolo." Although fitfully interesting as a performance doc, "We Are the World" is basically an exceptional case of humanitarian glitz (the music video version of the Jerry Lewis telethon); the Henley is the essence of high-tech balderdash, interchangeably a designer jeans commercial or a dream sequence out of *Miami Vice*; and the Petty is a prime example of what video would have looked like had there been MTV in 1967.

Roth alone seems to have grasped the nature of the medium: His exhibitionist posturing, hilariously smarmy in "California Girls," shamelessly hammy in "Just a Gigolo," redeems and deepens an otherwise undistinguished vocal performance. "Just a Gigolo"—a reflexive pastiche in which Roth invades noted videos by Lauper, Idol, Jackson and others; less deliberately postmodern than post-Woody Allen—owes more to Louis Prima and the Three Stooges and thus television, than to rock'n'roll as we know it.

The ability to construct, project, and market a persona has become the sine qua non of '80s pop as well as '80s politics. Only the most fanatical Springsteen purists would insist that it was not his capitulation to music video that sent his career into the stratosphere. Who knows? MTV may well supplant Hollywood as the new spawning ground of the stars—or worse.

Ghosts

Originally published as "Static Electricity" in *The Village Voice* (October 22, 1985).

THE CHANCE COLLISIONS and harsh molecular energy of the urban street have been Ernie Gehr's most consistent source of inspiration: films from his early *Reverberations* and *Still* through *Eureka* and *Shift* to the recent *Untitled* (1981) are all, in their ways, city symphonies—symphonies, that is, as they might have been conceived by as austere a composer as Webern or Berg. So too is Gehr's latest, *Signal—Germany on the Air,* which has its world premiere Saturday at Millennium. A 40-minute suite of "empty" compositions and puzzling pans, set mainly in a summery, but otherwise nondescript, urban intersection, *Signal* is deliberately anti-dramatic. As Walter Benjamin wrote approvingly of Atget, Gehr's landscapes "lack atmosphere."

Like Atget as well, Gehr could be said to photograph the street as though it were the scene of a crime. *Signal* marks the filmmaker's return to Berlin, the city from which his parents were driven in 1939. In this sense, as minimal as it may seem, *Signal* is a film about culture shock, about coping, about memory, about evidence, about the things that remain. (This latter notion is reinforced by the ebb and flow of pedestrian traffic past various clocks, lampposts, and fireplugs.) History as such first intrudes with Gehr's sudden shift to what appears to be a derelict factory on a barren lot. An unkempt multilingual sign identifies the building as the former Gestapo headquarters. Although this and the railroad lines Gehr also films may seem overemphatic in the wake of *Shoah* (with which *Signal* shares an underlying method—the discovery of the past in the present—as well as a motif), these cutaways serve to underscore the anti-atmospheric crosswalks with a backbeat of menace.

Gehr's best-known films, the ones that established his reputation in the late '60s and early '70s, are famous for their rigorous deployment of one or two formal devices. His recent work, though, has been less overtly systematic, and it's difficult on a single viewing to grasp *Signal*'s infrastructure. This is not just the most autobiographical, but also the least determined of Gehr's movies. (He's called it "almost a diary film.") Indeed, the casual intersection where most of *Signal* is filmed is like a metaphor for the movie as a whole. Some connections are made from shot to shot; more often, though, Gehr seems to be concentrating on the relationship between image and sound.

Signal is Gehr's longest sound film since *Still* and perhaps his most complex ever. The track is composed of chunks of ambient, asynchronous street noise; silence; and excerpts from the radio—which, in Berlin, broadcasts in French, English, and Russian, as well as German. Even more disturbing than the shots of Gestapo headquarters or the Berlin freight yards is a radio English lesson which teaches the phrases "You people are all the same," "Don't blame me," and "What are you accusing me of?" (As a kind of answering apocalypse, Gehr concludes the film with a thunderstorm concocted out of audio effects and end flashes.)

Ultimately, *Signal* is not just about how subtly sound transforms image; it's a movie about ghosts and unseen forces. Gehr has always been fascinated with film as an archeological trace ("a photo-memory of persons/objects in a cinematic force-field," as an early statement put it). In *Still* and *Eureka*, he literalized the past by re-presenting his landscape—through superimposition or re-photography—as the arena of present and absent energies. Here, the radio serves to make the invisible world concrete. As the signal shifts from station to station, the unfocused static deforms the placid bustle of the street.

The radio waves could be the breeze stirring the trees. The pedestrians swim and bob among these visceral transmissions; the total image seems suddenly so ethereal that the film's title, taken from a 1940s pulp magazine, becomes fact. Is the sound emanating from the phone booths or contained inside people's heads? As usual Gehr uses the simplest possible means to effect a subtle derangement in perception. *Signal—Germany on the Air* is a substantial addition to an oeuvre which is already among the most impressive in American film.

The purple rose of Soho

Originally published in *The Village Voice* (April 8, 1986).

PERHAPS BECAUSE IT takes her so long to fund and complete a movie, Yvonne Rainer tends to cram everything she knows into each one. *The Man Who Envied Women* is Rainer's first film in five years, and this bold, dense, and quirky rumination on love in lower Manhattan is the fitting climax to her Whitney retrospective. A bit long and occasionally repetitive, it's also startlingly frank. Rainer came to film from dance, and, in a sense, each of her works is a performance, juggling everything from the film's low budget and her performers' personae to, in this case, her own merciless ambivalence concerning sex, film theory, and artists' housing.

More than any other American filmmaker, Rainer has positioned herself at the intersection of the personal and the political. "It was a hard week," begins the film's unseen narrator who, like the film's maker, is a 50-year-old woman artist. "I split up with my husband and moved into my studio. The hot-water heater broke and flooded the textile merchant downstairs, I bloodied my white linen pants, the Senate voted for nerve gas, and my gynecologist went down in Korean Airlines 007. The worst of it was the gynecologist. He was a nice man. He used to put booties on the stirrups, and his speculum was always warm." Here is the characteristic Rainer movement—the deadpan montage of unlikely elements, the escalating crises, the brutally slapstick leap from the private to the public, unexpectedly cinched with a dancer's emphasis on pure physicality.

Its very title a sphinxlike provocation, *The Man Who Envied Women* is a sometimes confessional, often jokey stream of consciousness that alternates between the first and third persons, incorporating texts by Frederic Jameson and Raymond Chandler as well as chunks of urbane cocktail party chatter. No less than the dutifully overrated *Hannah and Her Sisters*, this is the war of the sexes in the realm of the sensitive: The streets of Rainer's Manhattan buzz with witty oneliners; her characters devote themselves to puzzling out the nuances of French poststructural theory. In one of the film's set pieces, two intellectuals get so tangled up in a discussion of Foucaultian power relations their mutual seduction almost never comes to pass.

Despite some discrete incidents, however, *The Man Who Envied Women* is less a narrative than it is a field in which, to go no further than the precredit sequence, elements as disparate as *Un Chien Andalou* and Bette Davis, Penguin Cafe Orchestra and KAL 007, City Council hearings and psychoanalysis are rubbed against each other in the hope of drawing sparks. A model for Rainer's associative, multilayered procedure can be found in the series of pictures her heroine has tacked up on her wall—the cover and two pages from *The New York Times Magazine*, a Central American atrocity photo, and an ad for estrogen supplements from a medical magazine. At irregular intervals throughout the two-hour movie, these images will be subject to all manner of political, semiotic, and psychosexual analysis, their relationship shifting as the layers of meaning accumulate.

In Rainer's films, sound and image, as well as men and women, nearly always operate at cross-purposes. When the protagonist's husband tries to rearrange the pictures, he only succeeds in making a visual muddle. (His typical appearance is a monologue delivered in front of the silent projection of some '40s melodrama.) Although the heroine of *The Man Who Envied Women* is often heard (her voice is that of dancer Trisha Brown), she's never seen, while two actors (Bill Raymond and Larry Loonin) play her estranged husband, Jack. With this strategy, Rainer not only reverses the premise of Buñuel's *That*

Obscure Object of Desire, in which a pair of actresses impersonated the eponymous object, she also literalizes the axiom of advanced feminist film theory that, in mainstream narrative cinema, woman is the object of the implicitly male gaze. If this is so, the existence of an unseen female subject overthrows the patriarchal tyranny merely by locating its organizing principle beyond the scope of the controlling gaze.

Rainer, however, is less programmatic than experimental. It's a truism that she's the avant-garde's most important woman filmmaker since Maya Deren (herself a former dancer); more likely, she's the most influential American avant-garde filmmaker of the past dozen years, with an impact as evident in London or Berlin as in New York. As a filmmaker, Rainer suggests Godard without his lyricism—or his glibness. At times, her stolid cinema of ideas resembles that of the West German director Alexander Kluge. There's a similar visual awkwardness—a mistrust of the appealing image coupled with an avoidance of the trashy one. The excitement in Rainer's films derives from shifts in tone and the genuine clash of ideas.

Her first two features, *Lives of Performers* (1972) and *Film About a Woman Who . . .* (1974), appeared amid a flurry of related quasi-narratives in which the women filmmakers served as their own protagonists, dramatizing issues of sexual and personal identity. Both method and theme link these films—which include Jackie Raynal's *Deux Fois* (1971) and Chantal Akerman's *je tu il elle* (1974)—to the psychodrama, the original genre of the American avant-garde, developed in the early '40s by Maya Deren and sustained for another dozen years by Kenneth Anger, Gregory Markopoulos, and Stan Brakhage. But, more influenced by Jean-Luc Godard than Jean Cocteau, the new feminist psychodrama has been cool, ironic, and behavioral—as opposed to the romantic, symbolist, Jungian psychodrama of the 1940s and '50s—developing in the context of a larger concern with the image of "woman" and the construction of sexual identity. (Not simply the concern of arcane film theory, the questions of what a "woman" looks like or how a "woman" is seen dominate the work of pop theoreticians as different in their audiences as Cindy Sherman and Cyndi Lauper.)

Rainer's films continue to suggest psychodramas even though, in *The Man Who Envied Women* as in her previous film, *Journeys from Berlin/1971,* her actual presence is limited. (Once a ham, always a ham, however. After leaving Jack an atonal singing message on his answering machine, Rainer abruptly pops into the frame and, addressing the audience—or, more specifically, the premenopausal women in the audience—gives herself the film's best line.) Still, as with Brakhage, albeit to far different effect, the protagonist of Rainer's psychodramas has become less the performer before the camera than the consciousness behind it.

That Rainer's work engages that of Godard and Brakhage, arguably the two most powerfully original filmmakers of the past 30 years, is another measure of her centrality. But addicted as she is to the life of her times, it seems perverse to segregate Rainer in an avant-garde ghetto. The relationship of psychodrama to the films of actor-auteurs like Charlie Chaplin or Barbara Streisand is a fallow field for academics. Nevertheless, it's apparent that, mutatis mutandis, Rainer has many points of contact with her fellow toiler in the vineyards of urban sophistication, Woody Allen.

Born a year apart, Rainer and Allen began the '60s as Greenwich Village performance artists before switching to film. Teenagers of the '40s, they've proved susceptible to Hollywood for both role models and guilty pleasures, however restrained by a stern reverence for the European art film. (That Rainer's models are Resnais and Godard and Allen's Fellini and Bergman could be conceived as the difference, circa 1963, between the Judson Dance Theater and the Bitter End.) Both are identified with specific out-groups; both use the incongruous juxtaposition of the great and the small as the basis for humor.

Like Allen, Rainer specializes in "grownup" movies. (*The Man Who Envied Women* is a sort of adult meditation on the infantile fantasy embodied in *An Unmarried Woman*.) Like Rainer, Allen has an intermittent interest in film as film. (The hilarious *What's Up, Tiger Lily,* made in 1966, actually prefigures the poststructuralist avant-garde in its use of language to undermine the authority of the image.) Both Rainer and Allen share a fascination with intimate relationships, a taste for overarticulate characters, a love of the urban milieu. Soap opera, psychoanalysis, and sendup are the touchstones of their art—which may have something to do with their shared inability to come up with a satisfying ending.

Rainer, however, is less sentimental than Allen, particularly in regard to what her heroine calls "the planned obsolescence of social relations." If the lengthy scene in which Jack lectures on Foucault (and incidentally much of the theory that underscores the film) seems destined for the dubious notoriety once accorded the interminable rehearsal sequence in Godard's *One Plus One,* Jack's smug soliloquies on his sexual code of ethics should have women viewers screaming and men wincing. "I'm not an average man, there's nothing predatory about me," he begins. "I've never seduced a virgin or intruded on a valid marriage."

The philandering Jack may be a theoretical feminist (the best excuse he offers his wife is that he's "a mass of contradictions—and what else could one expect under capitalism?"), but Rainer is always capable of bringing things down to earth. At one point, she follows the reading of a letter to Dear Abby in which "Available" complains about her boyfriend buying *Playboy* with a blunter formulation of her own: "Dear Abby, Is it bad manners or downright hostile if a guy jerks off in your bed?"

Rainer is also far more of a naturalist than Allen when it comes to casing the environment. Like his identification with the trendy, rich, and glamorous, Woody's proprietary love for New York (most evident in the sequence where *Hannah* shows off his favorite buildings) has inured him to the city's deterioration. Where *Hannah* trots through Manhattan like a blinkered cab horse, *The Man* schleps along on foot, documenting the evidence of decline. Allen's postgentrified Soho—with Max von Sydow angsting out in a sumptuous loft—is quite different than Rainer's workaday neighborhood; among other things, she exposes the flip side of the Allen persona by including, in her City Council hearing section, a remarkable sequence of art mogul Ivan Karp self-righteously oinking about the priorities of world culture to justify the cruelties of the Manhattan real estate market.

Still, Rainer is not wholly innocent here. Despite her more complicated politics, she shares Allen's nervous habit of salting the work with weighty (if street-smart) cultural references. *The Man Who Envied Women* invokes *Wavelength, The Mother and the Whore,* and Don Judd—not to mention "Foucault" and "Lacan"—in much the same spirit as *Hannah* includes nods to "Caravaggio," "Loos," "e.e. cummings," "Bach," and "Tolstoy."

If Rainer makes more of an attempt to integrate cultural discourse into her work, it's also true that, like Allen's, her films tend to flatter the audience as part of the cognoscenti. *The Man Who Envied Women* questions patriarchal power and masculine authority. Or does it? Throughout the film, Jack keeps citing Foucault. Does this make Jack an authority or Rainer? It's an open question: Rainer's very first film includes the admission, "I have always had a weakness for the sweeping revelations of great men." In this case, she might take a lesson from Mia Farrow in *The Purple Rose of Cairo*: "I've met the most wonderful man. Of course, he's fictional—but you can't have everything."

"He-e-ere's Jean-ee": TV à la Godard

Originally published in *The Village Voice* (April 22, 1986).

ANYONE OTHER THAN Jean-Luc Godard might be satisfied simply being the single most influential figure in film post-1960, pre-Steven Spielberg. But Godard, as always, is after bigger game—amazing stories broadcast to your home.

Godard was speaking wistfully of TV as early as 1968, but video technologies have seriously infiltrated his work (and vice versa) only since he teamed up with Anne-Marie Miéville. The pair's prescient *Numéro Deux* (1975) was shot mainly on videotape, set entirely inside a video editing studio, and played out almost exclusively on two TV monitors. The film even took a sitcom theme—namely the effect of late capitalism on the sex lives of a working-class family, but, unlike *The Honeymooners,* it's barely been recognized here as the masterpiece it is.

Godard spent the latter half of the '70s trying to crack French TV. Now, years after their original telecast, *Six Times Two/On and Beneath Communication* and *France/Tour/Detour/Two/Children,* received their New York premieres, along with *Scénario du Film Passion* and *Soft and Hard,* the more recent TV specials made for Britain's Channel Four. Showing these programs as projected video in a movie theater has the effect of turning extremely radical TV into marginalized movies. Still, in some ways, Godard's work is all one piece. Made between *Numéro Deux* and his 1980 "comeback" *Every Man For Himself*, *Six Times Two* and *France/Tour* at once elaborate *Numéro Deux*'s juxtaposition of factory and landscape and anticipate the opposition of work and love explored in *Passion*. *France/Tour* uses the analytic slo-mo that gave *Every Man For Himself* its original English title (*Slow Motion*), while the inspiration for *Hail Mary* might be found in *Six Times Two*'s interview with a schizophrenic woman who speculates on impregnation by the Holy Ghost.

Conversation is one of television's most durable spectacles, and, in a sense, both series are variations of TV interview shows. Of course, the assortment of interviewees (including children and schizos, unemployed laborers and working women, a mathematician and an amateur filmmaker, as well as various communications professionals) is no less purposefully eccentric than the usually off-camera interviewer, Jean-Luc Godard. Godard may be an insufferable know-it-all, but—his mind bursting with ideas and associations—he can be a brilliantly dogged questioner. No one is better at making the ordinary seem unfamiliar; Godard interrogates his subjects as though he's just arrived from Ork. As Gilles Deleuze noted in an enthusiastic critique of *Six Times Two*: "Generally speaking, you can only be a foreigner in a language other than your own. Here's a case of being a foreigner in one's own language . . . [Godard] has even perfected his Swiss accent for this purpose."

At once modest and self-aggrandizing, Godard simply called *Six Times Two* "an attempt at doing television differently." *Vive la différence*. Not since Ernie Kovacs has anyone made so madcap a try. Weighty it may be, but TV à la Godard defies the *Masterpiece Theater* treatment. (I would subscribe to Channel 13 simply for the pleasure of watching Alistair Cook peer earnestly out from his armchair and attempt to make Godard intelligible: "In the last episode, a pair of invisible cafe philosophers discussed problems of signification while Godard doodled expressively over the image. This week Godard himself is interviewed—his back strategically to the camera. . . .")

Watching this blitz of explicated advertisements, outré interviews, reflexive woolgathering, and electronic puns-and-anagrams, it's difficult to believe that, even in the land of Jacques Lacan and *Apostrophe*, anything so fascinatingly weird and blatantly demanding was ever telecast (however grudgingly) into anyone's living room.

Basically, *Six Times Two* sets out to explore the political economy of the media image. Like any self-respecting TV show, it adheres to a strict formula. The six programs are each divided into two 50-minute segments—the first elaborating a field of inquiry (work, women, history) and intended to be shown during the day, the second, an interview meant to be telecast that night. In the episode "Photography and Company," Godard focuses on the nature of professionalism while the corresponding interview, named "Marcel" for its subject, is with an amateur filmmaker. Who, Godard asks, is paid to take a picture? Who is paid to have their picture taken and who is not—why Christie Brinkley and not a napalm-burned Vietnamese peasant girl? At one point, a prize-winning news-photo of a barbaric military execution monopolizes the screen for 20 minutes while the photographer discusses the technical difficulties he encountered in producing this particular and, as it turns out, staged image of violent death. To underscore the philosophy of photo opportunity (or opportunism), the following segment has French Communist Party leader Georges Marchais denouncing television for the TV cameras.

Godard's position is radical, but it's not naive. As Frederic Jameson once observed at an academic conference devoted to "rethinking" TV, "Abolishing television as we know it would involve the abolition of the middle-class family as well." In "Before and After"—the first part of the final show, a critique of the entire series and the response it inspired, interspersed with segments from "real" TV—Godard suggests that, unlike the movies, television is watched *en famille*: "Television is a family business." The program ends with a speculation on the relation between adults and children, precisely the subject of *France/Tour/Detour/Two/Children*.

These 12 half-hour programs—the series title a play on that of a popular 19th century French primer—were completed in 1978. Although Godard wanted them to be shown in prime time over a two-week period, they weren't telecast until more than a year later and then, three programs at a time, in the late Friday night spot traditionally reserved for the films of great auteurs. Superficially closer to conventional television than *Six Times Two*, each episode of *France/Tour* follows an interview with either 11-year-old Camille or nine-year-old Arnaud (almost always shown in tight close-up) with instant analyses by two ostentatiously telegenic stand-ins for Godard and Miéville.

Unlike the old Art Linkletter show, on which kids were encouraged to say the darndest things, here it's the interlocutor whose unexpectedly clever, if not downright wacky, sayings inspire yocks, admiration, and embarrassment. Godard's wildly inappropriate questions are alternately metaphysical or leading: "How do you know you exist?" he wants to know. "Instead of your going to school, couldn't we say the school goes to you?" A long discussion about music and choice grinds to a halt when Godard asks Camille if, assuming such a thing were available, she would purchase a recording of God's voice. The verbal realm belongs to Godard, while the children's eloquence is entirely negative: They're stolidly self-conscious, admirably resistant, painfully stunted, desperately rational, and totally humorless, responding with single-word answers and an occasional "I don't know."

That Camille and Arnaud are interviewed at bedtime, before school, in school, watching television—engaged, that is, by the very institutions that "construct" them as children—supports Godard's continual equation of their state with that of prisoners or proletarians. In one episode, we see, over Camille's shoulder, children frisking in a schoolyard. Are they free or in prison? Godard asks. "Neither," Camille replies, although her continual, nervous glances toward her classmates leave no doubt that their imprisonment is preferable to hers. Later, Camille's classroom activities are not simply linked to class struggle;

Godard manages to inveigle out of her the complaint that it's unfair not to pay children to learn. (In another show, the more garrulous Arnaud is maneuvered into revealing that he's been bribed with a bicycle to submit to these interviews.)

Godard puts the children's recalcitrance in the context of a thoroughly alienated environment. Throughout, adults are referred to as "monsters," and each show begins with some invocation of their monstrous behavior. "It now appears that the monsters need oxygen and money," the Orkian Godard observes deadpan over sumptuously glacial footage of commuters exiting the subway. Elsewhere Godard and Miéville use slow-motion sequences of women working behind a restaurant counter to equate their bodies with machines. (The same point is made even more graphically in an office in which a very pregnant, stark naked secretary cheerfully takes dictation.)

Perhaps the most affectingly alienated sequence is the 11th program, subtitled *All,* whose centerpiece is a 10-minute static close-up of Camille at the dinner table, eating and grimacing while adult conversation swirls over her head. As Colin MacCabe observed in *American Film,* "In the heart of the family, the young girl inhabits an immense solitude." That this solitude may be the theme of the series is underscored by the last show's final sequence: a lengthy portrait set to a bombastic pop ballad in which a lonely middle-aged man in a toupee visits his gaudy neighborhood bar to drink "one for the road."

Although *France/Tour* failed to establish Godard as the French Norman Lear, he has since made two films for Britain's independent Channel Four. The first, *Scénario du Film Passion,* is Godard's version of a Disney documentary-cum-trailer like *The Making of 20,000 Leagues Under the Sea*—it even opens à la *Disneyland,* with Uncle Jean addressing the viewing audience: "Good evening to friend and foe." Like *Passion* itself, *Scénario* is filled with speculations about the cinema. Its most emphatic point is Godard's return to the image after his talk-heavy films of the '70s. Unlike TV newsreaders, whom he suggests are buggered by the images behind them, Godard covers his ass by taping himself looking at his film or else the white screen where it intermittently appears. *Scénario* is more ethereal than *Passion,* and also more sentimental (Godard kisses the image of Isabelle Huppert when it appears, speaks of turning a camera movement into a prayer, and offers an incantation to the empty screen.)

The more ambitious *Soft and Hard (A Soft Conversation on Hard Subjects)* blandly describes itself as a "talk between two friends," namely Godard and Miéville. The first half of this dialogue is mainly visual, counterpointing images of the couple working around the house. The division of labor is pronounced: Godard talks to his producers on the phone, while the chic and self-possessed Miéville threads something on the Steenbeck. Then she does the ironing, while he grabs a tennis racket and makes like John McEnroe. In the second half of the tape, Godard and Miéville discuss television and their work. But the subtext of the conversation is their relationship; in this sense, *Soft and Hard* is far more revealing than *First Name: Carmen* or *Hail Mary,* to cite two recent Godardian ruminations on the war between the sexes. In addressing their ostensible subject, Miéville starts out direct and pithy. Godard comes back aphoristic and vague. He waxes depressed. She cheers him up. "When you make a film it doesn't go unnoticed." "Yes," he agrees, "but for the wrong reasons."

Like Jean-Pierre Gorin before her, Miéville seems to function as Godard's guilty conscience. ("You know, your program about women was a bit weak," she tells him in one of the segments of *Six Times Two*. "You set them up, you question them, you more or less tell them how to reply, and then you're surprised that you can't find anybody [there].") Here, she criticizes the dialogue in Godard's recent love scenes. In the midst of these comments, Godard upstages her by noisily brushing the crumbs off the arm of his chair. (Jean-Luc may have his back to the camera, but he surely knows as well as Miéville where the microphone is placed.) "A phantasmagoria of crumbs," he weakly jests after this deafening interruption. Obviously thrown off balance, Miéville begins to express her insecurity. "You never doubt that what you have to say is interesting," she tells Godard—and the statement has less to do with his individual (and undeniable) genius than with her wistful recognition of his male entitlement. Later, Miéville comes back to this in a different way, explaining that she's hampered in her work by an undue respect for cinema. "How can you, knowing me, still think like that?" Godard asks in genuine surprise.

By the time Godard starts castigating TV as the "usurper" that has displaced the movies, you get the odd sense of a man playing George to his own Gracie. Cinema, he complains, is "the only means I have to understand and change myself." In television, however, he's found a superb means to dramatize his condition—and ours. If *The Jean-Luc and Anne-Marie Show* ever went weekly it could be the most amazing story of all.

Pagan rhapsodies

Originally published in *The Village Voice* (May 20, 1986).

THE BEST THING about Robert Gardner's *Forest of Bliss* is that it drops you off on the banks of the Ganges, skips the lecture, boosts the sound, and simply lets India (or rather, an "India") wash over you. There are no subtitles on *this* reality—it recognizes itself as an ethnographic fiction. Where once anthropology defined the Other, now it can only position that Other in relation to its own dubious self.

Gardner calls his Benares city-symphony "a 90-minute expansion on a split second of the panic dread I felt on first turning an unfamiliar corner onto the Great Cremation Ground and finding my way blocked by 'IT'"—IT being Death, which is Benares's lifeblood. This may be the oldest continually inhabited settlement in the world—it's been here for some 3000 years. Orthodox Hindus believe that to die in Benares is to attain *moksha*, release from the endless cycle of birth and rebirth; the decaying streets are clogged with funeral procession, and the air is acrid with smoke from pyres.

Dwelling on the senseless profusion of being in this gaudy theater of death, *Forest of Bliss* juxtaposes enigmatic rites of purification with quotidian filth. People bathe in the same muddy brown river where bodies and blossoms float. Cows saunter by sniffing at corposes and grazing on their garlands. Children's kites share the skies with baleful vultures. Less an ethnographer than an aesthete, Gardner is best known for *Dead Birds* (1963), a classic investigation of tribal warfare in the highlands of New Guinea. There, he went so far as to comment on the inner lives of his subjects. Since then, his films have become more purely experimental; what you see is what you get.

Two of Gardner's fiercely lyrical shorter films are *Sons of Shiva* (1984) and *Deep Hearts* (1978). The former depicts an elaborate, three-day ritual that effaces all caste distinctions among Bengali Shiva-worshippers in a blue haze of hash smoke and a blur of ecstatic dancing. As filmmaking, it's frankly sensational. Not only does Gardner revel in India's indigenously fauvist color schemes, but this archetypal hippie fantasy is presented in delirious slow motion.

No less unabashedly sybaritic, *Deep Hearts* documents the annual convention cum beauty contest held by the Bororo herdsmen of the upper Niger. Given this rarefied bash, Gardner's taste for extreme angles, fragmentary close-ups, and spatial distortions has the effect of making his subjects seem even more exotic than they already are. The Bororo are a strikingly tall and fine-boned people, and the filmmaker's nearly constant use of a wide-angle lens further accentuates their elongated bodies—wearing plumed headgear and feathered armbands, they posture and preen like a flock of Giacometti peacocks. These "primitives" aren't presented as doomed noble savages à la Leni Riefenstahl's *Nuba*. It's just impossible to draw the line between Gardner's aestheticism and theirs.

Forest of Bliss doesn't have the sustained visionary energy of the shorter films—the material is too overwhelming. But it's an astonishing catalogue of images nonetheless: carrion-seeking dogs and flaming orange garlands (made from marigolds the color of funeral pyres), toothless healers and hawkers of sacred fire. For urbanists, nothing exceeds the clamorous spectacle of these mean streets, a visual cacophony of beggars, bicycles, scooters, cows, canny gray monkeys that scamper over scarred plaster building facades as freely as squirrels in Central Park. Although people peer at the camera from the edge of the frame, Gardner is equally fascinated by the surface of the pavement: the mud and shit, the cracked stones, broken crockery, dead dogs, and crushed garlands that lie unnoticed underfoot.

Although Gardner's work has been praised by the likes of Stan Brakhage and Peter Kubelka as well as Margaret Mead, he's never gotten his due as one of his generation's most gifted, problematic filmmakers—a late romantic having much in common with Brakhage, Bruce Baillie, and their epigones. Of course, Gardner is possibly the one independent filmmaker in America who needs neither audience nor patron. Founder and funder of Harvard's Film Study Center, he is the epitome of privilege. Globetrotting is his perquisite. What's drawn him to the deserts of Eritrea, the mountains of Colombia, and the gaping maw of India, he explains, was a "persuasive suspicion" that those lives he might encounter had "a meaning which my particular technical and mental equipment could profitably address." To what end, Gardner leaves for us to debate.

Gardner is at once the establishment Gauguin and the avant-garde Indiana Jones. *Forest of Bliss* opens with a quote from the *Upanishads* by way of W.B. Yeats: "Everything in the world is eater or eaten, the seed is food and the fire is eater." You don't have to wonder which Gardner is. He devours cultures with regal authority.

Like Gardner, Trinh T. Minh-ha has an academic base, albeit somewhat narrower (she's a lecturer at San Francisco State). Unlike Gardner, she's non-white, non-Western, and female (as well as an immigrant), which may account for her somewhat different point of view. Trinh doesn't simply confront the Other, she is one.

The 40-minute *Reassemblage*—smuggled into the 1983 New York Film Festival along with equally outré items by Andrei Tarkovsky, Chantal Akerman, Ericka Beckman, and Mani Kaul—is a blatantly subjective film in which Trinh observes herself observing a Senegalese village. *Naked Spaces: Living Is Round,* which was screened earlier this year at Artists Space and will be shown at the Museum of Modern Art, ventures even further into counter-cinema if not postmodern ethnography. In the credits, Trinh pointedly places the word "director" itself under Derridean erasure (x'd out but readable).

Naked Spaces surveys the integration of ritual and work, the home and the world, culture and nature, in the traditional villages of six West African countries (Senegal, Mauritania, Togo, Mali, Burkina Faso, and Benin). Over the course of its two-hour-plus running time, the film effortlessly attests to the rich variety of the region's indigenous architecture. Trinh documents adobe cities and stilt-set river towns, villages nestled in the rocks and settlements splayed out across the bush, turreted straw houses and domelike huts. Each dwelling has its own blend of environmental logic and irrational splendor—simultaneously, as Trinh puts it, "a tool, a sanctuary, and a work of art."

Fittingly, considering her subject matter, Trinh's images are as unpretentious as home movies—exhibiting the same gorgeous overexposures, casual jump cuts, and, at times, jarring incompletion. Just as some shots refuse to take possession of their subject, Trinh's narrative declines to generalize about the Other (nor does she present her film as a unified whole). Not only is her use of sound purposefully erratic, there are times in *Naked Spaces* when representation decomposes into isolated details and pure sensation. More than a mosaic of impressions, however, the film is nonlinear, decentered, and deliberately unsettling.

Like *Reassemblage, Naked Spaces* sets out to challenge and criticize—not to mention derange—the conventions of the ethnographic film. In this, Trinh's major device is a half-confessional, half-epistemological, start-and-stop voice-over. A trio of voices (all female, with three different accents) performs a litany based on the recirculation of key phrases: "color is life," "the dead are not dead," "the earth is an overturned calibash," "the earth is blue like an orange." (Most of these are African sayings, although the last, as you might guess, is from surrealist poet Paul Eluard.)

Gardner's imaginative recasting of his subjects exaggerates ethnography's repressed imperial past; Trinh's surrender of directorial mastery over hers accentuates the sexualized interplay between subjects and their environment. These African houses are not only models of the universe but metaphors for the lovemaking they shelter ("the house, like a woman, must have secret parts to inspire desire"). Thus courtyards, at once interior and exterior space, hidden and open, are her particular concern. *Naked Spaces* itself has their circular structure, ending as it began, with a Senegalese village dance. "Light, air, water, woman, palm leaves, dust, children," one of the narrators intones—summing up the elements of the film as well as the contents of the courtyard.

Naked Spaces has a lot to say about the poetics of space, the function of roundness, and the origins of music. The last word, however, belongs to the Africans. The film ends with a saying that ethnographers might keep as frontlids before their eyes: "When you bend down to examine someone's anus, someone is bending down, observing yours." Living won't be round, nor space naked, until the denizens of Benares are able to document Robert Gardner documenting them.

As the Third World turns

Originally published in *The Village Voice* (June 24, 1986).

R AUL RUIZ IS a born storyteller, with an admirable disdain for narrative. The films he makes, mainly for French TV, at the astonishing rate of a half-dozen or so each year, are semiotic funhouses, at once gaudy and labyrinthine, as doggedly talky as they are visually extravagant. Ruiz, who exiled himself from Chile in 1973, is sometimes described as an aesthetic odd man out; actually he stands at the confluence of several traditions—film and television, the B-movie and the underground, third world and Europe.

Flamboyant impoverishment is Ruiz's trademark, and he compounds it with a bland, "underdeveloped" disrespect for European culture. Not long ago, perhaps in response to an observation made by his sometime collaborator Gilbert Adair, Ruiz knocked off Racine's *Bernice* in the manner of a Mexican hacienda meller. ("Except for his subject matter," Adair wrote, "Ruiz has never ceased to be a Third World filmmaker, for whom the Aristotelian unities respected by Racine constitute just another low-budget, B-movie parameter.") *The Top of the Whale* is one of Ruiz's more overtly political films—doleful satire of Western hubris, sending up anthropology, colonialism, and even the neo-Marxist equation between the proletariat and the third world.

Produced with Dutch financing in 1982 and subtitled "A Film About Survival," *The Top of the Whale* is set in an alternative future. It opens in the Soviet Dutch Republic, with a chance meeting on the terrace of the Hotel Malcolm X. Overlooking the bleak North Sea, a Dutch anthropologist and his wife Eva encounter Don Narcisso Cambos, a self-described "Communist millionaire," who mentions that he has the last two Indians of some massacred tribe at his Patagonian villa. As the anthropologist's specialty is "collective telepathy among primitive tribes," it's a foregone conclusion that the action will soon shift to somewhere under Capricorn.

For all its melodramatic music and colored filters, *The Top of the Whale* is less baroque than *The Three Crowns of the Sailor* and *City of Pirates,* the Ruiz flicks featured at the 1984 and 1985 New York Film Festivals. The angles aren't so extreme, and the compositions are less eye-popping (no shots from the inside of anyone's mouth). Even more than those, this film was made from nothing: two locations (an island off Rotterdam serves as Patagonia) and a handful of blatantly polyglot performers. Language is Ruiz's most potent special effect. *The Top of the Whale* lapses into and out of French, English, German, Spanish, Dutch, and the invented lingo of the Patagonian Indians. To a degree, Ruiz is satirizing the primacy of contemporary linguistic theory, but in common with poststructural filmmakers like Yvonne Rainer and the Wollen-Mulvey team, he uses language to derange an otherwise ordinary image. Of course, the Ruiz overlay tends toward the belligerently fantastic. A pointless anecdote suddenly becomes the description of a two-kilometer-high cat, a mirage created by a "natural video system."

Throughout *The Top of the Whale* Europeans bore each other with windy stories, while the Indians—a hilariously vacant yet menacing pair—make abrupt, seemingly random appearances. (As Eva tells Anita, her disconcertingly androgynous daughter, "Too much exploitation has made them strange.") While Don Narcisso waxes sentimental about the thousands of Indians massacred in Patagonia, the anthropologist tries to learn their language. Too bad for him that it appears to consist of one phrase; whatever he shows them, they call "yamas gutan." Later, he discovers that Indians exchange names each month and invent a new language every day. After all, they're telepathic. "I deserve a vacation in Rumania," he declares, leaving Patagonia for Europe.

Although—as Manny Farber wrote of Jean-Luc Godard—Ruiz is a master of "long stretches of aggressive, complicated nothingness," *The Top of the Whale* doesn't lack for events. Don Narcisso gives Eva the house, Anita is impregnated by a mirror (do we call this deadpan joke "Lacanic"?), Narcisso's assistant commits suicide by (what else?) cutting out his tongue. In the end, Eva succeeds in domesticating the Indians, training them to come for tea—there's a superb overhead shot of fluttering hands and cups—and to discuss Mozart in English. Can Ruiz be so tamed? I suspect we'll have some sort of answer when Cannon (who else?) is scheduled to release his big buck version of *Treasure Island.*

Avant to hold your hand

Originally published in *The Village Voice* (October 14, 1986).

THE WORD "GENIUS" buzzes around David Byrne's head like a noisy gnat; there hasn't been a pop star with so high-domed a fan club since the glory days of John Lennon or Bob Dylan. I enjoyed *Stop Making Sense* and compared to megalomaniacal yawners like *Imagine* or *Renaldo and Clara*, *True Stories* might seem as revolutionary as *The Battleship Potemkin*. But as precious as it is, the film all but begs for a shot of Flit.

From first image to last (both the road to nowhere, actually rural Texas), *True Stories* is a recognizable product of Byrne's distinctively postmodern sensibility. To make sure the point isn't lost, however, he appears in Stetson and string tie, tooling through the proceedings in a fire-engine red convertible. The film's high-tech cum postcard middle America—well-stocked supermarket shelves, tract houses under the sky, rat-a-tat-tat TV channel zapping—is meant to be the visual analogue to more songs about buildings and food. But some things don't translate, namely the disquietingly skewed clichés of Byrne's lyrics and the rhythmic propulsion of his disaffectedly impassioned delivery. Despite Ed Lachman's impeccable open-air photography, the images are as fastidiously framed as collectable art and as reassuringly monotonous as Muzak.

So, psycho killer qu'est-ce que c'est? Byrne's subject, as always, is the Brave New World of television, suburbia, and the schizoid consumer self. The film's major characters include the TV-addicted Laziest Woman in the World (Swoosie Kurtz), the vivacious Lying Woman (Jo Harvey Allen)—"I wrote 'Billy Jean' and half of Elvis's songs"—and, most crowd-pleasingly, Louis Fyne (John Goodman) an innocent lunk searching for love. (There is also Spaulding Gray who, considering that he doesn't have much of a character to work with, gives a polished, opaque performance as the town's visionary businessman.) That they're all Byrne's projections is hinted at in the sweetly solipsistic "Wild Wild Life" number but never particularly explored. *True Stories* lacks an edge; no one will ever confuse it with *Stop Making Sense*.

"Wild Wild Life," all fast cutting and visual repetition, demonstrates that Byrne knows how to direct a music video—after floundering around for half an hour, the film finally settles into a short-lived groove. (There's another charge of energy when, as the neighborhood voodoo priest, Pops Staples, sings "Papa Legba.") But although *True Stories* has the overdetermined pacing of a concert film, Byrne is after something else. Laurie Anderson's *Home of the Brave* took its cues from *Stop Making Sense* and here Byrne returns the compliment. Not only does he mimic Anderson's yodel in "Wild Wild Life," he ventures onto her oracular turf. *True Stories* is a Statement, and that Byrne lacks Anderson's cutie-pie delivery only makes it more painfully obvious.

In the *True Stories* tie-in book, Byrne acknowledges the influence of Robert Wilson, and the film goes further than anything yet—even the packaged epiphanies of Wilson's own videotapes—in popularizing Wilson's mise-en-scène. But the ideas in *True Stories* come from everywhere: *Our Town* and the Wooster Group and Errol Morris's documentaries and Kafka's "Nature Theater of Oklahoma" and particularly *Nashville*. Like Altman, Byrne casts a mesh of intersecting plots to discover what's really out there in the dark heart of America. But where Altman hid behind the clichés of Geraldine Chaplin, the more naively straightforward Byrne takes this village-explainer role himself. In a misguided concession to his audience, Byrne overnarrates the action. This sort of hand-holding is usually superfluous (who ever heard him talk so much?) and sometimes embarrassingly gee-whiz. Driving down some suburban street, he stops to contemplate the landscape: "Look at this. Who can say it isn't beautiful—sky, bricks . . ." (Is he really expecting an argument? And if so, from whom?)

The film has the texture of a TV special and, populated as it is by adorable little working-class wackos who insist that "there's more to life than this job," it's condescending in another way. After much riffing and jiving in the computer center or on the assembly line, *True Stories* more or less ends with a grand "Celebration of Specialness," in which low riders, lawn-mowing householders, and inept drum majorettes parade down Main Street. The film is somewhat utopian in its integration, but there's scarcely a yuppie (or any Talking Heads constituents) to be seen. A measure of unacknowledged contempt is mixed with Byrne's affectionate celebration of normality. He may be the resident mad artist, but everybody in *True Stories* is patently crazier than him.

Like *Nashville*, *True Stories* reaches a climax when one of the little people gets the opportunity to shine in the limelight. Louis ends the film by singing the smile button equivalent to Barbara Harris's grim what-me-worry? anthem: "People like us—we don't want freedom, we don't want justice. We just want someone to love." As Goodman puts it over, "People Like Us" has a pounding, twangy country beat—it's the best number in the film but it sacrifices the mildly satiric edge of Byrne's own rendition and only reinforces the sense that *True Stories* is as blandly positive in its platitudes as *Nashville* was glibly apocalyptic.

True Stories means to be very up and thoughtful (America as "the city of dreams"), but the epiphanies are thin, the score is sentimental, and the action drags. For a comedy, it's oddly pious. The film shellacks the viewer with chic artiness—it's postmodern to a fault. The book, the record, the videos, the puff pieces seem more authentic than the actual movie; when Byrne pulls into a mall to check out the shoppers, it's as though he's doing market research for himself.

As the movies become something other than a mass art, radical ideas take less time to work their way from the medium's edge toward its squishy center—witness the triumph of the midnight aesthetic that made commercial hits out of *Liquid Sky* or *Repo Man*. The late New York Film Festival was rife with more genteel examples, ranging from the "respectably" ersatz Bergman of *The Sacrifice* and the soft Bresson of *Thérèse* to the diluted Jarmusch of Jarmusch's own *Down By Law* and the domesticated Chantal Akerman of *Dancing in the Dark*.

It's both comical and telling that this last film, which is not only in English but directed by a man, has been most fervently embraced by the very critics who missed the boat on *Jeanne Dielman* ten years ago. Similarly, although scuttled by John Lurie's lackadaisical performance and Jarmusch's inability to construct a scene, *Down By Law* has been enthusiastically received by many who were nonplussed by *Stranger Than Paradise*. (That the film has been overpraised by nearly everyone, with exception of my colleague David Edelstein, was to be expected—what's unfortunate is that Jarmusch has been commended less for his compositional smarts and superb use of the long take, than for a strain of Saroyan-like cuteness that threatens to become virulent.)

Like *The Atomic Café, Stranger Than Paradise* was one of the more felicitous popularizations of avant-garde techniques. Jarmusch not only evoked a certain mood of New York posthip hipsterism, he synthesized a number of poststructural strategies including those developed in the mid '70s by Akerman and James Benning, whose 15-year retro is currently at the Whitney. Indeed, Benning's shaggy-dog narratives and long-take celebrations of banal middle Americana anticipate Byrne almost as much as they do Jarmusch.

Benning is best known for *11 × 14* (1976) and *One Way Boogie Woogie* (1977) and deservedly so—nothing he's made before or since equals the wit or energy of these playful narrative/landscape, sound/image deconstructions. For the most part, the early films on view this week are of interest mainly as tokens of Benning's struggle in the bleary aftermath of the '60s, to invent an avant-garde art appropriate to the American Midwest. Two exceptions are a pair of abstract road films *8½ × 11* (1974) and *The United States of America* (1975).

The films were breakthroughs and there's still a residual excitement: Benning takes raw chunks of the American scene—interstate highways, the commercial strip, AM radio—and hurls them on the screen like so many Duchamp urinals. *Pace* David Byrne, the "look at this" is implied.

Fear and trembling at the Whitney Biennial

Originally published in *The Village Voice* (June 16, 1987).

THE FRENCH CALL adolescence the age of film-going, and it may be that the movies you discover then set your taste forever. Certainly, my own life was altered in 1965, when I began frequenting a cruddy storefront on St. Marks Place and the even weirder basement of a midtown skyscraper. I knew movie-movies, but this was another world: oceanic superimpositions and crazy editing rhythms, films made from bits of newsreel and Top 40 songs, "plots" ranging from the creation of the universe to the sins of the fleshapoids, real people (often naked) cavorting in mock Arabian palaces and outer borough garbage dumps. Determined to learn more, I took out a subscription to *Film Culture*. That the first issue was half devoted to the grandiose schemes of a mad beatnik named Ron Rice only confirmed my sense that anything was possible.

The Village Voice of that era was totally committed to these so-called underground movies, and for a long time after I began reviewing films here, my ideal reader was me as an adolescent. Lately, that reader has turned reproachful. It's painful to imagine what he would think, wandering into the 1987 Whitney Biennial to watch the movies—sitting amid an impatient clutch of tourists and a few somber friends of the artist, bombarded by images rendered banal by MTV, reading program notes that could turn you off language altogether. What was once vital and freewheeling now seems sanctimonious, cliquish, and worst of all, superfluous. The onetime New American Cinema lives in its own peculiar ghetto—a handful of venues in New York, Boston, and San Francisco, various museums, media centers, and university film departments across the country—and a state of permanent frustration. Individuals persevere, but the movement seems moribund. For the average film buff, it's the shadow of a shadow.

In New York, the bastions of the '60s have nearly all crumbled: The Anthology Film Archives have been virtually shut since 1981, *Film Culture* has published two issues this decade, the Film-maker's Cooperative has not been able to issue a new catalogue in a dozen years. The Millennium endures but, far from self-congratulatory, the recent 20th anniversary edition of *The Millennium Film Journal* offers several lengthy, pessimistic assessments of the current scene. And the current Whitney Biennial offers the most dismal selection of avant-garde films since the Biennial began including the form in 1979.

It's not my intention to justify those who ignore the achievements of the American avant-garde. (A film critic who takes no account of Stan Brakhage or Yvonne Rainer has as much claim to serious attention as a historian who never heard of the Civil War.) Nor do I wish to discourage those who labor to extend those achievements. Their lot is tough enough: Film is fearfully expensive and hard to get right. The number of labs dwindle as the price of raw stock climbs—and even more than the rest of us, a-g filmmakers are oppressed by the waste and idiocy of most commercial movies. Still, it's clear to even the most sympathetic observer that something has gone horribly wrong.

Denied recognition in the culture at large—years ago, according to Vincent Canby, he and then *Times* critic Hilton Kramer decided that neither of them was capable of reviewing the crazy movies at the Whitney—avant-garde film further isolates itself from the mainstream, producing work that is increasingly sterile, derivative, and self-involved. Meanwhile, the starvation and squalor of ghetto life encourage a desperate, demeaning careerism—not to mention all manner of backbiting paranoid fantasies (one writer recklessly concocts the notion of a New York cabal, another maliciously suggests that a modestly successful and extremely gifted filmmaker "needs critical attention as badly as Bob Hope needs real estate"). That work of enduring value continues to be made under these conditions seems all the more remarkable.

In this sense, the film section of the Whitney Biennial is a paradigm for the scene as a whole: a pair of challenging films by first-rate artists (Yvonne Rainer's *The Man Who Envied Women*, Ernie Gehr's *Signal—Germany on the Air*), a few respectable efforts by established figures (James Benning's *Landscape Sui-*

cide, Warren Sonbert's *The Cup and the Lip*), a couple of brash, knotty, on-time films by relative newcomers (Trinh T. Minh-ha's *Naked Spaces,* Ericka Beckman's *Cinderella*), and a score of dreary mediocrities destined for oblivion—all blandly equated in an unilluminating, jargon-clogged catalogue essay.

The weakness of the Biennial selection is amplified, in that the Whitney has become the preeminent institutional force in American avant-garde film and curator John Hanhardt the avant-garde's single most influential programmer. The Biennial selection, which is subsequently packaged as a traveling show by the American Federation of Arts, is the most circulated exhibition of American a-g film. According to Hanhardt, no artist selected has ever declined to participate.

The malaise in avant-garde film is not a unique phenomenon—all movies have suffered in the past 15 years. It's not even singular in the context of the art world. Writing in *The Nation,* Arthur Danto worries that frenzied speculation will supplant the museum with the "private zoos" of wealthy collectors. For Danto, the Biennial's inclusion of 28 film and video artists (nearly 40 per cent of the total) seems "a brilliant counterattack by the Whitney curators against the museum's affluent enemies." Wouldn't it be nice! Never mind that Danto admits to having seen only one video and none of the films (although that in itself should tell you something), the real irony is that a major reason for the marginalization of avant-garde film is precisely the absence of a commodity to exploit.

WHAT IS THIS thing, "avant-garde?" The term is European, only recently applied to American-made films. Before, there was the grandiose New American Cinema or the exciting underground, and before that the tentative "experimental" film. "Avant-garde" has the connotation of a revolutionary elite, of subverting the status quo and advancing into some radiant future. Or is it only a pretentious academic label?

That the underground movies of the 1960s were greedily assimilated by TV commercials and rock videos, by porn (straight and gay), by midnight movies, and even by commercial features suggests that, in its heyday at least, the American avant-garde was some sort of literal vanguard: *Scorpio Rising* pointing the way toward *Easy Rider* and *L.A. Plays Itself, American Graffiti, Mean Streets,* and every MTV video ever made. But just as the militant counterculture of the '60s had little structural impact on the American political system, so the underground failed to transform the economy of American movie consumption. If anything, Hollywood movies are more grossly formulaic than they were 15 years back—and their audience is no less passive.

Thus, as it's currently applied to film, the term "avant-garde" defines movies that are less in advance of than simply *other* than the commercial cinema—those films that derange conventional codes of representation, that risk obscurity by confounding rigid expectations (including those of the not always tolerant official avant-garde). Is *Naked Spaces* a personal documentary or a Duras-like fiction? Is *Signal—Germany on the Air* an alienated diary film or a structural detective story? Is *Cinderella* a feminist puppetoon or a new wave operetta? Or are they something else? The avant-garde is the category applied to those films which elude categories. But the term is also deeply nostalgic.

Almost everyone agrees that the late '60s were golden. The era that began with Stan Brakhage's ultra-subjective *Anticipation of the Night,* his birth films, and subsequent epics, continuing through the beatnik underground and the world of Andy Warhol to end with the minimalist, modernist, structuralist tendency precipitated by Michael Snow's *Wavelength,* saw one of the richest, most diversified, and most underappreciated art movements in the 20th century.

Between 1958 and 1972, a disparate band of self-subsidized amateurs succeeded in transcending the Hollywood glitz mystique while opening movies up to formal possibilities that had largely lain dormant since D. W. Griffith designed the straitjacket of conventional narrative. By the mid '60s, the American avant-garde was a true oppositional cinema—supported by a popular base, with its own alternative venues and distribution co-ops, as well as a quasi-utopian ideology. Like the historical avant-garde, the New American Cinema saw itself as a vehicle for social transformation and self-transcendence—it criticized Hollywood, both directly and by example. The underground proposed to change the world by overthrowing the institution of moviedom, and it possessed a superb and irrefutable weapon—namely, the frank representation of eros on screen.

Underground filmmakers were among the shock troops of the '60s social turmoil, and many of them paid the price. But the rise of commercial porn deprived the movement of its greatest novelty, just as midnight movies would usurp the movement's popular base. Meanwhile, a chimerical respectability beckoned. Having attained a sort of apotheosis in 1971 with the establishment of the Anthology Film Archives, the temporary recruitment of an ex-Beatle into its ranks, the installation of regular film programs at the Whitney and the Museum of Modern Art, and the devotion of an entire issue of *Artforum* to its accomplishments, the New American Cinema retrenched behind academic bulwarks.

By the early '70s, almost all of the major filmmakers and a host of minor ones had come in from the cold to spawn a new generation of university-trained filmmakers. At first this looked like a victory, the creation of a beachhead. The structuralism of Snow and others was particularly well suited to academic film studies. As the celluloid era drew to a close and Minerva's owl took wing, movies produced an authentic, indisputable, Clement Greenberg-style modernism—one that drew attention to its own materials and axioms, that returned to ground zero to reinvent the medium from scratch. The delirious hedonism of the '60s gave way to a rigorous, ultimately punitive concern with "unpleasure." Small wonder the academic film a-g of the 1970s was as concerned with the production of theory as with the production of films.

The '70s were by no means a total loss. Despite the shrinking economy and the challenge of video, the decade saw a dramatic influx of women filmmakers, a welcome internationalization of the a-g scene, and the brief but influential punk neo-underground. Still, tolerated by universities and regulated by grants, pampered by apologists and ignored in the popular press, filmmakers abandoned the beatnik model of an anti-academic independent bohemia. Where once raving madmen became filmmakers, it was now the turn of genteel professors. Students studied avant-garde film in college, made a few in imitation of their teachers, and ventured out into the world to demand one-person shows at the Collective for Living Cinema. Correspondingly pushing the logic of the opening screening to a spurious limit, programmers placated their constituents by promiscuously dispensing shows, rather than championing the work they felt to be strongest.

Films like *Scorpio Rising* and *Flaming Creatures* were neither made for the avant-garde ghetto, nor contained by it; now avant-garde films appeared to illustrate particular doctrines or appeal to specific audiences. The rise of the institution subsidized mediocrity no less than genius.

THE AESTHETIC BOUNDARIES in the '80s have been blurred by numerous crossovers. That *The Atomic Café* and *Sherman's March* could enjoy commercial runs, that the National Society of Film Critics would name as best films *Stranger Than Paradise* and *Blue Velvet* (rather than *Gandhi* and *Hannah and Her Sisters*) indicate the popular acceptance of at least some a-g work. But the Biennial designates its own avant-garde. According to John Hanhardt, the film section is devoted to "the work of the individual artist who is creating and producing work outside the mainstream of commercial film production, distribution, and exhibition."

Hanhardt's parameters are American "independent" films made over the last two years ("I try to reflect on what's happened in that period") belonging to a "particular culture of opposition." But what exactly is that "culture of opposition?" And why does it apply more to film and video than to painting and sculpture?

Reflecting a major trend of the '80s, the '83 Biennial included one narrative feature, the '85 edition had three, and this year's has five. But the inclusion of independent features puts the Biennial in an untenable position. Is Lizzie Borden's *Working Girls* (57th Street Playhouse) less experimental than Lizzie Borden's *Born in Flames* (Film Forum, '85 Biennial)? Are Rachel Reichman's *The Riverbed* and Nina Menkes's *Magdelena Viraga* more formally a-g than *Sherman's March* or *Blue Velvet*? "*Blue Velvet* is a film I see in commercial release," Hanhardt told me. "I feel an obligation to support that work which is not enjoying marketplace support." (Of course—and he's the only curator in the Biennial who has to.) The artisanal modes of the '60s have clearly evolved into something else. But, defined as it is by what it is not, the Whitney's avant-garde can't be anything other than a mode of exhibition. The only thing that makes a film as conventional as *The Riverbed* Whitney fodder is its inability to find a commercial release. Not the media, but the American Federation of Arts package is the message.

Just as these features suggest subsidized equivalents of marketplace hits (with Leandro Katz's *The Visit* a sort of sub-Jarmusch punk-passé featurette), the work of Alan Berliner, Paul Glabicki, Barbara Hammer, and Stephanie Beroes are mediocre-to-embarrassing echoes of "established" a-g modes. It would be easy to put the blame for these botches on Hanhardt—and I think he should have held out more doggedly for excellence. But allowing for vagaries of taste, the quality of the Biennial depends on what's out there. If Hanhardt is suspicious of humor (consistently overlooking Joe Gibbons, George Kuchar, and—in video—Tony Oursler), he has proved responsive to criticism, validating Danto's observation that "the Whitney is open, uncertain, erratic, innocent, friendly and almost Chaplinesque in its readiness to dust itself off after a critical disaster and resolve to do better the next time around."

Consider this. In 1979, the film section was scored for its 17 : 1 male-to-female ratio; since that time, the percentage of women has steadily risen until now, when women filmmakers are a majority. In 1981, the Biennial was chided for excluding super-8; in 1983, the format was there. (It has since disappeared, although Hanhardt told me that "if there's strong work in super-8, I'm ready to show it.") In 1985, P. Adams Sitney suggested that Warren Sonbert's *Noblesse Oblige* should have been programmed with Ernie Gehr's *Untitled*; this year Sonbert's *The Cup and the Lip* is matched with Gehr's *Signal—Germany on the Air*, the only show of filmmakers from the Anthology canon.

Given the critical support their work has received, a few filmmakers are conspicuous by their absence (Marjorie Keller, Leslie Thornton, Su Friedrich, to name three). But I'm not convinced that their inclusion would have made an appreciable difference. Hanhardt may have missed the boat on a half-dozen or so films since 1979, but he has amply demonstrated his support for new talent—the average age in the film/video section is 38, and over half the artists are Biennial virgins. Yet for film, the Biennial is a succession of one-night stands: As the number of first-time filmmakers has risen, the number of those asked back has plummeted.

Some might suggest that the most serious omission is Stan Brakhage. (Certainly *The Loom* would have raised the level mightily.) But just as the Biennial only occasionally includes Willem DeKooning or Jasper Johns, suggesting in this way that these masters are above mere fashion, so the film section should not have to depend on Brakhage. If anything, this omission underscores the cruelest fate that the avant-garde has suffered—namely, the squeezing of successive generations within the same unyielding ghetto walls. In my alternate universe, Brakhage would be turning down dinner invitations to the White House, and Yvonne Rainer would be the subject of ga-ga profiles in *The New York Times Magazine*.

The history of art is not just the history of institutions but the history of individuals. A number of gifted filmmakers who surfaced in the late '70s have simply burnt-out—neither Vivienne Dick nor Manuel DeLanda has released significant new work in a half-dozen years—while, as Sitney observed in a review of the '85 Biennial, "No one has *commanded* attention since Yvonne Rainer moved from choreography to cinema." Of the younger filmmakers, Ericka Beckman is the closest to a consensus heroine—her stylistically assured,

graphically dynamic, relentlessly go-go work has been included in three consecutive Biennials, as well as the New York Film Festival (where it sparked a
near-riot), and has been reviewed in *Art in America, The Millennium Film
Journal,* and the *Voice.* But, unlike Rainer, Beckman (who teaches to support
herself and required two residencies at two universities to complete *Cinderella*)
hasn't much of an international reputation, nor indeed any reputation outside
her field.

I asked Hanhardt if he agreed with Sitney's assertion that no indisputably
strong artistic personality has emerged in the 15 years since Rainer's *Lives of
Performers.* "What about Jim Benning?" he suggested. "Or Bill Viola?" Benning's *11 × 14* is a decade old—but what's striking about Bill Viola is that he
works in video.

LET US PEER into the Radiant Future: This current Biennial is the first in which
film and video share a common exhibition space—and it's a significant move.
"There's an increasing dialogue between film and video," Hanhardt told me.
"For the first time, I've heard avant-garde filmmakers talk about the fact that
they're interested in video; and now I hear video artists say they're interested in
the theatrical presentation of their work." I've mainly heard filmmakers talk
about how much they hate video, but Bill Viola may be a case in point. Not only
did he make his stunning feature-length *I Do Not Know What It Is I Am Like*
specifically for projected video, but, with his combination of Brakhagian vision-
ary-romanticism and structuralist rigor, he extends the New American Cinema
by other means.

A credit to his medium, Viola is scheduled for a major retrospective at the
Museum of Modern Art later this year—the first ever given a video artist. In
general, however, video brings with it an air of lowered expectations. Whereas
film dominates the visual field, the video image is reduced and decentered,
typically shown on multiple screens. Several of the Biennial videos, most notably Steve Fagin's *The Amazing Voyage of Gustave Flaubert and Raymond
Roussel* (a tape as grandiloquent as its title), are would-be films; they cry out for
dream-screen presence. Others—ranging from Dan Graham's estimable *Rock
My Religion* to Juan Downey's pious *J. S. Bach* (the worst piece in the Biennial, a
glossy bit of irrelevance that treats the composer as a subject for *Live From Off
Center*)—benefit from avoiding film's weight.

Once the handmaiden of modern times, film (and not just a-g film) seems
headed toward its dotage. The technology is quaint, costly, and all but obsolete—although this scarcely spells the end of Cinema (high-resolution, projected video is on the way, and slide-tape shows may yet replace super-8 in the
bargain basement). And, even as movies are jostled by related forms, the plastic
arts have increasingly merged with the camera-based ones. The '85 Biennial, as
many observed, was awash in media-influenced work.

"I don't agree with the postmodern notion of pop culture being a place one
can operate in," Hanhardt admonished me, adding that he saw MTV as siphon-
ing off prospective a-g talent. But video, unlike film, is a strictly postmodern

development, and the Biennial contains a number of crypto music-videos. Postmodern artists characteristically rework popular forms in avant-garde terms: It's because Jarmusch, Lynch, and Borden emerge from art world backgrounds that films like *Stranger Than Paradise, Blue Velvet,* and *Working Girls* challenge the boundaries of the Biennial as well as the marketplace.

This strategy is literalized in two of the most impressive tapes in the video section—Joan Braderman's *Joan Does Dynasty* in which (shades of Ernie Kovacs, and special effects courtesy of Manuel DeLanda) the relentlessly hammy author is electronically matted into an episode of the prime-time soap to explicate the show's "world of unconscious desire," and Martha Rosler's more staidly formalist *If It's Too Bad to Be True, It Could Be DISINFORMATION,* which uses static to derange commercials and news reports on Nicaragua. As much desecrations as deconstructions, both tapes oppose the totalizing impulse of masterpiece art *and* the media. Like Hans Breder's slight but elegantly frantic assemblages, they take for granted that, in the postmodern world, TV has supplanted nature.

Although it's been said that the essential characteristic of postmodernism is the absence of vanguards, such guerrilla warfare suggests one valid avant-garde strategy. (The next underground is likely to be founded on the VCR.) In film, we have entered an era of near-instant, if vertical, assimilation. Where, 20 years ago, *Scorpio Rising* influenced everything on the horizon, from exploitation to agit-prop, now innovative underground movies are merely remade on a more grandiose scale: Vivienne Dick's super-8 movies are given the Cecil B. DeMille treatment by Lizzie Borden and Susan Seidelman. Indeed, rather than revitalizing the a-g, the super-8 underground of the late '70s had a salutary effect on independent film production.

Now, aspiring super-8 filmmakers do Lower East Side imitations of commercial genres (chiefly splatter and hetero-porn). Introducing last year's New York Film Festival Downtown, the organizers proudly announced "a marked shift toward short films emulating or parodying exploitation and cult films." The spectacle of neo-underground filmmakers doing belated, heterosexual imitations of John Waters, or mimicking the industrial barnacles that attached themselves to the original underground, is as pathetic as it is irrelevant.

I expect a few of these filmmakers, among others, firing belligerent protests off to the *Voice.* (And why not? I'm part of the institution, too.) It's always possible that something new and vital may emerge—and from the least likely source. I also hope something does. The impulse to make movies is far from dead, and it may be that the future is percolating at Charas or ABC No Rio or some other East Side emporium. But an authentic vanguard is a necessary vanguard—arising out of some deeply experienced crisis, either personal or cultural. It's worth remembering that, by and large, the underground films of the '50s and '60s were made by misfits, dropouts, borderline schizos, and gays, while the strongest a-g films of the '70s and '80s were overwhelmingly by women.

In 1978, Vivienne Dick made the underground films that could not have been made in 1965—and in that she wasn't alone. Issues of class and race are less resolved than ever: The energy to fuel a new avant-garde will have to come from someplace more marginal and excluded than the petulance of straight suburban white boys transplanted to Avenue B.

Bon voyeur: Andy Warhol's silver screen

Originally published in *The Village Voice* (May 17, 1988).

A NDY WARHOL THRIVED on paraphrase; he made movies that didn't have to be seen to make themselves felt. The rumor of their existence was sufficient to alter film history. Now these films can be examined in that altered light at the Whitney, and pilgrims may make some unexpected discoveries.

Between 1963 and 1967, Warhol virtually reinvented motion pictures from scratch. Presenting him with its 1964 Independent Filmmaker's Award, *Film Culture* wrote that he was "taking cinema back to its origins, to the days of Lumière, for a rejuvenation and a cleansing." This reinvention changed everything—and everyone. Regina Cornwell was the first to point out that Warhol's oeuvre influenced the structural filmmakers as well as their dialectical opposites, the punks. Further, he was a key figure in the histories of both ethno- and pornographic film, and had a decisive impact on the nature of screen documentary as well as acting.

Warhol's pragmatism redefined low-budget moviemaking. But, with ineffable passivity, he created a new notion of movie glamour—in part, because the camera gave him license to look.

THE FIRST WARHOL to be publicly screened, *Kiss* was originally a series of silent 100-foot camera rolls that were shown, a new one each week, during the fall of '63 as the "serial" at the Gramercy Arts Theatre, the then underground mecca. (Fourteen of these throbbing, three-minute osculations were spliced together; the result was characterized as a "lipsmacking revue.") With a directness of address unseen since Thomas Edison's epochal 1896 *The May Irwin-John C. Rice Kiss,* Warhol turned his camera on a motley collection of early superstars—including an uptight Baby Jane Holzer, avid Gerard Malanga, cool Marisol, romantic Ed Sanders, and steamy Naomi Levine—in various pairings (both hetero and homosexual), passionately, dreamily, solemnly, or campily chewing on each other's faces.

That was it. The simplicity of *Kiss* was followed by the more provocative and epic minimalism of *Sleep, Eat, Haircut,* and *Empire.* But *Kiss* not only announced Warhol's interest in the repetition of simple structures—simultaneously, if less obviously, it proclaims a fascination with sex, voyeurism, and orality (kissing, eating, smoking, and, eventually, talking) that would characterize his entire cinematic project. Playful as it is, *Kiss* establishes the archetypal

Warhol situation: the erotic, angst-ridden, adversarial one-on-one. These amplified, extended kisses—not to mention the performers' coping strategies—exert a powerful behavioral fascination. Innocent as *Kiss* is, it's nearly as intimate as hardcore porn and probably more revealing.

THE TRAJECTORY OF Warhol's film career leads inexorably toward pornography, which back in the early '60s scarcely enjoyed the sanctioned existence it has today. Thus *Blow Job,* arguably the most conceptual work of porn ever made, was prudently unadvertised for its world premiere at the Washington Square Art Gallery during the summer of 1964. (Five years later, the film would actually be shown—with the admonition to call the theater to find out its name—in movie-houses specializing in gay porn.) Although silent, *Blow Job* introduces language into the Warhol world. No film ever made has a more integral title.

An early Film-makers' Coop catalogue identifies *Blow Job*'s stars as "Willard something and Peter von something," blandly describing the movie as "a passionate matter handled with restraint and good taste." Restraint is the movie's subject; few films have ever been so rigorous in their logic. Over the course of eight 100-foot rolls, a would-be James Dean in a black leather jacket appears to be sexually serviced by someone outside the frame. As Stephen Koch observed, this 35-minute closeup must be the apotheosis of the "reaction shot." It's also a work of genius.

Tawdry and ethereal, *Blow Job* is Warhol's version of *Ecstasy.* The movie is a kind of silent aria. The star is dressed like a Method actor but, self-conscious as he is, he doesn't seem to be faking his response. His starkly lit face is a screen upon which we watch excitement ebb and flow. He looks up, closes his eyes, lolls his head back against the Factory's exposed brick wall—his consciousness apparently split between his own sensations and the extraordinary position in which he finds himself. Once or twice, our hero seems to acknowledge someone behind the camera (as well as below his belt). The camera, however, never budges. The frame is absolute. When the subject's hand intrudes to scratch his nose, it's like the introduction of a new character—an event. In the middle of the eighth reel he appears to climax. There's a bit of bucking and writhing, then an inadvertent attempt to slip out of the frame. Now the guy *has* to act cool. He lights a cigarette and the movie ends with him still smoking it.

OFFSCREEN SPACE IS an active presence in a number of Warhol flicks. "This is not just another pretty face but *Beauty #2,*" some unseen *yenta* announces at the start of this 1965 masterpiece. There's a false start and then a high-angle shot of Factory princess Edie Sedgwick and a minor cutie named Gino Piserchio, sprawled in their underwear across the striped sheets of an artfully rumpled bed. A dog (named Horse) is frisking around and the distracted couple is taking direction from someone (named Chuck Wein) just beyond the frame. It's as if they're there for his delectation. The setup suggests a pornographic circus, an *exhibición* in a pre-Castro Havana hotel room. Chugging vodka from a monstrous tumbler, Edie speaks of her costar in the third person: "Gino's going to sleep," she announces for no particular reason. "Are you German?" he asks, confused.

In late '64, Warhol had purchased a sound-on-film Auricon camera. (Perversely, the first movie he shot with it was the silent *Empire*.) *Harlot*—which premiered in January 1965, projected on a sheet at the old Cafe a-Go-Go—was the film that broke the sound barrier. Talkies followed at the rate of one per week, as Warhol consolidated his position as an avant-garde mogul. With Ron Rice's death and Jack Smith's traumatic reaction to *Flaming Creature*'s bust, the field was clear; underground movies entered their silver age. For much of the summer of 1965, *Vinyl*—which introduced Sedgwick—and *Beauty #2* were frequent attractions at the new Film-Maker's Cinematheque that Jonas Mekas had established in an off-Broadway theater on Lafayette Street.

Sound required actors. From Jack Smith, Warhol would later confide, he learned the knack of using "anyone who happened to be around that day," and filming "until the actors got bored." Every Warhol talkie was in some sense a screen test, but *Beauty #2* exudes an existential tension that's only grown more palpable in the 23 years since the film was made. The first reel suggests some monstrous Laurence Sterne digression in a de Sade novel. Sedgwick is totally, bizarrely poised, stomach sucked in, eloquently furling and unfurling her long, lithe legs. Chatting and giggling as though having tea at the Plaza, she refuses to disengage from offscreen even as the less articulate Gino removes his pants. He's wondering when to make his move, she's calculating how long she can keep stalling. There's an entropic yet hysterical pajama party ambience. Meanwhile the implacable, unseen Wein is pushing the couple to "get to know each other."

In the second reel, Wein begins reading from John Lennon's *A Spaniard in the Works*; his droning frees Edie and Gino to start some light making out. Then he stops and the question becomes, how much further can the couple on the bed go? Suddenly Wein's jealousy seems far more real than feigned. Briefly struck dumb as the couple goes back into the clinch, he does his best to make Sedgwick self-conscious: "Edie, you look like you were purchased at F. A. O. Schwarz. You can do better than that." Wein's taunts become the film's text, until Sedgwick finally loses it and throws an ashtray at him. (Ever-hopeful Gino keeps nuzzling, slyly coaxing down one of her bra straps.)

Image war and power struggle, *Beauty #2* maps one of the most extraordinary triangles in movie history. Simple as it seems, the film is a fantastically tangled vortex of controlling gazes. "What's a voyeur?" innocent Edie asks sophisticated Wein during some bit of lighthearted banter. She unconsciously reminds us that behind Wein (or rather, perpendicular to him) is Andy Warhol, the movie's metadirector and privileged phantom spectator.

BEAUTY #2 APPEARS all the more brilliant in the light of something like *I, a Man*. This 1967 feature opens with a head-on shot of a couple in bed arguing about whether she should take a shower or make coffee. The composition is crude, the color ugly, the acting transparent. Success has definitely spoiled Andy Warhol.

Encouraged by the unexpected appeal of *My Hustler* in late '65 and the commercial breakthrough of *Chelsea Girls* the following year, Warhol knocked off a string of semiporn features. *My Hustler* had been playing for much of the summer of '67 at the Hudson, a theater off Times Square; at the end of August it was succeeded by *I, a Man,* a title parodying that of a notorious Swedish skin flick. Its protagonist, according to Warhol, was originally to have been Jim Morrison. No such luck. The presence of a star might have redeemed this weary jape—but Tom Baker was barely an aspiring actor. *I, a Man* is not completely devoid of formal wit (a sequence of Baker playing guitar is amusingly deranged by strobe cuts), but basically the movie is a series of uninspired improvisations in which Baker tries to bed a succession of Warholian women, including the clownish Ingrid Superstar and the inscrutable Nico.

Despite a fair amount of nudity, the proceedings are uniformly flaccid except when, in a scene played out entirely in a hallway, Baker has to cope with the militantly lesbian Valerie Solanis. (She grabs his ass and demands he tell her how he keeps it "so squishy.") It took Warhol a mere four years to go from innocence to decadence. The worst thing about *I, a Man* is that everybody is acting like they're acting in "an Andy Warhol film."

EVEN AS THE Factory was churning out semiporn, they were still producing a number of more informal reels.

Most of these were subsumed into Warhol's last great gesture. This was * * * *, perhaps a hundred reels of film shown simultaneously in December 1967 in one 25-hour presentation of superimposed images from two projectors. By screening a pair of reels from this long since dismantled epic—unseen in any form for 20 years—the Whitney hints that the Warhol oeuvre may yet reveal obscure treasures.

"Katrina Dead," however, is not among them. The eponymous heroine is laid out on a table and surrounded by a half dozen mourners, notably Rene Ricard in diaphanous purple shirt. Ricard takes the lead in talking dirty and offering bitchy putdowns. (Given their generally abysmal sound quality, it's an iron law of nature in Warhol films that the shrillest, most querulous voices rule.) "She thinks she's Ondine in *Chelsea Girls,*" Ricard smirks of some would-be competitor. Then the real Ondine shows up, head swathed in a tatty green boa, to demonstrate how it's done. He upstages everyone—the sequence ends with him blithely gabbing away, having sprawled himself across the dead center of the screen.

"SUNSET ON LONG ISLAND" might be * * * *'s legendary coda—although, contrary to some descriptions, it's not a half-hour recording of the sun going down over the ocean. The mood is goofy and elegiac. It's late afternoon at the end of summer, and a number of Warhol creatures (including Ondine in a bedouin-style robe) can be seen in midshot frisking in the surf, their antics ener-gized by strobe cuts and purposeful overexposures. All the while, a British hippie with a guitar is improvising some sort of ongoing commentary along the lines of "Superstars on the beach . . . what a scene . . . trees sway in the breeze . . . the sun is almost gone . . . do you want to stay or do you want to go?" That his gently idiotic song is virtually continuous, while Warhol's camera hilariously shifts from setup to setup, destroys another cherished myth. This sequence was *edited*. The Whitney willing, maybe we won't have to wait 20 years to see the rest.

Raped and abandoned: Yoko Ono's forgotten masterpiece

Originally published as "Making a Spectacle" in *The Village Voice* (March 14, 1989).

FOR YOKO ONO, an artist who has frequently worked with the notion of "notoriety," fame has had the paradoxical effect of obscuring her actual achievements. Take *Rape*. The most powerful and disturbing of the various concept movies that she and John Lennon produced, it's also a work that, up until now, has been all but written out of film history—unclaimed by the British, cinetheoretical, and feminist avant-gardes, the victim of an inverted snobbery complicated by cultural amnesia.

Like Ono and Lennon's *Fly*, in which the Vasco da Gama of the insect world explores the Brobdingnagian terrain of a comatose nude woman for perhaps half an hour, *Rape* is a startlingly visceral experience—as blunt as its title. The premise for this 70-minute film comes from an Ono "film score," published in 1968: "The cameraman will chase a girl on a street with a camera persistently until he corners her in an alley, and, if possible, until she is in a falling position." The execution, which had its premiere over Austrian television 20 years ago this month, is one of the most violent and sexually charged movies ever made—even if flesh never touches flesh.

Angst-producing from the onset, *Rape* opens without titles: The camera zeroes in on an attractive, long-haired woman wandering through a picturesque London cemetery (suggestive of the park in *Blow Up*), meets her head on, and then tags along behind. It soon becomes evident that its prey, identified in auxiliary material as a 21-year-old Austrian named Eva Majlath, doesn't speak English. But she's basically amiable and makes numerous attempts to establish contact with the filmmakers in German and Italian. They are, of course, totally noncommunicative, ignoring even her request for a match, while shifting the camera to keep her always in frame.

The movie approximates real time. Whenever a roll of film runs out, the crew falls behind the subject, so that each new sequence begins with the exciting spectacle of their catching up to, and startling, her anew. After the third roll,

Majlath's composure gives way to annoyance. By the time the crew has followed her out of the park and into the street, she's angry and frightened—so spooked that she walks into a post and, at one point, nearly steps out in front of an oncoming truck. (No one in the street appears to pay the slightest attention to her plight.) When ultimately she hails a cab, the crew promptly climbs into its own vehicle, and the film's first movement ends with the camera still dogging her tracks as she walks morosely by the Thames.

Even more frantic and oppressive, *Rape*'s second half has the crew invade the small apartment where Majlath is staying. She paces like a caged animal, the camera's tight, hand-held close-ups mirroring her agitated movements as she compulsively combs her hair, babbles hysterically in German (tears of frustration streaking her elaborate eye makeup), and repeatedly attempts to open the apartment's locked front door. All the more violent for its sunbursts and white-outs, this section often becomes pure kinesis. Although Majlath hides her face or halfheartedly blocks the lens, the camera shows no restraint, swarming around her and opportunistically coming in closer whenever she appears most vulnerable. As the movie ends, she makes a phone call; the sounds of her distress continue over the credits. A brief coda has Ono and Lennon dourly distorted by an extreme wide-angle lens, singing something like "Everybody had a hard year."

For a simple movie, *Rape* raises a multitude of questions. Although Ono's score indicates that the film's subject should be chosen at random, this hardly seems the case. The film is clearly some sort of setup, although it's difficult to ascertain what kind. Majlath was obviously selected for her good looks, lack of English, and unfamiliarity with London; according to various accounts, the filmmakers obtained the key to her apartment from either her sister (whom she frequently invokes) or the building owner, then locked her in.

Although Majlath never completely panics or appears to imagine herself in physical danger, she doesn't seem complicit in her victimization—her anger and confusion are absolutely convincing. This, of course, is much of the fascination. In one sense, *Rape* is a particularly brutal dramatization of the Warholian discovery that the camera's implacable stare disrupts "ordinary" behavior to enforce its own regime. In another, the film is a graphic metaphor for the ruthless surveillance that can theoretically attach itself to any citizen of the modern world.

Indeed, although Ono has denied that this was her intent, it is hard not to see *Rape* as a reaction to the media coverage that she and Lennon had alternately courted and been victimized by at various stages of their careers. (It was shot in late November 1968, following a period of maximum, mostly adverse publicity; John was busted for hash on October 18, his divorce proceedings began November 8, and Yoko entered the hospital November 21; a week later, the album *Two Virgins,* with its scandalous nude cover, was released.) But *Rape* is more than just a hyperbolic representation of blanket media coverage; it radically challenges the viewer's privileged position.

Basically, *Rape* presents a beautiful, extremely feminine woman in peril, her situation overtly sexualized by the very title. (The opening graveyard provides a suitably gothic location.) Although this scenario is a movie staple, arguably *the* movie staple, the absence of a narrative strongly invites the audience to identify with the camera's (unmistakably male) look and recognize this controlling gaze as its own. In its realization, Ono's script becomes the purest illustration of Laura Mulvey's celebrated essay, "Visual Pleasure and Narrative Cinema," published eight years after *Rape* was made.

Rape differs from Jonathan Kaplan's *The Accused*, for example, in that its behaviorism cuts two ways. The sadistic aspect of "secretly" watching another person on the screen (and enjoying their powerlessness) here becomes a self-conscious and hence uncomfortable complicity. As Jonas Mekas observed when *Rape* was first shown in New York, "Two things are interesting to watch as the film progresses—one is the girl . . . and the other is the audience."

Jacobs' ladder

Originally published in *The Village Voice* (October 24, 1989).

THERE ARE ALL sorts of artists in this town—eight million in Soho alone. Some are polished and politic, socially adept pros with a market (and a trademark). Others are aggressively opinionated, self-defeatingly cranky, obsessively driven to make ephemeral works that confound explication and can never be sold. Ken Jacobs belongs to the latter type—which is one reason why this 55-year-old professor is one of the most extraordinary unknown personalities in the history of American movies.

A filmmaker since Eisenhower's second term, a teacher, a fabricator of elaborate shadow plays and inventor of a new form of 3-D movie projection, Jacobs is still best known for *Blonde Cobra* (1958–63), the portrait of Jack Smith he fashioned from footage shot by Bob Fleischner, and especially for *Tom, Tom, the Piper's Son* (1969–71), a 1905 one-reeler he refilmed as a feature-length "structural" extravaganza of close-ups, pans, freeze frames, and superimpositions. Jacobs calls *Tom, Tom* "a reverent examination . . . with a new movie almost incidentally coming into being." The same could be said of *Blonde Cobra*, another film-begotten film, as are many of his works.

Jacobs comes out of action painting, and one aspect of his project is film as performance—he may be the first moviemaker to take the projector seriously as his instrument, using an old Kalart-Victor to create dozens of unfixed *Tom, Tom*s in the course of his class lectures. His retro opens Friday evening with "*Southwark Fair*," a chapter from *The Impossible*, an ongoing piece scored for the apparatus Jacobs calls the "nervous system." Basically two interlocking projectors showing identical footage slightly out of phase, the nervous system embues flat movies with a shallow, intermittent three-dimensionality—"nervous" depth, a sort of perceptual corollary to Harold Rosenberg's "anxious object."

This set-up, which Jacobs has applied to material ranging from an ancient French stag film to newsreels of the American war in the Philippines, is a celluloid cyclotron, producing explosive energy from the collision of tiny image particles. As the projectors oscillate between two consecutive frames, or creep ahead a frame at a time, all action is converted into a hypnotic, strobelike twitch. These long, symphonic pieces are like a secret history of the 20th century, the ultimate *ballet mécanique*. The masses move in lockstep. The marketplace crowd in "*Southwark Fair*," drawn from the original *Tom, Tom,* are zombies conjured to life—there are few things more disconcertingly modern than the galvanized shuffle of these long-dead, film-imprisoned souls.

ALTHOUGH JACOBS KEEPS recycling *Tom, Tom* to show that this "primitive," ungrammatical strip of film is an inexhaustible welter of possibilities, he also makes movies from scratch—literally. *Star Spangled to Death,* his unfinished epic of the late '50s, the quintessential underground movie, is a monumental assemblage of pop detritus and urban debris. *The Sky Socialist,* an 8mm film made in the mid-'60s, is a dreamier gestic narrative that uses the language of happenings, rarefied and refined, to celebrate the Brooklyn Bridge. Jacobs's movies are ecstatically nonprofessional; the title of his 1958–60 *Little Stabs at Happiness*—four unedited camera-rolls of bohos hanging out—applies to them all.

Jacobs calls *Little Stabs* his "effort to be lifesize and available as a person . . . everything is lost for me when that tyrannical relationship takes place between the filmmaker and the viewer." Given the demands he may otherwise place on an audience, this sentiment is a bit disingenuous. Still, *Little Stabs at Happiness* is a triumph of sensibility over craft, one of the few movies that can be called truly inspirational.

His first movie, the ambitious but unpretentious *Orchard Street* (1956), exhibits an already honed eye for urban events and a fondness for apparent motion, not to mention an interest in the secondhand. The anthology *Sat. Afternoon Blood Sacrifice: TV Plug: Little Cobra Dance* (1957–64) includes a kinescope of Jacobs on the TV show *Play Your Hunch.* (A panel has to identify his film; Jacobs gets no further than saying "*Star Spangled . . .*" before one of the least-urgent special bulletins in the history of American broadcasting preempts his statement.) The last segment presents Jack Smith, head swaddled in old clothes, doing an undercranked dance on a tenement fire escape. Jacobs's early movies often feature Smith's most extravagant performances—in *The Death of P'town,* he haunts a New England graveyard, a "Vampire Fairy" with the elbows of a fullback—providing Jacobs with human energy that would later be sublimated into the film stuff itself.

Stan Brakhage, Jacobs's peer as a one-man assault team on official film culture, called one of his own domestic studies *An Avant-Garde Home Movie.* Jacobs explores this mode all the time—although he'd never use so condescending a title. For him, all home movies are potentially avant-garde. *Urban Peasants,* which opens the second show on Sunday, is 45 minutes of unedited 16mm camera rolls that record one extended family, mostly in front of their kosher butcher shop in some bleak Brooklyn backwater during the late '30s and early '40s. The footage is shown in silence; the filmmaker's only overt comment is to sepia-tint the sequence where the "peasants" visit Prospect Park, and to frame the film with two exercises from a record teaching conversational Yiddish.

Even before the first image of *Urban Peasants* appears we have had a six-minute lesson in Diaspora history called "Situation Three: Getting a Hotel." (The assumption is mind-blowing: Where in the world, with the possible exception of Birobidzhan, would one ever need to call room service in Yiddish?) A second excerpt, "Situation Eight: When You Are in Trouble," provides the film's double-edged punchline: "I am an American. . . . Everything is all right." Jacobs's deceptively simple juxtaposition makes it impossible to watch the homely clowning of his wartime, half-Americanized family without picturing the "situation" of their European counterparts.

THERE'S A BIT in *The Winter Footage* (1965–65)—a sort of warm-up for *The Sky Socialist* that demonstrates Jacobs's sensitivity to the uses of street trash, skeletal umbrellas, and broken toys—where, despite an attempt to block his lens, the filmmaker observes a professional crew shooting *A Fine Madness* under the Brooklyn Bridge. However suggestive, the coincidence of nonconformist creator coming across Sean Connery's Hollywood impersonation of same is an ordinary occurrence in the Jacobs oeuvre. No one has ever made richer, more varied use of what fortune brings to hand.

For Jacobs, "found" footage has less to do with appropriation than with appreciation. The bluntly titled *Perfect Film* is a 22-minute roll Jacobs discovered in a Canal Street junk bin and which he exhibits unaltered—an apparently random series of interviews and relevant exteriors taken by a TV news crew in the aftermath of Malcolm X's assassination. *Perfect Film* opens with a white reporter interviewing a black eyewitness (himself a reporter), and everything in this unmediated slice of celluloid takes on equal weight—the witness's faraway look, the way his experience becomes narrative, the camera-attracted mob (a Weegee crowd unfolding in time), the choice of camera angle, the interlocutor's tone. Meanwhile, other voices are heard. A white police inspector attempts to direct his presentation. A silent montage of streets, crowds, and cops sets off the recurring interviews. Even the dead Malcolm appears in a 30-second clip to say that Elijah Muhammad has given the order that he is to be killed.

More than a time-capsule, *Perfect Film* is a study of how news is made, literally. (As a meditation on the construction of truth, the film would make an interesting bill with *The Thin Blue Line.*) These out-takes have their own integrity. There's a structure here, even a revelatory drama. What's "perfect" is the demonstration that an anonymous workprint found in the garbage can be as multilayered and resonant, revealing and mysterious as a conscious work of art.

Jack Smith, 1932–1989

Originally published in *The Village Voice* (October 3, 1989).

SOMEHOW I GUESS I thought that Jack Smith would survive AIDS the way he survived poverty, landlords, neuroses, rip-offs, lack of recognition, life in New York, LSD, and the exploitation of *Flaming Creatures*. Given how little he ate, it's amazing Jack lived as long as he did—but then virtually every one of his performances was about the impossibility of its own coming into existence.

Jack Smith was an artist's artist whose boundless irony, formal integrity, visual wit, underdog passion, and fantastic pageantry were an inspiration and a source of ideas for generation upon generation of underground filmmakers, performers, and playwrights. His collaborators, appreciators, and acolytes included some of the most distinguished creators in town—Ken Jacobs, Andy Warhol, Susan Sontag, John Vacarro, Ronald Tavel, Richard Foreman, Charles Ludlam, Robert Wilson, Stefan Brecht, Vivienne Dick. I myself owe Jack a great deal. The first article I ever published in the *Voice* was on *Flaming Creatures*, and I can truly say that no art has moved me more deeply than the midnight slide shows and glacially paced performances Jack used to stage at the Plaster Foundation of Atlantis on pre-Soho Greene Street. (Permit me to recall some titles: *Gas Stations of the Cross Christmas Spectacle, Spiritual Oasis of Lucky Landlord Paradise, Orchid Rot of Rented Lagoon.*)

Long essays could be written about the rushes for *Normal Love*, or *The Secret of Rented Island*, Jack's 1978 production of Ibsen's *Ghosts* (who can even deal with the prescience of this?), played, at least the night I saw it, by a cast of stuffed animals and an NYU professor in a supermarket shopping cart, with Jack supplying all the voices. Jack Smith was a legendary character, like Alfred Jarry or Franz Kafka. And, even if he saw himself as plain "Donald Flamingo, just a local personality trying to make a living," he certainly didn't look or sound or act like anyone else. He was tall and skinny, and his distinctive, high-pitched drawl (fun to imitate, perfect for expressing feigned confusion) managed to evoke somnolence and hysteria in equal measure.

Jack could be very, very, *very* difficult, and although I was less a friend than a fan I knew him well enough to understand the ritual delaying tactics by which he distilled an audience down to its appreciative essence. (Important to note: He did work for an audience, and, unlike most avant-gardists, his audience was a popular one.) As an artist, Jack had a unique purity—his writings, his photographs, his films, his performances, his assemblages, his record collection, his costumes, his devotion to Maria Montez were all of a piece. Once he withdrew *Flaming Creatures* from Anthology Film Archives, his art was untainted by any institutional endorsement—an astonishing fact in this cruddy age, but then Jack Smith was, in every sense, a visionary.

He had politics as well. At the center of that "socialist" utopia Jack liked to imagine was a giant junkyard, a repository of discarded objects. "I think this center of unused objects and unwanted objects would become a center of intellectual activity," he once explained in *Semiotext(e)* (suggesting the journal be more catchily named *Hatred of Capitalism*). "Things would grow up around it." In fact, that center of unused objects is something Jack Smith created here, in this city, from the late '50s until last Monday. People tell me that Jack went easily, surrounded by friends. I really think his death marks the end of an era— for everyone who knew him and for New York as well.

Reviews and Appreciations, 1984–1989

White boys: Lucas, Spielberg, and the Temple of Dumb

Originally published in *The Village Voice* (June 5, 1984).

GEORGE LUCAS AND Steven Spielberg are the most successful filmmakers who ever lived, with the six top grossing movies in American history. Millionaires many times over, they can do whatever they want. Lucas even insists that what he would like to do are experimental, non-narrative films. But who's kidding whom? What these guys want, apparently, is *Indiana Jones and the Temple of Doom*. Free to do anything, they reinvent James Bond without the savoir faire.

There's a poetry to pulp—even *Raiders of the Lost Ark* could be read as a sort of kindergarten celebration of the Manhattan Project—and everyone knows most artists are engaged in working through the junk of their childhood. Few, however, seem as blithely uncritical as Lucas and Spielberg. When Kate Capshaw, who has the thankless task of playing *Indiana Jones*'s bimbo-in-residence, asks Harrison Ford why they're about to go off after the sacred Sankara stone of Pankot palace, there's a cut to close-up that turns his patronizing reply into a virtual manifesto. The reason, since you asked, is "fortune and glory." (You sense the undercurrent of bellicose anxiety here—can *Indiana Jones* muscle its way past *Jaws*?) The fortune, rest assured, will belong to Mssrs. Spielberg and Lucas. But the glory, on the other hand, is something grosses can't buy.

Strictly speaking a "prequel," this latest pastiche of the Saturday afternoon serials and adventure TV shows George Lucas loved as a kid picks up more or less where *Raiders* left off. Ford meets Capshaw during an intricately choreographed brawl in a Shanghai cabaret, and they dive out the window together, plunging through six canopies to land in a car driven by a 10-year-old street urchin (Ke Huy Quan), named Short Round in tribute to Sam Fuller's *The Steel Helmet*. Beating their pursuers to the airport, this surrogate family takes off in a plane, only to watch the crew bail out (and the fuel meter read empty), leaving them just a life raft with which to jump into space, go tobogganing down the Himalayas, sail over a cliff, tumble into a river, and ride the rapids to India.

Like *Raiders*, *Indiana Jones* is filmmaking at its most smugly mechanistic—the celluloid equivalent of a day in Disneyland, a point Spielberg brings home late in the movie with a reflexive action sequence that simulates an old-fashioned roller coaster ride. But *This Is Cinerama* notwithstanding, *Indiana Jones* spends most of its time in the Spook-a-Rama, activating one jack-in-the-box after another (the main one being your basic Kali cult writ large). I won't belabor the Freudian implications of the secret passage Ford discovers in Capshaw's boudoir (particularly in a film as breezily male supremacist as this one); suffice it to say it leads to a chamber of horrors inhabited by more roaches than the Furry Freak Brothers' crash pad and thence to the Temple of Doom, a flaming red-on-red set that suggests Maxwell's Plum as redecorated by Julian Schnabel.

Last weekend at Millennium, Jack Smith showed excerpts from a film once called *Normal Love* and now known, more accurately if somewhat less felicitously, as *Normal Fantasy,* which derives many of its images from the same stockpile of '30s and '40s exotica as *Indiana Jones.* The difference, however, is not simply that Lucas-Spielberg spend 100,000 times what Smith does to reach an audience 100,000 times larger. The difference is that where Lucas-Spielberg simply reproduce their childhood fantasies, Smith mediates his with adult realities. The result is infinitely richer and more poignant. Contemplative where *Indiana Jones* is frantic, *Normal Fantasy* has veiled, glitter-encrusted creatures washing the floor, savage Samoan-Aztec tribespeople clustered haplessly around their "Lucky Wishing Pool," or, most radically, the actual third world intruding upon a staged harem love triangle. What's more—Smith appears to identify with his creatures, all of them.

Although he's hardly thought of as a political filmmaker, Smith has made the most racially and sexually integrated of American underground movies. *Indiana Jones,* on the other hand, is inordinately racist and sexist, even by Hollywood standards. There's a kind of willful ignorance here, as though the magnitude of their success exempts Lucas and Spielberg from any moral considerations. Like white boys just want to have fun! As the film's only woman, Capshaw is compelled to play a bitchy gold digger (*her* desire for fortune implies no glory, that's for sure) who takes her ritual lumps toppling backward off elephants, being terrorized by jungle animals (while the boys argue over cards), yo-yoing up and down above the sacred lava pit, or discovering love while wrapped in the embrace of Indiana's equally fetishized whip.

Remaking the 40-year-old pulp serials they adore—without, apparently, pondering what it is that fascinates them so—these new Kings of the Earth have no qualms about reproducing 40-year-old assumptions as well. After all, it comes with the territory. The film's only humanized nonwhite is necessarily 10 years old. Indeed, when not pathetically down-trodden, the denizens of the third world theme-park where Indiana seeks his fortune and glory are all duplicitous, evil scum whose favored cuisine is a suitably yucky repast of raw snakes, giant beetles, and chilled monkey brains. For all its insistence on innocent pleasures and the primacy of entertainment, *Indiana Jones* is a joyless film—mean-spirited, preening, and lacking in grace.

All shook up

Originally published in *The Village Voice* (July 24, 1984).

NAGISA OSHIMA'S *Cruel Story of Youth* is the sort of movie that restores your faith in tabloid expressionism. Set in a world of strident rockabilly and lurid neon lights, boldly synthetic fabrics and flashy cars, turquoise telephones and motorcycle punks, this 1960 film is less Japan's *Rebel Without a*

Cause than its *Brave New World*. (Maybe it's both, like *The Cool and the Crazy* gone to *The Lost Civilization of Atlantis*.) Released briefly on the West Coast in 1961 under the suitably steamy rubric *Naked Youth,* the movie had its New York theatrical premiere almost a quarter-century later, yet it's weirdly contemporary—more new new wave than old new wave, the most hallucinatory youth film to open here since *Time Stands Still.*

Oshima's Fuller-like sensationalism has seldom been more apparent than in this, his second feature, made when he was 28. The opening titles are scrawled on newspapers; the colors are hotter than the soundtrack's intermittent rock 'n' roll sax; the film's sullen and sultry heroine, Makoto (Miyuki Kuwano), is like a cartoon teenage doll with her dyed bouffant hair and crinoline dresses. *Cruel Story of Youth* makes bravura use of the quintessential '50s wide-screen format (which had only recently been introduced into Japanese cinema with Akira Kurosawa's *The Hidden Fortress*). Oshima favors hand-held passages, skewed angles, and the sort of eccentric close-up that isolates a chin, a dangling cigarette, and a colossal phone receiver in one corner of an otherwise empty frame; he revels in startling effects, using them to map a superficially chaotic yet lethally repressive social milieu.

The film's herky-jerky plot development matches its jangling, flamboyant visual style. *Cruel Story of Youth* opens with Makoto and a girlfriend wandering around the Ginza, getting their teenage kicks by soliciting strange men to drive them home. Inevitably the virginal Makoto is attacked by one middle-aged creep only to be saved by Kiyoshi (Yusuke Kawazu), a dissolute university student who is being kept by an older married woman. A man of the world, Kiyoshi not only beats the would-be rapist but has the presence of mind to demand hush money as well.

The streets are filled with student demonstrators when next Kiyoshi and Makoto meet. The couple rent a boat on the previous night's hush money and wind up on a deserted industrial waterfront under a blazing sky. Kiyoshi offers to satisfy Makoto's sexual curiosity. She slaps him, he throws her in the dirty water. As the camera floats up into the glaring light, they have sex on the logs. It's a no-frills defloration; afterward Kiyoshi takes Makoto to his squalid room where they find another student couple in bed. The affair seems to be going nowhere—particularly when a gang of neighborhood hoodlums tries to put Makoto on the street—but, after her older sister Yuki attempts to nip young lust in the bud, rebellious Makoto moves in with Kiyoshi and promptly gets pregnant.

Kiyoshi and Makoto spend their evenings in a garish bar or else lounging about Kiyoshi's room listening to the radio. "Beethoven, bah!" he exclaims at one point, as though taking his cues from Chuck Berry. Oshima uses blaring rock 'n' roll to underscore the transitory nature of all the couple's pleasures, from motorcycling to cigarettes. When Makoto tells Kiyoshi that she's pregnant, he kisses her and they dance to the anarchic honking rockabilly for about 30 seconds, until Kiyoshi abruptly announces that "we can't have it born." In another memorable scene, they sit around drinking, Makoto in her slip, with another student couple, until the other girl gets insulted and runs out. If Kiyoshi's pad is an emblem of their illusory freedom, Makoto's ramshackle neighborhood—filled with construction sounds and iconic cement mixers—is a metaphor for the rampant growth of postwar Japan. Social welfare, such as it is, is represented by the sweaty, shabby clinic where Makoto gets an abortion. Yuki's old flame, a drunken medic in a bloodstained smock, runs the place in a dissolute parody of his idealistic younger self.

According to the Japanese critic Tadao Sato, *Cruel Story of Youth* was distinguished from other contemporary juvenile delinquency dramas (a genre known as *taiyozoku,* or "sun tribe" films) in that its protagonists were portrayed "neither as sad victims of society nor as daring rebels." Actually Kiyoshi and Makoto are both victims and rebels, up to a point. Their affair establishes the outer limit of acceptable sexual behavior. Indeed, Makoto—more victimized and hence more rebellious—is socially ostracized for her sexual acting out. Although the couple are resolutely apolitical, *Cruel Story of Youth* creates a dialectic that could take its subtitle from Wilhelm Reich's 1932 essay "Politicizing the Sexual Problem of Youth." It's apparent that their passion will be thwarted as long as things remain the way they are.

The film is as filled with unexamined sexual frustration as it is fueled by political rage. In Oshima's central metaphor, the couple become the willing agents of their own reification, using the hitchhiking ploy Makoto once played for thrills as a means to get money. In other words, they create a scam that permits them to turn a profit, punish society, and romantically (at least at first) recapitulate the way they met.

Although Makoto and Kiyoshi aggravate the film's various ineffectual adults by flaunting their romantic nihilism, the world of *Cruel Story of Youth* is so pervaded with cynicism, corruption, and sexual exploitation that ultimately they become the most innocent characters in the film. In despair at the "moral bankruptcy" of postwar Japan, Makoto's ineffectual father dodges confrontation, rushing off to work rather than asking his daughter where she's been all night. The sister and doctor who represent Oshima's generation, were part of the student demonstrations of the early '50s and have made an unhappy adjustment to the status quo, acquiescing in the blighting of their youthful dreams. "We have no dreams, so we can't see them destroyed," Kiyoshi boasts at one point. After they're arrested by the police—one of their marks having turned them in—he maintains that his only crime was getting caught.

This is a key assertion, because as Kiyoshi leaves the police station (released in the custody of his former mistress whose husband is a business associate of Makoto's mark), his sense of social justice is confirmed. On the steps, he encounters the idealistic doctor, who's just been arrested as an abortionist. So much for political idealism; the remainder of the film ties everything into a neat noose. Makoto has been sent to a juvenile detention home. Her father and sister come for her but she runs back to Kiyoshi. He says goodbye to his mistress (again) and goes with Makoto. The lovers jump into a cab but, of course, have no money to pay the driver. (The mistress, who has been following them in her

Buick, promptly appears and ironically foots the bill.) Their hopeless situation dawning on them, Kiyoshi and Makoto wander aimlessly through the Ginza. "The world makes us into tools," Kiyoshi finally announces and exercises his male prerogative by vanishing into the crowd.

In the end, Kiyoshi is surrounded by the hoodlum gang he's been dodging all film, while Makoto has reverted zombielike to her former means of excitement and been picked up hitchhiking by a middle-aged lech. As Kiyoshi is beaten to death he screams, and, in a haunting travesty of Japanese romantic convention, the faraway Makoto "hears" him. She jumps from the speeding car to her doom. Oshima tracks slowly along her torso, ironically superimposing Kiyoshi's opposite—as blunt and classic a closer as any Kabuki tragedy could provide.

For an American audience, *Cruel Story of Youth* is a fascinating example of Americanization in action. Although it's more likely that Oshima's cinematic models were Andrzej Wajda or François Truffaut than Hollywood action flicks, he's compelled to use American cars, clothes, and music as emblems of the modern world. The film is at once Americanized and anti-American, and its political complexity is a measure of Oshima's own. Born in 1932, the director came of age during the general strike of 1947 and was the leader of a left-wing student association at the height of the Korean War, his first films appearing during an equally strained and crucial period in U.S.-Japanese relations.

Nineteen-sixty was a year that proved as productive for Oshima personally as it was a watershed in the history of postwar Japan. The new U.S.-Japan Security Treaty—effectively locking Japan into the American sphere of influence—was announced in January, with President Eisenhower scheduled to visit in June. Mass demonstrations erupted that spring as *Cruel Story of Youth* was being shot, and Oshima uses documentary footage of students snake-dancing in the street. (In another topical touch, Makoto and Kiyoshi go to the movies and see newsreels of student demonstrations in South Korea, where the dictatorship of Syngman Rhee was toppled in April.) By the time *Cruel Story of Youth* was released in June, Eisenhower's trip had been long since canceled in the face of the escalating tumult.

Despite the largest mass movement—an alliance of students, intellectuals, university professors (including 75 per cent of the faculty at Tokyo University), housewives, and unions—and the largest work stoppage (five and a half million workers) in Japanese history, the security pact was ratified. This defeat notwithstanding, Oshima was consoled when *Cruel Story of Youth* proved a sensation. ("Through *Cruel Story of Youth,* Oshima became the darling of the age," Tadao Sato dryly observed.) Although saturated with the political tensions of the period, the film was identified with the current cycle of "sun tribe" films. As a corrective, Oshima quickly produced a follow-up, *The Sun's Burial,* in which—even less romantic than the protagonists of *Cruel Story of Youth*—his young subjects were followers of a right-wing militarist. Shot on location in Osaka's largest slum, the film rivals *Los Olvidados* in the ferocity of its vision, filled with routine rapes, murders, and rumbles.

Immediately after *The Sun's Burial* was released in fall, 1960, Oshima began production of his precocious masterpiece, *Night and Fog in Japan,* a scalding portrayal of the failure of two generations of left-wing idealists—his own and that of 1960—which makes painfully explicit all that can be read between the lines of his previous two films. Banned after four days (ostensibly because of the assassination of Socialist Party leader Inejiro Asanuma, but actually because of its bitter politics and unconventional film form), the movie immediately terminated Oshima's career at the Shochiku studio. Now that *Cruel Story of Youth* has belatedly arrived, one hopes that *The Sun's Burial* and *Night and Fog in Japan* won't be kept on ice another 25 years.

Stranger Than Paradise

Originally published as "Americana, Right and Wrong" in *The Village Voice* (October 2, 1984).

A DOWNBEAT PASTORAL just this side of sentimental, Jim Jarmusch's *Stranger Than Paradise* is a celebration of hanging out, bumming around and striking it rich—American (pre)occupations as deep-dyed as they are disreputable. The film is a stringent road movie cum character farce, with a trio of lumpen bohemians—a teenage immigrant from Budapest, her Americanized cousin, and his affable buddy—boldly emblazoned upon a series of gloriously deadbeat landscapes (the Lower East Side, the outskirts of Cleveland, the anonymous Florida coast). It's very funny and it's pure movie. No one will ever mistake this deadpan whatzit for a failed off-off-Broadway play.

Hair tortured into the world's most emphatic ponytail and bangs, the waif-like Eva (Eszter Balint) appears in America like some strange plant. (Call it a greenhorn.) But with her love for dated American slang ("bug off") and Screamin' Jay Hawkins, Eva is as confirmed a hipster as her older cousin Willy (John Lurie), who, no less stylized, is a hulking arrangement for stingy-brimmed hat and striped suspenders. Willy's sidekick, the diminutive, less savagely depressed Eddie (Richard Edson), has an even more rigorous dress code—matching *his* omnipresent fedora with a single ensemble in argyle sweater and gruesome plaid shirt.

Once seen, this threesome becomes absolutely indelible: the 19-year-old Balint, a child of the Squat Theater, carries messiness to blissful heights of brooding disarray. Lurie, a veteran of the late-'70s super-8 scene and a musician known for his work with the Lounge Lizards, is an astounding icon—a morose, menacing galoot with a propensity for pulling a fish face at unexpected moments. Edson, also a musician, has a mug out of a Ben Shahn etching that more than matches the mangled Lurie profile. Half the fun in Jarmusch's leisurely paced film is just watching these palookas breathe.

Stranger Than Paradise has lots of situations, if no real plot, and the action, such as it is, falls into three movements. The first, released by Jarmusch as an autonomous film in 1982, is simply called "The New World": Having fallen from the sky on the sullen Willy, Eva absorbs his *echt* American lifestyle ("Why is it called 'TV dinner?' What does that meat come from?") as well as the culture in general, smoking Chesterfields, reading comic books, and watching TV till dawn. After 10 days, she moves to Cleveland to stay with their ancient Aunt Lotte (played by Cecilia Stark as a superbly muttering Hungarian crone).

In the second movement, "One Year Later," Willy and Eddie are caught cheating at poker, borrow a car, and drive to Cleveland. There they play cards with Aunt Lotte ("I am the veenor," she flatly declares after every hand), accompany Eva and her date to watch kung fu films in a virtually empty theater, and visit the local landmark, Lake Erie. The final movement, tenderly titled "Paradise," has Willy, Eddie, and Eva pushing on to Florida, setting up temporary house in a shabby motel room, and then—with comic symmetry and typical haplessness—inadvertently dispersing across international boundaries.

Stranger Than Paradise is resplendent with the love of industrial ugliness. Our introduction to Cleveland is a rundown Greyhound terminal by a white-washed box optimistically called the Nite Life Cafe; Eva works at a hotdog-selling eyesore that looks like a miniature airplane hangar half-limned in neon. Even in "paradise," the film's unlikely deus ex machina is purchased in the most desolate gift shop imaginable. Lurie's spare score—a slow waltzing Bartok pastiche—adds a pinch of sweetness to this rummage-sale wasteland. The first time I saw the film, I wondered whether its sensibility might not wear thin; on the contrary, it takes a second viewing to fully savor Jarmusch's visual humor, internal rhymes, and masterful use of cliché. ("You can't win 'em all, it's the name of the game," the ever-conciliatory Eddie tells a raging Willy after they've stupidly blown their bankroll at the dog races.)

Structurally, the movie is a tour de force—a succession of brief vignettes punctuated by opaque film stock. There are no reverse angles, no point-of-view shots; each scene is a single take. Characters enter the frame as though it were a stage, and the effect is kabuki sitcom, yet powerfully naturalistic—an amalgam of Damon Runyan and Piet Mondrian that's a triumph of low-budget stylization. Jarmusch himself has come up with the film's best description, gleefully calling it "a neo-realistic black comedy in the style of an imaginary East European director obsessed with Ozu and *The Honeymooners*." My only caveat is that the film seems less black comedy than vaudeville—it's really a succession of black-out gags, some so absurd that you can sense the actors straining to keep from breaking up.

Jarmusch, 31, is an Ohio-born graduate of the NYU Film School and a onetime teaching assistant to Nicholas Ray. (He worked on Ray and Wim Wender's *Lightning Over Water,* among other local independent productions.) I was no great fan of his first feature, the 1980 *Permanent Vacation*—a plotless portrait of a teenage drifter, half post-punk verité, half Lower East Side tone-poem—but *Stranger Than Paradise* is a quantum leap forward in formal control. Without spoonfeeding his audience, Jarmusch manages to popularize the effects of some of the past decade's most powerful films.

With its dislocated travelogue, *Stranger Than Paradise* suggests Wim Wender's *Kings of the Road*; the transcendently shabby moonscapes evoke Chantal Akerman's *News from Home* and the absence of reverse angles her *Jeanne Dielman*; while the shaggy-dog narrative and vignette structure are anticipated by Jim Benning's *8½ × 11* and *11 × 14*. Jarmusch exhibits free-floating affinities to filmmakers as disparate as Ron Rice and Carl Dreyer as well, but *Stranger Than Paradise* is far more than the sum of its influences. The film is too strongly imagined and assembled to ever seem derivative. It's never less than wholly and confidently itself.

Jarmusch's movie has the timeless quality of a long-running comic-strip: It's as instantly familiar and ineffably weird as *Gasoline Alley* or *Moon Mullins*. Eva, Willy, and Eddie may be cartoon characters with unintelligible inner lives, but it's just that enigmatic two-dimensionality that makes *Stranger Than Paradise* so funny and gives the film, at once ethereal and hard-boiled, the look and feel of a classic. Tom Dicillo's august black and white cinematography compares with that of the most angst-ridden Bergman, but the world he depicts is as deliberately, comically, richly emptied-out as the most threadbare B-movie or cruddy TV drama. (The whole affair—props, sets, and costumes—could have been catered by the Salvation Army.) This is a film that goes beyond nostalgia toward some Platonic sense of Americanness.

The movie even manages to justify its clunky title. America *is* stranger than paradise—as Eddie says when they arrive in Cleveland, "You know, it's funny. You come to someplace new and everything looks just the same." The Hungary which Willy, Eva, and Aunt Lotte have separately fled is a purely negative conception—it only signifies the un-America. Actually, the idea of Willy as totally Americanized is a prize conceit. His America is the negation's negation. At one point, Eva takes Willy and Eddie to see Lake Erie. The wind is blowing, the snow is snowing, they lean over the rail and peer into a huge white void. It's one of the movie's most resonant bits. There really is no there there.

Double is my business

Originally published in *The Village Voice* (October 30, 1984).

THE POSTMODERN CRAZE for pastiche, quotation, appropriation reaches its Hollywood apogee in the voluptuously lurid, terminally flashy films of Brian De Palma. Unlike the more lovable Spielberg and Lucas, who synthesize their borrowings into seamless packages, De Palma flaunts his with cartoon garishness—and then perversely denies it. "I should listen to these nitwit critics?" he told Marcia Pally in a *Film Comment* interview filled with inadvertent disclosures, when she asked him why he kept quoting the shower scene from *Psycho.* "I don't cater to the public, why should I cater to the critics?"

Why indeed? If De Palma panders mainly to his own desires, the reader may be pardoned for wondering whether the director thinks *Body Double,* his current film, is bucking widespread lack of interest in softcore porn and bloody murder. The typically second-hand premise—lifted piecemeal from *Rear Window* and *Vertigo*—has an under-employed actor (Craig Wasson), who's just caught his girlfriend in flagrante and been fired from a low-budget horror flick named *Vampire's Kiss,* house-sitting a futuristic pleasure palace perched up high in the Hollywood hills. There he turns voyeur, spying on the exhibitionist antics of a mysterious neighbor (Deborah Shelton) who likes to dance half naked with the lights on before wearing her high heels to bed.

Someone is always spying on someone in *Body Double* (it's the film's most endearing trait), and the performance that hypnotizes Wasson is the movie's set piece. You get the feeling that, for De Palma, this is what movies (and sex) are all about. Accompanied by Pino Donaggio's prancing, perky, breathless post-disco theme—the music one might use to accompany an imaginary *Disneyland Blue* whose credit sequence begins with Tinkerbelle stripping off her gossamers and sitting on Pluto's face—Wasson's dream girl performs like clockwork for an invisible spectator.

Nearly as comic as this outrageous routine (which even climaxes Disney-style with the actress presenting her palpitating rump to the open window), is the contrast De Palma establishes between the planetariumlike luxury pad—a sinister lotusland of plants, fishtanks, and round, rotating beds—from which the sweaty-palmed Wasson watches the show and the all-white apartment where it takes place. If the latter is like a screen for Wasson's (and our) fantasies, De Palma visualizes the experience of peering in on her (and *Body Double*) as a delicacy fit for a pasha.

Unfortunately, it's not so simple. *Body Double* has a lot of frantic surface motion—usually an ominously gliding camera—and an overall lack of coherence. It's ultimately tiresome, although no De Palma film is without its tasty bits of business. *Body Double* is obsessed with video—as form, technology, and consumer item. De Palma makes witty use of the fast-forward scan mode, sets a comic scene in the adult section of Tower Records, and—at once brashly experimental, crassly pragmatic, and musically hip—plays havoc with his continuity by simply inserting a near-pornographic music video for Frankie Goes to Hollywood's "Relax" at a key moment in the action.

De Palma is the celluloid celebrant of the meretricious (his archetypal heroine is some variant of a hooker), and *Body Double* is long on pleasingly decrepit local color. Everything in this Hollywood is slimed with a residue of sweat and vinyl; even the sunlight seems made of tinsel. Although the imagery is less memorable than in most De Palma flicks, the dialogue is better than usual and so is the acting. (The pedantically obscene, relentlessly overplayed *Scarface* must have purged his system.)

Craig Wasson has the necessary callow innocence while, as a porn star supposedly modeled on Annette Haven (but sounding more like the director's ex, Nancy Allen), punky, platinum Melanie Griffith is unexpectedly charming—a tough tart with a child's squeaky voice. (Since she's also Tippi Hedren's daughter, her mere presence affords De Palma yet another kind of appropriation.) De Palma's favorite sleazoid, the nasally braying Dennis Franz, is an apt choice as the director of *Vampire's Kiss,* while, as a Hollywood cop, Guy Boyd is even better. This cold-eyed Joey Bishop type is the closest *Body Double* has to a resident superego. He interrogates Wasson like a bored talk show host, and briefly turns *Body Double* into a comic nightmare when he catches the harmless fetishist with Shelton's panties peeking out of his pocket.

But such primal moments are few. For all its primal ambitions, *Body Double,* like *Dressed to Kill* and *The Fury,* is pretty much an exercise in style. Previously, De Palma has been able to make genre conventions work even while hyperbolizing them. *Body Double,* however, suffers from a near total lack of suspense, while De Palma's propensity for pastiche has never seemed more blatant (or resulted in so little effect). Not content with appropriating elements from *Rear Window, Vertigo, Notorious, The Texas Chainsaw Massacre,* and *Driller Killer,* he rehashes scenes from his own *Obsession, Blow Out* and *Dressed to Kill.*

The elaborate sequence in which Wasson stalks Shelton through a multi-leveled shopping mall seems modeled after Angie Dickinson's fatal rendezvous at the Metropolitan Museum, but, despite the pyrotechnics, it misses the latter's pure narrative drive. "He's gotten so reflexive, he's disappeared up his own asshole," my companion remarked at the end of the movie, but it's more than that. After the honorable failure of *Scarface,* during which De Palma (who doesn't lack for self-admiration) had to subjugate his ego to that of Al Pacino, it was inevitable the director would come back singing "Hey lookit me, Ma!" with a vengeance.

With its frequent trompe l'oeil and intimations of trauma, the film *Body Double* most resembles is *Blow Out,* which, by transposing Antonioni's swinging London to downtown Philadelphia, effected an almost unbearably putrid representation of American social reality, with Watergate, Chappaquidick, the Kennedy assassination, Son of Sam, and the Bicentennial all conjoined in one ultraparanoid conspiracy. Like *Blow Out, Body Double* is a tawdry media circus that posits the consumption of images as the queasy essence of late capitalism. (De Palma would certainly appreciate the irony whereby all of human history could depend on the media perception of a single television show.) And like *Blow Out* as well, *Body Double* works overtime to remind the spectator of his/her spectatorship.

But where *Blow Out* was painfully cynical, *Body Double* is only cynical—an exercise in failed kickiness. When accused of misogyny, the misanthropic De Palma tends to shift the terms of political discussion by presenting himself as one of capitalism's necessary evils—*Blow Out* is so insistent on its self-conscious spectacle that it's virtually a capitalist *Man with a Movie Camera.* This near manifesto is De Palma's bitterest film: his alter ego John Travolta wants to tell the truth, but society just keeps pushing him back into his sordid little racket, dubbing the screams for *Coed Frenzy.*

Self-serving as its confessional schemata may be, *Blow Out* is also so controlled that, despite its continual barrage of distancing devices (ranging from actors applying make-up on camera to an elaborate demonstration of sync sound), many people identified sufficiently with Travolta (and Allen) as to feel upset and betrayed by the self-loathing despair of its superbly nasty punchline. De Palma likes to play with surfaces, but when he's at his best—in *Blow Out* or *Carrie*—the real horror lurks in the film's murky depths.

If *Blow Out*'s Moebius-strip plot hinges upon repetition, the best that can be said for *Body Double*'s more laborious circular one is that, as the title suggests, it's predicated upon a series of substitutions. The most complex of these involve Melanie Griffith (who not only stands in for Tippi Hedren and Nancy Allen but provides the sartorial model for Wasson when he's in his vampire drag). It wouldn't be cricket to reveal the rest. Suffice to say that when the heavy says to Wasson, "You ruined my surprise ending," he's being wildly optimistic.

The end of science fiction

Originally published in *The Village Voice* (December 25, 1984).

DAVID LYNCH may be the American director with the most direct pipeline to his unconscious. *Eraserhead* expressed a loathing of sex and procreation so visceral it virtually slimed its midnight cult, while *The Elephant Man* was far more disturbing than its sentimental script warranted. Similarly, *Dune,* Lynch's mega-million dollar adaptation of Frank Herbert's sword and sorcery classic, is steeped in an ancient, primordial nastiness that has nothing to do with the sci-fi film as we currently know it.

Dune suggests that Lynch is the first filmmaker who might be able to tackle H. P. Lovecraft. He has the right mixture of morbidity and naiveté, and he appears to be a resolute problem-solver. That doesn't mean he was the right choice to make *Dune,* although I can't imagine who would have been. A long time ago, in a far away galaxy, Haskell Wexler was supposed to direct a version for the producer of the *Planet of the Apes* series as the follow-up to *Medium Cool,* while Alejandro Jodorowsky, the now-forgotten director of *El Topo,* was involved in an abortive French version in the mid-'70s. (Jodorowsky planned to cast his own son as the messiah Paul Atriedes, with Salvador Dali, Gloria Swanson, and Mick Jagger in supporting roles.) Dino DeLaurentiis acquired the book in 1980 and originally hired Ridley Scott before the task fell to Lynch.

Published in 1965, Herbert's cult novel may be the kind of book you can only appreciate at a certain time in your life. Far be it from me to call something that's sold 10 million copies unreadable, but every time I sat down with it I slid into REM state after 20 pages. Lynch appears to have simplified the story (beside which the War of the Roses is a grade school primer) into your basic cosmic jihad. Without dwelling unduly on the religious overtones, he's visualized some of Herbert's more striking conceits while adding a few distinctive touches of his own.

Lynch gets a solo credit for the screenplay; but he's not primarily a narrative filmmaker and even with a stripped-down plot, the movie has the feel of frantic compression. *Dune* is plagued with clumsy exposition, much of it taking the form of whispered soliloquies. ("I *like* this Duke!" or "He's holding something back, and yet . . ." are typical of the film's buzzy, stilted stream of consciousness.) When not brutally self-evident, the dialogue is laughable, and Herbert's pretentious terminology doesn't help. But, although maladroitly written, the movie isn't badly directed. Lynch is all business when it comes to action, and the film's several firefights are sinuous, smoky exercises in shouts, routs, and confusion.

Although the script is a morass of clichés, *Dune* doesn't look like any science fiction film ever made. Whereas *Star Wars* was a raucous blitzkrieg in white, gold, and imperial blue, *Dune* is all earth colors—olives and grays and 15 shades of brown with a bilious orange to set them off. The film's preferred metal is not chrome but brass, its surfaces are not streamlined and shiny but dull, tarnished, and typically adorned with weathered Deco patterns. Ostensibly set in the year 10,991, Lynch's technology is far more mechanical than electronic. The style is lysergic Jules Verne—it's as though Lynch had designed a railroad coach that travels through hyperspace.

Dune has more wood paneling than the Harvard Club. The characters wear 19th century military uniforms and the bosom-suppressing gowns of 18th century Spanish infantas (in addition to assorted rubber bondage suits). The soundtrack is heavy with the roar of clanking machines, the sets are sodden with a steamy greenish miasma and the kind of lovingly detailed work—popeyed gargoyles, fluted bannisters—one spots in the background drawings of Disney's *Pinocchio*. The total effect is closer to the Victorian London of *The Elephant Man* than it is to Flash Gordon; *Dune* seems based less on old movies than old movie palaces. The center of *Dune*'s universe, where the Padishah Emperor (Jose Ferrer) hold court, is a fantastic vision of the men's room at Radio City or the lobby of the Brill building. *Dune* has the best sets of any film since *Blade Runner*.

As *Eraserhead* and *The Elephant Man* demonstrated, Lynch is a director of mood and texture, the queasier the better. *Dune* has the feel of a seventh grade science project run amok. It's often brilliantly disgusting. The film's villains are full of tubes and implants, their faces scarred with sewn-up orifices and weird skin grafts. Lynch's favorite characters are obviously the evil Harkonnens, who (when not attempting to conquer Dune) spend their time in a snot-green operating theater, casually butchering cattle or torturing cats. These baddies—who include the smirking Sting, Jack Nance (star of *Eraserhead,* his hair here dyed a carroty red), and particularly Kenneth McMillan—are leprously charismatic.

McMillan, who plays the pustule-covered archfiend Baron Vladimir Harkonnen as a kind of living pool of vomit, has a splendid time floating through the air dribbling food on his hapless confederates or bathing his face in motor oil. By contrast, the film's goodies are hopelessly blah. (Kyle MacLachlan, the hero, has the bland unctuousness and fistlike chin of the young Robert Vaughn.) In one of *Dune*'s more memorable exchanges, McMillan humiliates the hero's mother by letting fly a huge lunger right on her face. Lynch adds insult to injury by emphasizing this desecration with a juicily overamplified splat.

The Harkonnens have no womenfolk—one of *Dune*'s least savory conceits is making them crypto-gay leather freaks. (For pleasure, McMillan takes an epicene young boy and drinks his blood.) But then sex of any kind is apt to make Lynch squeamish. The humongous sandworms that tunnel beneath the desert of planet Dune are at once horrifically phallic and vaginal—these wriggling, static electricity-charged monstrosities erupt out of the ground and literally unfold into fantastic gaping maws. The film's most startling creature, a thing called the Spacing Guild Navigator, is a sort of hideous living brain with stunted vestigial arms that talks (so to speak) through what can only be described as a withered vulva (typically shown in tight close-up) complete with clitoris.

Against so violent a sexual backdrop—Lynch further manages to include two gratuitously slimy fetus shots—MacLachlan and his lady friend Sean Young (the beautiful replicant in *Blade Runner*) are ostentatiously chaste. *Dune* is full of squirting and squishing, and its most frightening monsters are lethal little hypodermic needles that dart and hover in the air like dragonflies. As in his earlier films, the slo-mo superimposition-filled dream sequences are among the weakest elements. Lynch is weirdest precisely when he's attempting to be most normal. The whole setup seems moments away from disintegrating before your eyes.

Dune is an obvious descendant of *Star Wars* (just as Herbert's epic space opera was a source for Lucas's), but—even allowing for Lucas's own brand of anti-eroticism—the two directors couldn't be more dissimilar. *Eraserhead* and *Star Wars* both appeared in 1977, equally expressive of the zeitgeist. But while one shot off into the stratosphere like a jet-propelled smile button to become the highest-grossing film of all time, the other—more suggestive of Johnny Rotten than Ronald Reagan and, by any standard, one of the most original American movies of the past decade—took years to find its cult.

The problem with *Dune* is that, unlike *Star Wars*, it has to be taken seriously. Lynch doesn't know how to distance himself from his own hackneyed script. He lacks Lucas's pop genius for pre-camp innocence and mindless rat-a-tat. The critical success of *The Elephant Man* notwithstanding, Lynch isn't a crowd pleaser. Where Lucas comes up with cute, cuddly wookies and ewoks, Lynch designs grotesque variations on human genitalia. Lucas's outer space is as cool, clean, and pure as one of Leni Riefenstahl's mountaintops. Lynch's is smeared with putrid globs of mysterious yech. It's about as pristine as an oil slick. There are moments in this movie when you simply can't believe your eyes.

THE DECADE BETWEEN *2001* (1968) and *Star Wars/Close Encounters* (1977) was likely the grimmest in sci-fi movie history. If the films of the '50s were paranoid metaphors for Communist invasion or nuclear catastrophe, those of the '70s were sodden bummers set in stagnant or devolved future societies (ranging from the grim postapocalyptic worlds of the five-film *Planet of the Apes* cycle to the cannibalistic Calcutta of *Soylent Green* and the tacky totalitarianism of *Clockwork Orange*).

Post-*2001* computer phobia reigned supreme. In *The Forbin Project,* a computer tried to become God; in *Logan's Run* a computer *was* God. In *The Stepford Wives* suburban hausfraus were replaced by compliant robots; in *Demon Seed,* Julie Christie was raped and impregnated by a sex-crazed computer. The most cherished leisure activities of American life came under brutal attack: *Westworld* and *Futureworld* carried the robot-crammed Disneyland theme park to its logical conclusion—as *Capricorn One* did the media manipulation of the evening news. *Rollerball* and *Death Race 2000* extrapolated sportsmania into a bloody, dystopian future. You don't have to be Dr. Siegfried Kracauer to see Nam and Watergate taking their toll. Seventies sci-fi was issue-oriented and earth-absorbed—parodies like *Dark Star* and *Flesh Gordon* aside, virtually the only sci-fi film of the period to take place in outer space was the ecology-oriented *Silent Running.*

Then in 1977, everything changed. *Star Wars* returned science fiction to outer space (where it has by and large remained), while *Close Encounters* infused the genre with a heady dose of Von Danikenism. Rationality was on the run: By now the notion that astronaut gods invented algebra, built Machu Pichu, and destroyed Sodom and Gomorrah is probably more widely believed in America than Darwin's theory of evolution.

Resurrecting the space invader-UFO genre, *Close Encounters* led the way back to the '50s—but with a difference. Whereas the humans of the '50s were menaced by everything from bloodsucking carrots and giant ants to mysterious pods and bellicose Martians, the new extraterrestrials were positively saintly. Meanwhile, in pastiching the space opera, *Star Wars* brought glitzy high-tech and aggressive innocence to the serials of the '30s and '40s and the primitive TV of the early '50s. (Is it a coincidence that the rebels in *Star Wars* are interested in the restoration of the status quo ante?) The sci-fi movies of the '70s were depressed sociological extrapolations; *Star Wars* and *Close Encounters* were both devotedly feel-good. If science had ceased to be a religion, the new science fiction offered itself as the vehicle for new religious fantasies to bring us together. Which brings us to the messianic meanderings of those two seasonal offerings, *2001* and *Starman.*

Starman, the more Von Daniken of the two, has been widely publicized as the film Columbia chose to develop instead of *E.T.* (an even more blatantly religious film than *Close Encounters*). Maybe so, but the commercial message of the 1982 blockbuster has had ample time to register. In his youth, John Carpenter made the funniest of all *2001* parodies, *Dark Star,* a low-budget vision of spaceship-as-hippie-crashpad that ended with an astronaut surfing off into the cosmic void. Perhaps trying to change his horror-purveying image, he's here succumbed to slavish Spielbergism, from the film's opening crypto Kodak ad through the reverent little theme that underlines all the action to the White Christmas glow of its heartclutching closer.

The film's premise has an affable alien visiting earth in the form of Karen Allen's late husband, a Madison, Wisconsin, housepainter. Jeff Bridges, perhaps the most charming male star in Hollywood pictures, plays the alien like an intelligent dog—hyper-alertly sniffing the breeze. His most daring attempt to disarm Allen is robotically mimicking Frank Sinatra's rendition of "New York, New York" (which he has apparently learned from the transmissions of Voyager 2).

Sappy but not boring, *Starman* blithely reverses the fears of *Invaders from Mars, Invasion of the Body Snatchers,* and particularly *I Married a Monster from Outer Space*—in which one's loved ones turn out to be soulless things. (Typically, the film ignores the provocative case-study angle: Allen's fantasy that her husband has died and been resurrected as a monster from outer space. Nor does it have much fun with the idea that back on his home planet Bridges is, as he tells Allen, an *unmarried* slime mold.) Charles Martin Smith, the nerdily sincere star of *Never Cry Wolf,* portrays a sympathetic scientist—the one earthling besides Allen who can grok Bridges's plight—and the riffs he plays with his superiors are the exact opposite of those in *The Thing,* where the carrot-symp scientist was a pathetic (and dangerous) dupe.

The Starman's mission to earth is extremely vague if not totally irrational. There's no apocalyptic warning, he just wants to make us feel good. ("You humans are at your best when things are worst," he illogically tells Allen.) Like E.T., his real purpose is to reverse the past. Not only does the alien invoke a happier vision of the innocent '50s, it also heals the wounded nuclear family. Given America's 50 per cent divorce rate, that may be a miracle only a flying saucer can provide.

AS THE STARMAN has the power to start a car engine with the touch of his hand, you can't help but wonder what miracles he can perform in the sack. Although he needs to pick up some technical pointers by watching *From Here to Eternity* on TV, it turns out to be nothing less than fathering the messiah. Hallelujah, for sure. *2010* is even more directly concerned with divine intervention.

Like Carpenter, *2010*'s director-writer-producer-cameraman Peter Hyams is a veteran of the sci-fi genre (his previous films include *Capricorn One* and the crypto-western *Outland*), and his sequel to Kubrick's "ultimate trip" moves along, explaining away every ambiguity in the original from HAL's breakdown and Keir Dullea's transformation to the nature of the monolith. For some, this may be superfluous, although at the screening I attended, "Thus Spake Zarathustra," the first monolith, and particularly HAL's voice were greeted with rapturous applause.

Set (no matter what the title says) in a contemporary universe of ugly futuristic kitchens and cluttered, corrogated furniture, *2010* is a film of rampant clichés. Observe the guilt-ridden NASA chief (Roy Scheider), the uptight scientist who loves computers more than people (Bob Balaban), the icy, Ninotchka-like female commissar (Helen Mirren), the John Lithgowesque paradigm of anxiety (John Lithgow). It's also a fount of impeccable special effects—the "natural" world is virtually never shown—the best of which is a Russian spaceship whose crew is played almost exclusively by recent émigré actors, all doing their versions of the wild and crazy guys. ("Issier than cake!" one says when embarking on a particularly dangerous probe. "Eetz a piss of pie.")

Nothing if not topical, *2010* posits the U.S. and USSR on the brink of war over a crisis in Central America as a joint Soviet-American mission goes in search of the spaceship that got farblundjet in *2001*. Hyam's script eliminates the Chinese who complicated Clarke's 1982 novel, making the film a less complicated plea for détente. It may be preposterous that the hardheaded Russians let themselves be seduced by an incoherent run-in with the ghost of Keir Dullea, but it's obviously the thought that counts. Although much of the dialogue is Russian, you better believe that once the voice of God starts beeping out on the video terminal it's strictly English, pal.

The cosmic miracle that concludes *2010* shocks the Americans and Russians into burying the swords, while ruining the nightclub business forever. As a further sop to Moral Majority fanatics pissed at missing the Rapture, divine will is expressed in the crassest of capitalist terms. "We're only tenants of this world," someone reverently observes. "We've been given a new lease—and a warning from the landlord." That's a thought for Christmas: God as Donald Trump.

Ralph and Alice and Ed and Trixie

Originally published in *Film Comment* (October 1985).

A neo-realistic black comedy in the style of an imaginary East European director obsessed with Ozu and *The Honeymooners*.
                    —Jim Jarmusch, describing his *Stranger Than Paradise*

THEY MAY YET raise the *Titanic,* excavate Troy, or unearth Judge Crater, but I doubt any archaeological find will generate more excitement this year than the announcement that Jackie Gleason had opened his vaults and discovered no less than 75 hitherto believed lost episodes of *The Honeymooners*. One expedition to the basement and the extant examples of the Great One's supreme creation nearly tripled.

Last aired between 1952 and 1955 during the halcyon days of *The Jackie Gleason Show,* all 75 were snapped up by Viacom International for cable telecasts. (In the meanwhile, 20 were "previewed" at the Museum of Broadcasting in New York, where the rapturous reception that had greeted four earlier lost-and-found *Honeymooners* reportedly inspired Gleason to go digging for more.) The remarkable thing is that the new "lost" *Honeymooners* are less Stone Age precursors to the 39 telefilms that have thrived in reruns lo these 30 years than prime examples of a fully developed concept.

Brooklyn bus driver Ralph Kramden, his long-suffering wife Alice (originally Pert Kelton before Audrey Meadows assumed and became synonymous with the part), and their upstairs neighbors, the Nortons (always Art Carney and Joyce Randolph), first appeared in late 1950 during Gleason's stint on the old DuMont network's *Cavalcade of Stars,* where they formed the nucleus of one skit among many. By the time Gleason jumped to CBS two years later—Meadows having replaced the ailing Kelton—*The Honeymooners* was the centerpiece of his show. Indeed, there was a time during the first Eisenhower administration when it would be the centerpiece of the entire CBS schedule—if not America's Saturday night. After struggling and prevailing against NBC's *All-Star Review* during the 1952–53 season, *The Jackie Gleason Show* gathered momentum throughout '53–'54 to place third in the Nielsen ratings (behind *I Love Lucy* and *Dragnet*) by late spring. The program reached its peak of popularity in June 1955, when Gleason stood atop the TV heap—although *Lucy* would finish first for the entire '54–'55 season, as it had for the previous two.

His popular if not aesthetic decline was just as rapid. For '55–'56, Gleason (now known as "Mr. Saturday Night") made an extremely profitable deal to split his weekly spot. The first half hour was to be a variety show he would produce, followed by a half-hour *Honeymooners* telefilm. Although the 39 episodes that were the fruits of this experiment have been rerun hundreds of times in some markets, they were clobbered in their original ratings by Perry Como, the show barely finishing in the top 20.

THESE DAYS, URBAN sophisticates are apt to appreciate *The Honeymooners* for its beatnik poverty and minimalist aesthetic. "There is a ritual, ceremonial, almost kabuki-like flavor to *The Honeymooners,*" writes David Marc in his indispensable *Demographic Vistas.* "Each story is told by means of a series of 20 or 30 highly stylized morphemic units." The familiar routines, the iconic costumes, the no-frills set (Ralph and Alice's almost ostentatiously barren kitchen) presented in every episode from the same static camera position have the timeless quality of a long-running daily comic strip. "The only modern convenience in this house is this can opener," Alice complains in "Santa and the Bookies" (12-12-53).

Yet, the Kramdens' kitchen is a complete and highly charged universe—its epic richness is underscored by one of Alice's most famous exercises in conjugal sarcasm. Comparing her realm to Disneyland (which opened, amid much fanfare, in 1955), she identifies her back window view with Fantasyland, the perpetually malfunctioning sink with Adventureland, the stove and icebox with Frontierland. All that's missing, she concludes, is "the world of Tomorrow"—

thus setting up the literal punch line as Ralph proposes addressing that absence by sending her to the moon.

The lost *Honeymooners* enrich the syndicated shows emotionally even as they take the edge off their formally rigorous stylization. Typically four eight- or nine-minute "acts," the rediscovered episodes escape more frequently from the less-is-more confines of the Kramden apartment—most often to the local pool-room or the front stoop, but also to assorted movie theaters, restaurants, and street corners, as well as Ralph's and Ed Norton's places of employment. The apartment itself is less fixed and more stagey (extravagant cracks appear in the plaster, the curtainless window casts a painted reflection). Still, the essentials are all in place—the mysteriously denuded window, the ancient icebox that is the prime signifier of Kramden poverty.

In "The Move Uptown" (4-24-54), Ralph and Alice attempt to leave Brook-lyn for a relatively lavish apartment in the Bronx. Their relocation is, in part, predicated on their ability to sublet their Chauncey Street dive—a task that would require the ingenuity needed to sell the Brooklyn Bridge. A succession of mainly immigrant families come to examine the apartment; a single glance sends most of them fleeing in horror. Ralph takes this more or less in stride, but when one couple actually stops to marvel at the antique icebox, he flies into a rage and throws them out. The episode ends, gratifyingly enough, with Ralph trashing the apartment in the vain hope that he will be evicted by his invisible, penurious landlord—revealed in "Principle of the Thing" (4-30-55) to be Jack Benny.

But if the lost *Honeymooners* clear up several minor enigmas (e.g., Trixie Norton's real first name), the essential mysteries are left veiled. The Kramden bedroom, for example, is never shown.

Fuller's scripts are grotesque jobs that might have been written by the bus driver in *The Honeymooners*: "OK, I'll give you five minutes to clear out. If you're not out, we're going to burn the place down."

–Manny Farber

THE ELEGANT SIMPLICITY of *The Honeymooners*' formula is exceeded only by its superb execution. As Marc has noted, virtually every show is concerned either with Ralph's hare-brained schemes to better his lot or his equally doomed attempts to assert authority over Alice. Similarly, two relationships provide most of the comedy: Ralph's sarcastic bickering with Alice and his Laurel-and-Hardy-like rapport with Norton.

In the world of *The Honeymooners,* Norton is the natural man—stupid, relaxed, fundamentally satisfied with his lot (which is, of course, working in the sewer). Playful rather than driven, he willingly participates in Ralph's ventures, if only for the enjoyment that his neighbor's discomfort invariably affords him. Norton's inspired foolishness—a matter of poetic loose connections and mala-propisms, idiosyncratic rituals, and occasional idiot officiousness—is the show's most surreal element. Alice, by contrast, is the reality principle incarnate.

Motherly but insulting, she refers to Ralph as her "266-pound baby," and caustic banter aside, her specialty is the terrifying calm she exhibits in the face of her husband's Vesuvian tantrums, her basilisk stare of seasoned contempt as, hand on hip, she begins, "Now you listen to me, Ralph . . ."

For Ralph, Norton is an object of friendly contempt, sexual solidarity, and intermittent male rivalry, while Alice is a Kali-like being eliciting fear and hatred as well as veneration. "This Is Your Life" (1-1-54) is one of the various episodes in which he suspects her of carrying on an illicit affair. (So far as I know, Alice never suffers a corresponding suspicion.) "Fourteen years I fractured myself driving a bus to take care of her," Ralph screams two minutes before reversing himself, after imagining that she might actually leave him: "I'm gonna treat her like a queen!"

BUT AS INSPIRED as Audrey Meadows and (especially) Art Carney are, they are eclipsed (figuratively as well as literally) by the stupendous character they support. There's Shakespeare's Falstaff, and then there's Gleason's Kramden—succinctly characterized in *The Honeymoooners' Companion* as "a fat, jealous, conclusion-jumping, big-mouthed bus driver with an ego that is dwarfed only by his waistline." Possessed of a hair-trigger temper—the loss of which could well have inspired Zero Mostel's transformation into a rhinoceros in Ionesco's play—Ralph wakes up in a walk-up tenement and a constant state of irritation. Indeed, one of the *The Honeymooners'* best built-in gags (all the more splendid for never being truly articulated) is the hilarious and appalling mental image one conjures of this frustrated, hostile, short-fused bully piloting a bus through midtown Manhattan.

In some respects, the Fifties mass cultural figure Ralph Kramden most resembles is Carl Barks' comic-book version of the similarly tantrum-prone Donald Duck. Philosophically opposed to both Alice and Norton, Kramden (like Donald) is continually looking for the one great business idea that will catapult him into the economic stratosphere, or even the middle class. (That Manny Farber could envision the script of *The Steel Helmet* or *The Crimson Kimono* as one of Kramden's get-rich-quick schemes is a joke of which I will never tire.) Despite his pretty wife and steady job, Ralph is a failure.

Lonely, thwarted, and frightened of authority (Gleason's overwrought cowardice is one of his prize routines), Kramden espouses a male supremacist philosophy so blatantly compensatory that it becomes a virtual critique of macho.[1] In "The Battle of the Sexes" (11-13-54), Ralph teaches the henpecked Norton his credo: "Tell her, 'I'm the King of the Castle—and you're nothing!'" ("Those words should be recorded and played at every wedding instead of 'Here Comes the Bride,'" Norton riffs, possibly to avoid commenting on the notion of the Kramden apartment as a "castle.") But however aristocratic Ralph's pretensions, he does not believe in noblesse oblige. The would-be tyrant is stingy—not simply with Alice but with Norton as well.

In "Kramden vs. Norton" (1-5-55), Ralph conspires to take his buddy and their wives to a cheap neighborhood movie rather than a nightclub as agreed.

When Norton wins a TV (an unlikely door prize for a theater in 1955 but the universal object of desire—and thus the exact opposite of the Kramden ice-box—on *The Honeymooners*), Ralph flies into an implacable rage: "Da set belongs to me!!!" (Ultimately the case winds up in night court.) That Kramden is Gleason's funniest creation goes without saying. It is Gleason's genius, however, that he makes this bellicose, gloating, ungenerous blowhard not just sympathetic, but profoundly moving as well.

I knew a hundred guys like Ralph Kramden in Brooklyn.

–Jackie Gleason, *American Film* (1982)

THERE IS A rediscovered episode, "The Honeymooners' Christmas Party" (12-19-53), in which Alice—bitchier here than on the syndicated shows—sends Ralph out on Christmas Eve to bring back her preferred brand of potato salad. As a result, the hapless bus driver is away from the house when, one after another, a half-dozen of Gleason's other alter egos (including Joe the Bartender, the Poor Soul, Reginald Van Gleason, and several anonymous tradesmen and delivery boys) come calling. Although designed as a tour de force for Gleason, the show is actually a tiresome washout. Struck by Gleason's lack of range, one waits impatiently for Ralph's return.

Indeed, Ralph scarcely seems to be a performance, so utterly did Gleason inhabit the role. But is it a hundred guys he is playing or is it one? Gleason's father, for whom he was named, was an alcoholic failure who deserted his family when Jackie was eight. For Gleason, the Depression began at least five years before the stock market crashed. "The set for *The Honeymooners* was exactly our living and dining room—we had a different kind of stove but that was it," he told *American Film*. The Kramden's address, 328 Chauncey Street, is that of the Bushwick tenement where Gleason and his mother lived at the time of her death in 1935; the building's facade is fairly accurately reproduced by the lost *Honeymooners'* exterior sets.

Clearly, Kramden is an integral part of Gleason's identity. Despite the versatility he demonstrated in his Hollywood performances, Gleason has made intermittent attempts to revive *The Honeymooners* throughout his career, most notably during the mid-Sixties, after his formula had been successfully travestied (and grotesquely denatured) by *The Flintstones*. Based in Miami—where Gleason moved in 1962 and (according to a contemporary *Look* magazine profile) lived like a "sultan"—the Sixties' *Honeymooners* was inflated to suit the boom-boom years. Gleason and Carney sported new (and younger) wives and enjoyed a more properly bourgeois lifestyle, even though many of the show's scripts were remakes from the "lost" era.

The extent of Gleason's psychodrama becomes evident in the context of the hour-long programs which in 1954 and 1955 defined the nation's Saturday nights. As David Marc describes it, Gleason was "Brooklyn's answer to *Le bourgeois gentilhomme*."

Opening his show with a Busby Berkeley-style number by the June Taylor Dancers, entering from the wings amidst an entourage of his personally auditioned Glea Girls, daintily lifting a coffee cup from a saucer to take a sip of you-know-what, the Great One bellowed, "How sweet it is!" and mugged for the camera while his audience—often composed of old neighborhood cronies brought in from across the river—went berserk. Ostentatiously displaying his expensive tastes in booze, broads, and life itself, the Cincinnatus of the Brooklyn tenements wallowed in the admiration of the masses.

The show's blowsy, "sophisticated" theme, its glamorous opening (successive dollies in on the dangling earrings and plunging necklines of a series of gorgeous Glea Girls), the Depression era opulence of the June Taylor Dancers, the star's grand entrance and his brazen slogan, created a multi-faceted spectacle of abundance. It was only within the security of this gilded frame, perhaps, that Gleason could explore—and his Saturday night audience endure (from the relative security of their suburban sofas)—the grim comedy of deprivation that was his masterpiece.

Viewers apparently keep dialing in to find out whether Ralph actually will crank up and let Alice have one "Pow! right in the kisser!" Male viewers in particular seem to get a vicarious satisfaction out of watching a man prepare to clobber his spouse.

—TV Guide, 10-1-55

THE LIFESTYLE REPRESENTED in *The Honeymooners* is at least as suggestive of the Thirties as it is of the Fifties. One would have to return to the early Thirties, to vintage W.C. Fields or the first Warners talkies, to find a corresponding atmosphere of lower-class meanness. Despite its near-obligatory kiss-and-makeup fadeout, the show is notable for its startling lack of sentimentality. When Gilbert Seldes wrote of *The Honeymooners'* "harshness, often too realistic to be funny," he was speaking not just of economic impoverishment but of emotional suffering as well.

"Ralph and Alice dramatize the bickering of the loveless," Seldes observed in his perceptive 1956 essay, "and the emotion delivered with the authentic ring of truth is actual dislike. . . . A scene of high-pitched recrimination between [the Kramdens] reminds us of voices overheard across areaways and on back porches just before doors slam or crockery is smashed." Or the screaming starts. *The Honeymooners* may be the most intense representation of ongoing marital discord ever put before the American public. In no other sitcom has the threat of domestic violence ever been so tantalizing (even titillating) a constant. "Just once, just once!" Ralph snarls in each and every show, brandishing his fat finger in Alice's sneering face. "One of these days, POW!!!"

Nor is Alice's infinitely postponed trip to the moon the show's only taboo. Students of Leslie Fiedler should note that where Ralph and Norton are several times compelled to share a bed, Ralph and Alice have never been so depicted—

and the Kramden bedroom is a structural absence. In some ways, food is the displaced expression of sex, particularly insofar as it demonstrates Ralph's dependence on Alice. When Alice and Trixie walk out on their spouses in "The Battle of the Sexes," the men are literally starved into submission. Similarly, dissatisfaction with Alice's cooking is Ralph's most persistent domestic gripe. "No wonder I'm getting those crazy suppers," he explodes with the force of a sudden revelation in "This Is Your Life," having jumped to the conclusion that Alice is in the habit of sharing afternoon cocktails with an imagined lover. "Every time she cooks them, she's loaded!!!"

Whatever the state of the Kramden's sex life, however, the absence that *The Honeymooners* cannot conceal is that of offspring. Among other things, *The Honeymooners* is one of the few child-free domestic sitcoms of the Fifties, and the possibility that the Kramdens might not want children—amidst the greatest baby boom that the Republic has ever known—is kinkier than any sexual aberration. Thus, in "Santa and the Bookies," Ralph discovers the baby clothes that Alice is surreptitiously knitting to pick up some Christmas cash (she's not permitted to work) and is thrilled by the possibility that she's pregnant.

It may be that the Kramdens' childlessness is even more intrinsic to their identity as a couple than is their continual bickering. The punchline of a celebrated *Saturday Night Live* parody later has Alice knocked up, rather than knocked out. (That Norton is revealed to be the father adds another wrinkle.[2]) Alice's phantom pregnancy provided one of the comic situations in "The Second Honeymoon," an hour-long special that reunited Meadows and Randolph with Gleason and Carney in 1976 for a 25th anniversary celebration. Indeed, the Kramdens' unsuccessful attempt to adopt a child was the subject of a one-hour special ten years earlier, for which Meadows also emerged from retirement. This was actually a reprise of a lost show, "The Adoption" (3-26-55), which might reasonably be among her favorites. For it is the episode that forever establishes the Kramdens' childlessness as a loss rather than an absence and thus throws the entire *Honeymooners* enterprise into a particularly harsh and poignant light.

"THE ADOPTION" OPENS with a call for the Kramdens on the Nortons' phone (Trixie obligingly lowers her receiver down through the Kramdens' kitchen window). Ralph and Alice, we discover, have registered with an adoption agency and are now to expect a home visit from a social worker who will report on their suitability as parents. The news delights Alice and sends Ralph into an overheated reverie about his son, Ralph Jr. "We wanted this more than anything else in the world," he expansively tells Norton, setting the table for the tragedy to follow.

Act II reveals that the Kramdens have borrowed furniture (including a refrigerator) from all their neighbors, turning their Thirties hovel into a Fifties Potemkin village. Beside himself with anxiety, Ralph naturally accuses Alice of being "jittery" and neurotically plies the social worker with sandwiches. In the middle of the interview, the ice man shows up demanding the four dollars the Kramdens owe him. Ralph totally mishandles the crisis. Rather than simply paying the bill, he loudly accuses the ice-man of having come to the wrong apartment—the Kramdens have a refrigerator after all. Sensing a deadbeat, the ice-man escalates the argument until the social worker has to take notice. Now the humiliated Kramden is forced to make a direct bid for sympathy, pathetically bleating, "I want a kid." Surprisingly, she agrees. "I don't think I've ever been in a home with a greater desire for a child," she says, turning a phrase with a ghostly resonance for every successive *Honeymooners* episode.

Sure enough, the next act finds the Kramdens (supported by the Nortons) in a hospital waiting room. The baby is brought out and predictably it's a *girl*. Just as predictably (but no less shockingly for all that), Ralph goes berserk, buttonholing the doctor and demanding a son: "A girl! A girl!! Nobody wants a girl!!!" For once, Alice proves unable to cope with her husband's tantrum; so mortified she lacks the strength to argue, she retreats with the Nortons. Meanwhile, the doctor (who, as played by show regular George Petrie, has the professional demeanor of a backstreet abortionist) is called away, leaving Ralph alone with the baby and Gleason to play an expert solo. He begins by telling the infant not to take his rejection personally—"If I wanted a girl, you'd be the one"—and ends by belligerently refusing to surrender the child back to the doctor's care.

The drama concludes where it began, in the Kramdens' kitchen—now festooned with diaper-draped clotheslines. Ralph and Norton are amusing little Ralphina, ineptly fashioning a nipple out of a rubber glove and squirting each other with milk. Alice returns with bad news—in the form of the doctor—in tow: The baby's natural mother has changed her mind and wants the child back. Ralph, naturally, flips. "I've had the kid for a week! I'm in love with her!" he trumpets, while Alice, who appreciates the hopelessness of the situation, is simply stricken. (Meadows' performance is exemplary in its underplaying.) The scene concludes with the most agonizing demonstration of Ralph's powerlessness imaginable. As rage is spent (and his awe of authority returns), Ralph retreats into a pitiable fantasy of being Ralphina's secret benefactor, her anonymous "Santy Claus." Then he dazedly exits, leaving Alice alone and shaking with silent sobs.

The grandeur of this episode lies in its elevation of the child to metaphor. Ralphina is the embodiment of all the Kramdens' failures, the epitome of everything they lack—including, apparently, the capacity to comfort each other. It is at this point that the Kramden kitchen becomes as mutely eloquent as a Beckett stage set, and Ralph's monstrous figure but a fragile bulwark against the void.

---

[1] In this sense, Kramden is the perfect subject of fascism—in thrall to authority and content to reproduce his own exploitation in the domestic sphere. For all Ralph's bellyaching, a trade union is one of *The Honeymooners'* key significant absences; instead, Kramden and Norton belong to a ludicrous fraternal organization (replete with much bogus pageantry and arcane ritual), the International Order of Friendly Raccoons.

A political reading of *The Honeymooners* is long overdue—it would be useful to chart the curve of Kramdens' popularity against that of the similarly loud-mouthed, lower-class, conclusion-jumping Senator Joseph McCarthy. (It's interesting as well that Farber associates Kramden with Sam Fuller, the lumpen-Americanist par excellence, before Sylvester Stallone.) Although Archie

Bunker, Ralph's most notable successor as a TV prole, is clearly modeled on Kramden, *The Honeymooners* is as true to its historic moment as *All in the Family* is to its, in avoiding politics. "The People's Choice" (10-23-54) flirts with the idea of Ralph as a political icon, then uneasily backs away.

²Here *SNL* precipitated another latent aspect of *The Honeymooners*. Norton's appetite for food exceeds Ralph's; left alone, he frequently raids the Kramden icebox. In general, Norton is less repressed than his buddy—more apt to bring up the prospect of ditching their wives for some illicit fun and also more flirtatious, albeit brainlessly so. (Bumping into Alice at the start of "This Is Your Life" he extravagantly doffs his hat and exclaims, "I beg your pardon, my fair mam'zelle.") According to *The Honeymooners' Companion*, Trixie is a former "burlesque queen."

Shoah: The being of nothingness

Originally published as "*Shoah*: Witness to Annihilation" in *The Village Voice* (October 29, 1985) and "*Shoah* Business" in *The Village Voice* (January 28, 1986).

CLAUDE LANZMANN'S *Shoah* is not simply the most ambitious film ever attempted on the extermination of the Jews; it's a work that treats the problem of representation so scrupulously it could have been inspired by the Old Testament injunction against graven images. "The Holocaust is unique in that it creates a circle of flames around itself, a limit which cannot be crossed because a certain absolute horror cannot be transmitted," Lanzmann wrote in a 1979 essay, ostensibly about the mini-series *Holocaust*. "Pretending to cross that line is a grave transgression."

Shoah, which takes its title from the Hebrew word for "annihilation," doesn't cross that line, it defines it. For much of its nine and a half hours, the film seems formless and repetitive. Moving back and forth from the general to the specific, circling around certain themes, *Shoah* overwhelms the audience with details. For those who demand linear progression, Lanzmann's method may seem perverse—the film's development is not a temporal one. "The six million Jews did not die in their own time, and that is why any work that today wants to render justice to the Holocaust must take as its first principle the fracturing of chronology," Lanzmann has written. Although *Shoah* is structured by internal corroborations, in the end you have to supply the connections yourself. This film throws you upon your own resources. It compels you to imagine the unimaginable.

Length aside, *Shoah* is notable for the rigor of Lanzmann's method: the eschewing of archival footage and narration in favor of contemporary land-scapes and long interviews (shown mainly in real time) with those who, in one form or another, experienced the Holocaust. "The film had to be made from traces of traces of traces," Lanzmann told one interviewer. Like the Swedish *Chaim Rumkowski and the Jews of Lodz* or the Hungarian *Package Tour,* two recent documentaries with less global perspectives on the war against the Jews, *Shoah* embodies a powerful and principled restraint. Like Syberberg's *Hitler, a Film from Germany,* it refuses to "reconstruct" the past, thus thwarting a conventional response and directing one to the source of one's own fascination.

Lanzmann, however, is scarcely as theatrical as Syberberg. In some respects, his strategy resembles that employed by Jean-Marie Straub and Danièle Huillet. The Straubs' 1976 *Fortini-Cani*, for example, punctuates readings by the Italian-Jewish-Communist poet Franco Fortini with long ruminations upon sylvan vistas where, 30-odd years earlier, the Nazis massacred a group of Italian partisans. Lanzmann shares the same conviction that the past surrounds us, that history is inscribed (if only through its erasure) on the present. In his *Holocaust* piece, he approvingly quotes the philosopher Emil Fackenheim: "The European Jews massacred are not just of the past, they are the *presence of an absence.*" This is why, while the vast Auschwitz complex has come to epitomize the Nazi death machine, *Shoah* emphasizes Treblinka—a camp built solely to exterminate Jews, a back-countrysite razed and plowed under by the Nazis themselves in an attempt to conceal all physical evidence of 800,000 murders.

The landscapes in *Shoah* are no less tranquil than those of *Fortini-Cani*, but they are haunted beyond the mind's capacity to take them in: Piney woods and marshy fields cover mass graves, a brackish lake is silted with the ashes of hundreds of thousands of victims. The camera gazes at the overgrown railroad tracks, end of the line, site of a ramp where a quarter of a million Jews were unloaded then hurried along with whips to their doom; it considers the postcard town of Chelmno where, one day after Pearl Harbor, the first Jews were gassed in mobile vans, using engine exhaust. What can be more peaceful than the ruins of Birkenau's snow-covered cremos and gas chambers? Of course, not every vista is so scenic. In one unforgettable camera movement, Lanzmann slowly pans down to the brown winter grass covering the rusty spoons and personal detritus that still constitute the soil of Auschwitz.

What binds these landscapes together are the trains that chug through Europe bound for Poland and the east. Lanzmann even managed to find an engineer who drove the Jewish transports. One of the film's recurring images is that of a train crossing the Polish countryside or pulling up in Treblinka station, with this very engineer, now wizened and bony as some medieval Death, looking back towards his invisible freight. In the argument of *Shoah*, these trains underscore the extent of bureaucratic organization needed to commit genocide, the blatant obviousness of the transports, and, finally, the existential terror of the journey. While the Jews were systematically deprived of water, the railroad crew was plied with drink. Through a translator, the former engineer tells Lanzmann the run was so harrowing the Germans were forced to pay a bonus in vodka. "He drank every drop he got because without liquor he couldn't stand the stench," the translator explains. "They even bought more liquor on their own . . ."

If landscapes give *Shoah* its weight, interviews provide its drama. Over and against these images of present-day Poland and Germany is the testimony of witnesses ranging from Jewish survivors to Polish onlookers to Nazi commandants. But the film is as filled with silence as with talk. Nine hours' worth of subtitles barely make a comfortably margined 200-page book. Pauses, hesitations, are often more eloquent than words. The evident torment with which Jan

Karski, a onetime courier for the Polish government, recalls two clandestine tours of the Warsaw Ghetto carries an expressive charge far beyond his pained, halting description. Indeed, his face gray with agony, Karski breaks down and bolts off camera before he can even start.

Moreover, words are belied by expressions. Among the most scandalous aspects of *Shoah* are Lanzmann's interviews with the Polish residents of Chelmno and Treblinka. Although there are exceptions, their blandly volunteered memories and perfunctorily offered concern ("it was sad to watch—nothing to be cheery about") are almost more damning than the casual anti-Semitism ("all Poland was in the Jews' hands") the interviewer has little difficulty in provoking. Real malice only surfaces in tales of "fat" foreign Jews "dressed in white shirts" riding to their death in passenger cars where "they could drink and walk around" and even play cards. "We'd gesture that they'd be killed," one peasant adds, passing his finger across his throat in demonstration. His buddies assent, as if this macabre signal was itself an act of guerrilla warfare directed at the Germans.

If the sequence induces the unbearable mental image of trains run by drunken crews, packed to overflowing with a dazed, weeping human cargo, careening through a countryside areek with the stench of gas and burning bodies, jeered at by peasants standing by the tracks, this and more are corroborated by the surviving Jews: "Most of the people, not only the majority, but 99 per cent of the Polish people when they saw the train going through—we looked really like animals in that wagon, just our eyes looked outside—they were laughing, they had a joy, because they took the Jewish people away."

As for the Nazis, it's hard to know which is worse, the pathetic evasions of the avuncular Franz Grassler, onetime deputy commissioner of the Warsaw Ghetto, insisting that the Jews knew more about the final solution than did their jailers, or the affable, expansive Franz Suchomel, an SS Unterscharführer at Treblinka, expressing a grotesque camaraderie with the people he was killing. Among other things, *Shoah* precisely details the means by which the Jews were compelled to participate in their own destruction. Meanwhile, the testimony of Suchomel and others, such as the former head of Reich Railways Department 33, demonstrates that genocide—by which the Nazis proposed to have the Jewish vanish *without a trace*—posed incredible logistical difficulties, solvable only by a modern, mobilized bureaucracy. It is here that the language of problem-solving takes on a hallucinative unreality. Suchomel allows that at its peak, Treblinka "processed" 12,000 to 15,000 Jews each day ("we had to spend half the night at it"), a train-load of victims going "up the funnel" in two or three hours. Unlike at Auschwitz, prisoners at Treblinka were gassed with engine exhaust. "Auschwitz was a factory!" Suchomel explains. "Treblinka was a primitive but efficient production line of death."

You watch this in a state of moral nausea so strong it makes your head swim. Nor does Lanzmann ease you into the flow. *Shoah* opens at the site of the Chelmno death camp, with one of the film's few narrative voice-overs observing that of the 400,000 Jews who were sent there only two survived. (Later we meet them.) The film's second part begins with another sort of horror, Suchomel singing the Treblinka anthem:

> *Looking squarely ahead, brave and joyous,*
> *At the world,*
> *The squads march to work.*
> *All that matters to us now is Treblinka.*
> *It is our destiny.*
> *That's why we've become one with Treblinka*
> *In no time at all.*
> *We know only the word of our commander,*
> *We know only obedience and duty,*
> *We want to serve, to go on serving,*
> *Until a little luck ends it all.*
>   *Hurray!*

Each morning, he explains, the newly arrived Jews selected for slave labor were taught the song: "By evening they had to be able to sing along with it." (Even now I can't get this idiotic martial melody out of my head. In Jean-François Steiner's *Treblinka,* it is reported that, after the day's work, Jewish laborers were compelled to stand at attention and repeat these words for hours—as well as sing the anthem as they marched.)

Lanzmann's most detailed interviews are with former members of the Sondercommando—the Jews who were kept alive at Treblinka and Auschwitz to stoke the annihilation machine. "We were the workers in the Treblinka factory, and our lives depended on the whole manufacturing process, that is, the slaughtering process at Treblinka," one explains. Only the naive or the pitiless can call them collaborators. In a sense, these men hyperbolize the dilemma of Jewish survivors in general—it is one of the Holocaust's cruelties that every Jew who survived is somehow tainted. One woman who managed to weather the war hiding in Berlin describes her feelings on the day that the last Jews in the city were rounded up for deportation: "I felt very guilty that I didn't go myself and I tried to escape fate that the others could not escape. There was no more warmth around, no more soul . . . [only] this feeling of being terribly alone. . . . What made us do this? To escape [the] fate that was really our destiny or the destiny of our people." A terrible fate, an absolute isolation are ideas that recur in *Shoah* again and again.

If the Nazis are all too human, the survivors are as mysterious as extra-terrestrials. What is one to make of the urbane, ironic Rudolf Vrba smiling as he describes cleaning the bodies out of the gas chamber, or the beseeching eyes of Filip Müller, survivor of five liquidations of the Auschwitz special detail? (His relentless discourse—an account of undressing corpses, shoveling them into the cremo, witnessing the last moments of thousands of Jews, some knowing, some not—is delivered in a tone of perpetual amazement, as though always for the first time: "It was like a blow on the head, as if I'd been stunned.") Unlike other accounts of the Holocaust, *Shoah* deliberately minimizes acts of individual heroism—to have been a Jew in Hitler's Europe was to have had the most appalling kind of heroism thrust upon you. "I began drinking after the war," the grim, noble-looking Itzhak Zuckerman, second-in-command of the Warsaw Ghetto's Jewish Combat Organization, tells Lanzmann. "It was very difficult. Claude, you asked for my impression. If you could lick my heart, it would poison you."

People have been asking me, with a guilty curiosity I can well understand, whether *Shoah* really has to be seen. A sense of moral obligation is unavoidably attached to such a film. Who knows if *Shoah* is good for you? (One hopes, probably in vain, that reviewers will declare a moratorium on the already debased currency of movie-ad hype.) There were many times during the screening that I regarded it as a chore and yet, weeks later, I find myself still mulling over landscapes, facial expressions, vocal inflections—the very stuff of cinema—and even wanting to see it again. The published text can in no way substitute for the film itself; the "text" of *Shoah* can only be experienced on the screen. On the other hand, the book is quite helpful in grasping Lanzmann's structure. For, if at first, *Shoah* seems porous and inflated, this is a film that expands in one's memory, its intricate cross-references and monumental form only gradually becoming apparent. One resists regarding *Shoah* as art—and, as artful as it is, one should.

This movie transfixes you, it numbs you, and finally—with infinite solicitude—it scars you. There are moments when you simply can't bear to look at another human being; *Shoah* is something that you experience alone. (If it teaches us anything, it's the meaning of the word "inconsolable.") The film ends in Israel—as it has to—with a member of the Jewish Combat Organization describing his fantasy, while searching the empty ruins of the Warsaw Ghetto, of being "the last Jew." (After he finishes comes a coda of trains implacably rolling on . . .)

Leaving the theater, you may recall one survivor's account of a secret mission out of the Ghetto to "Aryan" Warsaw: "We suddenly emerged into a street in broad daylight, stunned to find ourselves among normal people. [It was as if] we'd come from another planet." The horror of it is, that planet is ours.

I FIRST HEARD the bitter pun "there's no business like *shoah* business" while working at YIVO, an institution almost exclusively staffed by Holocaust survivors or their children. The joke acknowledged the seemingly limitless appetite for Holocaust materials, mainly as fund-raising tools within the Jewish community, but also as a source of identity—even a perverse ethnic pride—as well as the antidote to the fascination with Nazism.

The joke also observes that nothing in this world is beyond recuperation. Elie Wiesel has dedicated himself to keeping the Holocaust pure, so to speak, and untrivialized. In doing so, his insistence has become so official and automatic that he himself has become a mass-culture cliché—the gaunt, tragic-eyed Holocaust survivor. On the surface, Claude Lanzmann's *Shoah* would seem to be another candidate for this sort of recuperation. But the film's nine-and-a-half-hour length, among other things, helps it to resist easy assimilation despite the extravagant reviews I quoted several weeks ago.

Shoah is the latest example of an epic genre, born with *The Sorrow and the Pity*, but also including the TV miniseries *Holocaust* and *The Winds of War*, Fassbinder's *Berlin Alexanderplatz*, Edgar Reitz's *Heimat*, and Syberberg's *Our Hitler*, which attempts to elevate memory to the level of myth (or antimyth), to lay bare the central event of the century before it vanishes from living history. Whether confronting the events of World War II or the origin of barbarism in the heart of western civilization, these films are susceptible to a nostalgic appetite for eternal verities—cooking up the past into a digestible narrative complete with ending. With the exception of the Syberberg film, *Shoah* is the only one of these to refuse this closure and rethink the problem of representation.

That so advanced and lucid a filmmaker as Ernie Gehr would independently develop strategies parallel to *Shoah*'s (with his recent *Signal—Germany on the Air*) is a kind of backhanded acknowledgment of Lanzmann's formal intelligence. There's a sense—mainly in its use of real time and existential drama—in which *Shoah* has as much in common with *The Chelsea Girls* as *The Sorrow and the Pity*. It's even closer to Jean-Marie Straub and Danièle Huillet's *History Lessons*, in which the camera dramatizes the search for historical verity by circling around a central absence, and their *Fortini-Cani* or *Too Early, Too Late*, both of which interrogate now-peaceful landscapes, the sites of past atrocities, for what a believer might call the silence of God.

Documentary is a tricky concept, made even more so by celluloid halls of mirrors like *The Atomic Café* and *One Man's War*—films that "document" earlier films. Archival footage carries its own baggage. But although *Shoah* is largely oral history, Lanzmann's eschewal of illustration triggers a primitive response to the photographic image. Looking at a photograph, one sees *through* the composition and imagines what has been pictured. Hence, Lanzmann's fanatical attention to detail; this is a film which can only unfold in the mind's eye. The question that underlies *Shoah* is, how did the Holocaust happen? Lanzmann sets out to answer this both in terms of practical logistics and human sensations. How was it done, how did it feel?

Much of what has been written about *Shoah* glosses over the film's provocations—its repetitions, its absences, its Talmudic system of cross-references. Review after review contains a flash of recognition—to experience the Holocaust onscreen is still, on some level, to experience the Holocaust—followed by a movement to put the film at arm's length. "If this isn't the best film of 1985, what does that category mean?" one well-known TV critic asked his partner. (What *does* that category mean? Less than a month later, he answered his own question with *The Color Purple*, an altogether more upbeat film about brutality and oppression.) In light of the extravagant praise *Shoah* has received, Pauline Kael's notorious negative appraisal in *The New Yorker*—which reportedly held her copy several weeks before tacking it onto the December 30 reviews of *Out of Africa* and *The Color Purple*—would seem particularly nervy. But Kael's response is something more complex than a personal distaste.

If *The New Yorker*'s review has convinced some people that *Shoah* isn't worth seeing, one could also sense a backlash at the meeting of the National Society of Film Critics this year. *Shoah* was not above criticism after all. Sitting through it may even have been, as Kael suggested, "a form of self-punishment." There was a free-floating embarrassment among some of Lanzmann's partisans, complemented by a revisionist line that the film's significance was historical (or documentary) rather than cinematic, and even by a certain amount of open hostility. During the three ballots necessary to arrive at a best picture, *Shoah* was always in the running (it finished fourth). At strategic intervals throughout the process, one critic kept petulently pointing out that we *would* be voting a best documentary while, during the voting for that category (which *Shoah* easily won), another gaggle of reviewers indicated their disdain by ostentatiously casting ballots for *Pee-Wee's Big Adventure*.

If there has been very little written so far about *Shoah* from a formal point of view, there has been an undercurrent of criticism which I've heard expressed in conversation but, until Kael's piece, hadn't seen surface in the press. Basically, this critique involves the notions that Lanzmann treated the Polish peasants unfairly and that his aggressive interviewing techniques violate the boundaries of propriety.

The charge that the film is anti-Polish was leveled by the Polish government soon after *Shoah* opened in Paris. (Later tactics shifted and the film was acquired by Polish TV, which followed telecast excerpts with a round-table denunciation of Lanzmann and, according to a report published in *Variety*, the suggestion that the film was fictional.) The basis for this is Lanzmann's interviews with the peasants who lived near the death camps at Chelmno and Treblinka. These eyewitnesses express various degrees of ordinary anti-Semitism, more an indication of indifference than hatred, a cultural climate rather than an ideology, but no less startling for that. One would have imagined that the extermination of their Jewish neighbors would have left a more thoughtful residue. In this, *Shoah* reveals a syndrome touched on in *Now . . . After All These Years*, a West German documentary about a town that had once been half Jewish. The older inhabitants remembered the Third Reich as an embarrassing drunken spree in which otherwise good people acted as perhaps they shouldn't have, but that was a long time ago, and in any case, they'd been punished for it by the war; there seemed to be no empathy for the Nazis' victims, as though the centuries-long Jewish presence in Germany was transitory—certainly no great loss.

While *Shoah* documents that anti-Semitic attitudes persist in the very place where millions of Jews were sent, as the Nazis put it, "up the chimney," it has been observed that Lanzmann interviews only one Pole who seems to have helped the Jews. But just as the subject of the film is the Jews who were exterminated, not the handful who survived (hence the absence of escape stories), *Shoah* necessarily focuses on prevailing attitudes rather than exceptional deeds. (In her recently published *When Light Pierced the Darkness: Christian Rescue of Jews in Nazi-Occupied Poland*, Nechama Tec points out that the Polish Gentiles most apt to risk their lives to help Jews were almost invariably—albeit in wildly different ways—extraordinary, nonconforming individuals, and, in group terms, peasants were the class least likely to offer assistance.

Anyone familiar with the history of pre-World War II Poland knows that, during the 1930s, traditional anti-Semitism was elevated to a quasi-official policy. Anyone familiar with the history of postwar Poland knows that 1968 saw a quasi-sanctioned anti-Semitic campaign resulting in the emigration of some 30,000 remaining Polish Jews (most of them assimilated, many of them Communists). And anyone who followed developments during the 18 months of Solidarity is aware that—even in the absence of a Jewish community—anti-Semitic rhetoric surfaced in both the union and the party. Yet, according to *Variety,* representatives of Polish TV collected the peasants interviewed and had them confess that they were paid by Lanzmann to make up their anti-Semitic remarks.

Kael is only a few steps behind this assertion that *Shoah* is a fabrication. In one of the most remarkable passages in her review, she implies that, "eager to seize on signs of ignorance and prejudice," Lanzmann is somehow responsible for what he has uncovered. Obviously the Polish authorities were embarrassed that Lanzmann could stand outside a church in which, 40-odd years before, the town Jews were rounded up, beaten, and then transported to nearby gas chambers, and find a large crowd of worshipers ready to characterize that event as punishment for the Jews' murder of Christ. But why would an American critic find this excessive, even phony—an attempt to con the audience with, as Kael puts it, "Woody Allen's convention of village idiots"? (And why, one might well ask, Woody Allen?)

The essential question here is one of identification. If one doesn't identify with the Jews in *Shoah,* one is left with the Poles—stand-ins for the rest of the world, which was not, after all, unduly preoccupied with the fate of European Jewry at the hands of the Nazis. Indeed, in its structure *Shoah* encourages the viewer to identify with the victims. As Timothy Garton Ash wrote in *The New York Review of Books* in a piece that's extremely well-informed on precisely the issue of Polish anti-Semitism and *Shoah*'s representation of it: "This deadly repetition, this exhaustion, this *having* to sit through it, is an essential part of Lanzmann's creation. He deliberately uses the dictatorial powers of the director to lock you in a cattle wagon and send you for nine and a half hours down the line to Auschwitz." (The implications of this can return in the least-expected contexts. Watching the latest, sub-Spielberg remake of *King Solomon's Mines*— a succession of death-defying, exhilaratingly narrow escapes—I was suddenly reminded of *Shoah,* a film about death in which, over and over, no one ever escapes.)

This may contribute to the objections I've heard about Lanzmann himself, his "arrogance" and "self-indulgence." Yes, he is single-minded, relentless, and sometimes abrasive. So are many filmmakers, but Lanzmann has the guts to show himself thus on the screen—it's necessary to his method. (Marcel Ophuls—who called *Shoah* "the greatest documentary on contemporary history ever made"—writes, "for a Jewish filmmaker to ingratiate himself in this particular context would have been akin to the frantic, laughable, and eventually unsuccessful attempts of so many of our elders to blend into the landscape.")

When people refer to Lanzmann as tasteless or pushy, as a fetishist or a ghoul, who do they really mean? In the wake of Bitburg, it should be evident that Jews, Jewish suffering, Jewish moral indignation are no longer fashionable. On the contrary. You can read the boredom in Richard Corliss's glib lead in *Time*: "Why is this holocaust different from all other holocausts?" Although Corliss eventually gets around to fashioning a sort of answer to the question, his first suggestion is that the distinguishing factor may simply be publicity—"in raw nightmare numbers, the Nazi extermination of the Jews ranks below the Soviet Union's systematic starvation of the rebellious Ukraine in 1932–33 [10 million by Stalin's count] . . ." Typically, Kael is a lot more blunt. "*Shoah* is a long moan," she wrotes. "It's saying 'We've always been oppressed, and we'll be oppressed again.'"

If Kael misses Lanzmann's carefully constructed point about the uniqueness of the Holocaust (in Jewish as well as world history), her profoundly hostile reaction—perceiving the film as a stand-in for paranoid Jews wallowing in self-pity—suggests a view of the Holocaust I believe more widespread than generally acknowledged. On one hand, the Jews are faulted for passively going to their doom; on the other, for making themselves tiresome by refusing to shut up about it. Both charges blame the victim; both have a dialectical engagement with what could be termed the Gentile world's indifference. Dwelling on the minutiae of genocide, the nexus of events (including—does one really have to say it?—European anti-Semitism) that made the Final Solution possible, *Shoah* is the most ambitious attempt ever to make the extermination of the Jews tangible. For Lanzmann, the Holocaust was an impossible, perhaps incomprehensible event—requiring time and effort and a multitude of facts to begin to understand it. For Kael, his entire enterprise can be reduced to "a Jew's pointing a finger at the Gentile world and crying, 'You low-lifes—you want to kill us!'"

Given her contempt for *Shoah*'s "lack of moral complexity," the coarseness of Kael's own formulations are astonishing. "If you set him loose," she writes of Lanzmann, "he could probably find anti-Semitism anywhere." Imagine, he actually found anti-Semitism at Treblinka. Who knows, if he's not tied up again, he might even find it in *The New Yorker*.

Only make believe

Originally published in *The Village Voice* (February 11, 1986).

UNLIKE *ROCKY IV*, which it displaced as the nation's number one box office attraction, *Iron Eagle* is spaced out and airy. There's a sort of voluptuous vapidity to the whipped cream cloud formations and the wheeling aerial stunts.

This is a place where nobody suffers and the sun always shines. Death is a matter of radar blips and gorgeous explosions—the film is definitely post-vid game as well as post-MTV.

Directed by Sidney Furie, *Iron Eagle* is a relatively benign, or at least relatively abstract, example of the Hollywood genre the Soviets have, with more wit than one would expect, labeled "war-nography." Their pun isn't even as facile as it seems: Archer Winsten's ironic (?) pull-quote—"Anyone who fails to respond to *Iron Eagle* has no red blood at all"—makes you wonder if the film he's touting isn't really *Spread Eagled (and Bodacious)*. *Rambo*, *Red Dawn*, and *Rocky IV*, the key exhibits in the Soviet diatribe, purvey hypothetical wars the way porn films traffic in hypothetical sex. Indeed, the same arguments could be made as to whether such films are behavioral primers, pathetic substitutes, social symptoms, or all three in one. The only thing beyond question is that porno is a lot less respectable (and maybe even profitable) than warno these days.

Iron Eagle's premise, as any subway rider knows, has an American jet pilot shot down and placed on trial for "the crime of being an American." That is, he supposedly violated the airspace of a North African nation which, with a nod to the film's structuring absence—this is, after all, a man's world—we might term "Labia." (It's ruled by a flaky military dictator whom, given the movie's fear of you know what, I'll call "Colonel Cut-off-he.") Faced with a do-nothing State Department, the pilot's sweetly hulking teenage son, Doug (Jason Gedrick), teams up with the irascible yet tenderhearted Chappy (Lou Gossett), a reserve colonel working as the base mechanic (gimme a break), to borrow a pair of F-16s and bring back Dad themselves. Gossett's Chappy, the film's only real character, not only places *Iron Eagle* in the oft-debased tradition of *The Pathfinder* and *Huckleberry Finn*, he gives it a spurious moral weight. A black superpatriot makes everyone feel good; a black guru makes even Doug seem hip.

Given the nuke-'em-high scenario—a mixture of *Star Wars* and *Uncommon Valor* in which fighting for the absent father is elevated to a divine principle—much of the film is bizarrely low-key. Gossett aside, the actors seem to be reading their lines off a teleprompter. There's a long Spielbergistic sequence in which Doug's gang of army brats runs rampant over the base getting supplies and data together. (The spectacle of a tubby little four-eyes commandeering the base computer prompted the patron behind me to riposte "Intelligence? Goddamn!" with juicy disgust.) Contrary to Jay Maeder's wonderful pull-quote—"*Iron Eagle* is bringing audiences to their feet screaming!"—the crowd at the RKO National was pretty subdued, its concentration broken only by occasional cries of "Where they get this dialogue from?"

Who needs language? Or logic? Has anyone noticed that *Iron Eagle* blunders right into the disjunction between Reagan and Rambo, the master of fantasy and the fantasy of mastery? No one in the movie even pretends to approve of the State Department's policy that leaves Doug's dad a hapless hostage. "Christ, we're holding all the aces!" one guy exclaims. "Why do they act like it's a pair of twos?" So tell me, who's they? When someone brings up Iran, Doug's friend (the only black on the air base besides Chappy and thus shamelessly exploited as a mouthpiece for the film's most jingoistic sentiments) becomes irate. "That was different," he explains. "Mr. Peanut was in charge then. Now we got this guy who don't take no shit from no gimpy country. That's why they call him 'Ronald Ray-gun.'"

Given this provocative use of the triple negative, it almost seems churlish to observe that, in the context of *Iron Eagle,* it is Ronald Ray-gun's government and not Mr. Peanut's which has wimped out by refusing to invade Labia. But who cares? The real point is: Would you rather be (i.e. have) a Ray-gun or a Peanut? In the real world, the real Reagan once resolved this contradiction by endorsing *Rambo*—identifying himself as a member of the audience just like everyone else, learning what he was supposed to do next time. *Iron Eagle* is the mythological next time—it resolves everything with the happiest ending imaginable. Not only does Colonel Cut-off-he get vaporized in man-to-gook combat, but all the fathers are resurrected, and Doug is even admitted to the Air Force Academy, bad grades and all.

Iron Eagle is so positive it eschews the primal hatred of technology found in the Stallone films. "God doesn't give people things he doesn't want them to use," Chappy reassures Doug. (So much for deterrence: As the subway ad says, "Waiting time is over.") But, Reaganite good-vibes aside, the most ideologically cogent thing in the film is the structural importance of rock music. When he's flying, Doug must have rock 'n' roll to hit a target. Even Chappy requires a dose of James Brown to do some problem solving. But, a few quaint bars of "There Was a Time" notwithstanding, the *Iron Eagle* score is overwhelmingly a series of white-bread masculine headbangers with some piquant transformations as a result: Twisted Sister's "We're Not Gonna Take It" becomes a patriotic anthem, Queen's "One Vision" a paean to the new world order.

The use of the Spencer Davis Group's "Gimme Some Lovin'" during the Labia destructo orgy is almost too Freudian to be true, but the song this movie really craves is, of course, "Born in the U.S.A." You can easily imagine matching explosions to *that* mighty beat. POW-rat-tat-tat-tat-tat-POW!

Still Krazy after all these years

Originally published in *The Village Voice* (June 3, 1986).

OF ALL CLASSIC comic strips, George Herriman's *Krazy Kat* was the most brilliantly formulaic. For over 30 years, the daily installment climaxed more often than not with the strip's eponymous star taking a well-aimed brick on the head. You might call it a "riff" if you were inclined to be musical.

Krazy Kat—which ended as a strip during World War II and has now been anthologized for the first time in decades by the team of Patrick McDonnell,

Karen O'Connell, and Georgia Riley de Havenon—is based on an eternal triangle, a setup that confounds conventional animal (if not necessarily human) behavior. Kat loves mouse and is, in turn, adored by dog—thus establishing an equilibrium based on longstanding obsession and mutual misunderstanding.

The strip is a rondo of unrequited love. Ignatz, a spindly splenetic mouse, despises Krazy; his greatest pleasure is beaning the hapless Kat with a brick. For Krazy, however, the brick is proof that Ignatz cares: "L'il Ainjil, he has rewarded my watchful waiting," Krazy beams after being conked. The doggedly faithful Offissa Pupp, hopelessly in love with the oblivious Kat, jails Ignatz after each assault. Thus, in a sense, every cliché comes true and all the characters get what they want. *Krazy Kat*, many commentators feel obliged to observe (as they don't for example, of *War and Peace*), is a fantasy.

No less than Charlie Chaplin, its only pop rival for the affection of Jazz Age aesthetes, *Krazy Kat* synthesized a particular mixture of sweetness and slapstick, playful fantasy and emotional brutality. The strip acknowledges life's school of hard knocks and then negates it. Herriman's quintessential image is Ignatz crowning Krazy with a brick—the trajectory marked "zip," then "pow" (or sometimes "bop") as the missile bounces upwards off the back of Krazy's head. The image is as visceral as a drawing can get—the monomaniacal mouse is into his Walter Johnson-like follow-through, while Krazy is knocked forward at a 45-degree angle by the force of the blow. A bump is never raised, yet as Krazy pitches stiffly toward the earth, a dotted line culminating in a little heart issues from the Kat's forehead. Usually, the fantastic vista of Coconino County, Herriman's version of Monument Valley, can be glimpsed in the background.

If *Krazy Kat* was one strip that never ducked the violence inherent in the term "punch line," it owed considerable charm to its subject's personality— the Kat's romantic optimism, philosophical ramblings, amiable propensity for ukelele-accompanied song ("There is a heppy lend, fur, fur a-wa-a-ay"). The strip has no mystery greater than that of Krazy's sex. Most observers assume it is female. In one 1920 Sunday page, the Kat even carries a banner for women's suffrage (Ignatz is thinking he'll support the movement until he discovers who holds the placard aloft: "I'm for no 'party' that has that 'Krazy Kat' in it").

Unlike Krazy, Herriman refused to commit himself. "I don't know. I fooled around with it once; began to think the Kat is a girl—even drew up some strips with her being pregnant," he wrote. "It wasn't the Kat any longer; too much concerned with her own problems—like a soap opera. Know what I mean? Then I realized Krazy was something like a sprite, an elf. They have no sex. So that Kat can't be a he or a she. The Kat's a spirit—a pixie—free to butt into anything. Don't you think so?" His certainty is less than overwhelming.

Herriman's mystical sense of his creation is epitomized by a 1917 Sunday page in which the Kat asks a Ouija board who his enemy is, receives the answer I-G-N-A-T-Z, and refuses to believe it, stomping the Ouija board (which, of course, turns out to belong to Ignatz) into a crumpled accordion. In an often reprinted box at the bottom of the page, Herriman apologizes to the spirits on Krazy's behalf: "You have written truth, you friends of the shadows. Yet, be not harsh with Krazy. He [sic] is but a shadow himself, caught in the web of this mortal skein. We call him 'cat,' we call him 'crazy' yet he is neither." Herriman goes on to conclude that even after Krazy passes into the shadows, "you will understand him no better than we who linger on this side of the pale." Is Krazy then a sphinx without a secret?

This spirit of Krazy-ness governs every aspect of Coconino County. In marked counterpoint to the strip's rigorous formula is its delirious, insistent flux. Herriman's attitude toward his graphic details was one of jazzy insouciance. Not only was the *Krazy Kat* logo a mutable, unstable design but, in blatant contradiction of the continuous action, panels typically alternate between day and night (the latter often signified by a crescent moon resembling a decrepit mobile fashioned from a warped Frisbee).

Albeit taken literally from Monument Valley (where Herriman spent much time after the mid-'20s), the landscape of Coconino County was wildly fluid, shimmering more drastically than the most extravagant mirage: One typical strip opens with Krazy and Ignatz talking on a hillside, the second panel places them in a suburban yard, the third further up the hill, the fourth on a drawing tacked to a wall, and the fifth against some nondescript horizon. The sixth and final panel finds the pair back in the yard, standing by a wall from which Ignatz meaningfully extracts a brick.

At once crude and delicate, Herriman's line seems almost free-associational in its spontaneity. Actually, his drawings are masterpieces of dramatic economy, achieving miracles of individuation and expression through body language and suggestive absences. Less is usually more: Because Ignatz has no mouth, for example, his eyes become beacons of preternatural alertness on an otherwise blank face. Like Paul Klee's, this work often looks like inspired doodling, but don't be fooled; as much as it celebrates Herriman's quasi-automatic drawing, the Abrams anthology emphasizes his canny vulgar modernism. From the late '30s on, the dailies are full of referential gags—characters address their creator, make their own drawings, or use erasers to alter reality. In one 1940 strip, Krazy heaves a brick against the side of the frame—it ricochets like a banked billiard ball up and off the top of the frame to slam her on the head. In another, Ignatz makes strategic use of a black brick, having successfully predicted the placement of the strip's all black frame.

In the mid-'20s, Herriman's fanciful Sunday layouts were standardized to give newspapers greater flexibility in running them. As Herriman chafed under this new format, the authority figure of Offissa Pupp came to the fore; even so, the layouts of the late Sunday pages have the sort of impacted, tightly integrated curvaciousness—not to mention burnt, sandy colors—of classic SoCal bungalows. Although some of the more extravagant Sunday pages are wordless (one 1918 example is an extended, chilling riff on trench warfare), *Krazy Kat* is as distinctive for its use of language as it is for its other particulars. Krazy speaks with a kind of stage Yiddish accent, tempered with miscellaneous Sam Wellerisms: "Oh what a unheppy ket I am these brickliss days—oy-yoi-yoi!" Offissa Pupp specializes in ineptly highfalutin (often self-pitying) speeches: "Krazy burns a late candle tonight—I trust it attracts neither moth nor mouse." Only Ignatz, as the reality principle (he's also a householder with a large family), speaks relatively plain English.

Krazy Kat counted Wilhelm DeKooning and Jack Kerouac among its fans; the strip was always a cult writ large. When Herriman died in 1944, it was only being syndicated in 35 newspapers, as compared to the more than 1000 that carried *Blondie*. Indeed, William Randolph Hearst was Herriman's incongruous patron; he liked the strip and he kept it going. (According to McDonnell, O'Connell, and De Havenon, he even forced Herriman, humble to a fault, to accept a raise.)

As Herriman's creation is widely held to have been the greatest of comic strips, theories of *Krazy Kat* abound. Gilbert Seldes's pioneering 1922 appreciation (reprinted in the Abrams book, it first appeared in *Vanity Fair*) compared Herriman to the Douanier Rousseau. For Seldes, Krazy was a combination of Don Quixote and Parsifal (with Ignatz his malign Sancho Panza, if not Kundry). Twenty-four years later, when the strip was posthumously anthologized, e. e. cummings furnished a suitably high-toned introduction. In his view, the "humbly poetic, gently clownlike, supremely innocent, illimitably affectionate" Krazy was nothing less than the spirit of democracy itself struggling against the excesses of individualism (Ignatz) and the stupidity of society (Offisa Pupp).

More recently, Arthur Asa Berger has seen the strip as an existential parable; by Franklin Rosemont's anarcho-surrealist lights, *Krazy Kat* is "utopian in the best sense, signifying the imaginative critique of existing values and institutions, and the presentation of imaginary alternative societies." There is also a belligerent view that *Krazy Kat* has no meaning. In reviewing the 1946 anthology for *Partisan Review,* Robert Warshaw saw the strip as inspired nonsense, comparable to Lewis Carroll: "We do best to leave *Krazy Kat* alone. Good fantasy never has an easy and explicit relation to the real world." (Although Warshaw admired the strip's "fresh quality of pure play," he expressed a decidedly *Partisan* anxiety over its "complete disregard of the standards of respectable art.")

The Abrams book provides material for some new theories. Herriman was a notoriously private person and particularly vague about his background. (On his death certificate, his daughter maintained that his parents had been born in France; colleagues used to refer to him as "the Greek.") With some difficulty, McDonnell, O'Connell, and De Havenon have researched Herriman's background and confirmed the long-standing rumor that he was of African descent: Born in New Orleans in 1880, Herriman was classified as "colored" on his birth certificate, and his parents were listed as mulattos in that year's census.

Catholic and French-speaking, the so-called "colored Creoles" of New Orleans were a tight-knit, sophisticated elite, descended from "free persons of color" who emigrated from the West Indies. Although the 10,000 or so who lived in New Orleans in the late 19th century were mainly professionals and shopkeepers, their position rapidly eroded with the institutionalized segregation that followed the end of Reconstruction. Indeed, it was just at this time—

around 1886—that Herriman's family left New Orleans for Los Angeles, where his father found work as a barber and a baker. In 1900, George rode the rails to New York City. By 1903, he was on staff at the *New York World.*

McDonnell, O'Connell, and De Havenon suggest Krazy Kat's distinctive patois might be a memory from the Creole quarter of New Orleans. That's scarcely the only aspect of Coconino County the revelation of Herriman's background throws into new light. One wonders about the folk stories Herriman might have heard as a child, and Krazy's vaunted Egyptian heritage now seems like something more than a casual conceit. "Remember Krazy, my child, you are a Kat—a Kat of Egypt," she's told by Kleopatra Kat in one 1919 Sunday page, which also gives the origin of the mouse's custom "to crease his lady's bean with a brick laden with tender sentiment."

In view of Herriman's origins, the persistent comparison of *Krazy Kat* to the rhythm and spontaneity of jazz takes on an added resonance. The comics and jazz appeared on the American scene at roughly the same time. But how many comics shared Krazy's distinctive formal mixture of sweetness and rough-and-tumble, consistency and improvisation. Jazz, as Franklin Rosemont points out, was full of "crazy cats." Jelly Roll Morton, another Creole given to fantasy and hyperbole, was only five years younger than Herriman. It was he who saw the riff as both jazz's background and foundation.

"Krazy Kat was not conceived, not born, it jes' grew," Herriman is quoted as saying. His admission is startling both for its equation of Krazy with Harriet Beecher Stowe's Topsy and for its echo of James Weldon Johnson's statement about the origin of "the earliest ragtime songs." Johnson, another Herriman contemporary, published his novel *The Autobiography of an Ex-Colored Man* two years after Krazy's spontaneous debut. In fact, *Krazy Kat* did jes' grow out of the cracks of another Herriman strip, *The Dingbat Family* (a/k/a *The Family Upstairs,* for the Dingbats' unseen nemesis). The strip published on July 26, 1910, contains an incidental gag: the Dingbats' cat had his bean bonked by a brick-wielding mouse. Eureka!

The relationship between this cat and that mouse soon became a sort of sub-strip beneath the main action; in late 1913, they were spun off into a comic strip of their own. Thus, the Kat was an eruption from below—not just from the underworld of *The Dingbat Family* and the lower depths of American popular culture but also from Herriman's unconscious. Ishmael Reed's *Mumbo Jumbo*—which is dedicated to, among others, "George Herriman, Afro-American"—uses that concept of Jes Grew as a metaphor for jazz (and popular culture in general).

From the first, Herriman's comic strips revolved around compulsive eccentrics—one wonders if he wasn't the most complex of them all. His love for Monument Valley, his identification with indigenous Indian culture, his fondness for western Stetsons—not to mention Krazy's sexual ambiguity and unrequited passion—take on a certain poignancy in view of what must have been an ontological insecurity regarding his own identity. Herriman's most African feature was evidently his tightly curled hair—it's striking that, in virtually every photograph, he's wearing a hat.

Does *Krazy Kat* then exorcise the sort of gut-twisting anxiety and guilt engendered by passing for white in a segregated culture? Are these brickbats signs of love? Is Coconino County an American utopia? Denial, raised to the sublime, is what *Krazy Kat* is all about.

Blue Velvet

Originally published as "Return to Normalcy" in *The Village Voice* (September 22, 1986).

BLUE VELVET IS a film of ecstatic creepiness—a stunning vindication for writer-director David Lynch. *The Elephant Man* was crippled by a sentimental script, and, while brilliantly disgusting, the foredoomed *Dune* succeeded mainly on the level of production design. This is the first time since his midnight classic, *Eraserhead,* that Lynch has vented the full force of his sensibility, and the result is astonishing.

Continually unpredictable, albeit far more straightforward than *Eraserhead, Blue Velvet* is generically a teen coming-of-age film crossed with a noir. But Lynch, whose blandly gee-whiz affect has been compared by more than one startled interviewer to that of an Eagle Scout, is weirdest precisely when attempting to be most normal. (He attacks the material with the sublime discordance of Charles Ives singing "Rally Round the Flag.") *Blue Velvet* could be described as *Archie and Veronica in the Twilight Zone* or John Hughes meets Luis Buñuel or *The Hardy Boys on Mars,* but no single phrase captures the film's boldly alien perspective, its tenderness and disgust.

Ostensibly set in the present, *Blue Velvet* suggests the 1950s the way *Eraserhead* evoked some entropic, postnuclear future. The film celebrates and ruthlessly defamiliarizes a comfortable, picture-postcard facade of malt shoppes, football fields, and rec-room basements—not to mention Roy Orbison and film narrative itself. For Lynch the veil of appearances is precisely that; he effortlessly attains the downbeat visionary quality Francis Coppola was groping for in the overwrought *Rumblefish.* "It's a strange world," the denizens of Lumberton are wont to tell each other every time Lynch lifts up the rock of middle-American niceness.

In one sense, *Blue Velvet* is the continuous subversion of apple-pie normalcy (call it "Blue Velveeta"). In another, it represents a terrifying collapse of authority that, as if through a trapdoor, plunges Lynch's college-age protagonist, Jeffrey (Kyle MacLachlan, the aggressively innocuous star of *Dune* and a kind of air-brushed doppelgänger for Lynch himself), into a murky vortex of sex, death, and mutilation, where corruption of the body and corruption of the body politic are part of the same mindless cosmic drama.

Lynch is basically a non-narrative filmmaker, and even when *Blue Velvet*'s plot becomes apparent, you still can't help but wonder what the "normal" version of the script might be. From the opening evocation of idyllic Lumberton ("the town that *knows* how much wood a woodchuck chucks"), the film is instantly and insistently bizarre. To the accompaniment of the lachrymose Bobby Vinton title ballad, the camera caresses an incandescent white picket fence fronted by glowing red roses—a kind of kryptonite Kodachrome effect that dissolves into graciously slo-mo calendar images of friendly firemen and solicitous crossing guards. For all these guardians of public safety, however, the surface of Lumberton seems as gaudy and fragile as an Easter egg, and sure enough, it's immediately shattered by ridiculous catastrophe: Watering his lawn, Jeffrey's father is stung by a bee and collapses. For Lynch, this is like a message from beyond—he uses an escalating series of mega-close-ups to literally rub your nose in the terrifying profusion of life.

Did I say nose? Returning home across a vacant lot after visiting his grotesquely hospitalized father (tubes everywhere, head clamped in place by a strange contraption of rods and screws), Jeffrey discovers a severed, slightly moldering, ant-covered human ear. Like a good Lumberton lad, he gingerly puts it in a paper bag and brings it to the police station (primly decorated by projects from the local primary school). "Yes, that's a human ear all right," Detective Williams (George Dickerson) assures him with the impersonal solicitude of an airline captain or a hologram. With his haunting juxtapositions, brazen non sequiturs, and eroticized derangement of the ordinary, Lynch has affinities to classic surrealism. But Lynch's surrealism seems more intuitive than programmatic. For him, the normal is a defense against the irrational rather than vice versa. (After a while, one notices the never commented upon gold ring that pierces Jeffrey's lobe.)

The story behind the ear becomes Jeffrey's obsession, leading him—with the ambivalent help of Sandy (Laura Dern), Detective Williams's engagingly gawky teenage daughter—to explore the Deep River apartments, a musty dive out of *Eraserhead*, where the lushly carnal, bewigged Dorothy (Isabella Rossellini), a nightclub chanteuse at once madonna and whore, makes her enigmatic home. The film features a dual sexual initiation that's all the more powerful for only being partially expressed. *Blue Velvet* is a film about what goes on behind closed doors. "I don't know if you're a detective or a pervert," Sandy complains to Jeffrey. "That's for me to know and you to find out," is his Lynch-like reply. "There are opportunities in life for knowledge and experience," he tells her, eyes agleam—and later, after he has crossed the Deep River Rubicon, spying not only on Dorothy but her sinister associate, Frank (Dennis Hopper), he says, "I'm seeing something that was always hidden. I'm in the middle of a mystery."

So are we all, and Jeffrey's baptism in the Deep River is best experienced without too much prior knowledge. Suffice it to say that *Blue Velvet* is ornately framed by the euphemistic "facts of life" (birds, bees, flowers), while the heart

of the film is a 20-minute sex scene replete with voyeurism, rape, sadomasoch-
ism, implied castration, all manner of verbal and physical abuse, elaborate
fetishism, and a ritualized kinkiness for which there is no name. It's a sequence
Alfred Hitchcock might have given a year off his life to direct—appalling,
erotic, appallingly funny, and tragic.

Given the surprises and secrets of *Blue Velvet*'s story, I'm inclined to write
around the film's action and celebrate its texture—the hilariously stilted educa-
tion-film dialogue (people will be quoting it for years), the transcendently seedy
compositions, the dank aroma of skid-row porn that even the sunniest scenes
exude, Dorothy's definitively lugubrious rendition of the title ballad. While
Eraserhead had a dreamlike flow, *Blue Velvet* is hallucinated and hyperreal. The
colors are oversaturated, the motion is blandly discontinuous. There's a schizophrenic vividness that's underscored by the film's microcosmic backdrop and
absolute representation of moral qualities. "I'm *not* crazy. I know the difference
between right and wrong," Dorothy assures Jeffrey pathetically, as if by rote.

Blue Velvet is a triumph of overall geekiness—a fat man in shades walking a
tiny dog, the deadpan Dick-and-Jane detective who wears his gun and badge in
the house, the references to Jehovah's Witnesses, the strategic use of the world's
loudest flushing toilet. As the demiurge of raunchy, lower-class sexual menace,
Dennis Hopper is a virtual Harkonnen on Main Street—a violent, volatile
hophead, periodically dosing himself with ether to further addle his turbulent,
fuck-obsessed stream of consciousness. (In a smaller role, the epicene Dean
Stockwell is no less indelible.)

Of course, Lynch's representation of innocence is just as perverse as his
world of experience, and no less aggressive. Large chunks of *Blue Velvet* are
disconcertingly skewed evocations of paradise along the lines of the singing
description provided by *Eraserhead*'s simpering, disfigured radiator lady: "In
Heaven everything is fine. You've got your good thing, and I've got mine."
Jeffrey's crazed naïveté—"Why are there people like Frank? Why is there so
much trouble in this world?" he shrieks—is more than matched by Sandy's
sensitively stunted worldview. Enraptured by her own vision, she recounts a
dream of robins bringing a blinding light of love. (Typically, the scene is set in
the vicinity of a discreetly illuminated church.)

There hasn't been an American studio film so rich, so formally controlled,
so imaginatively cast and wonderfully acted, and so charged with its maker's
psychosexual energy since *Raging Bull*. But *Blue Velvet*'s unflinching blend of
raw pathology and Kabuki sweetness is pretty much sui generis. One doesn't
know what to make of it, which may be as disconcerting for some as it is
exciting for others. The audiences with which I've seen the film have left the
theater stunned. *Blue Velvet* is a film about repression. It keeps turning in on
itself in successive movements of revelation and denial—Rossellini's hissed
"What did you see?" followed by Hopper's lunatic "Don't you fucking look at
me!"—and going over my notes, I was astonished at the details I had forgotten.
I don't think mine is an isolated case. In some respects *Blue Velvet* is as

exhausting as it is exhilarating—movies have become so depleted one scarcely expects to be confronted with this much *stuff*. The more you see it, the more you get.

P.S. *Blue Velvet* was Lynch's intended follow-up to *Eraserhead*, and I assume that, on some level, Dino De Laurentiis backed the film as Lynch's payoff for the thankless task of directing *Dune*. De Laurentiis is better known these days for epic schlock (*Death Wish, King Kong*) than commercial neorealism (*Bitter Rice, La Strada*), but considering *Dune*'s failure to set the world on fire, a lesser producer would scarcely have thought twice about giving Lynch the shaft. It's a strange world, all right: De Laurentiis is not just a man of his word, he's also a patron of the arts.

At war with ourselves

Originally published in *The Village Voice* (December 23, 1986).

Vietnam is awkward, everybody knows how awkward, and if people don't even want to hear about it, you know they're not going to pay money to sit there in the dark and have it brought up.

—Michael Herr, *Dispatches*

ELEVEN YEARS AFTER the Vietnam War sputtered to an end, it remains as dark and primal as a murder witnessed by a two-year-old. Our language hasn't evolved to describe it. There is still no official account of what happened (let alone consensus), no agreed upon narrative line, no Pearl Harbor or Iwo Jima, no Remember the Alamo or Four Score and Seven Years Ago.

The war had a murky beginning and an unsatisfying end: It's hardly coincidental that the most popular movies it inspired were hypothetical sequels in which *we got to win*, or that, however high they soared, the most artistically ambitious of Nam films, Stan Brakhage's *23rd Psalm Branch* and Francis Coppola's *Apocalypse Now*, couldn't help but go down flaming in futile pretension and intellectual disarray.

Visceral and driven, a highpowered dirge, Oliver Stone's *Platoon* belongs with these two—divided against itself as well, it solves the narrative problem by being all middle. *Platoon* is based on Stone's own army experiences; it's set in the shadows, late 1967 near the Cambodian border. Chris (Charlie Sheen) is Stone's alter ego, a tormented idealist from a well-off family who left college and enlisted out of an inchoate sense of duty. "You volunteered for this shit, man?!" an incredulous black comrade explodes and, hearing Chris's egalitarian rationale, adds disgustedly, "You gotta be rich in the first place to think like that."

With Chris wandering through the battle zone as if in a dream, Stone's is definitely the grunt's eye view. *Platoon* is a gutsy corrective to the fantasies of bellicose noncombatants Milius and Stallone. Stone puts continual emphasis on war's physical discomfort; in this steaming jungle, no one is vermin-free, every-one's feet are in some stage of rot. The film's power resides in its details—the grunts talking about their "bad feelings," the bandanas and fetishes of the men who've gone native, the ongoing intra-platoon sniping (between lifers and draftees, black soldiers and white, heads and straights), the base psychedeli-catessen with gas mask candelabras and a poster of Ho Chi Minh in the corner, the uptight sergeant who chews gum the way someone else would work a rosary, the teenage psychopath who thrives on war's chaos.

Platoon opens with a quote from Ecclesiastes and a burst of Samuel Bar-ber's doleful "Adagio for Strings": Awkward as ducklings, a gaggle of green recruits is reborn in Nam (literally discharged from the belly of a plane), gaping at the body bags they pass going the other way. The mixture of arty detachment and wrenchingly vivid detail sets the film's tone. Stone is relentlessly uneven. *Platoon* is often crudely lyrical (Chris smoking a joint in the orange dusk with the Jefferson Airplane buzzing in his head) and often just crude (to dramatize the schisms within the platoon Stone cuts from a group of dopers listening to Smokey Robinson and shotgunning reefer through their automatic rifles to a sullen redneck petulantly singing the praises of "Okie from Muskogee.") But, crudely rendered or not, the incidents in *Platoon* have the authority of events that have been witnessed.

In a questionnaire on war films, Sam Fuller—who was wounded twice as an infantryman during World War II—maintained that it was impossible to "show war as it really is on the screen," adding that it might be preferable to "fire real shots over the audience's head" and "have actual casualties in the theater." Fuller's combat films, which include the first to treat Korea, thrive on impossible situations: "In war all characters are psycho. Everyone is at a nervous animal pitch. Vomit is inevitable." Sergeant Zack, the ostensible hero of *The Steel Helmet* (1950), shoots an unarmed POW point blank; although softened by their producers, *Fixed Bayonets* (1951), *Merrill's Marauders* (1962), and *The Big Red One* (1980) are no less anti-inspirational. "The reaction I would like to my pictures is, 'only an idiot would go to war,'" says Fuller. When I interviewed him in connection with *The Big Red One*, he crowed that, after seeing a preview, a three-star general told him it had "no 'recruitment flavor.'"

Fuller would appreciate *Platoon*. Hardly a glamorous gook-shoot, combat is here a mixture of incredible confusion—panic and shrieks and men dying with their eyes open—and shrill hyperexcitement. The film's climactic battle has the base-camp itself under assault, with the men in the field haplessly retreating from foxhole to foxhole until air support arrives. The aftermath is a shocking antidote to Stone's periodic benders of terminal corniness. The sur-vivors return to consciousness in an enormous crater, some deliberately wound-ing themselves, others cutting the ears off dead enemies or rifling their corpses.

Stone has a relentless camera and a taste for sunbursts. He's addicted to the visual equivalent of purple prose, but he can bring you up short in admiration. *Platoon*'s climactic battle has a startling theatrical beauty—it's a lethal shadow play in which flares and parachute probes scoop a shallow, deadly proscenium out of the hellish jungle night. *Platoon* is a tangle of shots, but it's surprisingly agile. Stone has the discipline to cut away from a juicy image; the narrative never gets caught in the underbrush.

Stone's lapses have more to do with inner necessity than commercial consideration, and his switch from amoral schlock to leftwing pulp has been one of the more intriguing developments of 1986. (He might be the thinking person's Cimino.) In the harsh, elegiac light of *Platoon, Salvador* seems also to be about Vietnam, with James Woods a one-man platoon running around a tropical hell in an adrenaline-laced purple haze. *Platoon* isn't as wild as *Salvador,* but it's subject to the same sentimentality and simple-minded moral schemata. The incongruously sweet Sergeant Elias (Willem Dafoe) is the platoon's guardian angel. Dafoe has been used mainly as a heavy in films, but as Elias he's too good to be true, his pale, harsh features lit by an inner glow. ("Do you believe in this?" Chris asks him. "In '65, yeah," Elias replies. "But not now.") Elias is the spirit of human decency, and his fate is a metaphor for the tragedy of American involvement.

Elias's opposite number is Sergeant Barnes (Tom Berenger, also cast against type), an imperious monster who seems to have been stitched together from the remains of a half-dozen corpses. "I don't need this shit to escape reality," he says contemptuously to the heads, sneering at a joint. "I *am* reality." The war between Barnes and Elias for the soul of the platoon is as about as subtle as the prologue to a medieval morality play—still, Stone feels compelled to make it even more obvious in the film's gratuitously maudlin ending: "We did not fight the enemy," intones the fatuous voiceover. "We fought ourselves, and the enemy was in us."

Platoon continually engages *Apocalypse Now* (in part through Charlie Sheen's uncanny resemblance to his father). But, unlike Coppola, Stone is more interested in the chaos of combat than the overall spectacle. *Platoon* is more painful to watch than *Apocalypse Now*; it's less explosively pleasurable, and it never hits the visionary. But, in a curious way, the film gains from the stolid absence of overview. Stone's evocation of My Lai is more harrowing than Coppola's, because he leads you step by step into the terrifying breakdown of restraint, the situation unravelling from two points of view. After discovering one of their platoon eviscerated and strung up, the grunts arrive at a nearby village. They are all vibrating with fear, frustration, and rage, and the contagion, which is only stoked by the incomprehensible jabbering of the prospective victims, affects even the most easy-going of the platoon. Chris uses his automatic rifle to make the village idiot dance, before another soldier wipes the dazed smile off the dink's face by bashing in his skull with a rifle butt.

This could be the Nazis in Poland, and, in a sense, it is. By so deliberately unpacking an atrocity, *Platoon* achieves a timeless quality: This is war. The film is so monumental an unburdening, it's eerily lightheaded. When Stone scores a long-shot of the torched village with Barber's "Adagio," the effect is akin to the distancing that comes with traumatic shock. *Platoon* is as tactile as mud, but it's also dizzy with grief.

CLINT EASTWOOD'S ELECTION to public office only certifies his political career—such Eastwood tropes as the demonic underclass and the establishment loner have dominated American political discourse for the last 15 years. Ronald Reagan appropriated Dirty Harry's "Make my day" tagline, and in *Heartbreak Ridge,* Eastwood returns the compliment, taking the president literally and using the conquest of Grenada to offset the loss of Vietnam. In art as in life, the structuring absence is that of the 241 marines who were blown to bits two days earlier in Beirut. That the Lebanon crisis would not surface even as a subject for barracks jitters or maudlin flagwaving is proof of Eastwood's bad faith.

As a movie, *Heartbreak Ridge* is just as tortuous as David Edelstein suggested last week. Still, for those of us who find Eastwood the epitome of American pathology, it holds a certain grim fascination. Even if Eastwood were not the icon who presided over the end of the Western and the birth of the anti-Miranda urban policier, his unprecedented 18-year reign as a top male attraction would make him a potent figure in national myth. It also seems to have made him a legend in his own mind. While John Wayne never wasted a moment pondering what was this thing "John Wayne," Eastwood's self-consciousness became apparent as early as *Play Misty for Me.*

Since *High Plains Drifter,* the last convincing Western to come out of Hollywood, Eastwood's most interesting movies (*The Gauntlet, Bronco Billy, Tightrope*) have all been ferociously introspective—their theme is nothing less than the social construction of masculinity as mediated by superstardom. Eastwood's public psychoanalysis reached its furthest extent in *Tightrope,* a dirtier version of *Dirty Harry,* in which the star cast himself as a cop who has to arrest women to enjoy them while stalking a killer who acts out his own conscious and unconscious desires, up to and including incest. Eastwood isn't as clever as Woody Allen (Woody would never have been so uncool as to take out a full page ad in *The New York Review of Books* as Eastwood did for *Tightrope*), but given his type, he's far more exotic.

Bracket Allen's psychodramas with Eastwood's and it becomes apparent that, no less than *Hannah and Her Sisters, Heartbreak Ridge* is a meditation on middle age. Indeed, Eastwood's sense of anachronism is more visceral than Woody's hypochondria. When Eastwood gazed into the abyss in *Tightrope,* it must have winked back. The defensive self-parody which Edelstein slyly attributes to Eastwood's fear of Pauline Kael, here reaches grotesque levels. Our hero is a Fulleresque dogface who studies *Vogue* to understand his ex-wife, creates a phony generation gap—"shut your face, hippie"—to justify his existence, and abuses his men with a nonstop stream of homophobic innuendo. (Although this macho free-association is considerably more subversive coming from the likes of Karen Finley, it apparently so offended the Marine Corps that they withdrew their endorsement.) Eastwood plays his leatherneck jerk with a certain dogged brio, but just as he fails to deal with the fact of Lebanon, he lacks the nerve to deny this asshole a shred of vindication.

Eastwood wants nothing less than total approval. With a befuddled energy that belies its overall somnolence, *Heartbreak Ridge* tries to ride a Hollywood trend and (one hopes) breaks its back. This foredoomed attempt to get relevant rewrites *An Officer and a Gentleman* from the point of view of the Lou Gossett character while using a black actor (Mario Van Peebles) as the correspondingly diminished "Richard Gere." In short, the film is a middle-aged *Top Gun*—with all the crabbiness and contradictions that implies.

Top Gun sexualized everything. *Heartbreak Ridge* sexualizes nothing, least of all its star. Indeed, the anti-eroticism is contagious: In a final bit of bushwah, Eastwood persuades the libidinal Van Peebles to give up a personal harem to reënlist in the marines. Whatever their reasons, the Marine Corps was right. The film doesn't work: Eastwood's attitudinizing notwithstanding, there's no recruitment flavor.

Full Metal Jacket: Dressed to kill

Originally published in *The Village Voice* (July 7, 1987).

S TANLEY KUBRICK HAS the autodidact's love of big ideas and the technocrat's faith in big machines—and the cynic's mistrust of both. Kubrick would be a true engineer of the soul if he could only believe in one. There's a ruthless solipsism to his compositions; they're at once forcefully singleminded and powerfully simpleminded, everything subordinated to the illustration of one concept. Control freak that he is, the director is continually rediscovering monotheism.

Spontaneity is not among Kubrick's virtues. He hates interviews—as well he might, having once defined a director as "a kind of idea and taste machine" and a movie as "a series of creative and technical decisions." From *The Killing* to *The Shining,* Kubrick's films are exercises in cosmic problem-solving (one of which solved the problem by blowing up the world). Since *2001,* they've been carefully preplanned, painstakingly executed Major Statements. To call *Full Metal Jacket* studied is to say the obvious. Five years in the making, Kubrick's Vietnam film mixes the brilliant and banal, sometimes within the same sequence. The title is marine jargon for a full complement of field ammunition, and having pondered the situation, Kubrick comes prepared to play. *Full Metal Jacket* is sometimes unpleasant and often wrongheaded, but it's more than once indelible and hardly ever boring.

One of the ideas in *Full Metal Jacket* is that killers are made, not born. It's the exact reverse of *Clockwork Orange,* in which the naturally vicious Alex is conditioned to be "good," but it only confirms Kubrick's thesis that humans are essentially puppets to be jerked this way or that by their lofty controllers. *Full Metal Jacket* opens with a 45-minute boot camp sequence in which the recruits are objectified from the credits on. Heads shaved, names changed, these "maggots" are subjected to a brutal regimen of exercises and insults by a fanatical drill sergeant (Lee Ermey). The process is already overfamiliar from *An Officer and a Gentleman* and *Heartbreak Ridge,* but because Kubrick is so relentlessly schematic, he's able to effect the sense of a streamlined, killer mechanism. Ermey, a former marine sergeant who served in Vietnam and was technical adviser on *Apocalypse Now* and *The Boys in Company C,* has none of the twitchy, actorish charm of a Lou Gossett or Clint Eastwood. He's compellingly unlovable—just part of the process.

The movie's first 15 or 20 minutes are the sergeant's screaming litany of abuse; not until well into the action is there even cross-talk. The sequence is a true tour de force and, apparently, an accurate one—several people I know report being buttonholed at screenings by total strangers, former marines compelled to testify that this is exactly how it was on Parris Island. Close to clinical, Kubrick's basic training cantata allows ample room for his sadism and black humor. It's filled with bleak vaudeville routines: the sergeant leading the men in singing "Happy Birthday" to Jesus on Christmas Day, or marrying them to their rifles. The substitution of violence for sex, which was the subtext of *Top Gun,* is here overt: "This is my rifle, this is my gun—this is for fighting, this is for fun," the maggots are compelled to chant, nervously grabbing their crotches every time they say the word "gun."

Although with its bald, slug-like recruits and symmetrical compositions, the marine barracks seem as stylized as one of the milk bars in *A Clockwork Orange,* Kubrick's mise-en-scène is ostentatiously simple. A few trademark dollies aside, there's very little camera movement. The vignettes are deliberately paced and elegantly linked. Like nature, Kubrick abhors a vacuum, or rather, he lovingly abhors one. His most memorable images are often outsized, if not megalomaniacal sets: the War Room in *Dr. Strangelove,* the rocket ship in *2001,* the corridors of the Hotel Overlook in *The Shining.* The flat Parris Island landscape here becomes nearly their equal—a vast prison of space.

Molded by the architecture, the sequence is rigorously overdetermined. Only two recruits are given personalities: the film's resident wise guy and nominal hero (Matthew Modine), aptly dubbed Pvt. Joker, and the barrack's fuckup (Vincent D'Onofrio), whom Ermey calls Pvt. Pyle—as in Gomer, as in hemorrhoid, as in manure. The film's first conversation comes, perhaps a half hour into the action, when Joker is promoted to squad leader and shows Pyle the correct way to make up his bed. Pyle is amusingly, appallingly helpless. He can't do one pull-up, and he can't stop smirking, especially when the sergeant pushes his raging snout into Pyle's chipmunk face and calls him "a worthless piece of shit."

Wide-eyed and bashful, D'Onofrio resembles a big baby—at one point, he's made to march with his pants down around his ankles, sucking his thumb—and he's the only bit of humanity in the whole oppressive landscape. We know he's dead meat, but Kubrick tips his hand when the sergeant begins citing Lee Harvey Oswald and University of Texas sniper Charles Whitman as ex-marines. The camera dollies into Pyle's puffy face, and suddenly he's talking to his rifle and making like Jack Nicholson in *The Shining,* knitting his brows and flashing *sampaku* with a lunatic low-angle stare. It's a stunning miscalculation, effectively turning a fastidious essay in brutalization into a student film with a $30-million budget—so crude it feels as though the director were lost in the space between his ears.

Adapted from former military correspondent Gustav Hasford's 1979 novel, *Full Metal Jacket* uneasily shares the original's two-part structure, dashing the rational machine of basic training on the crazy reef of actual combat. Joker, now a correspondent for *Stars and Stripes,* reappears in Vietnam with "Born to Kill" scrawled on his helmet. (To compound the irony—we just spent three-quarters of an hour watching this wild card being redesigned to kill—he wears a peace button, the better to sucker dumb officers into arguments on the essential duality of human nature.) Joker is bitterly callow, if not aggressively supercilious. "I wanted to meet people of an ancient and interesting culture and kill them," he goofs. Actually, Joker is set to interview Ann-Margret when hell breaks loose with the 1968 Tet offensive.

Sent to a combat zone outside Hue, Joker is woofed by mega-marine Animal Mother (Adam Baldwin), the film's Rambo clone and an eerie, muscle-bound echo of Pvt. Pyle. A practiced clown, Joker tries to squelch him with his John Wayne imitation. Animal Mother is unfazed—"You talk the talk, do you walk the walk?"—but Joker's "Wayne" is among Kubrick's prize conceits. In more ways than one, Vietnam was John Wayne's last war. Not only did Wayne take it upon himself to make *The Green Berets,* his name comes up time and again in interviews with veterans; Wayne epitomized the American fighting man before the model broke down. If Francis Coppola represented the war as the ultimate mixed-media extravaganza, for Kubrick it's just a particularly degraded form of show business—an impersonation act. Joker's camera has battle-crazed grunts smiling through interviews, striking their own John Wayne poses, or mouthing meaningless clichés.

Still, Kubrick never quite transcends his own aestheticism. He choreographs a formation of marines slinking through some atrocious rubble as if to parody his own love of camera movement. And the death arabesques during a mad firefight, with each shot bringing a slow-motion Miró explosion of blood, are acutely tense and oppressive in part because they're as ruthlessly scheduled as the Washington shuttle. This prolonged variation on Ten Little Indians, in which one by one marines are driven out into the open to be dispatched by sniper fire, is the closest Kubrick comes to constructing a model for Vietnam's quagmire. The last hour of *Full Metal Jacket* is set during the precise turning point of the Vietnam War, but the movie has far more to do with War (and war movies) than it does with Vietnam.

Platoon offered the grunt's eye–view of the war and *Apocalypse Now* a series of spectacular, self-canceling metaphors, but both films put versions of the My Lai massacre at their centers—American atrocities against a civilian population. (Masterpiece of neurotic projection that it was, *The Deer Hunter* reversed this and had devious VC torturing naïve Americans.) Supremely unimpressed with our loss of national innocence, Kubrick blows it off with a bit of business in a low-flying chopper—someone about to barf while another guy takes target practice at civilians, chortling, "Ain't war hell, hahahahaha."

War movies, too. The commander who proclaims, "All I've asked my men is to believe my orders as they would the word of God," or, "Inside every gook is an American trying to get out," is the rankest sort of combat cliché. A guy picks up a stuffed toy and gets blown up—hasn't he seen *The Steel Helmet*? Perhaps Kubrick is striving for the archetype; certainly *Full Metal Jacket* has intimations of the cosmic. Rather than jungle, the battle scenes are set in a flaming, post-apocalyptic landscape of bombed-out buildings and grotesque billboards (the opposite of Parris Island's placid green). For the blasted city of Hue (where 10,000 soldiers and civilians died in early '68), Kubrick used a section of London's East End that had itself been attacked during the Blitz (as well as used in the last remake of *1984*), embellishing it with 200 palm trees imported from Spain. The effect is as harshly artificial as the look is purposefully inorganic—it's the Dehumanized Zone.

Another Kubrick concept suggests that war is based on a denial of the feminine. (This might be an idea gleaned from Klaus Theweleit's *Male Fantasies* were it not so true of Kubrick in general—listing the number of significant female roles in his oeuvre would scarcely require the fingers on one hand.) Two of the film's three women are Vietnamese whores, a significant absence in previous Viet films and here resplendent in their own sexual full metal jackets. One struts around like a Tina Turner perpetual motion machine, negotiating her price while crooning, "Me so horny," and—this is a movie of ideas after all—TB-ishly coughing behind her hand. The third woman is a pigtailed Vietcong warrior whose capture provides the film's most startling moment and, immediately thereafter (in a sequence that inverts the coda to *Paths of Glory*), its disastrously unconvincing moment of truth.

Full Metal Jacket has two climaxes, and Kubrick manages to botch both of them in a paroxysm of obviousness. Still, frayed as it is in places, the film knots several strands in its maker's career. Kubrick Sardonicus (*Lolita, Dr. Strangelove, A Clockwork Orange*) meets Kubrick Anti-warrior (*Fear and Desire, Paths of Glory, Dr. Strangelove*), while Kubrick the Genre Deconstructor (*The Killing, 2001, The Shining*) acknowledges Kubrick the Blockbuster (*Spartacus, 2001, Barry Lyndon*). Although *Spartacus* drove Kubrick into exile, at least since *2001* he's been Hollywood's official genius: an intellectual David Selznick. The maestro may see himself as the heir of the beleaguered Orson Welles, but he's more a canny barnstormer on the model of Abel Gance (whose *Napoleon* Kubrick has termed "very crude" and "really terrible").

In the maiden issue of *Premiere*, David Denby identifies his eagerness for *Full Metal Jacket* with "a mostly conventional nostalgia for something now gone—the Hollywood that presented a certain number of huge, exciting events every year." I'm not sure I know which huge, exciting events Denby had in mind—*The Best Years of Our Lives, The Ten Commandments, Dr. Zhivago, Roxanne*—but what's interesting is that, although far from being the most gifted filmmaker of his age, Kubrick is able to mobilize such anticipation.

Kubrick has us all buffaloed; he's a master of PR. Who else could inspire the requisite *Arts and Leisure* scribe to begin by comparing him to God and then reverently record his divine critique of a Michelob commercial: "They're just boy-girl, night-fun, leading up to pouring the beer, all in 30 seconds, beautifully edited and photographed." Pud-pull or put-on? The *Times* even missed Stanley's punch line. "Economy of statement is not something that films are noted for," he observed. Well, not Abel Gance's anyway.

For all his heaviness, Kubrick has an irrepressible facetious streak, most obvious in his use of music, grafting "The Blue Danube Waltz" onto *2001* or dropping "Singin' in the Rain" on *A Clockwork Orange*. *Full Metal Jacket* is filled with tasty pop juxtapositions; however dubious Kubrick's sarcasm in using "Wooly Bully" to underscore combat fatigue or "Surfin' Bird" as a backbeat for a bit of the old ultra-v, he has better taste in music than Oliver Stone (even if his use of Top 40 hits from the prepsychedelic mid '60s seems carelessly anachronistic). Indeed, *Full Metal Jacket*'s triumphant appropriation of the generational anthem that begins "Who's the leader of the club that's made for you and me" is as smart and funny and resonant a cheap shot as any wise guy jest in Kubrick's career.

It's also as contemptuous. Neither ecstatic napalm d'or spectacle nor personal unburdening, this is one distanced film—directed as if gazing through the wrong end of a telescope from the perspective of *2001*. What fools these insects be? *Full Metal Jacket* seems to have been made with less burning conviction than disciplined revulsion. Joker must be speaking for his creator when, at the end of the film, he proclaims, "I am in a world of shit, but I am alive and I am not afraid."

The other, woman

Originally published in *The Village Voice* (September 29, 1987).

ASSURED, PRURIENT GLITZ, Adrian Lyne's movies seem more designed than directed, conceived for shopping malls and VCRs. *Flashdance* and *9½ Weeks* may not be postmodern, but they're post *Modern Screen*. Like Tony Scott, another veteran of Brit TV spots, Lyne specializes in delivering a one-dimensional concept with maximum surface action and a slick, queasy sheen. But unlike Scott, Lyne seems to brood over just what exactly his movies are selling. Lyne has an instinct for the archetypal as well as a taste for the tinny— so perhaps it shouldn't surprise that his thriller *Fatal Attraction* is both efficient and resonant.

Based on a 45-minute featurette made by screenwriter James Dearden, *Fatal Attraction* applies Murphy's Law to the extramarital fling. It's bedroom horror rather than farce. Working overtime through the weekend while his wife and child are out of town, corporate lawyer Michael Douglas is unexpectedly reunited with publishing exec Glenn Close, the intriguing, frizzy-permed Medusa with whom he'd recently exchanged pleasantries at a job-related book party. A drink expands into dinner and dinner becomes the weekend. But the ostensibly sophisticated Close refuses to obey the conventions of the one-night stand; when Douglas politely loses interest, she becomes unpleasantly obsessed and then positively vengeful, an implacable threat to him and his family.

Like all Lyne's films, *Fatal Attraction* has a terrific hook. According to the statisticians of *The New York Times* "Living" section, half of all married men and at least a third of married women have had illicit affairs, with a hefty chunk of the rest lusting in their hearts—but it's an activity of which virtually no one approves. *Fatal Attraction* is confident it's on to something; the film's first 20 minutes are humid with offhanded references to fooling around. "Are you discreet?" Close mischievously asks, ostensibly referring to Douglas's legal practice, after the waitress brings their brandy. "I think so," he lamely replies, setting her up for a provocative, "Me, too . . . So where's your wife?"

Although Close is meant to be hot, there's nothing here to match the relentlessly lascivious spectacle of *Flashdance* or the theatrical sex of *9½ Weeks*. Not that Lyne completely stays out of the kitchen. He cuts from the restaurant to the memorable visual pun of Douglas and Close going at each other with splendid abandon as she's perched on the ledge of a dish-filled sink. (It's not quite as visceral as the quicksand crib David Lynch concocted for *Eraserhead*, but, to add to the verisimilitude, the tap splashes on.) The preview audience greeted this scene with anxious laughter—more cannily than *9½ Weeks*, *Fatal Attraction* addresses the inherent ridiculousness of (other people's) passion. Lyne's camera maintains a cool objectivity as the enthusiastically engaged couple stagger toward the bed, an ignored coffee pot madly perking away.

With her heavy eye makeup and basilisk stare, Close gives her femme fatale immediate intimations of craziness. It's a physically rangy performance, at once frightening, imperious, and vulnerable, that continually teeters on the edge of melodrama—and sometimes kabuki. (By the middle of the film, Close's face is one step from a death mask, even as her black leather wardrobe has become increasingly pale and ethereal.) Close's previous films tended to blur rather than define the strong classical lines of her face; Lyne frames her features to make them even more alarmingly angular. The psychological kicker is that Anne Archer, who plays Douglas's wife, is lit as though *she* were the sex toy. Soft, rounded, radiating wet-lipped reassurance, Archer is the object of desire rather than an object who desires.

Affable, but hardly a smoothy (his features seem to have sunk into the sediment of his face), Douglas bumbles between the women, negotiating his dilemma with a barely submerged hysteria that lends reverb to Close's. For a high-powered lawyer, he seems strangely fuzzy-tongued, ineptly explaining his whereabouts to his unsuspecting wife, and he's pointedly nonpredatory. In virtually all their early interactions, Close comes on so strong Douglas has to give in. Although she's the self-destructive one, he's set up to be the passive victim—consequently his morning-after response can only be a cipher. *Fatal Attraction* not only eliminates the possibility that Douglas might have eventually called Close (they did, after all, have dynamite sex and a meeting of the minds), it incinerates his ambivalence in the heat of her desire.

As thrillers go, *Fatal Attraction* plays fair; it goes light on the red herrings and, perhaps due to its previous life as a short, has a pleasing structural integrity, based on a number of free-floating symbols and key repetitions. As the return of the repressed for Douglas, Close always repays him—in spades. (Even the final, seemingly gratuitous shocker is prepared for early in the film.) Enriched by the judicious use of a child's point of view, the film's second half takes on a malign fairy-tale aspect, involving the opposition of a good mother and a bad one and the looming question of whether Douglas or Archer will ultimately kill the witch. (Less a dating film than a Rorschach test, *Fatal Attraction* should provoke some mordantly hilarious postscreening discussions.)

Given its psychosexual possibilities, one might well wonder how Hitchcock or De Palma would have handled Dearden's script. Either would surely have raised the kink quotient but, at the same time, might have trivialized the material: Lyne is slick, but he doesn't share the two chill-masters' contempt or black humor. He makes an attempt to give everyone at least a patina of humanity. Close, who is identified with the seduced-and-abandoned Madame Butterfly (in a scene where her tormented loneliness is contrasted to the beer-commercial bonhomie of the married couple and their friends), is not only the film's heavy but its most complex and morally ambiguous character—and, in her refusal to be ignored, far from unsympathetic. Still, there's no mistaking *Fatal Attraction* for anything other than an '80s film. It's the nuclear family *über alles,* for Close no less than Douglas.

Fatal Attraction opens with the image of the family as a beleaguered beacon of safety burning in the night—Douglas and Archer bustling around a naturalistically cramped Manhattan apartment in their BVDs as their six-year-old daughter clutches her pet dog and watches TV. (In an echoing scene with intimations of *Stella Dallas,* Close will spy on this domestic bliss and then, magnificently, vomit.) Hardly the heterogeneous carnival of *9½ Weeks,* New York here is congested, noisy, and malign. Indeed, the nuclear family is plotting its escape to the suburbs even as Douglas begins his entanglement with Lady Chaos. The very spirit of the metropolis, Close lives in hell, her loft located above a stylized version of the West Village meatpacking district, a nocturnal landscape of carrion and fire.

In the world of soap operas and country-western songs, adultery is something like the Greek tragedy of the American middle class; and in this respect, *Fatal Attraction* is right on target. Douglas is neither rich enough to buy his way out of trouble, nor poor enough to let this particular woe slide into a morass of other miseries. That Close attacks his property (which includes his family) rather than his person is slyly comic, never more so than when she destroys his Volvo. As a presumably honest lawyer, Douglas represents social order. But what is the law? And who does it serve? "Jesus Christ, be reasonable!" he begs Close during her first hysterical outburst. "You knew the rules." The image of beleaguered patriarchy haunts the movie; when Close and Douglas exchange family confidences, it's of troubled memories of their respective fathers.

If the Lyne oeuvre has any single theme, it's the spectacle of female self-realization (as enacted for a male viewer). *Foxes, Flashdance,* and even *9½ Weeks* are eroticized versions of old-fashioned women's films. One doesn't have to skew *Fatal Attraction* terribly far to see it as the tragedy of a partially-fulfilled woman who wants it all (career, family, sex, salsa) and winds up with nothing. (It's more than a little striking that Close shares the name "Alex," by no means a common one, with the heroine of *Flashdance*.) Almost despite itself, *Fatal Attraction* has a feminist subtext—while some women may find Close as threatening as she's intended to be, others will enjoy the reversed situation of a guy terrorized by a malign female lunatic.

Long before the film's end, Close has metamorphosed from the Other Woman into the Other, Woman. She materializes unexpectedly, leaves disembodied messages, seems to pass through walls. She's wraithlike, uncanny. (Perhaps we should use the German equivalent *unheimlich,* "unhomelike," precisely because the housewife Archer is so totally *heimlich.*) It's not just that Close is scripted to turn threatening and emasculating ("You're scared of me, aren't you?" she taunts Douglas. "Fucking faggot!"), she inexorably becomes a locus for a host of obliquely acknowledged male phobias: the horror of pregnant women, the fear of menstrual blood, the threat of voracious sexual demands.

When Close demands that Douglas "face up to his responsibilities," she's the negative aspect of every man's wife or mother. But she's also something more, and this is what gives the film an unexpected poignance. To keep *Fatal Attraction* within the rules, her character shoulders the full weight of irrational passion. Jealousy and rage know no gender but, Bess Myerson and Jean Harris notwithstanding, I'd hazard that more women than men have been hounded by rejected one-night stands. By the film's patriarchal logic, however, all desire must be projected onto Close.

It's inevitable that *Fatal Attraction* will be read as a metaphor for the age of AIDS. But this cautionary tale taps into something more fundamental—society has never needed a sexually transmitted killer virus to seek to regulate individual libidos. *Fatal Attraction* is a metaphor for just how devastating sex itself can be. If the film only hints at the male urge to create families and abandon them, it's stunned by the power of love to make people disrupt their lives, lose control, suffer delirium, forget who they are, leap into the abyss. Just below the surface, *Fatal Attraction* illustrates the bleak wisdom of popular songs and the craziness implicit in the idea of "love at first sight" or "it had to be you." The film is compelling because, ultimately, there's no such thing as safe sex.

Written on the Wind

Originally published as "Twister" in *The Village Voice* (October 27, 1987).

T HE MOST VIOLENT and hyperbolic of family melodramas, Douglas Sirk's *Written on the Wind* may be the quintessential American movie of the 1950s. The film turns a cold eye on the antics of the degenerate superrich, with Robert Stack and Dorothy Malone as two overaged juvenile delinquents, one a lush, the other a nympho, the wayward offspring of a Texas oil billionaire. Trash on an epic scale, it's a vision as luridly color-coordinated, relentlessly high-octane, and flamboyantly petit bourgeois as a two-toned T-bird with ultrachrome trim.

Written on the Wind has risen steadily in critical esteem since the Sirk revival of the early '70s. The film is not only the ancestor of *Dallas, Dynasty,* and the other imperial soaps that ruled prime time during Reagan's first term but, in its delirious pessimism, it's the Hollywood corollary to Allen Ginsberg's "Howl." But then who in America would have been sufficiently alienated to appreciate Sirk's brilliance at the time of the movie's original release?

To watch *Written on the Wind* is to enter a semiotic jungle and encounter a ferocious irony. Sirk, who achieved his greatest success directing glossy soap operas for Universal, was one of the century's more drastically displaced persons. In his youth, he studied with the great art historian Erwin Panofsky and translated Shakespeare's sonnets, knew Brecht and staged Kurt Weill's last German production. Sirk was a European intellectual, and, if not exactly Adorno in Hollywood, he was nevertheless temperamentally suited to appreciate the exuberant one-dimensionality, the fantastic *Ersatzkeit* of his adopted culture. Long after he returned to Europe, Sirk maintained that he would have made his Hollywood swan song, the monstrous *Imitation of Life,* for the title alone.

Written on the Wind is not simply kitsch—it has a lurid classical grandeur that suggests Norman Rockwell redecorating Versailles (or Jacques-Louis David painting Vegas). Sirk dots the screen with stylized patches of hot canary and flaming turquoise, doubles the image with reflections, skews it with shock tilts, slashes it with flagrantly unmotivated shadows. *Written on the Wind* is the original Technicolor noir. It's fabulously ill, it reeks of autumnal rot. "It is like the Oktoberfest," Sirk's admirer Rainer Werner Fassbinder once wrote. "Everything is colorful and in motion, and you feel as alone as everyone [else]." And, as with the Oktoberfest, a good many of the characters are stumbling around sloshed.

The movie is at once overexcited and detached, embodying a distinctively contemporary attitude that some have associated with the postmodern. Although Sirk keeps things hyper with much brisk cutting on movement, his camera consistently dollies back, transforming point-of-view shots into two-shots, to emphasize relationships and prevent easy identification with his characters. Throughout, Sirk deploys mirrors and rear-screen projection in the service of a distanced antinaturalism. Nature is even phonier than the barren forest of oil rigs that signifies the Hadley wealth; it's like a museum diorama in which everything has its didactic place. A tree exists only to show the initials that were romantically carved there 15 years before and have been perfectly preserved ever since.

There's a monumental Edward Hopper quality to the town pharmacy—the emptiness, the stylized light pattern, the thicket of banners emblazoned "Buy Quality Drugs Here"—that epitomizes the film's frantic affect and seductive flatness. It is in that drugstore that *Written on the Wind* has its natural home. The images are as flashy and iconic as the cover design of a paperback novel. Everything in the film is exaggerated, heightened, concentrated—and theoretical. The lizardlike, liver-spotted patriarch of the Hadley clan (Robert Keith) sits beneath his painted image; his drunken son (Stack) careens through a rear-screen projected wasteland that might have inspired Antonioni's *Red Desert*; his daughter (Malone) makes love to a photo of the film's star and universal object of desire (Rock Hudson), a Hadley serf who spurns her advances because he's in love with her sister-in-law (Lauren Bacall).

Sirk is less a director of actors than a master of blocking, arranging his performers in stylized postures as though they were modeling for liquor advertisements or the Anaheim Palace of Living Art. Malone, who drives a flaming red sports car to the weak-willed Stack's glaring yellow one, is a human jukebox, a virtual taxonomy of '50s come-hither looks, an outrageous erotic construction (based, it becomes apparent, on sexual frustration). Brandishing her tits and licking her lips (she's obviously inherited the lizard's hyperactive tongue), she's Hadleyworld's J.R., the spirit of wanton destruction. The tormented Stack crowds the screen while flinching away from the camera—with his constricted delivery and crooked gait, he's a walking metaphor for tortured ambivalence. Bacall awakes on her wedding night to find him lying aslant—like some cornfed Adonis who's been slain in the marriage bed. (Then, in one of the film's most haunting images, she adjusts his pillow to discover the pearl-handled revolver he's tucked underneath.)

A genius at juggling volumes, doling out light, positioning the camera, Sirk is also supremely tactile, with a sculptor's flare for juxtaposing unexpected textures. Everything in *Written on the Wind* feels sealed in plastic, airbrushed to the point of reflection. The sets are a hermetic succession of furniture showrooms. Like Frank Tashlin, Sirk anticipates the commodity artists of the 1980s. *Written on the Wind* revels in the spectacle of immaculate consumption; it feasts on the decor of a posh Miami Beach hotel. The suite, which Stack has furnished for Bacall with an absurd abundance of fruit, flowers, gowns, handbags, and silk underwear is a cross between a midwestern funeral parlor and a djinn's palace. It's the setting in which the Bacall character experiences *herself* as a commodity, becomes fascinated and ashamed, and flees—but not very far.

No director has ever made more expressive use of decor or the objective correlative. *Written on the Wind* creates a shorthand lingo of fast cars, cigarettes, and booze. This is a universe where people dress like mood rings and surround themselves with totemic fetishes: the model oil-rig phallus that dominates the patriarch's desk, the silver poodles that guard Bacall's calendar, the crimson anthuriums and étagère of perfume bottles that decorate Malone's boudoir. (In this strategy, Sirk's most perceptive disciple is not Fassbinder but Errol Morris, who uses the telling personal effect to turn a talking head into a talking sarcophagus.) Nothing is funnier than the little bits of world culture, ancient statues and abstract paintings Sirk scatters as tchotchkes throughout the Hadley mansion and the film.

"What used to take place in the world of kings and princes has since been transposed into the world of the bourgeoisie," Sirk told Jon Halliday in a long and justly celebrated interview. The Hadleys are Sirk's embodiment of America, a small-town family grown rich beyond measure. But rather than staid burghers, these yokels are laughably (and magnificently) petit bourgeois—the emotionally deprived rich kids acting out their domineering father's rapacious desires, one craving sex, the other seeking oblivion.

In opposition to these hysterical Hadleys are the ostensibly normal Bacall and Hudson. While the Hads are weak, passionate, and rebellious, the Had-nots are moralizing, smug, and pantingly eager to please the old man. The supposedly independent Bacall is all too cooperative; once married into the family, she makes her reports directly to Dad. Hudson, the film's nominal hero, is no less ambiguous—his overweening virtues serve to cripple Stack even as they stifle Malone. Hudson is little more than a broad-shouldered absence and, despite his evident resentment, the father's tool—the foreman in the film's *Metropolis*-blunt class structure. (Below him are the lustful white workers Malone vainly tries to pick up and the subterranean black slaves who exist only to open doors and pour drinks.) Indeed, Hudson is actively fawning on the old man, as a sinister police car simply marked "Hadley" drives up with Malone and her latest lower-class swain in tow.

Where the Hads are direct, the Had-nots are devious. Hudson submits to the father's rule, using Malone to act out his Oedipal desires. Here, as Fassbinder pointed out, "the good, the 'normal,' the 'beautiful' are always utterly revolting; the evil, the weak, the dissolute arouse one's compassion." One cares for the grotesque Malone because her continually thwarted sexuality poses the greatest threat to the patriarchal order. Indeed, in the film's most hilarious excess, her inflamed strip-mambo literally knocks the father dead. By contrast, Stack can only desecrate the rule of the father, as when, in a paroxysm of impotence, he smashes a bottle of bottleg cornmash against the side of Dad's big white house. Even so, his character manages to find a place in the chain of patriarchal oppression when his violence aborts Bacall's pregnancy.

Written on the Wind is not simply epic trash but meta-trash. As the pulp poetry of the title suggests, it's about the vanity of trash, set in a world Sirk finds poignantly innocent. (There's a wonderful, if belated, gag that no one is quite sure exactly where Iran is.) This is the land of simulacrum, a hall of mirrors in which the reflection of an image substitutes for the image itself. Malone disposes of both male Hadleys (freeing Hudson to possess the film's only possible mother, which is to say, Bacall) and sentences herself to eternal sexual frustration. She's left to fondle her father's oil-rig dildo, the image of the dead patriarch smiling benignly from above, as Hudson and Bacall make their escape. The last shot is of a black servant closing the gate; you expect him to roll up the lawn and strike the set.

London burning

Originally published in *The Village Voice* (November 11, 1987).

I N *MY BEAUTIFUL LAUNDRETTE*, director Stephen Frears and writer Hanif Kureishi achieved the unrepeatable—offhandedly serving up a lyrical knuckleball that, however unpredictably it fluttered, arrived with a thwack exactly on target. Their follow-up collaboration, set in a kindred multiracial, omnisexual milieu, is more of a power pitch. As showy and confrontational as its title, the pair's *Sammy and Rosie Get Laid* starts as an incandescent blur, then accelerates.

Sammy and Rosie is a boldly hectic, an orchestrated frenzy with a sardonic, hip tone. "My aim in life," Kureishi said recently, "is to get as much filth and anarchy into the cinema as possible." After invoking Margaret Thatcher as their malign muse, Frears and Kureishi quickly map a series of intersecting fates, crosscutting from playful subway buskers to robotic special police, from a boho photographer's studio to a pensioner's dreary flat in a series of half-minute bites. The film is a succession of these mad juxtapositions. No sooner is a middle-aged black woman shot dead by the cops in the middle of her kitchen than Frears places a pert set of white buttocks in the middle of the screen.

The eponymous Sammy and Rosie are a married couple in their late 20s who met at university and maintain student-style digs in the sort of gentrifying slum where liquor stores resemble armed camps and real estate deals are clinched mid-riot. As in *My Beautiful Laundrette*, Kureishi uses the central relationship to mirror his own mixed heritage—the dissolute accountant Sammy (Ayub Khan Din) is the son of an infamous Pakistani politico, the militant social worker Rosie (Frances Barber) is the daughter of an English bigot. But here the landscape is mixed as well, a ghostly Karachi superimposed over London. The atmosphere is pungently hellish, decayed, and vibrant—half ideological battleground, half Asian souk. The subways are filled with crazies, the streets home to beggars, while hordes of thrift-store hippies can be found living, cooking, farming beneath the crumbling concrete bridge of a once modern superhighway.

Acerbic and defensively callow, Sammy sports a manicured mustache and an American mistress (Wendy Gazelle). He's a pleasure-seeking yuppie while the downwardly mobile Rosie, whom he clearly adores, is the more polemical of the pair. A benign and condescending smile crinkles Rosie's heart-shaped face when she cites "freedom and commitment" as the twin pillars of their open marriage. Ample and confident, she's a feminist party animal who keeps pictures of Virginia Woolf and Jacques Lacan in her study, believes "jealousy is wickeder than adultery," attends lectures on semiotics by Colin MacCabe, employs a pair of Third-World lesbians as her political conscience, and claims to be writing *The Intelligent Woman's Guide to Kissing in History.*

Into this p.c. paradise plunges a real life political monster—Sammy's father Rafi (Shashi Kapoor), a former cabinet minister fleeing his enemies, brandishing a fistful of money, and seeking to recapture his past, personified by Alice (Claire Bloom), the proper Englishwoman he loved and abandoned. "For me, England is hot buttered toast on a fork in front of an open fire . . . and cunty fingers," Rafi muses, exiting his cab in the midst of a police riot. "Before I die, I must know my beloved London again. It is the center of civilization, tolerance." Rafi is the movie's moral epicenter; by his presence alone, the retired torturer raises questions whether Sammy and Rosie should have a child or split up, denounce the old rogue to Amnesty International or take his money and move to the suburbs, possibly with him in tow. ("He could have the basement—or 'dungeon' as we could call it," Sammy offers his unhappy spouse.) To complicate the situation, Rosie has a fling with a squatter named Danny (Roland Gift of the band Fine Young Cannibals), an enigmatic figure with a Flash Gordon widow's peak who lives in a poetry-inscribed trailer and follows Rafi through London's smoky streets, pursing his lips in an affable, flirtatious smirk. "If I lived here, I would be on your side," Rafi glibly assures Danny, the old wog addressing the new.

Although *Sammy and Rosie* is a treasure trove of best acting nominations, it's stolen by Kapoor, the Robert Redford of India (last seen here as the raja who seduces Greta Scacchi in *Heat and Dust*). Plump and (for the first time) middle-aged, Kapoor appears swaddled in Saville Row suits, a ruthless charmer and uncomfortable, garrulous sybarite. Of all the characters, his urbane Rafi is the most superficially British (both he and his son could have been drawn by David Low) and appallingly sympathetic. As in *My Beautiful Laundrette,* Kureishi lavishes his best lines on the older generation. Self-involved and world-intoxicated, Rafi gives social confusion a human form: "Come, I will show you my life—a geography of suffering," he offers, raisings his dhoti for the delectation of his son's mistress. ("Do you chant?" she wants to know. "Chant what, my dear?" he asks.)

Possibly Frears's quintessential film, *Sammy and Rosie* combines the svelte urban apocalypse of *Bloody Kids* with the Anglo-Pakistani complexities of *My Beautiful Laundrette.* It conjoins the metaphysical pretensions of *The Hit* and the sexual politics of *Prick Up Your Ears* to showcase the director's smooth touch with cramped chi-chi restaurants and chaotic parties. In one of the more elaborate set pieces, an urban uprising—complete with flaming cars, smashed shop windows, looters posing for photogs, hovering police helicopters, and even a chorus line—is mirrored by Sammy's own frantic overstimulation. Rafi wakes to find his son simultaneously snorting coke, jerking off, listening to Shostakovich, and scarfing a Big Mac. But for all this, most of the fireworks are verbal. *Sammy and Rosie* is a film of continual talk—everyone wisecracking, reflecting, bantering, engaging in chatty lovemaking, offering homilies on racism, the family, corruption, and sex. It's a barrage of witty metaphors, an intellectual action film. "This is liberalism gone mad," someone says around the time when *Sammy and Rosie* gets leaden, tripping over its own need to be snappy, bright, and shocking 24 hours a day.

Kureishi has said that *My Beautiful Laundrette* was originally intended to be a multigenerational *Godfather*-like epic. *Sammy and Rosie* is far more compressed, but it has a swarming baroque quality. Precipitating the earlier film's latent magic realism, this one is less elegantly oddball and more purposefully emphatic. Frears and Kureishi continually shoot for the big effect and, although some of the walking metaphors fall flat, more often than not they achieve it—as when Rafi's cool is blown by catching the lesbians, one of whom is Pakistani, *en flagrante* and the screen is seared by fantastic subtitled insults. More radical cheek than chic, the film hoists its banner when the image splits in thirds to feature a trio of adulterous interracial couples coming together while serenaded by "My Girl" as performed by the Rastafarian version of Sergeant Pepper's Lonely Hearts Club Band.

Ambitious as it is, *Sammy and Rosie* is almost too much a good thing. It's rich but exhausting. Undoubtedly this incident-crammed vaudeville could have been thinned out (although it becomes more satisfying on a second viewing). Still the frantic spectacle lacks for feeling. All the characters are wounded and needy, as poignantly self-deluded as they are energetically pragmatic. And all of them have their reasons. The film's comedy of manners isn't cynical so much as unsentimentally humanist. Which is to say that Frears and Kureishi aspire toward *The Rules of the Game*—as well as changing them.

Divided city

Originally published as "Earth Angel" in *The Village Voice* (May 3, 1988).

THERE'S SOMETHING ALCHEMICAL about the way Wim Wenders's *Wings of Desire* transmutes gravity into airiness, weltschmertz into spectacle. A fantasy that has nothing to do with special effects, *Wings of Desire* posits a supernatural Berlin where unseen presences hover over the city. This at times astonishingly original film is at once solemn and soaring, somber and intoxicated; it's steeped in the sadness of ordinary life but is also powerfully entrancing.

The film's German title, *Der Himmel Über Berlin* (The Heaven over Berlin), more vividly evokes the juxtaposition of spirit and matter. From the beginning, Wenders adopts a dizzyingly overhead angel's-eye view. His leading seraphim, Bruno Ganz and Otto Sander, see the world in sumptuous black and white and, although their presence is sometimes sensed by alert humans, they are visible only to each other. Alone or as a pair, they ride the subway, comfort the dying, bear witness to suicides, and generally practice a sort of ecstatic brooding over the city's daily routines.

Passing through crowds, peering over people's shoulders as they suffer extreme crises, the vigilant angels tune in on individual frequencies—they're like radio receivers for human brainwaves. (An ideal audience, they're endlessly solicitous and ever entertained.) Hardly creatures of light, Ganz and Sander are as sober as solicitors and as conservatively dressed, their hands in the pockets of their gray flannel topcoats. Sander is appropriately reserved but Ganz is truly remarkable—it's difficult to imagine another actor inhabiting the role. Ganz radiates such empathy he could be the strontium 90 in the milk of human kindness.

The movie's first 45 minutes are a form of astral projection. There's no narrative and the angels' journeys are totally unpredictable. (The construction is less dramatic than elastic—there's a continual streamlined rush, a stretching and snapping of time and space.) The camera soars over the autobahns, swoops into housing tracts, peers out an apartment window, then in a single, impossibly smooth movement, glides across a courtyard from one crowded flat—a couple of weary, anxious parents listening to their son's inexplicable rock music—into another, where kids cluster around a glowing video game.

It's a measure of the movie's sweetness that a library serves as seraphim central. Wenders's angels are drawn to the vast multileveled reading room of the Staatsbibliothek—a fluorescent neo-Bauhaus structure, half international style, half postwar Warsaw, not far from the Wall. Here celestial voices mix with the soft murmur of a hundred minds. (Later, we see the library emptied out except for the angels and the Turkish night cleaners.) Bending over the readers, the angels are enraptured by the flow of thought, Ganz listening with concert-hall concentration. When Sander tunes into an elderly man played by the octogenarian Curt Bois, the movie suddenly melts into the past—the library gives way to newsreel footage of liberated Berlin, dead children laid out amid the ruins.

AN URBAN STREAM of consciousness as well as city symphony, *Wings of Desire* reinforces one's sense of Berlin, or at least West Berlin, as an island—a place isolated onto itself, reachable mainly by air. Berlin has been called a city in exile and, better than any film I've seen, *Wings of Desire* captures the place's stoic melancholy, its somnolence, its self-absorption, its leaden brutality, its deep sense of loneliness and desertion.

Wings of Desire is shot in a silvery black and white, so that Berlin seems dusted with celestial soot. (The cinematographer is the 79-year-old Henri Alekan, responsible for Cocteau's *Beauty and the Beast* and half the French quality films of the '50s.) But, despite this glamorous sheen, the film has the tough urban lyricism one associates with movies celebrating New York. The camera caresses ancient metal bridges and fondles peeling houses, wanders across desolate stretches of Kreuzberg and dwells upon the Wall until even the city's stainless-steel modernity and Scandinavian sense of order seem wounded and incomplete. The empty buses, near-deserted Schnell Imbiss stands, and hard-edged advertising posters of Wenders's Berlin suggest an abandoned *Metropolis,* while the Wall makes the city seem as stylized as Venice.

In Bois—a onetime child star, Reinhardt actor, refugee, Hollywood bit player (the pickpocket in *Casablanca*), member of Brecht's Berliner Ensemble— Wenders has a living relic of the city's past. Bois, in fact, was the subject of a documentary made by Ganz and Sander. A few blocks from the Staatsbiblio-thek, the old man wanders through the mud and wild grass searching for Potsdamerplatz, the city's lost center, now bisected by the graffiti'd Wall. Once Berlin's Times Square, this overgrown nowhereland is illuminated by flood-lights rather than neon; this city generates negative geography the way others do urban renewal.

As in Ernie Gehr's brilliantly minimal *Signal—Germany on the Air,* Berlin is here a ghost town, the site of unseen forces. Ganz and Sander perch on the ruined steeple of the city's famous Kaiser Wilhelm church or nestle on the shoulder of the statue of Winged Victory that gazes east towards the Branden-burg Gate. Meanwhile, an old-fashioned circus (Wenders names it after his cinematographer) pitches tent in a barren lot off Friedrichstrasse, a boulevard severed by Checkpoint Charlie and, past it, the former site of Berlin's movie studios. The angels are not the city's only present absences. "The film is drawn to these empty spots, as if they had a magnetic charge," Wenders told me when I interviewed him last February in Berlin.

The impossibility of reconciling German history is parodied, after a fash-ion, by a film within the film. Peter Falk, playing himself, arrives in Berlin to star as an American detective in a German war movie. Ganz visits the set (an actual World War II bunker) where costumed SS men and Hitler youth mingle with exhausted old people and Jewish deportees. These historical phantoms comple-ment Ganz's longing to be corporeal. His first monologue is a wistful celebra-tion of physical sensation, of weight, the desire "to feel what it is like to take your shoes off under the table." Outrageously ephemeral and bluntly materialis-tic, *Wings of Desire* articulates the two poles of German ideology while map-ping Berlin as a metaphysical site. As Maurice Blanchot observed: "Berlin is not only Berlin, but is also the symbol of the division of the world"; its Wall marks the border between Truth and Error, Good and Evil, Freedom and Bondage.

Ganz's yearnings are crystallized when he discovers the aerial artist at the Alekan Circus (French actress Solveig Dommartin). The film switches briefly to color as Ganz watches her rehearse and then again when, under his tactful gaze, she sits on the edge of her trailer's bed, naked back to the screen. Dommartin, who makes her film debut as the trapeze performer, is grave and statuesque, with a wide, generous mouth and a corona of frizzy hair swept over to one side so that she suggests an electric Michèle Morgan. With her broad shoulders and strong dorsal muscles, she's no sylph—it's easy to appreciate Ganz's fascina-tion, based less on desire than *Dasein.* Later, Ganz follows Dommartin to a bombed-out rock club and watches her dancing by herself (like everyone else) to the voluptuously dirgelike industrial-noise drone of Crime and the City Solution. Even the punks are dreamers in Wenders's Berlin.

WINGS OF DESIRE is Wenders's first German movie after an ambitious but problematic series of American productions that, paradoxically, helped make him the most garlanded European director of his generation. Far more than Herzog or Fassbinder, Wenders was in love with the myth of America, Hollywood, rock 'n' roll—playing out his increasingly tortuous affair over the course of *The American Friend, Lightning Over Water, Hammett,* and *Paris, Texas.*

"I was in America so long that German became my second language," Wenders told me. *Wings of Desire* was inspired by his 1984 relocation to Berlin, which he considers the only German city with a sense of the past, and his simultaneous reading of Rilke ("the most beautiful use of the German language"). The screenplay was subsequently polished and developed by Wenders's erstwhile collaborator Peter Handke; the result is surely Wenders's strongest outing since his 1976 *Kings of the Road*—that most tender and horrific exploration of German postwar anomie—charted an ERG at once empty and imprisoning where, as one of the protagonists complained, "the Yanks colonized our subconscious."

Falk aside, *Wings of Desire* owes nothing to Hollywood—it belongs to a specifically European tradition of adult fairy tales that includes Cocteau's *Orphée* and early Fellini. Before shooting began, Wenders screened three films for his cast and crew: Walter Ruttmann's 1927 documentary *Berlin: Symphony of a Great City,* Marcel Carné's 1942 medieval fantasy *Les Visiteurs du Soir,* and Roberto Rossellini's 1947 neorealist drama *Germany Year Zero,* made in French-occupied Germany as the Carné film was made in German-occupied France. *Wings of Desire* manages to mix all three, but more than that, it seems steeped in a specifically German feeling of being positioned outside of history, a helpless phantom. Ganz articulates his desire to become human as a need "to conquer history for myself"; the angels have their last meeting in the *echt*-German twilight zone, the eerie no-man's-land between the two structures of the Wall.

A free-floating homesickness is something Wenders shares with Rilke, but for Wenders this has become an absolute condition. In the *Duino Elegies,* Rilke writes that "every angel is terrifying," presumably because mortals prefer to cling to the visible world. A materialist in spite of himself, Wenders reverses Rilke's overarching theme—the abandonment of the ordinary world to quest for the invisible, eternal one—even as he illustrates the final lines of the last *Duino* elegy: "And we, who have always thought of happiness as *rising,* would feel the emotion that almost overwhelms us whenever a happy thing *falls.*"

Ganz's fall provides the film's only story. And, abetted by Falk's cute Columbionics, the film fluffs up to meet the lapsed angel towards the end— garish color sears your eyes after two hours of pearly black and white. Given Ganz's childish pleasure in every new tactile sensation, it's staidly cornball that

Wenders opts to climax with a celebration of mature hetero love, but the actual ending is deliriously risky. When Ganz and Dommartin finally meet—in an empty bar, across an uncrowded room—she makes her five-minute speech right into the camera: ". . . There's no greater story than ours." Although this baldly romantic ending strains her resources—Dommartin's heartshaped face is more pleasant than sublime—I'm not certain Garbo could've have carried it off. Still, the movie has built up so much good will that one tends to regard the scene benignly, the way Ganz and Sander consider the denizens of Berlin.

There are times when Wenders and Handke's sentimental streak makes you want to abolish language—*Wings of Desire* has so perfectly realized a visual style. This movie shimmers across the desert of current releases like some myrrh-scented breeze. The first time I saw the film I thought it was a knockout; on second viewing it already seemed a classic.

Name that 'toon

Originally published in *The Village Voice* (July 5, 1988).

AS EVERYONE WITHIN TV range surely knows, *Who Framed Roger Rabbit* is this summer's eighth wonder of the world—an animated epic, a *Newsweek* cover story, a *New York Post* page one, the Disney studio's $40 (or is it $50) million gamble, a technological marvel, a masterpiece of vulgar post-modernism, the greatest film Frank Tashlin never made but a triumph for director Robert Zemeckis and presenter Steven Spielberg, the Looneytune to top all Looneytunes.

Providing its own short subject, *Roger Rabbit* opens with an impressively nerve-shredding pastiche of a vintage Warner Brothers cartoon. This fully animated, pseudo-Bob Clampett job has the hysterical Roger tying himself in knots, as he chases his diapered charge across a kitchen as vast and perilous as the Grand Canyon. Casting reflections and throwing shadows, the manic rabbit survives scalding, baking, drowning, and electrocution—only to plunge his cartoon vehicle into the context of a "live action" studio after he blows his cue by seeing birds, not stars. "What the hell was wrong with that take!" the gravel-voiced baby asks the cartoon's human director.

It is the premise of *Roger Rabbit* that, once upon a time (which is to say in 1947), Hollywood was populated by cartoon stars as well as flesh-and-blood ones, and that these Toons, including contract-player Roger, had their own studios, their own neighborhood of Toontown, and their own peccadillos. When Roger's humanoid wife Jessica seems to be stepping out on him, the studio hires a hard-drinking human detective (Bob Hoskins) to investigate the case. Ensuing complications enable the filmmakers to mix animation and live action on a scale unseen in the quarter-century since *Mary Poppins*—which, perhaps not coincidentally, was the greatest financial and critical success of Walt Disney's career.

As far as animation goes, *Roger Rabbit* far surpasses *Mary Poppins*, even as it substitutes hardboiled nostalgia for Disney's traditional saccharine tone. The Toons maintain the illusion of volume while conforming to the most extreme Warner Brothers cartoon conventions: projecting eyeballs, insane torso stretches, bizarre facial contortions. Roger crashes through a window, leaving a frantic silhouette punched out of the glass. Humans and Toons don't just share space—they physically mix it up. When Roger and Hoskins are cuffed together, the Toon drags the human under a bed and slams him into a desk. If the Toon weasels brandish real guns, Hoskins can retaliate with his customized, animated Yosemite Sam pistol and talking Dum-Dum bullets.

Hoskin's wide-eyed doubletakes, tight smile of menace, and dyspeptic glare of disbelief carry more than their share of the film's comedy—but part of the joke is that this squat, solid toughguy is a sort of cartoon character himself. (Even in more conventional roles, Hoskins strikes viewers as potently stylized. Reviewing *Mona Lisa*, Pauline Kael approvingly quoted her date's remark that the actor was "like a testicle on legs.") On the whole, Hoskins exhibits considerable savoir faire, punching out humans and Toons alike, while extending his range to a game song-and-dance routine. Hoskins must have felt he was going mad, playing straight man to a nonexistent rabbit, and the underlying fury sharpens his performance. After watching him drive an anthropomorphic cartoon cab with the screaming rabbit wrapped around his neck, you figure he deserves a Purple Heart even more than an Oscar.

Costar Roger, a lanky hare in maroon overalls and a polka-dot bow tie who breaks plates on his head for laughs, is a dim p-popping cousin to Avery's brilliantly obnoxious Screwy Squirrel. He's a credible icon but will likely be upstaged by the errant Jessica. A dizzying ensemble of curves with a Veronica Lake peekaboo do, Mrs. Rabbit appears more pulchritudinous than even the heroines of Avery's *Swing Shift Cinderella* or *Red Hot Riding Hood*. This outrageous construction in slink and bounce might start a new trend in inflatable sex dolls. Hoskins bangs his head on her Mansfield-sized mammaries (which do everything but play the drums). When she blows a kiss, it flies through the air and, like some sinister sci-fi creaturette, affixes itself to his cheek.

Although "nature" is continually stylized through outsized props and exaggerated makeup, *Roger Rabbit* never brings to fruition that garishly cartooned reality anticipated by filmmakers as disparate as Joe Dante, the Coen brothers, and Pee-Wee Herman—or realized, a half dozen years ago, in the quasi-underground *Forbidden Zone*. Hoskins aside, the humans can't compete with their Toon associates. Nor are they meant to. Zemeckis crisply cuts on Toon movement to keep the illusion of coexistence going. But because the film drags when Toons aren't on screen and overaccelerates when they are, there are moments when *Roger Rabbit* is less great than grating. The movie was conceived in the Avery spirit, but only the most hardcore Averyite could endure a dozen of the master's cartoons spliced end to end.

Because the ghettoized Toons are little id monsters—creatures of impulse who would sooner self-destruct than miss the opportunity to indulge some corny gag—the film has aspects of allegory, both racial and psychological. More than the site of cuddly run amok, Toontown is perceived as a source of chaos and menace (as well as urban renewal). But given the movie's frantic pace, the suggestion that the Toons represent something other than jabbering drawings is scarcely developed. The evil Judge Doom (Christopher Lloyd) wants to rein in the Toons; there are times when you see his point. Toontown is a place of hilariously abrasive cuteness. Nothing in the movie is funnier than the bilious expression on Hoskin's face, as he drives through a landscape in which everything from raucous bunnies to swaying trees is singing and dancing. It's as if he's experiencing the horror of Disneyland on Mars (or magic mushrooms).

Just as the Moscow Summit might be considered the Great Communicator's last hurrah, so *Who Framed Roger Rabbit* suggests the last efflorescence of Spielbergism—that is, the process by which the subversively self-reflexive practice of the French New Wave was recuperated in the service of building bigger, better, and blander entertainment machines. At one point in *Made in U.S.A.*, Anna Karina describes the movie she's in as "a Walt Disney film with Humphrey Bogart." *Roger Rabbit* is that Disney film—belatedly but literally. And it's not half so mindboggling as the genre-busting combo envisioned by Godard (or his audience).

There probably hasn't been a more elaborately, seamlessly intertextual Hollywood movie since *Dead Men Don't Wear Plaid*. Half the sightgags are a homage to Chuck Jones—and most of the rest are steals. Not only do Mickey Mouse and Bugs Bunny appear in the same epic free fall, but the cameos include virtually every animation house—Lantz's Woody Woodpecker, Fleischer's Betty Boop, and, most effectively, M-G-M's Droopy Dog are all on the scene. Still, no assumptions are unmasked, the universes all blend; the real subtext here is the war of the trademarks, Warner and Disney.

If Roger combines Bugs's species with Daffy's energy, Porky's nerdiness, and a generic Mel Blanc voice (actually Charles Fleischer), the set itself belongs to Walt. There's an early explosion of Toon nonsense, with Dumbo buzzing the studio office window, and a gaggle of Fantasia chorines—ostriches, hippos, brooms—dancing around the commissary. True, Daffy gets the better of Donald in their dueling-piano stage act. ("This is the last time I work with someone with a speech impediment," Daffy tells the crowd.) But when Roger wants to admire real genius, he plunks for *Goofy Gymnastics*.

Warners sets the tone, but Disney calls the shots: when, in the film's final seconds, policeman Porky appears to stick his head in the closing iris and stutter "Th-th-th-th-that's all folks!" he's vaporized by Magic Kingdom super cop Tinker Bell. *Who Framed Roger Rabbit* is definitely a wonder. But it may leave you with a feeling familiar to those who have visited Disney's Magic Kingdom—this spectacular technology has given birth to a mouse.

Hal Willner plays Disney: Never mind the mouse ears

Originally published in *The Village Voice* (October 25, 1988).

A NYONE WHO'S EVER visited Walt Disney World knows that the so-called Magic Kingdom is the most aurally intrusive place on earth. You can't go anywhere without being assaulted by "Zip-a-Dee-Doo-Dah." Paralyzing the cerebral cortex, this quintessential mickey-mouse Muzak is meant to evoke childhood, security, wonder—the whole dodo of happiness. And, unless you're some kind of beatnik deviant, it does.

Bush hasn't yet pledged allegiance, but Disney is the closest thing America has to an official culture. Thus the revisionist boldness of producer Hal Willner who, having previously given pop highbrows Nino Rota, Thelonious Monk, and Kurt Weill the gonzo all-star treatment, turns the Disney songbook over to the likes of Yma Sumac, Betty Carter, and the Replacements. Drawing heavily from the classics (*Pinocchio, Snow White, Dumbo*), Willner's *Stay Awake* (A&M) is straight Americana for bent Americans. In the history of the Disney cosmos, there's only one precedent, the studio's rehabilitation of bawdy Ukelele Ike as the voice of prissy Jiminy Cricket.

For all the Moody Bluesoid earwax that frames the performances, *Stay Awake* is less concept album than concept art. Dealing with Disney-dreck, there are three strategies: hip sincerity, hip "sincerity," and bebop. Sincerity takes the material at face value; "sincerity" recognizes that there's something intrinsically appalling about it, and that's what makes it great. Sincerity is easily assimilable into the Disney universe; "sincerity" would give us enormous pleasure if, by some corporate oversight, it were. Willner straddles both options when he has Ringo Starr romp through "When You Wish Upon a Star" with the original TV show arrangement and a fat, burbling solo by Herb Alpert.

Nothing here is as sincerely sincere as Barbara Cook's recent *The Walt Disney Album* (MCA), complete with Nancy Reagan thank-you note in the press kit. If the Roches, Natalie Merchant, and Michael Stipe treat "Little April Showers" as glee-club fodder, Yma Sumac's bombastic "I Wonder" presents *Sleeping Beauty*'s big solo as it deserves to be belted out at Bayreuth—all wordless trills and extraneous noodling. Sincere? My Disney-bred daughters couldn't distinguish Sumac's Inca-shriek from the anemic original. Sincere or "sincere," you still must face the awfulness of the music. Suzanne Vega doesn't: her a cappella version of Mary Poppin's lullabye, "Stay Awake," is self-importantly purist, less suggestive of Willner's Brechtian bias than her longing to have been included on his Weill album. Neither does Bonnie Raitt with Was (Not Was). Her bloozy "Baby of Mine" becomes a triumph for Disney and a minor camp pleasure for anyone familiar with the song's grotesque-pathetic context: a mother elephant poking her trunk through prison bars to cradle her mutant offspring.

More sincere than "sincere" are guy-groups who avoid embarrassment with obscure uptempo numbers. Los Lobos's "Monkey Song," from *The Jungle*

Book, lacks edge. It's straight out of the Enchanted Tiki Room. Buster Poindexter's mambo-ized "Castle in Spain" gets arcanity points for being from the 1960 *Babes in Toyland,* but the Replacements' sourly raucous interpretation of "Cruella DeVille" (*101 Dalmations*) as Vegas lounge scuzz is more a personal purgative than anything you'd want to listen to twice. The best of the male bond-a-ramas is Sun Ra's "Pink Elephants on Parade." A near-normal arrangement of the ditty heralding Dumbo's psychedelic freakout, it is sung with such falsetto enthusiasm that it might almost be about something—like maybe the segment of the population you don't see on *Soul Train.*

"Sincerity" is a harder act to pull off, if only because it involves putting your particular kidculture in historical perspective. NRBQ treat the authoritarian "Whistle While You work" as an inanely cheerful Fender bender, in which they carefully drift off the beat. Conceptually superior, which is to say less likely to be co-opted, is Sinéad O'Connor's chilly "Some Day My Prince Will Come," a terminally depressed dirge that all but leaves a trace of spittle in your ear. (O'Connor has the advantage of being a foreigner; to underscore the political correctness of her version, she plays the guitar as if scratching chalk on the blackboard.) In a less self-aware dayroom performance, James Taylor croons "First Star to the Right" (saccharine even by Disney standards) with the same toneless gusto he uses to chant everything else. Irony hurts, but its absence is far worse.

Louis Armstrong was probably the first musician to demonstrate that it's possible to make something out of any kind of crap. (Take his 1930s recording, "Shine." Not only does Armstrong knock this monotonous racist fluff into exuberant self-affirmation, he refuses to enunciate the eponymous epithet—substituting a riff beyond any transcription.) Every once in a while, someone is driven mad by the vapidity of official American culture and takes up the challenge: John Coltrane interprets "My Favorite Things," Wilson Pickett covers "Sugar, Sugar," Phil Spector produces a Christmas album. As far as this sort of transcendence goes, *Stay Awake*'s brute existence compensates for the individual duds.

So what's the pick hit? Betty Carter performs her routine 'round-about-midnight alchemy on "I'm Wishing," improvising frantic parallel lyrics to Snow White's wistful lament but without engaging it. Some people are moved by Aaron Neville's lugubriously soulful "Mickey Mouse Theme." To me, it sounds like side two Motown filler. (Besides, Stanley Kubrick has already given that particular generational anthem a definitive kiss-off in *Full Metal Jacket.*) My personal Armstrong award goes to Tom Waits for scoring the Dwarf marching song "Heigh Ho" for kettle drum and police siren. The day they play this Martian field holler on the Disneyworld sound system, you'll know that something more epochal than Snow White has finally woken up.

Lost in America: Jean Baudrillard, extraterrestrial

Originally published in *The Village Voice Literary Supplement* (March 1989).

IS JEAN BAUDRILLARD our Jerry Lewis, or are we his? Given the French genius for appreciating American popular culture, it was only a matter of time before America itself—the Burger King K-Mart and Eyewitness News drive-in, the plastic parthenon, the whole airbrushed "Have a Nice Day" theme park that we've all grown to love or ignore—would return to enchant us à la française. Jean-Luc Godard never got to make his Vegas movie but do not despair: Jean Baudrillard's *America,* appearing in English just as the author seems poised to pass from intellectual fashion, is an ambivalent paean to that "museum of power" we call home.

For the most part, *America* is fun. Although ambivalent on democracy, Baudrillard is less a postmod Tocqueville than a giddy Gene Kelly in reverse, kicking up his heels on some (in this case, mental) Metro soundstage: "American banality will always be a thousand times more interesting than the European—and especially the French—variety." Only offhanded social theory, *America* is more of an epic poem or the treatment for a science fiction film—it zips along like a logorrheic version of *Koyaanisqatsi,* the continental U.S. visualized as an awesome planet of freeway deserts, urban jungles, and monumental enigmas.

Baudrillard is on a hallucinatory journey to the end of night, where California oil-drilling platforms stand sentinel till dawn "like grand casinos or extra-terrestrial spacecraft." He has grasped the *E.T.* metaphor and he's not about to let go. The Mormon tabernacle in Salt Lake City is "straight out of *Close Encounters,*" the museums of Washington suggest an attempt "to gather all the marks of earthly endeavor and culture . . . for the benefit of a visitor from outer space."

The author is, of course, that alien visitor—the distinguished observer from a distant galaxy, at once obnoxiously superior to and ridiculously dazzled by the life-forms he detects: Sure, Marxism and fine wine don't really cross the ocean, but "the latest fast-food outlet, the most banal suburb, the blandest of giant American cars or the most insignificant cartoon-strip majorette is more at the centre of the world than any of the cultural manifestations of old Europe." The mall, as Baudrillard prophesied in "Consumer Society" (albeit using the quaint appellation "drugstore"), is the acme of Western civilization—the sublimation of life, where work, money, and even the seasons disappear.

It was in America, Baudrillard told an interviewer, that he suddenly found all his themes manifest in a concrete form. Small wonder he believes that America embodies the imaginary or that he calls it an "achieved utopia." In 1981, Baudrillard conceptualized Disneyland as a sort of innoculation, an official fantasy designed to make the rest of hyperreal America seem authentic by comparison. Now he's moved on to a higher truth: "It is Disneyland that is authentic here! The cinema and TV are America's reality!" (Walt Disney would have agreed. He once told Billy Graham that the "fantasy" started outside Disneyland's gate.)

Having given up on Europe sometime after 1968 (and slipped his Marxist moorings during the next decade), Baudrillard constructs America as the inevitable, not-so-radiant future. Oscillating between condescension and envy, Baudrillard resolves his ambivalence by pronouncing America "the only remaining primitive society," that is to say "the primitive society of the future"—a land without a past, privileged (or condemned?) to live in the eternal, what-me-worry? now. Geographically, the search for the pure and primitive leads Baudrillard to imagine America as desert and desert as the ecstatic negation of all culture. (At one point, in his neo-Dada delirium, he is moved to suggest that the desert demands a human sacrifice, most appropriately a beautiful woman.)

In the semio-gaga, happily solipsistic tradition of Roland Barthes's *Empire of Signs* (an appreciation of the "novelistic object" the author chooses to call "Japan"), Baudrillard perversely holds that America is a coherent, crystalline entity—"a giant hologram, in the sense that the information concerning the whole is contained in each of its elements." Clearly, this is not the America of trade unions and multiple-use zoning. Nor is it America the relentless social laboratory—Baudrillard's formulations are far too static. He takes his cue from our departing maximum leader. Like Reagan, Baudrillard prefers a higher form of banality, an "astral America," an America suspended in the heavens, lost in the cosmos, a constellation, a starry night, a myth, a . . . movie. Years of watching westerns, musicals, and crime films have prepared him for the neon excrescences of this crazed and arid planet where "cinema does not assume an exceptional form, but simply invests the streets and the entire town with a mythical atmosphere."

A theorist for the age of Reagan! A Parisian in America! Everything Baudrillard sees is as excessive and overdetermined, violent and stridently colored as a Warner Bros. cartoon. New York, "the center of the world," appears like some monstrous Babylon (with Central Park as its hanging garden), a city of "wall-to-wall prostitution" where Baudrillard is spooked by the "terrifying diversity of faces" and "the mad" who walk free. Every motel room has a television and every television is endlessly transmitting otherworldly, seductive, mind-boggling gibberish—the canned laughter of the gods.

Infuriatingly oracular even by poststructuralist standards, indispensable for describing the discombobulated sensation of living in our national mediacracy, Baudrillard has received rote bashing for his ill-defined terms, overheated style, and unsystematic analysis. These faults serve him well here—where theory is reduced to aphorism—as does his most endearing shortcoming. For Baudrillard's greatest sin is that, like most of us, he pretends to extrapolate reality from television.

Smile button ironically pinned to his lapel, poster of Marilyn ostentatiously taped to his wall, Baudrillard is the poet laureate of Reagan's reign. In a certain sense he has become American himself—and not just because for five years he has reigned supreme over American art journals, film theorizing, and conferences on postmodernism. At the least, Baudrillard's rhetoric fulfills Tocqueville's believe that, because of democratic levelling and individual self-absorption, American poetry would be compelled to overcompensate, "surcharged with immense and incoherent imagery, with exaggerated descriptions and strange creations; and that the fantastic beings of their brain may sometimes make us regret the world of reality."

Or rather, hyperreality. Indeed, Baudrillard takes TV more seriously, more literally, than any social thinker since Jerry Mander. For him, this ubiquitous medium is something like *Don Quixote*. Fiction doesn't simply invade or replace reality, it depletes it. Transforming everything into a consumable image, it empties the world—leaving that which we call "life," the pale imitation of television. Reality is judged by how well it conforms to our telereceived images. Is Dan Quayle really another Robert Redford? Is *Favorite Son* the avatar of Dan Quayle?

If many of Baudrillard's insights are rooted in the '60s—drawing upon Marshall McLuhan's *Understanding Media,* Jacques Ellul's *Propaganda,* Guy Debord's *Society of the Spectacle,* and Walter Benjamin's then rediscovered "The Work of Art in the Age of Mechanical Reproduction," not to mention the acid-ravings of the ordinary hippie in the street—it is because that is when the full implications of teledemocracy began to be felt. Back then, Baudrillard was hooked on advertising; he argued that the vapors of illusion clouding men's minds arose from the manufacture and exchange of commodities, except that with the rise of the soft sell, exchange value was more important than use value. The ideologies of competition and freedom, not to mention the "total organization of everyday life," had migrated from the sphere of production to that of consumption: "Individuals no longer compete for the possession of goods, they actualize themselves in consumption [and that] consumption, in so far as it is meaningful, is a systematic act of the manipulation of signs." Like, when the going gets tough, the tough go shopping.

With its breathless prose and rhapsodic appreciations, *America* often reads like *On the Road*: "Snapshots aren't good enough," Baudrillard gushes during the first of many drives through the desert. "We'd need the whole film of the trip in real time, including the unbearable heat and the music." Like Kerouac, Baudrillard celebrates the sensation of speed, the appetite for distance, the enchanting emptiness of the open freeway. "Europe has never been a continent," he writes, marvelling at the hugeness of the American sky or pondering "the wall of crystal that imprisons California in its own beatitude."

None of this is exactly unfamiliar. It's the lysergic Moloch of Allen Ginsberg's poems or *Highway 61 Revisited* as refracted through the clammy prism of *Nova Express*—and yet, given Baudrillard's particular brand of antisociology, *America* has an alienated quality all its own. For one thing, it's radically depopulated, or rather inhabited by phantoms. Baudrillard's quintessential American is the lone jogger, infuriatingly plugged into his own personal Walkman, "sleepwalking in the mist like [a shadow] escaped from Plato's cave."

This America has no soundtrack, no voice—save Baudrillard's. (Despite a perfunctory nod to "smash hits on the Chrysler stereo" in his first sentence, he doesn't blast the radio when he drives.) The silence makes your ears ring. Baudrillard's America has the emptiness of an Edward Hopper landscape. When he writes of "the unspeakable house plants, lurking everywhere like the obsessive fear of death, the picture windows looking like Snow White's glass coffin," he is describing the setting of *Magnificent Obsession* or *Written on the Wind*. This is America the hyperreal—the media-saturated world of self-referential signs, the endless round of simulations without an original.

By Baudrillard's lights, and some semiotic Gresham's Law, these tawdry "simulacra" have superseded what used to pass for reality. (The masses, he argues, subvert this regime only through their passivity.) Now, diminished yet uncontestable, the United States dominates the world as its own two-dimensional image, the triumph of advertising. The American flag waves as the planet's supreme trademark. American power is a special effect concocted by Industrial Light and Magic.

No American can understand this. Such is the price of life among the stars for the primates of Tomorrowland. Americans have no sense of simulation, Baudrillard explains for our benefit, because they are themselves simulation—in its most developed state, of course. College professors are, for him, the worst (not unlike those top-of-the-line "clickers" in *Creation of the Humanoids* who believe they are human and loath "clickers" with a racial antipathy). Naturally, such academics are his most vociferous fans.

The American silent majority may or may not be subversive in its unconscious imitation of itself, as M. Baudrillard has argued elsewhere. But he is convinced that his own authenticity is intact; Baudrillard is the last non-simulacrum in *America*. *Voilà*: it took the French to introduce designer jeans. Baudrillard is selling us back to ourselves with his name flamboyantly stitched on our pockets. Which is why Parisian cultural theory will always be a thousand times more interesting than the American—and especially the American academic—variety.

The last Western

Originally published as "Once Upon a Time in America" in *The Village Voice* (May 16, 1989).

THE LAST REAL Western made by Sam Peckinpah (or anyone else, for that matter), *Pat Garrett and Billy the Kid* is almost insanely elegiac. The colors are ultra magic hour, and the characters are obsessed with growing old. In this rereleased *film maudit*, directed from Rudy Wurlitzer's screenplay, the end of the Western is inextricably bound up with the waning of the '60s, not to mention the twilight of the filmmaker's career.

Peckinpah, who'd been trying to make a Billy the Kid film for at least 15 years (one early attempt mutated into Marlon Brando's ineffably perverse *One-Eyed Jacks*), inherited a script that Wurlitzer had written for *his* erstwhile soulmate, Monte Hellman. The failure of *Two-Lane Blacktop* diminished Hellman's bankability, but the Peckinpah'd result—with weathered James Coburn and pudgy Kris Kristofferson in the title roles—proved anything but commercial. The movie first appeared 16 years ago this month after a well-publicized battle with M-G-M boss James Aubrey and, doubly disowned by Wurlitzer, inspired extremes of praise and invective. Even more than most Peckinpah movies, it's almost pure fetish object.

At 121 minutes (15 longer than the release print), the "director's version" was evidently one of many. According to Roger Spottiswoode, who coedited the movie, this particular cut was stashed away by Peckinpah after a sneak preview. In addition to recovering several lost scenes, the reissue restores Peckinpah's mildly convoluted structure. The movie opens in 1909 with old coot Garrett gunned down in an ambush, then spirals back to 1881 to juxtapose this belated assassination with Billy and the boys taking target practice. The newly civilized Garrett rides into Fort Sumner to warn the free-spirited Kid that he's now representing the law. "How does it feel?" Billy taunts his old buddy. "It feels like times have changed," is the doubly weary answer.

As terminally autumnal as it is, the movie carries more than a trace of Wurlitzer's absurdism (and taste for haute-bohemian fashion). But the abundant violence and leathery camaraderie, ritualistic killing and mucho macho posturing, the incidental cockfights and lip-smacking whiskey guzzling, the rub-a-dub-dub, four-whores-in-a-tub partying and the towheaded kids who amuse themselves by swinging on the hangman's noose are all pure Peckinpah. Wurlitzer undoubtedly contributed to the countercultural ambience, but it was the grizzled, bandanna'd director who gave the movie the sense of a giant family squabble, pivoting on Garrett's inchoate love for his old range buddy, the Kid. This is one intensely romantic flick.

Indeed, back in 1973, *Pat Garrett and Billy the Kid* was the hippest of Westerns—not just post-*Wild Bunch* and post-Sergio Leone, but post-*El Topo*, post-*Antônio das Mortes,* even post-*Last Movie*—filled with righteous outlaws and lines like, "There's gonna be some hard times coming down." Much of the action seems to segue from one commune kitchen (or bedroom) to another. Almost ridiculously rich in scene-making, the movie is as densely populated as a Warhol flick: In addition to the two nominal stars, it offers a pair of then hot pop icons, Bob Dylan and Rita Coolidge, in supporting roles, along with an astonishing collection of veteran *secondarios* (Slim Pickens, Katy Jurado, Elisha Cook, Harry Dean Stanton, Jack Elam, and Mexican director Emilio Fernández). Even Jason Robards turns up as General Lew Wallace, military governor of New Mexico (and future author of *Ben-Hur*), to deliver the capitalist rap on the need to eliminate Billy.

The movie's spookiest aspect is its sense of America having killed an outlaw part of itself and then having that part come back—will all due media fanfare. If

Billy and his pals are proto-Rolling Stones, the wealthy cattle baron Chisum (played by John Wayne, no less, in the 1970 vehicle of the same name) is their highly unsympathetic idea of the devil. Less worthy revisionists than would-be visionaries, Peckinpah and Wurlitzer play connect-the-dots with history. The battle of Stinking Creek, in which Garrett captured Billy in an isolated cabin, is staged so that wounded outlaws play poker in a tough-guy delirium, with Dylan baying out his first rendition of the movie's theme song ("Bill-EE, they don't like yuh to be so FREE-E-E") as, arms outstretched, the grinning outlaw surrenders.

The most amiably ironic of '60s action heroes, Coburn is weary and relentless—the silverhaired grim reaper in pursuit of Kristofferson's unlikely sacred monster. The successor to Johnny Mack Brown, Buster Crabbe, Robert Taylor, Audie Murphy, Paul Newman, Dennis Hopper (who played Billy on the TV show *Sugarfoot*), Dean Stockwell (the actor "Billy" in Hopper's *The Last Movie*), Jean-Pierre Léaud (star of the 1973 *Une aventure de Billy the Kid*), and Michael J. Pollard (eponymous antihero of the preceding year's *Dirty Little Billy*), Kristofferson is a plump-faced dude with a modified Monkee shag—shamelessly pulling a tight, self-mocking smile, an attempted Jack Nicholson tic.

Kristofferson is fatuous, but Peckinpah works with it; there's an antiheroic bit of business in which Billy dons his sombrero, mounts a horse, and is promptly dumped in the center of Main Street. Nor is he exactly a selfless Robin Hood. One of the movie's most brazen killings has the beleaguered killer challenge decrepit Jack Elam to a duel and win by cheating first. In a nerdily conceived role as Billy's temporary sidekick, "Alias," Dylan is something of an embarrassment—he's badly postdubbed and gets extremely limited mileage out of an angelic smirk. (His part did not appear in the script; the abundance of pointless close-ups that Peckinpah lavishes on him must have been stipulated in the performer's contract.)

Even more than Kristofferson, Dylan is meant to be the signifier of hip. When Emilio Fernández appears to invite Billy to Mexico, Alias portentously presents the Mexican soul bro with a knife: "It has a good edge." A surefire laugh line, the sentiment reeks of countercultural smugness. Still, Dylan's music is intrinsic to the film—his sensuously minimal quasi-Mexicoid score (surely the best thing he'd done for the movies since singing "It's All Over Baby Blue" at Donovan in *Don't Look Back*) gives the movie a pleasingly stoned circularity.

The mode is voluptuously static. One of the key sequences has the dogged Garrett trading unprovoked potshots with some anonymous homesteader who is floating by on the river *en famille*. If not exactly a saga of hanging out, *Pat Garrett* is still an extremely desultory quest through a wilderness worthy of *Conan the Barbarian*. Hardly a masterpiece of suspense, the movie drifts toward the inevitable face-off with the lazy fatality of an eddying rowboat approaching the falls.

In the end, Billy is cornered one cold night—Fort Sumner filling up with hombres wandering through the fog as Kristofferson and Coolidge bed down with sad hippie smiles, Dylan moaning appreciatively on the track. The real

Garrett shot the real Billy unarmed and asleep. Here Peckinpah revels in the ambiguity of so brutal an execution: Garrett sits impassively outside Billy's window, generously (or voyeuristically) allowing him one last bit of pleasure before he waylays him en route to a postcoital snack.

For a Peckinpah film, the death sequences are amazingly languid—as lengthy (if not as loquacious) as those in a Shakespearean play. The scene in which, having been coaxed out of retirement by the implacable Coburn, fat old Slim Pickens buys it in a confused gunfight is the dark heart of the movie. Fatally wounded, Pickens leaves his comrades and, like some bull elephant, painfully lumbers away from the action down to the river to die. His wife (Katy Jurado) follows him, and their exchange of glances, as the movie brilliantly grinds to a halt (allowing him a few more precious moments of life), is at once startlingly gratuitous and utterly intrinsic.

This is the sequence which inspired Dylan's "Knockin' on Heaven's Door." In Peckinpah's version only the implacably mournful background chorus wells up on the track to send Pickens to another world. It's no less bravura, but those familiar with the movie's release version may experience a sense of missed catharsis.

Suddenly, last summer

Originally published in *The Village Voice* (June 27, 1989).

WHAT GOES AROUND comes around, bigger than ever. Like the mindless, autostimulating "waves" that course through the stands at American ballparks, product familiarity celebrates itself: The record weekend grosses racked up by *Indiana Jones and the Last Crusade* are echoed by the spontaneous rhythmic applause greeting the appearance of that unmistakable ambulance-cum-smogmobile 10 minutes into Ivan Reitman's *Ghostbusters II*.

Truly, no value in America is more sacred than a trademark, nothing more comforting than the assembly line production of Mom's Apple Pie. It scarcely matters whether *Ghostbusters II* strokes or satirizes the viewing public—this film will gross a zillion. The nostalgia mode has become a permanent fixture of our cultural economy. What goes around comes around, as often as it can: *Ghostbusters II* isn't a sequel so much as a fond remake, a simulation of the original (and its epoch). Scarcely half a decade after the actual event, we're treated to a partial replay of the summer of 1984, that fabulous New Morning which saw the Olympics staged in Los Angeles (83 gold medals), Ronald Reagan out on the hustings (525 electoral votes), *Born in the U.S.A.* topping the charts (10 million units sold), Indiana J. rocking the Temple of Doom (109,000,000 simoleons), and the Ghostbusters exorcising Central Park West (21,000,000 more than that).

It *was* a heady moment. And, the highest-grossing movie perpetrated by anyone other than George Lucas or Steven Spielberg, the original *Ghostbusters* is the most popular film comedy ever made—as well as one of the most ideologically intriguing. (What's it all about? The movie wasn't all that funny. Many reviewers considered it sub-Abbott and Costello.) Hardly pre-sold, the original *Ghostbusters* was a cult run amok. During the '84 campaign, Democrats and Republicans alike realized that the party that controlled the summer's smash hit (or at least its logo—you may remember the rival Ron- and Fritz-buster T-shirts) would win the election, and the Dems had about as much chance of that as carrying Orange County. More than *Star Wars* or *Rocky*, *E.T.* or *Rambo*, *Ghostbusters* was the perfect embodiment of Reaganism—and not simply because, like the president, it celebrated "the indispensable defense science of the next decade."

At once cynical and idealistic, *Ghostbusters* was hailed by *The Wall Street Journal* for its glorification of the free enterprise system. The movie was business school perfect—celebrating the creation and exploitation of a false need. *Ghostbusters* brilliantly inscribed its own advertisements within its text (as Bill Murray exulted after the first successful exorcism, "The franchise rights alone will make us rich beyond our wildest dreams.") Taking the supernatural as a given and then satirizing not belief in the occult but rather the special effects movies that appeal to it, *Ghostbusters* approximated the psychic sleight of hand by which our presidential *Zeitgeistmeister* conjured crises and victories to save us from our psychosomatic ills. (Not the least of the movie's tricks was preempting this very analysis by attributing it to the film's ridiculous Environmental Protection Agency agent—the designated "pencil-dick"—who accused the Ghostbusters of fabricating apparitions to dispel them.)

So, *Was geht herein, kommt herein.* In virtually every regard, *Ghostbusters II* is more of the same—perhaps a bit kinder and gentler. That K-G feeling is ubiquitous: In the current *Premiere,* Spielberg explains that he made *The Last Crusade* in part "to apologize" for *The Temple of Doom,* which "was too dark, too subterranean, and much too horrific." (Are these his euphemisms for too racist, too sexist, and much too successful?) There is a kind of pallid new New Morning in America (partly because the old Z-meister is gone and partly because he's not around to make it happen anymore), and, a number of thrilling sewer scenes aside, what *Ghostbusters II* and *The Last Crusade* have in common is their concern for establishing family ties. In *The Last Crusade,* the search for the absent father is identified with nothing less than the quest for the Holy Grail—"I didn't come for the Cup of Christ, I came to find my Pop!" Less Oedipal in its conflicts and less reverential in its worldview, *Ghostbusters II* provides its protagonists with offspring rather than parents.

"Five years later," the film begins. There's a suggestive close-up of organic slime oozing from a crack in the sidewalk and—presto!—Sigourney Weaver is perambulating an eight-month-old infant, jokingly called Oscar. The opening sequence, which sends the tot's carriage careening off into heavy traffic, crosses the central heartclutcher in *Potemkin*'s "Odessa Steps" with the trajectory of that venerable, one-gag kiddie classic, *The Slant Book*. Thus, as heavily dependent on baby F/X as it is on animation and miniatures, *Ghostbusters II* is part of the boomer boom that, in movie terms, encompasses everything from *The Wonder Years* to *Pink Cadillac* (Clint Eastwood's answer to *Raising Arizona*) to Max Spielberg (the most influential four-year-old on planet Earth).

In keeping with this downhill coast into adult responsibility, there aren't as many cigarettes consumed here as in the original *Ghostbusters*—not to mention the persistent alienation effect of Murray and Aykroyd's rampant middle-age spread. Still, children will be pleased to find the same abundance of ecto-mucus and hyper-goo. (If anything, the intervening triumph of the Garbage Pail Kids and the marketing of play Slime has significantly enhanced the yuck quotient.) While initially the Ghostbusters are has-beens, reduced to doing birthday parties for "ungrateful little yuppie larvae," the movie's whole agenda is to render Bill Murray patriarchal—or at least, good-with-kids. Indeed, *Ghostbusters II* is so suffused with socially channeled testosterone that the climactic pissing contest will even establish archnerd Rick Moranis as potent. (The token black member of the team, Ernie Hudson, is no less marginalized than in the original.)

This is important because the 'busters are, after all, public servants—affable disaster specialists with a selective sense of wonder. A billion-dollar logo aside, their trademark is a juicy contempt for those literal-minded bureaucrats who are constrained by the reality principle. Thus, *Ghostbusters II* hews to the original pattern of free-market catastrophe, misguided state intervention, and the triumphant rehabilitation of the entrepreneurial spirit (here somewhat inflected by a half-hearted populism). Having inadvertently caused a third New York blackout, the 'busters are put on trial—redeeming themselves when they save the judge from the familiar squadron of blobby, toothsome apparitions.

Like its model, *Ghostbusters II* grounds its fantasy in Manhattan local color. Indeed, in the absence of a surefire hit single, the movie's most persistent leitmotiv is its insistence on the city's negative aura. "Being miserable and treating other people like dirt is every New Yorker's God-given right," the Kochoid mayor proclaims in a line that deserves to haunt the upcoming mayoral campaign. "Only a Carpathian would come back to life now and choose New York," Murray smirks. (That's not the only weird lifestyle decision. It's even harder to figure why Sigourney Weaver would return to dating and choose Murray. The city's deterioration matches his own.)

The Last Crusade may have the hottest sex scene in any Spielberg film (albeit played for laffs largely below the frameline) and a Nazi rally where Hitler gives Indy his autograph, but, as relentlessly overdetermined as it is, it's far less entertaining than *Ghostbusters II*. Reitman's bad taste is as irrepressible as the blob beneath the city: The dread pink slime violates Weaver's apartment as she fills Oscar's bath, erupting out of the tub in the form of a giant penis, which sends her scampering for the relative safety of Murray's boudoir. More frequently, however, the ooze is associated with afterbirth. As the film's resident geek couple, Moranis and the Ghostbusters' gumsnapping secretary (Annie Potts), broach the possibility of having a child. Reitman cuts to a trio of megaslimed 'busters emerging from a manhole in front of the Metropolitan Museum of Art.

One can appreciate Reitman's Dada gesture in locating the center of evil in New York's preeminent cultural citadel; his movie is frequently so disjointed as to seem virtually avant-garde. Even allowing for its supernatural premise, *Ghostbusters II* makes little narrative sense. The two cosmic threats—the malign painting of the Carpathian potentate, Vigo, which bids to manifest itself in little Oscar and take over the world, and the viscous river of gunk that courses beneath Manhattan, feeding on the city's bad vibes—are only tangentially related. At best, *Ghostbusters II* is a free-associative semiotic barrage, studiously evoking the original even as it giddily addresses all manner of contemporary anxieties. This psychic spritz is the film's central pleasure. The topicality of some images is positively uncanny—the phantom jogger rounding the Central Park reservoir, the totemic use of the Statue of Liberty.

In the Ghostbusters saga, no less than in the legend of Indiana Jones, evil invariably has a foreign accent. But where Spielberg has a taste for villainous Nazis, Reitman—a child refugee from the People's Republic of Czechoslovakia—is, understandably, more taken with the specter that once haunted Europe. Nothing overt, of course. As his green-card jokes suggest, there's just a vestigial insecurity. Reitman remains an outsider, having grown up in Canada— it was, perhaps, with a double dip of alienation that he orchestrated an American invasion of his birthplace in the underrated *Stripes*. Still, the satire of East European malevolence is the most heartful thing in *Ghostbusters II*. (The parody goes well beyond standard Bela Lugosi stuff. The monstrous Vigo may be an excessive stand-in for Gorbie, but the opening send-up of *Potemkin* is unmistakable—Peter MacNicol, who plays the depraved nudnik Janosz, strongly suggests a puny Eisenstein.)

What Reitman can't quite muster is the appropriate nationalist fervor. It's an odd feeling watching *Ghostbusters II* in the aftermath of Communism's well-publicized collapse, particularly as the movie ends with a mad cacophony of patriotic symbols. The film's one element of social realism is the Balkanization of New York. Compelled to rally the city, the 'busters are at a loss, ultimately brainstorming Liberty as a positive version of the Stay-Puft Marshmallow Man (only in Czechoslovakia or Tiananmen Square would the Statue of Liberty have such clout). Brought to life by a combination of cosmic ick and Jackie Wilson, the Lady, as they were calling her back in the centennial summer of '86, strides across the bay and marches up Fifth Avenue. (There's a last, wonderfully anarchic moment when she squashes a cop car as heedlessly as King Kong trampling a native hut.)

Here, along with the energy beams of Ghostbuster's patented proton packs, the movie's various trademarks converge. Like a mob of revelers transported from Times Square, the crowd outside the Metropolitan starts singing "Auld Lang Syne." (Which new year is it?) In the world of Ivan Reitman, this could be considered sentimentality—I think.

Street scene

Originally published as "Pass/Fail" in *The Village Voice* (July 11, 1989).

THERE'S BEEN A lot of ink spilled already on *Do the Right Thing,* and there's sure to be a lot more—the Spike Lee film may be the only summer movie that encourages any discussion beyond the "oh, wow." You can't avoid having a point of view; this film won't just wash over you. Indeed, some commentators seem to think that the operative fluid won't be ink, but blood and tears.

The effect of motion pictures on human behavior is a question that's been debated for nearly a century, but *Do the Right Thing* is being treated in some quarters as a blueprint for catastrophe. Let's start by observing that the experience of this movie is complicated and perhaps chastening, but also skillfully organized and not exactly unpleasurable. *Do the Right Thing* is bright and brazen, and it moves with a distinctive jangling glide. Set on a single block in the heart of Brooklyn on the hottest Saturday of the summer, it offers the funniest, most stylized, most visceral New York street scene this side of Scorseseland.

Lee is a deft quick-sketch artist. His Bed-Stuy block—a dank pizza stand, a Korean grocery, a storefront radio station, a half dozen decrepit brownstones— is as humid as a terrarium and as teeming with life. Taunted by a moving chorus of heedless high school kids, the tormented, borderline Radio Raheem (Bill Nunn) stalks the neighborhood with his humongous boombox. Meanwhile, a retarded stammerer (Roger Guenveur Smith) peddles a double portrait of Malcolm X and Martin Luther King. The irascible Mother Sister (Ruby Dee) stares contemptuously out her window at the beer-sozzled busybody known as Da Mayor (Ossie Davis), as a trio of street corner philosophers shoot the breeze beneath their portable beach umbrella, badmouthing Mike Tyson, the Korean greengrocer, and the proud and foolish Buggin' Out (Giancarlo Esposito), an irate hiphopster looking for a fight. Someone opens the hydrant. The cops turn it off. People get on each other's nerves. Da Mayor saves a kid running for the Mister Softee truck. The sun starts going down; you're waiting for the catastrophe.

Do the Right Thing has a surplus of data; it's filled with low angles and crowded, panoramic frames, the characters peering over each other's shoulders like good and bad angels in a medieval morality play. Everyone interacts with everybody else; the diminutive hero Mookie (played by Lee) threading his way among them, delivering pizzas, dispensing advice, dropping in on his girlfriend. The other unifying presence is Mister Señor Love Daddy, the DJ who broadcasts 24 hours a day. If Mookie is a black everyman, Mister Señor Love Daddy is the celestial spirit of the neighborhood, at one moment offering a celebratory litany of black artists, at another calling time out to end a cathartic montage of ethnic slurs.

Lee, himself, isn't quite so mellow; his portraits are affectionate but not exactly flattering. Few black filmmakers have ever been this bold and it's telling that, in a movie as filled with intricate checks and balances as this, he would make the most obnoxious, least articulate character the ultimate victim. Everyone has his or her own agenda. Mookie is introduced counting his money, then nuzzling awake his sister Jade (the filmmaker's sister, Joie Lee) as Sal (Danny Aiello) pilots his battered white Cadillac toward his "famous" pizzeria, warning his squabbling sons, "I'm gonna kill somebody today."

Do the Right Thing is Lee's first film with white characters and, if not as vivid as the blacks, they're not exactly faceless stereotypes. The bored cops cruising in and out of the neighborhood are hardly identical to the guy who gets drenched, or the gentrifier who inadvertently scuffs Buggin' Out's sneakers; the passive, easygoing Vito (Richard Edson), who drops out of the narrative, is distinguished from the stupid, angry Pino (John Turturro), who *wants* to move out: "I'm sick of niggers. It's like working on Planet of the Apes." And, given a weary dignity by Aiello, the patriarch Sal is a complex creation.

Crude but hard-working, the pizza-man is the movie's sole embodiment of the American Dream. "I never had no trouble with these people," he tells unhappy Pino. "They grew up on my food, and I'm very proud of that." It's Sal's fantasy that his sons will someday inherit this empire of nourishment—in a moment of generosity he even declares that there will always be a place for the hired hand Mookie. Sal's success is comprehensible, his paternalism has a human face. "Who does he think he is," Radio Raheem wants to know when Sal compels him to turn down his boombox, "Don Corleone and shit?"

Lee, who hates comparison as much as the next filmmaker, has more than once expressed his distaste for being dubbed "the black Woody Allen." Still, one would be hard-pressed to come up with another auteur who has as much of himself invested in his work. Like Allen, Lee is a control freak who typically has his own person inscribed at the center of his films. But, unlike Allen, Lee has no firmly established persona. What exactly is the relation between Mookie and Lee?

Do the Right Thing's fictional pressure cooker suggests Lee's own. In this steaming Saturday world, Mookie (brilliantly named after the most lovable of Mets, so that his name will haunt us all summer long) is responsibility writ small. He works. He maintains some interest in the mother of his child. He counsels his friends. So when the crunch comes, what right thing will Mookie do?

A DARING MIX of naturalism and allegory, agitprop and psychodrama, *Do the Right Thing* begins, literally, where *School Daze* leaves off—with a Brechtian call to "wake up"—and, as confrontational as it is, the movie sustains more moment-to-moment interest than most of the year's releases combined. The choppy, fragmented narrative seems much smoother on second viewing, once you get the spiral structure. The flow is teasingly eruptive: Like Julien Temple, Lee designs his production numbers with an eye toward MTV. The movie opens with a surge of rock-video energy and a burst of prurient militance as Rosie Perez in boxer shorts pugnaciously gyrates to Public Enemy's "Fight the Power." This anthem has an irony that only becomes apparent when the film is over.

Someone is sure to call *Do the Right Thing* a rap movie. Certainly, it's a language-intoxicated film, filled with mainly feckless, fast-talking men and invariably judgmental, fast-talking women. "What I ever done to you?" Da Mayor asks haughty Mother Sister. "You a drunk fool," she spits back like a gatling gun. "Beside that?" he demands. Jade is usually on Mookie's case, while Tina (Perez), his awesomely strident lady friend, is in a class by herself: "If you listened to me, I wouldn't have to repeat myself like a fucking radio." *Do the Right Thing* is clamorous with sign language, but this is the only negative reference to the medium that, supporting Marshall McLuhan's notion of the tribal drum, provides Lee's somewhat idealized village with its social cohesion.

Lee has already taken a fair amount of criticism for sanitizing his street scene. But the real issue is not the absence of drugs or street crime; the real issue is racial solidarity. No black character on this street may exploit another for economic gain. Thus, no black character can operate any sort of business or hold any real authority. No black character, save Mookie (and the ethereal Mister Señor Love Daddy), is shown to be gainfully employed. Where *School Daze* offered a critique of black racism and class conflict, *Do the Right Thing* presents no essential divisions within the black community. Discontent is signaled by the endless series of personal turf wars, the movie touching lightly on the pain in having your sense of self bound up in a pair of sneakers or a radio, the relative merits of this major league pitcher or that pop music superstar.

Like Scorsese, Lee fills out his films with his own fetish objects and family members. The latter subtext comes complete with an undercurrent of sexual paranoia. When Jade (who is, after all, the woman with whom Mookie lives) visits Sal's and gets fawningly special treatment, Mookie flips out. "All Sal wants to do is play hide the salami," he tells his disbelieving sister. That the scene is played in front of a "Tawana Told the Truth" graffito gives it an added ambiguity. Is Jade an unwitting candidate for abduction and gang rape? Does Mookie believe Tawana told the truth? Does Lee? Or is the sign only a sign of the times, a bit of street scene verisimilitude?

Walls are important in this movie, mainly for what they say. A Hispanic mural is visible in many scenes. And the site of the *Kulturkampf*, after all, is the sweaty wall of Sal's Famous, covered with (and restricted to) framed publicity photos of the Italian celebs who, whatever else they do, will never ever drop in for a slice.

ANOTHER DIRECTOR MIGHT be satisfied putting stuff on the screen that's never been there before, but Lee is driven by his own demons, not to mention constituencies ranging from the Fruit of Islam, who protected his set, to the Universal executives who bankrolled the film (after Paramount, the studio of Eddie Murphy, put the project in turnaround). Thus, *Do the Right Thing* is not a career move in any conventional sense of the term. As Da Mayor tells Mookie in a fit of melancholy, "Always do the right thing." Yeah, sure. But just what is that anyway?

There are a number of powerful black personalities in American show business, but Lee is unique, having gone further on his own terms than any other black filmmaker in American history. Neither Ossie Davis nor Sidney Poitier, Melvin Van Peebles nor Michael Schultz, has been able to move from success to success, generating his own projects and controlling his own persona, to become a spokesman, a symbol, and a force to be reckoned with. For that alone Lee is destined to be patronized and slighted, lionized and attacked, spoiled and abused, put in his place and denied his place. (Why was it not immediately recognized, for example, that his was the missing voice in *New York Stories*—and not only for the obvious demographic reasons?)

Lee's films are markedly free of filmschool references (*Do the Right Thing*'s homage to *The Night of the Hunter* is a rare exception), but to a certain degree his project seems to involve rewriting the movies of the '70s. If his first feature, *Joe's Bed-Stuy Barbershop: We Cut Heads,* was an archetypal regional/independent, his breakthrough, *She's Gotta Have It,* can be seen as a cannily revisionist *Sweet Sweetback's Baadasssss Song. School Daze,* his would-be blockbuster, combines, overhauls, rewires, and subverts a number of mondo youth films, including *Animal House, Grease,* and *Saturday Night Fever.* Not as grandiose as its predecessor, *Do the Right Thing* appears to address Michael Schultz's 1976 *Car Wash,* coincidentally the last movie directed by an American black to be shown in competition at Cannes (where, less problematic than Lee's, Schultz's film won an award for its score).

Anticipating *Do the Right Thing* in its workday structure and radio mysticism, as well as its high-grade ensemble acting, *Car Wash* is suffused with frustration and powerlessness. What Lee does, among other things, is to bring the story back home, moving the L.A. car wash owned by a middle-aged white ethnic to a black neighborhood and transforming it into a pizzeria (even as the car wash's mainly black labor force is reduced to Mookie). That the whites in *Do the Right Thing* are virtually all Italian-American not only suggests Howard Beach but an assault on the media counterrevolution begun by *The Godfather* and effected with *Rocky,* by which, with the blessing of white America, Italians supplanted blacks as the national minority of choice.

Do the Right Thing is truly tribal; it lacks the horror of the industrial world. Indeed, *Car Wash*'s space-age shoeshine parlor makes Lee's movie seem cozily old-fashioned. (A kindred social realism might have dictated the replacement of Sal's Famous with a bombed-out Burger King—half junk food factory, half armed camp.) But while *Car Wash* reeks of mid-'70s post-Orgy burn-out—it's one of the saddest movies ever made about the cost of earning a living in America (there's never been a more chilling disco refrain than the title song's exhortation to "work and work and work and work")—*Do the Right Thing* seems more a metaphor for the '60s. It requires human sacrifice and a taste of the apocalypse for the climactic integration of Sal's Wall of Fame.

Do the Right Thing might have ended there, with flames devouring the image of Al Pacino (making room for a picture of Eddie Murphy?). But, didactic as he is, Lee reserves the right to tie up some loose ends and balance a few equations with a coda that stops the film dead. Even the well-choreographed riot is clumsily adjusted to "do the right thing" by evoking Selma, Alabama, as well as Michael Stewart, while allowing the industrious Koreans—previously hassled by Da Mayor, Coconut Sid, and Radio Raheem—to be accepted into Lee's particular rainbow coalition.

"I built this place with my bare fucking hands," Sal tells Mookie on the grim morning after. "Do you know what that means?" Mookie may not, but Lee certainly does—something effaced in the closing minutes. This final scene, which should have the impact of the father-son battle the narrative never delivers, disintegrates into feeble self-justification. Mookie accepts his pitiful reparations (something less than 40 acres and a mule) and, less than convincingly, promises to go back to Tina and his son (oddly adding, "if it's all right with you"). Mister Señor Love Daddy informs us that the mayor has convened a blue ribbon panel to protect private property, and suggests that his listeners register to vote; Lee delivers an antiviolence quote from Martin Luther King and an apparently contradictory, pro–self-defense quote from Malcolm X.

If Lee's convoluted ending hedges his bets, that shouldn't obscure the enormous risk that the film takes. In addressing racism and racial violence, while refusing to take an unambiguous stance for (white) civil order, Lee risks being blamed as the messenger of bad news—if not an outright demagogue. Already Joe Klein, *New York*'s expert on race relations, has speculated at length as to whether *Do the Right Thing* will cost David Dinkins the primary: Not only do "a great many white New Yorkers" hold Dinkins answerable for the gang-rape of a white jogger, Klein reports, but "unfortunately, Dinkins will also have to pay the price for Spike Lee's reckless new movie . . . which opens on June 30 (in not too many theaters near you, one hopes)."

So will Ed Koch have to pay the price for the urban bad vibes in the reckless *Ghostbusters II*? *New York*'s target audience notwithstanding, Klein predicts that while white liberals debate *Do the Right Thing*'s message, "black teenagers won't find it so hard . . . *white people are your enemy.*" In spite of this hysterical accusation of cinematic wilding, it seems obvious that (1) most black teenagers don't have to see *Do the Right Thing* to have feelings about white people; (2) there is no monolithic, unthinking response to this film, anyway; and (3) the vast majority of Lee's fans would probably rather star in his next movie than torch the bijou where it's shown.

But even if black teenagers are angry enough to burn it down, Spike Lee didn't invent that destructive rage or American racism. Did George Bush need *Do the Right Thing* to get himself elected by running against Willie Horton? Americans spent the past eight years under a Teflon smile button whose pleasure it was to deny that racism had *ever* existed in America—let alone that it might actually be a live social problem. New Yorkers have lived for the last 12 years with a mayor who has recklessly played one ethnic group off against another and then congratulated himself for his evenhandedness. And whatever one thinks about them, these experiences (as even Klein must know) are qualitatively different, depending on your race.

The ending of *Do the Right Thing* is certainly upsetting (and upsettingly incoherent), but its pathos and self-defeat are real. In the absence of an organized movement, honest political leadership, and a realistic sense of American life, the alternative for those this system denies will be to fight whatever comes to hand, even if they are only the powers that *seem* to be.

New York Film Festival: Societies of the spectacle

Originally published in *The Village Voice* (October 3, 1989).

T HE NEW YORK Film Festival is always good for a Sunday think piece, and this year there's no shortage of movies to think about. Some even address the contemporary world—the ramifications of communications technology, the not-unrelated end of Russian hegemony in Eastern Europe, the corresponding loss of American economic preeminence.

A three-and-a-half-hour evocation of the Hungarian home-video business, *The Documentator* is set in 1987—two years after the local leadership realized that the VCR revolution posed a threat to "socialist morality," even though, unlike in Poland, Magyar home video was less a matter of guerrilla newsreels than black-market porn. (Now socialist morality has all but vanished; last month, the Hungarian Workers Party cynically created a corporate entity with an English-language name, "Next 2000," to protect its portfolio of resorts, garages, and computer systems.) If events have overtaken this film, *The Documentator* is still the first postcommunist movie I've seen, albeit no less Marxist for that.

This epic assemblage, made by István Dárday and Györgyi Szalai from all manner of archival footage, depicts Budapest as a sleazy Eurotown where the Diners Club logo has replaced the hammer and sickle, and a single day's take at the protagonist's video store is 10 times the monthly salary of the average Hungarian worker. A vast, visually exciting political cartoon, *The Documentator* has an abundance of sight-gags, very little dialogue, and all manner of juxtaposition. In some respects, it's a throwback to '60s hubris; Dárday and Szalai, who call their movie a "film novel," are groping for a new form. The credit sequence offers a compressed history of 20th century warfare from grainy battlefields to brash color-and-disco video games. A subsequent montage introduces all the film's elements: sex, violence, advertising, surveillance.

Russian tanks may be irrelevant, but the legacy of Soviet filmmakers remains: The movie engages Sergei Eisenstein's sensational "montage of attractions," Dziga Vertov's encyclopedic kino-eye, Esther Shub's historical compilation films. The intellectual categories are Marxist too. (From time to time, the proles appear—getting drunk in a dive named "Hell," dressing up on TV in 18th century costumes—complaining about low pay, high prices, and constant work.) *The Documentator* continually flips the dialectic of glitz and squalor, fiction and documentary, personal drama and history.

Virtually everything in this mad, ambitious movie is mediated by the TV monitor, punctuated by the squeals of car tires and orgasm. Vérité-style mono-logues alternate with mindless sensationalism, sometimes in the same frame. The use of archival footage takes the last few Márta Mészáros films several steps further: In one set piece, newsreels of Budapest '56 occupy one large monitor and three smaller ones, the soundtrack segueing from a '30s paean to the Five Year Plan to a radio report of Stalin's death. *The Documentator* is a film taxonomy, quoting everything from Italian horror flicks to Wim Wenders's *State of Things*; a so-called "intermission" offers five minutes of Hungarian commercials for toilets, bikinis, tax helpers, designer work clothes, state objet d'art insurance, "superbike" motorcycles, and *The Documentator II*.

The minimal plot concerns a sordid romantic triangle consisting of the middle-aged Raffael, the dour, bearded intellectual of East European tradition (here, the owner of a white Oldsmobile and mighty mogul of the bootleg video market), his smashing concubine Chip—a blond bombshell with cheekbones up to her hairline—and the leather-clad second-in-command they call Rambo (although his mode of attire more closely suggests RoboCop). Healthy young animals, Chip and Rambo live in their own romantic movie, which Raffael ultimately turns into a closed-circuit spectacle.

The eponymous documentator is not only hooked on surveillance devices, he's a history-junkie, obsessed with the idea of creating a video lexicon of the 20th century. Thus the self-absorption of everyday life, parodied in the narrative and magnified by commercials, is set against the televised drama of Great Events. Even as his feckless employees cavort in the nude, Raffael spends his free time cross-referencing his image archive. (Undermining his lack of commitment, the filmmakers ponder images of Prague '68 with Raffael wondering how to categorize them: *war, coup d'état, demonstration, reform, revolution, counterrevolution,* or *fight for freedom?*) A visionary who narcissistically tapes his own Nietzschean credo while maintaining that cheap video will democratize expression, Raffael embodies the dilemma of the Hungarian movie industry as it maneuvers between a 40-year tradition of state-subsidized "research" and the new imperative to create crowd-pleasing blockbusters.

The filmmakers have this problem themselves: They identify their techniques with advertising even as they make visible much of what we have become immune to. The juxtaposition of rural poverty with a televised speech by Party Secretary Károly Grosz (his platitudes interspersed with random quacking from the barnyard) aside, *The Documentator*'s most politically daring moment is the pithy critique one economist offers of the current crisis. Citing the traumas of modern Hungarian history, the tradition of national self-deception, and the unexpected violence of 1956, he raises the possibility that public ignorance of the country's real economic situation could lead to a similar explosion. (Indeed,

The Documentator has a quintessential Hungarian ending—the police arrive and everything comes to naught.)

This is a film of high energy and deep pessimism. The failure of socialism creates a vacuum that can only be filled by the shit of capitalism.

THE ELECTRONIC IMAGE is no less omnipresent in Atom Egoyan's witty, sinister *Speaking Parts*. The third feature by this talented young Canadian immediately establishes a Cronenbergian sense of dread, crosscutting between a lone mourner in a video-equipped crypt and the ominous impersonality of a hotel laundry room.

For Egoyan, video is at once a phantasm and a commodity, a private hallucination and a nexus of social relations, a doppelgänger and an Other, a form of truth and a source of mistaken identity. A disturbed chambermaid, obsessed with an aspiring movie actor, haunts a video store where the clerk analyses customers on the basis of their rentals and supplements his income making VCR tapes of weddings and orgies. A monstrous TV producer issues instructions or kudos via closed-circuit vidscreen—later, a doomed, mutually manipulative couple usurps his technology for a more advanced version of telephone sex.

Not primarily a narrative filmmaker, Egoyan thrives on urban anxiety and excels in scenes based on the deadpan staging of a single monstrous gag. The lapses in continuity and relative absence of street life or connecting shots subvert *Speaking Parts*'s sleek, generic look. Indeed, the film's overall lack of resolution only heightens its intimation of an image underclass breeding in the barrios of the North American metropolis.

ROGER & ME, Michael Moore's enormously engaging documentary, addresses itself more directly to ways by which history awards some speaking parts and consigns the rest of us to be extras.

The movie's ostensible subject is Flint, Michigan—birthplace not only of Moore but the United Automobile Workers of America. Strategically personalizing his material, Moore briefly evokes his childhood and stormy stint as editor of *Mother Jones*. The loss of the latter position sent him back home just as General Motors shut 11 factories, threw 30,000 workers on the scrap heap, and inspired his attempt to bring GM Chairman Roger Smith to Flint for a documentary film.

Working the same circle of postindustrial hell as Tony Buba, the documentary-celebrant of the equally depressed Braddock PA, Moore makes a disarming Virgil. You can't get more vox populi than this heavyset guy in a baseball cap making one unsuccessful attempt after another to penetrate GM headquarters or the Detroit Athletic Club—the sense of turf-conscious class warfare accentuated by the evictions that serve as the movie's grim running joke.

Funny and demagogic, *Roger & Me* comes closer than any documentary I've seen to offering an overview of the past decade. The film opens by harking back 30-odd years to the golden age of working-class prosperity and, although

Ronald Reagan only drops in briefly to share a ceremonial pizza with a group of unemployed auto workers, his surrogates are everywhere. The movie swarms with vapid TV personalities and patriotic cheerleaders, and Moore's metaphors for the class struggle can be effectively mordant. Factories close and Taco Bells proliferate; Flint's proletariat work as human statues, sell their blood, raise bunny rabbits for food. As Flint becomes the most violent city in America, crime control becomes the major growth industry, and the more adaptable of the laid-off find work as jailers for the rest.

In a desperate Reaganite ploy, Flint attempts to reinvent itself as a tourist attraction. The city fathers subsidize a luxury Hyatt hotel and squander $100 million on an indoor theme park where the attractions include a miniaturized version of the old downtown, and an auto worker singing a love song to the robot that has replaced him on the assembly line. Everything fails. Flint finishes last in *Money* magazine's list of America's 300 most desirable places to live, while a *Nightline* exposé is aborted just before airtime when the show's equipment truck is hijacked by an unemployed worker. By the end of the movie, even GM's tireless local lobbyist is laid off.

Roger & Me is everything *Mother Jones* isn't—gutsy, populist, outraged, and outrageous. Still, the critique of Reaganism cuts two ways. Moore makes shameless use of Christmas and frequently lays on irony with a trowel. The Toronto Film Festival audiences with whom I saw the movie loved the spectacle of American kooks and American degeneration. Indeed, the only place where they might not appreciate this comic operetta *Kapital* would probably be the Hungary of *The Documentator*.

Brave new image world

Originally published in *The Village Voice* (November 28, 1989).

HAS FRANKENSTEIN CONQUERED the universe, or what? You step off the elevator at the Whitney's "Image World" and the 300 zooming, blaring TV monitors of Nam June Paik's *Fin de Siècle II* smack your head like so many pounds of bricks.

Paik's computer-programmed video wall is impossible to take in—the glowing image-waves rippling across the room to the accompaniment of chanted uh-oh polyrhythms are instant sensory overload, rampant media muscle flexing. All attempts at focusing fail. There's analytic Cubism, there's Jackson Pollock, and then there's *Fin de Siècle II*—pinwheeling, flipping, fissuring, melding, mirroring, multiplying, disintegrating, devouring, totalizing. You'd have to be a cretin to worship this icon, and a Cromwell not to enjoy it.

The premise of "Image World"—which includes more than 100 works in various media by some 65 artists or artists' collectives and more than 250 films and videos—is to explore artists' responses to that postwar American landscape defined by the curators as the "specific media culture of teletransmissions, channels, feedback, playback, and interface." The relationship of modern art to the mass media may be the oldest aesthetic conundrum of the American half-century but it's scarcely the least relevant one. The conventional reading of art history is that modern art and mass culture have developed dialectically, that the *kulturkampf* of the age is the struggle between mass-cultural concealment and high modernist revelation, while postmod, on the other hand, is predicated on blurring the opposition (and even the distinction) between high and mass.

Sounds good, but ever since *Life* profiled Pollock in 1949 ("Is he the greatest living painter in America?"), there's been a new dialectic: the struggle between the media within and the media without, between the way we process and the way we are processed, between the artist as the subject of the media and the artist as its object, between aesthetic appreciation and *Entertainment Tonight*. Just what is painting in the light of TV?

PAST THE *fin de siècle* is the cramped little gallery one curator termed the "Orientation Room." For Hilton Kramer this has to be the antechamber to hell. Abandon all hope: "Those looking to art as refuge from the outside world will not find comfort here," the wall text proclaims.

The room is papered with Peter Nagy's techno-art timeline, matching great moments in the history of modernism with newsprint-quality reproductions of electronic commodities. Pages clipped from old magazines are fixed under Plexiglas along the floorboard, a little procession of simulacra in an endless band. Three TV monitors, one for each of the last three decades, spew out five-second bites from *Star Trek*, Watergate, *Cosby*, et. al. The "real" art includes Jeff Koons's encephalitic Bob Hope *tchotchke*, a coffee can emblazoned with an Ansel Adams landscape (kinda Duchamp's urinal in reverse), and Jenny Holzer's accusatory plaque: YOU DON'T CARE WHAT'S REAL. Oh yeah? Propelled as if by a forcefield, one staggers next door to the room of the forefathers.

Here, in relative splendor, is Pop's Art: Rosenquist, Wesselmann, Lichtenstein, Warhol. Fluxus, posited in the exhibit catalogue as a counter (mass) culture for its use of film, TV, and postage stamps in a neo-Dada, Cage-inflected manner, occupies the center. On the far wall are the Coca-Cola classics: Warhol's tastefully muted *Double Elvis* and gorgeous *Red Disaster* (multiple electric chairs plus a matching color-field), and Rauschenberg's 1963 *Die Hard*. The Rauschenberg is in scope and color, like the Bruce Willis film, and just as action-packed on its own terms: Balloons land, space capsules splash down, choppers hover, the Statue of Liberty shakes. It's the Ravenna mosaics to Paik's Sistine Chapel.

Pop Art, as we know, accepted the new Nature, embraced its own status as a collection of secondhand images, welcomed the interpenetration of modernism and the media. Pop Art took from advertising and it also gave back. But Pop Art did not pioneer the notion of an art-world superstar. Past the fussily doctored magazine ads and reworked movie posters, the sculpted newspapers and giant Cibachromes that punctuate the exhibit's back room like so many footnotes, is a shrine to celebrity. Below a row of signed and airbrushed art-world personality pictures suggesting Sal's Pizzeria's Wall of Fame, a display case offers a batch of the most outrageous of artist-placed *Artforum* ads, like Ed Ruscha in bed with two babes, Lynda Benglis astride a hyper-gnarly dildo. But who's fucking who? The media hot-wires global consciousness the better to propagate a modernist mythology that inflates art's moral authority even as artists become the most glamorous entrepreneurs in the whole supermarket-place.

One of the landmarks of postmodernism was surely the Museum of Modern Art's 1980 Picasso exhibit, where one's appreciation of the art was rivaled by one's appreciation of the crowd flow techniques borrowed from Disneyland. Now, scarcely a year goes by without the Modern or the Metropolitan or both mounting comparable cultural spectaculars—incorporating modernism into the media. And of course vice versa: MOMA's recent Warhol show perversely attempted to prune the unmanageable Warhol oeuvre—movies, videos, magazines, photographs, self-promotion, advertisements—back to painting. (We await with trepidation MOMA's impending "High and Low: Modern Art and Popular Culture," designed to demonstrate that "the popular and commercial arts are not inert or anonymous genres that have been exploited, but close partners to modernist innovation, with separate histories of invention and evolution.")

So, to crib the title of another recent Whitney show, just what is the desire of the museum here? Is "Image World" to be a church or an amusement park, an afterschool program or a stock exchange?

SO FAR AS movies go, it's strictly potluck. Coming as they did from a dissident cadre within the media itself, underground movies were the political wing of Pop Art. Bruce Conner's *A Movie*, Kenneth Anger's *Scorpio Rising*, Ken Jacobs's *Star Spangled to Death*, Jack Smith's *Flaming Creatures*, Mike Kuchar's *Sins of the Fleshapoids*, Andy Warhol's *Vinyl*, and Dennis Hopper's *The Last Movie* all turned Image World inside out. Some of these are even included in the exhibit, although the film and video annex is so generous in mixing and matching every sort of avant-garde classic, Hollywood movie, and independent doc as to be a self-canceling mishmash. The best way to view the films is as installation, a random flow of imagery serving to confuse the exhibit's figure and field in the manner of the apocalypse wallpaper at the New Museum's "Signs of Chaos" show.

TV, of course, is more of an active intervention. Indeed, left to its own devices, *Fin de Siècle* is capable of colonizing other works. The video wall transmits such powerful signals that, until adjustments were made, the three Orientation Room monitors, not to mention the old black-and-white set imbedded in Wesselmann's *Still Life #28,* were picking up Paik's kaleido-gonzo effects. TV is the subject of any number of pieces—maybe even all of them. And what's not about TV would seem to be in competition.

If you hit it at the right moment, the exhibit homestretch has the pleasing cacophony of a Crazy Eddie's showroom. Essentially decorative, Dara Birnbaum's *P.M. Magazine,* demurely picture-enclosed TVs, interface with Robert Longo's disco-splayed poseurs. David Salle's *Pewter Light* may seem like an inert wallflower, particularly if you're reeling away from Bruce Nauman's bilious *Clown Torture,* four stacked monitors, some upside-down, with two video projections—spiteful entertainment with a ball-and-chain.

The most powerful installation by far is by Gretchen Bender, who basically proposes a new way to watch the tube. Her *TV Text and Image* offers nine sets, each tuned to a different channel, each with a phrase superimposed on the screen: PUBLIC MEMORY, PEOPLE WITH AIDS, NARCOTICS OF SURREALISM. So simple you could make it at home, this conceptual version of *Hollywood Squares* is an earthwork in the media landscape, even more a triumph of synchronicity than Paik's video wall. (The last time I was there, someone had turned the sound up on MTV, so that Billy Joel's media litany was added to the semio-stew.)

Complicating your pleasure while giving a new meaning to the notion of "close-captioned" TV, the piece is Brechtian in several senses but very nearly upstaged by Jeff Koons's extravagantly hideous, life-sized white porcelain and gold-trimmed Michael Jackson whatzit. It's remarkable: Koons has created something uglier and (at least temporarily) even more compelling than TV. I'm reminded of Harold Rosenberg's mid-'70s observation that "the struggle to merge art with the world of actuality is America's ritual vanguardism."

THE MEDIA ITSELF isn't making much of "Image World." Nor are the art mavens. What's more, to judge from the cramped space the exhibit occupies, the Whitney may be hedging its bets as well. The word on the street is " '80s retro." But this is one more way of fending off the obvious.

After all, the reinvestment in painting is as much a part of the '80s retrenchment as junk bonds, Star Wars, *Family Ties,* and safe sex. How else to explain the benign neglect that shrouded two of the key '80s exhibitions—the Whitney's 1982 Paik retro and the Modern's 1987 Bill Viola show (or the recent Ken Jacobs show at the Museum of the Moving Image)? If video-installation and film-performance are beyond the art-world pale, art-world consciousness has scarcely proved immune to televisual thinking. Witness the parallel phenomena of bogus pluralism, continual reruns, and multiseason hits. (What current artist has shown the staying power of *Cosby?*)

The autonomous artist is a creature of the marketplace, but the artistic vanguard has traditionally hitched its wagon to techno-advance. So where does that leave the painter of modern life if not in the position allegorized by *Action Painting II,* Mark Tansey's mock-academic painting of painters painting mock-academic paintings of a missile midlaunch? There's a bluish cast to this frozen moment. The least one can say for "Image World" is that it illuminates the surprisingly slow process by which film, video, and photography have begun to break the stranglehold of painting and sculpture on this thing called art.

Noh exit

Originally published in *The Village Voice* (November 21, 1989).

HISTORY MAY ULTIMATELY judge Jim Jarmusch to be the hipster's Frank Capra—a canny sentimentalist with an "aw-shucks" hammerlock on the national dreamlife—but there's a reason why he remains the hottest young filmmaker on the international circuit. While Spielberg and company produce hyperbolic simulations of Hollywood B-movies, Jarmusch reinvented the B's no-frills aesthetic. His minimalist vaudevilles (complete with dialect humor) are irreducibly, confidently American. They have the musical repetition and abstract vernacular of black-and-white sitcoms, '50s doo-wop, and pre-Vietnam comic strips.

Still, Jarmusch is not a simple celebrant of retro stylistics. His obsessive running gag is the re-presentation of America through alien eyes. More and more, this seems to have been a particularly '80s trope, informing everything from the mega-hit *E.T.* and the indie triumph *Liquid Sky,* through the disposable comedy of *Splash,* its ideological cousin *Moscow on the Hudson,* and Eddie Murphy's *Coming to America,* to a subtitled sleeper like *Bagdad Café* and the eccentric post-Wenders excursions of *Mitteleuropa* wiseguys Péter Góthar, György Szomjas, and Aki Kaurismäki. It is as if that wondrous New Morning in America could only be confirmed from the uncritical, born-again perspective of a mermaid, Martian, or Hungarian immigrant.

Mystery Train—the Jarmusch shown to great acclaim at the 1989 New York Film Festival—goes down this road one more time. The movie consists of three successive, albeit simultaneous, stories, each set in Memphis and involving foreign protagonists (who inevitably wind up spending the night at the same sleazy fleabag, the Arcade Hotel). The credit sequence introduces the most endearing of these outlanders—a young Japanese couple, stolid Jun (Masatoshi Nagase) and perky Mitzuko (Youki Kudoh), as they Amtrak through Tennessee, Elvis singing the title song, and a succession of automobile graveyards whizzing past the window.

Celebrant of this sort of entropic Americanarama, Jarmusch is the postmod Walker Evans, a cartoon Robert Frank, for whom the whole roadside United States is a vast moldering museum. (Call it Desolation Row.) No less than the Cleveland of *Stranger Than Paradise* or the New Orleans of *Down By Law,* his Memphis is a stage set—empty, rundown, ineffably cool—through which Jun and Mitzuko wander, carrying their bright red suitcase peasant-style on a bamboo pole, as uncomprehending as they are appreciative of the native life forms they encounter. *Mystery Train*'s first third would make an apposite short subject on a bill with one of Nagisa Oshima's early '60s youth films, set as they are in a stridently Americanized Japan. Even so, Jun and Mitzuko represent something of the director's own point-of-view.

Although *Mystery Train* is his first movie with black speaking subjects, Jarmusch has long been recognized as an apostle of White Negroism. (Self-consciously hip as he is, how could it be otherwise?) In the Jarmusch cosmos, old-timey Negroes—as opposed to militant blacks or self-defined African Americans—are the essential Americans. Jun and Mitzuko know that they've arrived when one thanks them in Japanese. The teenage immigrant in *Stranger Than Paradise* signaled her a priori love of America through her allegiance to Screamin' Jay Hawkins's "I Put a Spell on You," and Screamin' Jay himself turns up here as the Arcade's nightclerk. (Resplendent in crimson jacket and matching tie on black shirt, he's hilariously restrained—as proud and skittish as a tethered race horse.)

Always adept at characterizing his movies, Jarmusch has described *Mystery Train* as a minimalist *Canterbury Tales,* the stories of religious pilgrimages made to the shrine of Sun Studio. This is most explicit when Jun and Mitzuko gaze up at a statue of Elvis the way an earlier generation of Americans might have gawked at Michelangelo's Pietà; like the Greil Marcus book of the same title, *Mystery Train* is consecrated to the enigma of the greatest White Negro of them all. Thus, the movie provides a comic counterpoint to the mortician splendor of William Eggleston's sacrophagal Graceland studies. The Arcade offers no TV, but provides an icon of Elvis in every dank room.

Indeed, *Mystery Train* is the most ironically ethereal of posthumous Elvis movies—celebrating the deity whose "disappearing body," as Canadian "panic" theorists have it, is "a flashing event-horizon at the edge of the black hole that is America today." Mitzuko recognizes the face of Elvis on both the Buddha and the Statue of Liberty, and it is precisely because Luisa (Nicoletta Braschi), the Italian protagonist of the movie's central (and weakest) episode repeatedly misunderstands the Elvis references dogging her 12-hour Memphis layover that He reveals Himself to her in an appropriately ridiculous mystical vision.

Ultimately, the King is made physically manifest in the form of onetime punk idol Joe Strummer, here playing the pugnacious and pompadoured Englishman dubbed "Elvis" by his black buddies. In the course of the film's final episode, this pseudo-Presley demonstrates that he can be as feckless and violent as any real American. Embarking on a drunken spree, he shoots an unpleasant liquor store owner with the same sodden *esprit* his namesake might have used to plug a TV, dragging along two cronies (performance artist Steve Buscemi and former TV host Rick Aviles) on an absurd journey to the end of the night that, perhaps too loosely, knots the movie's separate narrative strands.

Easier to enjoy than champion, *Mystery Train* builds up enough momentum in its first half-hour to sustain the ride. *Stranger Than Paradise* was the near-seamless synthesis of a quarter-century of underground movies, and Jarmusch may never again achieve its swallowed-up perfection. *Down By Law,* a tactical retreat from this one-shot classicism, seemed a glossy gloss on the previous film. (Serving mainly to establish the director's commercial credentials, *Down By Law* narcissistically reveled in its own capacity to embody a self-proclaimed "sad and beautiful world.") Now, having lowered expectations all around, Jarmusch returns with a more realistic display of his strengths and weaknesses: *Mystery Train* is never so slight that it lacks charm. Invention may flag, but not so much as to distract from the inspired comedy of its best moments or the clarity of its conception.

Like each of his films, *Mystery Train* is a confessional in which Jarmusch tells all that he knows about America. What's new about this installment is that the foreigners are tourists rather than immigrants. Their investment in this country is passionate but transitory, and, for that reason, *Mystery Train* seems the most melancholy of Jarmusch films—and perhaps the most self-reflexive. It's suggestive that it was bankrolled by JVC, the Japanese electronics giant that pioneered the VHS video format. First Columbia Pictures, then Radio City, Ronald Reagan, and now this. No wonder Jarmusch's worldview seems preserved in amber. Unlike his forebears, he may never go Hollywood or grapple with the echt-American dilemma of selling out; his innocence can remain intact, his "independence" has already been bought.

The worst years of our lives

Originally published in *The Village Voice* (December 26, 1989).

BORN ON THE FOURTH OF JULY is the most visceral of weepies—a vast oozing wound of a movie. Oliver Stone's second Vietnam film, based on a harrowing memoir by the severely disabled Viet-veteran Ron Kovic, is awash with bodily fluids. Powerful and unflinching, crude but compelling, this is a movie to remind you that blood and guts (not to mention sweat and tears) are the sort of abstractions that leave a puddle on the floor.

Nearly two-and-a-half hours long, *Born* opens like an episode of *The Wonder Years*, with Tom Cruise's incantatory voiceover: "It was a lo-o-o-ng time ago." The sun is refracted in the trees, the kids are playing war ("You're dead and you know it!"). This reference to the last scene in *Platoon* provides the first proof that Stone has no fear of the obvious. Indeed, he wants to get your tear ducts pumping even before the credits end. Stone piles "innocent" patriotic displays upon Little League heroics, ladles family togetherness over JFK's inaugural address. The air swirls with spring buds, it's the last American paradise. This is the "American Pie" of movies—a distended dirge, as coarse as it is clever, that bids to lodge itself in your brain. Permanently.

The eldest son of a large Catholic family from Massapequa, Long Island, Ron (Cruise) grows up during the postwar boom in thrall to a mother whose rampant Momism (an odd remnant of '50s pop psychology) combines anti-Communist rhetoric and sexual repression in equal measure. Young Ron is totally gung ho, wrestling for God and country (and crying when he loses), mouthing better-dead-than-red platitudes to his more cynical friends, enlisting in the marines as soon as he graduates high school. Vietnam is the fall, and

Stone builds upon his prior mythology by having the robotic recruiter played by Tom Berenger, the evil angel from *Platoon*.

If the archetypal movie 'Nam is green jungle, the terrain here is parched and brown, as if drained of its vibrance by constant reproduction. Combat is signaled as unrepresentable. A confused firefight is made more so by the alternation of stolid pans and brain-slamming returns—as though the camera were mounted on a typewriter carriage—while the sound comes and goes of its own accord. Indeed, Stone's visualization of the scene in which Ron suffers his wound is far less graphic than Kovic's unforgettable written account of paralysis and panic (grown marines calling on Jesus and screaming for their mothers).

Not until Ron winds up in the field hospital—a butcher shop piled with leaking, twitching bodies—does *Born on the Fourth of July* wrap its hands around your throat. The next circle of hell (and one of the most horrific sequences in any American movie) is a Bronx VA hospital, a miserable hovel with urine on the floor, rats in the bedpans, and junkies in the closet. Disaffected black orderlies give enemas and hose down the wounded, while the still-avid Ron watches a telecast of the '68 Chicago police riot ("Love it or leave it, you fucking bastards") and wonders what he, a Vietnam veteran, is doing in this world of excremental slime.

It's to Stone's credit that *Born on the Fourth of July* never forgets that the ultimate purpose of war is to inflict injury—to puncture, maim, and destroy human body tissue. Nor does it allow the viewer to repress the nature of the metaphoric injury that the Vietnam war wreaked on American manhood. To see *Born on the Fourth of July* is to understand, once again, Rambo's profound, quasi-therapeutic importance as an American icon. Indeed, as *Platoon*'s relatively naturalistic battlefield challenged *Rambo*'s fantasy arena, *Born* unmasks *Rambo*'s compensatory appeal. While Stallone's perfect Nautilus-built pecs assuaged America's mutilated masculinity, Kovic's book, Stone's movie, and Cruise's gritty performance are all intimately concerned with the failure of the body.

This collapse extends to the dissolution of Ron's patriotic character armor. In the film's most disturbingly choreographed scene, he spins drunkenly around a Massapequa barroom (as it spins around him). More than an act of will, Cruise's performance has the quality of a convulsive rebirth. Moist and drooling, shooting pool and picking fights, desperately hitting on a half-amused, half-petrified hippie chick, he's rapping and wheeling under the strobe until he falls out of his chair—then goes home to complete his degradation, waking up the neighborhood, blubbering about killing women and children, and screaming the word *penis* until his mother breaks down in tears. It's a scene as painful as the dry heaves: "Who's gonna love me? Who's ever gonna love me, Dad?" the drunken paraplegic wants to know.

Although nothing else in the movie has the horror and the pathos of these middle sequences, they are sufficient to propel the events to an uncertain conclusion—Ron's moral regeneration as an antiwar activist—and even overwhelm the film's obvious flaws. *Born on the Fourth of July* can be as operatically strident as *The Deer Hunter,* it's only rival as a there-and-back-again epic. Stone has a simple belief in catharsis and a maddening propensity to nudge the audience. The film is thick with unnecessary voiceovers and superfluous flash-backs. Does Kovic enlist out of high school? Let's have the prom feature the Shirelles' "Soldier Boy." Is Mom in an advanced stage of denial? Let's have her change channels from a demonstration to a rerun of *Laugh-In.* Is there a scene in a hippie coffeehouse? How about a Baez-oid chanteuse singing "A Hard Rain's A-Gonna Fall" (a golden oldie even then). Is there a student demo? Get the actual Abbie Hoffman to address the crowd, and never mind that he looks closer to 60 than the '60s.

Naïve as can be, *Born on the Fourth of July* lacks the evil humor of the year's other major Viet-film, *Casualties of War.* While the detached De Palma is coolly working something out, the overinvolved Stone is struggling to work something through. (If he were any more earnest, he'd be the Elie Wiesel of Vietnam.) Thus, it's difficult to gauge the irony of Kovic's turning-point re-habilitation in another Third World brothel. As neither *Born* nor *Platoon* addresses Vietnam as a realm for sexual acting out, one wonders if Stone recognizes this Mexican interlude as the symbolic return to the 'Nam that it is. (It is here too that Ron encounters a "good," if fallen, angel in the *Platoon*ic form of Willem Dafoe.)

Ultimately, Stone's solipsism is more generous than De Palma's narcissism—he wants to relive Vietnam for all of us, for the national good. For all the muscle-flexing camera pyrotechnics, Stone is always ready to go slow and tragic. More than any other American filmmaker, he's in touch with his grief over Vietnam—but what is that grief exactly? Stone's heartbroken evocation of American innocence betrayed is indistinguishable from his celebration of American super-ficiality. What happened to that suburban Eden where every A&P seemed an arena of possibility? Why did Vietnam bring the fast-food degradation of the national life?

Despite (or maybe because of) a decade spent stripmining our resources, it's increasingly apparent that the Vietnamese conflagration marked the acme of American empire. *Born on the Fourth of July* is like the jolt that failed. Stone's sincerity is weirdly self-congratulatory. He denies his nostalgia even as he indulges it.

Trips

five

Two weeks in another town:
India and its film festival

Originally published in *The Village Voice* (March 4–10, 1981).

NEW DELHI, WHERE I spent two weeks at the Eighth International Film Festival of India, has an eerie lack of congestion. Built by the British in 1911 as the capital of the Raj, it's a monument in negative space—a vast expanse of government buildings, deluxe hotels, and walled estates, insulated from each other and the rest of India.

In Bombay, for example, the ride from the airport to the high-rise beachfront takes you through some of the most wretched slums on earth; when your car stops at an intersection six-year-old beggars fling themselves against the windows like moths pelting a lightbulb. There are no squatters and ditch-dwellers in New Delhi. Still, the capital is not precisely suburban. A dozen miles out of town, past the power lines, is another planet: The fields blaze with yellow mustard seed, the hills are dotted with temples, women in electric blue or flaming orange saris walk along with earthenware jugs balanced on their heads. Camels are the major source of locomotive energy and the only signs of modern technology are the highway itself or an occasional capsized transport truck.

Over the last two millennia, ten cities have risen on the Delhi plain. Old Delhi, the ninth and only a few minutes from the capital by car, is as mellow as Times Square on acid. Crossing the street is an act of faith, it's best to follow the cows. You walk out of a restaurant and into the last reel of *Freaks*—legless cripples and smiling lepers advancing on all sides out of the darkness. But you can't really walk anywhere in New Delhi. The British designed the city as a series of traffic circles and radial roads; almost nothing can be approached in a straight line. The hotels and movie theatres are spread out all over town. Festival delegates wait anxiously for official buses or shuttle from place to place on three-wheel motorcycle rickshaws. "Which palace was it you wanted, sir?" an elderly driver asked me. There's some grumbling because we're being housed at the first-class Janpath rather than the deluxe Ashok (both are government hotels). The Ashok is currently the headquarters for Sir Richard Attenborough, whose $22 million production *Gandhi* has built its sets on the outskirts of town.

The festival itself is a five-ring circus with an official competition, an "informational section" composed of noncompetitive foreign films, a market, several directorial tributes, and a twenty-one-film Indian Panorama. Most of the Western critics are here for the latter, which is devoted to the latest products of India's tenacious noncommercial or "parallel" cinema, and where the proportion of worthwhile films turns out to be gratifyingly high. The information section is mainly attended by Indians—India imports relatively few films—and includes eight Hollywood movies. The two war flicks, *Apocalypse Now* and *The Big Red One,* are regarded with understandable suspicion, while *Manhat-*

tan is taken in stride ("Diane Keaton plays her usual self with high-brow blabber to boot," wrote the *Hindustan Times*). *Being There* is the most highly regarded, perhaps perceived as our *Angi Vera*.

Much of the informational fare is familiar, but by no means all of it. In addition to Andrei Tarkovsky's *Stalker*—a brilliant, brooding allegory that intermittently resembles a Soviet *Eraserhead*—there's a love story from Mongolia, a feminist film from Tunisia, a Kenyan biopic of Idi Amin. There are also two propaganda shorts, from Kuwait and Afghanistan. While the first oozes assurance with Exxon commercial glibness, the second could have been cut with barbed wire and spliced with adhesive tape. Its soundtrack is startlingly crude; the notorious photo of Zbigniew Brzezinski brandishing a tommy-gun at the Khyber Pass—roundly booed—is scored to the menace music of a radio spook show, and there's a toneless voice-over spoken in phonetic English.

The market offers veteran K. A. Abbas's astonishing *Naxalites*—a kind of pop, left-wing *Third Generation* on the Indian Maoist guerrillas of the early '70s that opened with the "Internationale" being beaten out on a tribal drum. The screening is attended by a contingent of North Koreans, identifiable by the enamel portraits of Kim Il Sung pinned to their lapels. Afterwards the distributors pass out mimeographed copies of the censor's objections ("delete part of the scene in which a policeman accepts bribe," "reduce in length the repulsive close shot of vomitted blood"). Less corporeally, the flier for *Oceans of Love*— a Hindi life of Christ—promises to show His "crucification, reasurrection, and assumptions." As it turns out, the film delivered a few perky ragas and a palm tree leaf dance as well.

The vast conference room that houses the market displays is almost always empty, a single tape of a James Bond trailer beaming out over "the TV of Tomorrow" into the void. The most fascinating thing here is the Sovexport booth, decked out with AIP-style posters that conflate drawn ray-guns, disintegrating airplanes, and ample cleavage to promote such little-known Soviet fare as *The Hijacking of Savoy, Pirates of the XXth Century, Air Crew, The Stellar Inspector,* and *Rallye*. The last, a tale of art smuggling set against the backdrop of a Moscow-Warsaw-Berlin road rally, sounds particularly promising, but when I ask the lone and seemingly baffled Indian who mans the display when the films will be screened, he tells me that none of them are scheduled until two weeks after the festival ends.

By comparison, the competition holds few surprises. The Delhi festival has to scrounge for leftovers from Cannes, Berlin, and Venice. (The American entry, for example, is *The Fish That Saved Pittsburgh*.) First place is shared by a Bulgarian feature, *The Unknown Soldier's Patent Leather Shoes,* and one of the Indian entries, *Aakrosh,* which although a deserved choice wasn't even the best film in the Panorama. Indian officials are floating the idea of turning the competition into a third world film festival. None now exists, and showcasing the cinema of developing nations would give the Delhi festival an added raison d'etre and a stronger identity. Still, India is not so much a part of the third world as it is a world unto itself.

Some statistics: India's population is estimated at 650 million. This is roughly equal to the population of Europe, plus the western half of the Soviet Union. However, India has only one-third the land mass and at least as much cultural diversity. Scots have more in common with Sicilians than many Indians do with each other. Before the coming of the British, the subcontinent was divided into hundreds of separate states. There are perhaps 20 major languages, not a few of which use their own alphabets.

This is a land of a thousand contradictions. India has atomic bombs and temples consecrated to rats, weather satellites and homes for old cows. It has a minister of tourism who dismissed the problem of industrial waste in the Ganges by insisting that nothing could pollute the river's holy waters, and more scientists than anywhere on earth except the U.S. and the Soviet Union. There is actually a surplus of doctors and medical technicians; thousands of them have gone abroad to staff hospitals throughout the Persian Gulf and East Africa.

India is the world's 10th leading industrial nation. Virtually no consumer goods are imported, nearly everything is manufactured at home. But just as the Indian economy cannot absorb all of its trained professionals, neither can it afford to automate and compete for world markets. Jobs are the highest priority. Every government position is seemingly divided into four. Clearing customs or mailing a parcel plunges you into a miasma of redtape. If the clerk whose job it is to stamp your document is out of the office, it's a good bet that no one else will do it for you. There are hierarchies everywhere, imbued with the subtleties of caste. The elevator operators and bellhops in the posh hotels have assistants, the assistants have apprentices, and the apprentices have understudies. Over half the population has no assured source of income and earns $50 or less per year. Only 5 per cent make as much as $600.

There are about a half-million Indians with incomes high enough to pay tax, and an equivalent number of TV sets. Everyone else goes to the movies. "Movies are not just an *aspect* of Indian culture," says the narrator of *The Great Indian Film Bazaar,* the *That's Entertainment*-style compilation film that closed the Panorama, "movies *are* Indian culture." Indeed, India has long since surpassed Hollywood and Japan as the world's movie capital, last year breaking its own record by producing some 750 films in 16 different languages. Well over three billion tickets were sold—and the number of admissions is substantially depressed by the shortage of theatres.

Movie ads fill two or three pages of the skimpy English language dailies with ecstatic prose-poems: "Century's Most Controversial Film—Spicy Dialogue and Hit Songs/Defying All Oppositions—Smashing All Records/8th Houseful Week of Tremendous Rush." Films can run for years; the ads occasionally note "Brand New Print!" Bombay and Madras, the two major film centers, churn out hundreds of escapist extravanganzas—not only for India, but for Africa, the Middle East, and parts of the Soviet Union as well. Stars and songs are their key ingredients. Rare is the film of whatever genre that doesn't include at least four musical numbers. (Invariably, these are dubbed by special performers known as "playback singers.") Despite their epic length, the best of these films have a gaudy, kitsch vitality. Although the parallel cinema is basically a neo-realist repudiation of the Bombay talkies, it's significant that several of the Panorama's strongest films deployed commercial conventions for their Brechtian potential.

As the movies supply India with its popular music, so the movie stars constitute a popular mythology. Six hundred film magazines detail the opulent lives and sexual escapades of the "filmi folk," running articles like "Is Deepak Parasher a Homosexual?" or items on a famous femme fatale's one-night stand with a Kuwaiti stud. The most scurrilous publications are in English. (*Film Mirror,* bizarrely a-grammatical, is a moral majority nightmare, combining near-pornographic gossip with ads for Sovexport and Aeroflot.) In a sense, the stars have replaced old-style maharajahs, if not the Hindu deities themselves. One middle-aged businessman told me that when he was a boy, the old people of his town used to prostrate themselves before the screen. There's a distinct resemblance between the movie posters that cover market walls and the divinity pictures that hang in every shop. The huge Day-Glo cutouts of the stars that tower over theatre facades in lieu of marquees are almost a parody of the god-festooned roofs of Hindu temples.

For years, the southern state of Tamil Nadu has been governed by M. G. Ramachandran, familiarly known as MGR, a onetime matinee idol whose political party started out as a fan club with Dravidian nationalist overtones. According to MGR, he stands for "the best of capitalism combined with the best of communism." In any case, MGR's career has blended show biz and politics to a bewildering degree. During his first campaign he was shot and wounded by the actor who played the heavy in many of his films. Once elected, he paid off his debts by moonlighting in a few more films. (While I was in India, MGR was awarded an honorary degree by a fundamentalist outfit in Arizona. "What Plato dreamed of 2500 years ago," read the press release, "Dr. Ramachandran has achieved in Tamil Nadu—a state ruled by an artiste.") Nor is MGR an isolated phenomenon. The sheriffs of Calcutta and Bombay are both film-world figures and during the last elections a group of Bombay movie stars launched their own political party, which evidently collapsed after a government tax raid.

Madame Gandhi aside, stars like Rekha or Sashi Kapoor may be India's only national figures. The huge, half-empty government auditorium where the festival's opening ceremonies were held took on an atmosphere of discreet hysteria when a half-dozen Bombay film stars filed in and sat down. Within moments a living lightshow of photographers had interposed itself between the stars and the stage. The minister's speech droned on, the ushers abandoned their posts to request autographs, and still the wall of paparazzi stood three feet from their subjects, firing off shot after shot of people who by now had to be the best-documented beings on the face of the earth.

There is, of course, a certain ambivalence—if not hostility—implicit in all this adulation. The Sikh driver who took several of us on a daytrip to Jaipur would only admit to seeing one film a year. Almost simultaneously, he revealed an encyclopedic knowledge of stars and directors, as well as a set of fiercely held opinions. He refused to attend the movies with his wife, he said, because she liked them all indiscriminately. Moreover, he had forbidden his five children to go to the movies until after they were married. What, he finally demanded, did we think of Indian movies? "I think a few of them are marvelous and many of them are stupid," one colleague replied. The driver considered this. "By stupid," he asked at length, "do you mean sexy?"

Were it not for government censorship, some will tell you, the Indian cinema would be completely overrun by sex and violence. Indian movies are subject to stringent government control (albeit, *pace Naxalites,* rarely regarding political content). This censorship is strict without being standardized, and hence is the subject of much confusion. Until 1977 there was an absolute, but unwritten, ban on kissing. With nudity beyond the realm of possibility, an on-screen kiss is still an event. But commercial movies are far from chaste. They've developed an erotic code that has a nutty vulgarity all its own. Musical numbers feature suggestive lyrics, coy bedroom acrobatics, or rainstorms that plaster the heroine's sari to her body. Lengthy scenes of attempted rape are another main-stay. ("In reality," grumbled one film mag letter, "the villain could have raped the heroine at leisure and made good his escape with a cigarette on his lips.")

Recently, the government has entered film production in a big way, putting up $6 million toward the cost of Attenborough's *Gandhi*. (The rest of the financing is British.) For the last few months, *Gandhi* has been a major national issue. "Can you imagine the Vietnamese giving Coppola money to film *Apocalypse Now?*" one cineaste asked me. Holy men have fasted in opposition to the project, former prime minister Desai has threatened to sue Attenborough, and filmmakers are naturally bitter about the government subsidy. But that's not all of it. Gandhi himself is a controversial figure, particularly on the left. At one point, the gadfly director Mrinal Sen declared that he would apply for govern-ment funds to make an *anti*-Gandhi film. Not to be outdone, the Soviet festival delegation held a press conference to announce *their* plans for co-producing a biography of Nehru. ("Why don't you tell them you'd like to produce an Indo-Soviet life of Stalin?" one Indian journalist whispered to another. "Not me," came the reply. "I want to go to Moscow this year.")

The *Gandhi* set is located on a dusty plain several miles outside Delhi. They've reconstructed the Mahatma's ashram and are shooting interiors on the day I visit, so there isn't very much to watch. Intermittently, one sees "Dickie," as the London contingent calls Attenborough, striding purposefully about, lost in concentration. Most of the crew appears to be British. Lunch is steak and kidney pie. European extras are paid $36 per day; their Indian counterparts get a bit less than $2. The film festival has given *Gandhi*'s unit publicist two reasons to be grateful. On the one hand, the festival provides a ready pool of Western journalists to be invited on location; on the other, it has given the Indian press something else to froth about.

The day the festival opened, the lead editorial in the *Hindustan Times* ran: "Film Festivals held in India provide an opportunity to the well-heeled and well-connected to engage in a little titilation. If there is no nude scene the film is bound to be a flop. If there is the slightest exposure of the female form, people will beg, borrow and steal and consider the effort worth the humiliation. On the surface, of course, it is all in the interests of art, cinema verite, avant garde and so on. But the mass of skin is the message. It could not be anything else for a people so sexually frustrated as the Indians."

As though in confirmation, the cover of *Film Mirror*'s festival issue features a bevy of undraped blondes. Inside, a completely straight-forward festival guide is illustrated by cliches culled from 11 films, some of which have been creatively retitled. (*The Long Riders* here becomes *The Love Rides*.) The magazine sells out in 24 hours. Festival delegates are soon accustomed to being stopped and queried as to which films are "hot." One rickshaw driver complains to me that he had spent 10 rupees—perhaps half a day's pay—to see the Ghanaian film *Love Brewed in the African Pot*, only to find that it was not about sex but class conflict. "I could have made that film myself," he says with disgust. Nevertheless, he remains optimistic. "Sex is rising. They cannot stop it. Sex is rising day by day."

Actually, it is the expectation of sex that is rising. Alongside hatchet jobs decrying the "international flop festival" as "a squalid mess," the Indian press publishes frequent accounts of disturbances at neighborhood theatres showing festival films. Seventy-six seats are reported ripped at a screening of an Egyptian film. Disappointment with a Spanish movie causes patrons to riot and demand their money back, then kick in the theatre doors when refunds aren't forthcoming. At another cinema, a discrepancy between what is advertised and what is shown divides the audience into two warring factions, one barricading the theatre doors while the other threatens to burn the place down.

Meanwhile, at the government auditorium hosting the competition, the war between the press and the festival turns into open combat. It is alleged that reserved press seats are being given away to "well-connected gatecrashers." At one screening, several journalists claim to have been forcibly ejected from their seats and clubbed by police. The next night, at the presentation of the official Hungarian entry, a similar shortage of seats prompts festival delegates and members of the press to disrupt the screening by pounding on doors, overturning chairs, climbing on tables, and blocking the projector with an improvised banner. The rest of the audience showers the demonstrators with abuse and projectiles, while the public address system issues garbled ultimatums. After the jury walks out, the rattled Hungarians succeed in stopping the show. ("At first I thought they just didn't like the film," one told me.) But it takes an emergency appearance by the minister to quell the pandemonium.

Nothing even remotely similar to this event occurs at any of the Panorama screenings I attend. Nevertheless, as amplified by the press, this distant thunder reverberates throughout the rest of the festival. On our way back from the *Gandhi* set, our car passes two drivers engaged in a heated dispute by the side of the road. Gazing out the window, a British critic absently remarks: "I'd say the potential for vah-lence here is quite *nearly* as great as in America."

Havana 1983

Originally published as "Our Man in Havana" in *The Village Voice* (April 10, 1984).

"**E**VERYONE WHO COMES to Cuba has been brainwashed. Skillful propaganda has told them Havana is a haven of heaven." That's Steve Ryan talking; see his indispensable "Havana: Sucker Trap of the Caribbean," published for your edification in the February 1957 issue of *Exposed* magazine (the one with Diana Dors on the cover). "Forget the Maine" is Ryan's message. Remember the dirt, the beggars, the shoeshine urchins, the porno postcard vendors, "the thin, ragged women carrying babies too hungry to cry," the guy who makes his living exhibiting a bedraggled, cawing *perico* trained to fire a cap gun, the hordes of hookers who can barely wait for nightfall so they can "flow over the city like a tidal wave in search of *americanos*."

What's the story? "When Batista took over in 1952," Ryan explains, "he sat on an empty wallet." The ousted Carlos Prío "had scattered eight million in bribes during his term and Batista was stuck with the tab. The only hope for solvency was to find an angel. Ninety miles away sat the United States . . . fat, pompous, sex happy—and loaded." Hey meester, you want *muchachas*, gambling, 24-hour crap games, a daiquiri at Señor Ernest Hemingway's favorite bar, a night at Tropicana *el cabaret más fabuloso del mundo,* plus live sex show in a three-peso hotel room? You name it, you got it. "This is Cuba," warns the implacable Steve Ryan. "Geared to American tastes . . . with moral standards so low you'd need a submarine to reach them."

Well, a lot of things have changed since 1957, but Havana remains a cornucopia of '50s imagery. Even modest bungalows out in the suburbs sport curlicue grillwork and harlequin mosaics, jazzily tapered columns brandishing kidney-shaped sun roofs. Half the cars on the road are Eisenhower-era De Sotos and Buicks, patched and repatched and painted tropical colors: mint green, dusty pink, hot canary, blazing turquoise. Driving west along the seawall on the Malecón freeway you see the terraced towers of palatial hotels, blindingly white against the diaphanous December sky. Vegas strip garish, Miami Beach deluxe, they rose even as Fidel and *los barbudos* were making revolution in the Sierra. There's the Capri with its rooftop swimming pool and Salón Rojo nightclub, the Riviera (built, they say, by Meyer Lansky) with its free-form fountain sculpture and ancillary, blue-domed something or other, once a mambotorium inaugurated by Miss Ginger Rogers. Amazingly, the Hilton logo is still decipherable on the glass doors of the renamed Habana Libre. Of course, the former casino is now the Salón de Solidaridad, and there's the inevitable *Vietnamita* exposition downstairs by the dollar shop, where you can buy a handstitched leather platter bearing the likeness of Che Guevara for only $140.

The French have moved over to the Libre, but all the rest of us foreigners, here for 10 days for the fifth Havana Film Festival, are holed up at the Hotel Nacional, around the corner from Casa Czechoslovakia, a block and a half from the spot where Sergio Corrieri picked up Daisy Granados in *Memories of Underdevelopment,* not far from the concrete umbrella of the people's Coppelia Ice-Cream Center (more flavors than Baskin-Robbins). Built in 1927, the Nacional is a stately dowager with a flaming past. It was here that the officers of the old regime resisted the first coup staged by then-sergeant Fulgencio Batista. In 1957, Steve Ryan called the hotel "a pile of money sitting on a rock overlooking the Malecón" with a "controlled gaming room" as "hallowed as a church." When the Nicaraguan revolutionary priest Ernesto Cardenal stayed here 13 years later, he noted with pleasure that "young proletarians"—white and black—were chatting in the lobby "with the confidence once possessed by millionaires." Now the place is full of Aeroflot personnel—beefy pilots and no-nonsense stewies taking their r&r . . . only 90 miles away! The flotskis even have their own lounge up on the fifth floor, complete with fridge, TV, blackboard, and bound copies of *Pravda.*

Outside the Nacional, brazen young swindlers in Bruce Lee T-shirts offer to sell you pesos at twice, three times, four times—the record is seven times—the official rate of exchange. But if you've read your Steve Ryan, you know that "gambling in Cuba is about as safe as stepping in front of the Super Chief." Every day there's a new story making the rounds about some gringo *shmegegge* exchanging his dollars for a worthless mess of Batista money, Mexican pesos, or just a fat wad of paper sandwiched between two legitimate bills. Although trafficking in pesos begins at the Miami Airport—one couple on the tour swears that some Hare Krishnas tried to make a deal—you can't walk out of the hotel without being approached. These kids are persistent, too. The most entertaining way to handle it is to adopt the self-righteous persona of an American Communist. Some guy offers you five to one and, in your sternest pidgin Spanish, you say *Pero compañero, esto es contra la ley*—But comrade, that is against the law. When he doubles over with laughter, you make your escape.

The truth is, there's not so much to do here with pesos anyway. ("This is a city that is bound to please a monk, a meditator, anyone who in the capitalist world has decided to withdraw from the world," Ernesto Cardenal noted. "Here there is no bourgeois joy, but here there is true joy.") Havana's hot, dusty neighborhoods are dotted with *curiosidad* shops that wouldn't seem out of place on Canal Street, selling miscellaneous pieces of hardware, old radio tubes, and secondhand camera parts (as the ancient autos attest, the Cubans are masters of recycling). But most stories open late, close early, and don't stock much besides cotton shirts, cheap toys, translations of *The Godfather* frugally designed to save paper, and jars of preserved Bulgarian figs.

One day there's a book fair, and someone unearths a 1936 American tourist-guide called *Cuban Tapestry.* We consult it like the *I Ching* and learn that "Cuba, is foreign. Havana is foreign. No amount of contact with big Tío Sam, across the Florida strait, will ever make the island capital an American city. The Cuban likes his huge good-natured 'uncle,' for alone among Latin Americans he senses no covetousness in our attitude towards him. He believes the United States his awkward, bungling, but sincere champion. . . ."

FREEDOM IN CUBA can be defined as freedom from the United States. Cuba is not simply the first Latin American nation to successfully defy big Tío Sam, it has openly opposed U.S. policies for the last 25 years. And, although the forced reorientation of the Cuban economy is a shock from which the island has yet to recover fully, it is certainly arguable that the U.S. trade embargo has helped Fidel Castro more than it has hurt him. The lack of consumer goods is a sign of revolutionary virtue. The American threat encourages national unity, permits total mobilization, and fosters a heady sense of geopolitical adventure.

Before the revolution, Cuba enjoyed one of the highest per capita incomes in the tropical world. But this apparent prosperity was founded upon 25 per cent unemployment, landless peasantry, institutionalized political corruption, a continual oscillation between dictatorship and democracy, utter dependence on foreign capital, and the vagaries of the American market. Only two years before *Cuban Tapestry* was published, the American greenback was the lone paper currency used in Cuba. Until the Triumph of the Revolution, the U.S. ambassador was the island's second most powerful man (at least), and the U.S. safely regarded Cuba as its most reliable ally. The Cuban economy was actually a subset of the American one. Cuba sold the U.S. sugar and bought virtually everything else—from nuts and bolts to TV sets and automobiles—at the company store. Americans owned Cuba's major banks and biggest factories as well as 90 per cent of the island's utilities. The U.S. exerted greater influence here than in any Latin American country, with the possible exception of Panama.

Now handmade signs on every block routinely excoriate *yanqui asesinos*, and—our naval base at Guantánamo aside—the official U.S. presence is reduced to the so-called "Interest Section," located on the ground floor of the former American embassy, an incongruously large glass building on the Malecón. Opposite the entrance is a lurid neon sign with a rifle-toting Cubano giving the raspberry to a frothing Tío Sam. Every time the Interest Section gringos walk out their front door they get zapped in the face with the same pink, yellow, and orange blinking message: *Señores Imperialistas, No Les Tenemos Absolutamente Ningun Miedo!* We're not scared of you! (Not exactly so: many Cubans are convinced that if Reagan is reelected, he will certainly invade them. "We expect another Vietnam," one official told me. "We have the whole island prepared.")

To get inside the Interest Section—which I did, accompanying a friend who had her passport stolen in an after-hours dive called *El Gato Tuerto*, the One-Eyed Cat—you have to first convey your business to the bored Cuban soldiers posted around the building, then convince the teenage American marine manning the reception area that you're kosher (impossible, actually; the fact that you're in Cuba automatically means you're not). While he deliberates, you practice your upside-down reading by noting the handy Spanish phrases taped to his desk: What is your name? What do you want? Please go away! Once inside, you find an ostentatiously over-air-conditioned waiting room decorated with framed travel posters of San Francisco and Aspen, and furnished with a plastic Christmas tree and an expensive load of useless, pseudo-oak cabinets. Not since the Miami airport have you seen such waste. The inner courtyard can barely contain the satellite dish (major league, albeit not as huge as the one the Cubans use to monitor American TV). Some nest of spies: the single secretary turns out to be an employee of the Cuban government. Next to her desk she keeps an institutional-size can of Tang. A week in Havana and this seems exotic.

After 24 years of embargo, modern Americana is so rare in Cuba that you're jolted when you see a Viceroy baseball cap, a bootleg Michael Jackson tape, or a cup fashioned out of a Coca-Cola can. Only the most obscure Disney characters—individual dwarfs out of *Snow White,* the rabbit from *Alice in Wonderland*—are to be found on walls and storefronts. The almost complete eradication of Mickey Mouse is no less striking than the absence of Jesus Christ. As you walk around Havana, gawking at the homemade signs of a fanged Tío Sam devouring Grenada—*Abajo el Imperialismo Yanqui!*—that embellish each block's Committee for the Defense of the Revolution bulletin board, people will inquire whether you're Argentine or German or, most often, Russian. When you tell them that you're a *norteamericano,* they're taken aback or amused, occasionally nostalgic, but never, in my experience, hostile.

It's astounding how many Cubans seem to have lived on East 103rd Street between 1947 and 1949. There's still an emotional bond; we do, after all, share the same national sport. Once upon a time, Cuba had the Havana Sugar Kings—baseball club of Sandy Amoros, Vic Davalillo, Tony Taylor, Leo Cardenas, Bert Campaneris, Tony Perez, Camilio Pascual, Elio Chacon—International League farm team for the Cincinnati Reds. In 1958, the Sugar Kings were mired in last place and all but bankrupt. After the Triumph of the Revolution, Fidel offered to bail the team out. "The Sugar Kings are part of the Cuban people," he is reported to have said. "It is important for us to have a connection with Triple-A baseball." The 1959 season was a tumultuous one and, as fate would have it, July 25 turned to July 26 with the Sugar Kings and the Rochester Red Wings tied 4-4 in the bottom of the 11th. The patriotic Cubans began celebrating their revolution's name day. A party erupted, out came the congas, but when Red Wing third-base coach Frank Verdi was grazed by a spent bullet, the game was called on account of gunfire in the stands.

There was a lot of angry talk then of yanking professional baseball out of Cuba—the details can be found in Howard Senzel's *Baseball and the Cold War*—but the red-hot Sugar Kings went on to win the International League championship and then the Junior World Series. This was the time of miracles— when the last could be first, and the revolution opened Cuba's beaches, nightclubs, and parks to all. By the 1960 season, however, relations between revolutionary Cuba and the Republican mainland had grown perilously frayed. On July 6—shortly after the American-owned oil refineries refused to process the Russian crude that Fidel bartered for the sugar the U.S. wouldn't buy—Secretary of State Christian Herter summoned baseball commissioner Ford Frick to Washington. Three days later, some evil alchemy transformed the Havana Sugar Kings into the Jersey City Jerseys. Severed from Triple-A, Fidel howled with rage. It was one more act of treachery and aggression against the Cuban people: "Violating all codes of sportsmanship, they now take away our franchise!"

So much for socialist baseball in the capitalist world. Nine years ago there was talk of a U.S.-Cuban series, but that got scotched by Henry Kissinger on account of the situation in Angola. Meanwhile, Cuban amateur teams have continued to dominate international play. Thus it's with keen anticipation that we socialist baseball fans take a powder from the festival for a Sunday doubleheader at Latinoamerica Stadium. Free admission and open seating notwithstanding, the ballpark is emptier than Shea on a weekday in August. You just march down to the first-base line and help yourself to a box. Does this indifferent turnout indicate a lack of interest in two mediocre clubs—the Havana Metropolitanos and the Guantánamo Guantánamos, respectively 14th and 12th in the 18-team league? Yet, it is only December; the season is young. The first game is a classic, with Los Metropolitanos beating Los Guantánamos 3-2, when R. López lofts a J. Matos fast ball over the left-field wall for a *jonrón* in the bottom of the 10th. (Guantánamo retaliates in the nightcap by peppering hapless R. Arocha for *jit* after *jit* to build a 7-0 lead by the middle of the third.)

Contrary to Senzel's memories of the Sugar Kings ("a slick and speedy ball club and so colorful," "they used to bunt a lot, hit and run a lot, try to steal home, and execute other daring feats"), the games are low-keyed to the point of somnolence. The fans are almost all men, many seem to be pensioners basking in the sun. Our entrance causes a mild stir, and—*qué coincidencia!*—here's one of the festival guides remarkably unsurprised to see us. "Sit anywhere," he invites us. "How about here?" It is interesting to note that while the Cubans employ cheap and durable aluminum bats (illegal in the major leagues), they have—despite the embargo—adopted the designated hitter, *el bateador designado.*

There's no *cerveza* to be had; instead, vendors sell hits of sweet black coffee in the sort of tiny paper cups mental hospitals use to dispense Thorazine. Could that be why, despite some atrocious calls—including a foul ball down the third-base line that goes for a two-run Guantánamo double—there are neither rhubarbs on the field nor razzing from the stands? Or does the crystal light of the four o'clock sky have everyone dazzled? Far from shooting off machine-guns, the fans are so well socialized they scoop up the foul balls that are hit their way and toss them back onto the field.

IN REVOLUTIONARY CUBA, not just sporting events but health care, public telephones, and burials are free. Day care, too, for the children of working mothers. Education is universal and compulsory. Cuba-watchers say the rural areas have been developed at the expense of the cities, and Havana is still doing penance for its sinful past. The capital is shabby but clean, delapidated yet orderly. You can drive your rented Russian compact totally off the map, out to where the pavement ends by the cement factory in the deepest estuary of Havana Bay, and the hovels you find are only hovels—small, run-down stucco houses that appear to be electrified. They're not tin shacks stacked up on cardboard boxes fronting on a raw sewage canal. Even in this alley of poverty, the kids look healthy and well-fed, playing baseball in the street and wondering what in the world you're doing there. If this were Mexico City or Rio de Janeiro, you might fear for your life. But Havana isn't Port-au-Prince, let alone New York. You can stroll for miles at midnight through the central city, the dark streets illuminated only by the blue glow of TV sets, and never experience the slightest anxiety. Mugging Russians, we joke, must be a capital offense.

JUST AS SOVIET communism will always suffer from the reality of the Russian winter, so Cuban communism will always benefit from the island's eternal summer. Often, as you walk, you get a whiff of salsa and catch a glimpse of some steamy living room, crowded with dancers. Every open window yields some fantastic arrangements of plastic flowers, porcelain animals, crumbling plaster, and icons of Che. Revolutionary martyr, advocate of the New Socialist Man, Che is a far more popular household deity than Fidel; his resemblance to JC can't be denied. Bus drivers keep his image on their decal-decorated dashboards, next to pictures of their *novias,* commemorative pennants, and plastic kittens with bobbing heads. There's an orange neon portrait of Fidel on the Malecón advising that *La Revolución* can never be crushed, but his most widely distributed image is that of public servant supreme—a silk-screened poster of the leader dressed in fatigues, a rifle slung over his shoulder and the ambiguous command *Ordene!*

The Catholic Church seems to have been driven totally underground—or else to Miami—but there are vest-pocket shrines to José Martí in every neighborhood, and many Cuban documentaries attest to a burning religious fervor. Such films are no more objective than a Pepsi-Cola spot and no less revealing for their blatant artifice. *Che hoy y siempre* (Che Today and Always) is the latest in a series of graphically innovative shorts by the Chilean exile Pedro Chaskel. They're formal variations on a sacred theme, not unlike medieval altarpieces. Miguel Torres's *Condenadme, no importa* (Condemn Me, It Does Not Matter), taking its title from Fidel's "History Will Absolve Me" speech, is another kind of holy relic. It's incredibly well-faked "documentary" footage purports to record the failed Moncada raid of July 26, 1953, Fidel's trial and subsequent imprisonment. The filmmaker has already made one previous pseudo-documentary, *Crónica de una infamia,* concerning a 1949 incident in which a drunken U.S. marine desecrated a statue of José Martí with his *yanqui* urine. He plans another such "reconstruction of a history that has no documents" to celebrate the January 1959 Triumph of the Revolution.

Luis Felipe Bernaza's *Aquí y en cualquier parte* (Here and in Whatever Place) is a "love song" to "the new heroes of the Revolution," the young Cuban soldiers in Angola. Lyrical shots of combat training are mixed with choreographed guerrilla rituals and the vocal accompaniment of some dulcet *compañera.* Along with Israel, Cuba must be one of the most highly mobilized societies on earth. Militia manuals are available in all bookstores. The ministries, politburo, and central committee are dominated by military men. The army has a film studio as well, and produced Belkis Vega's *España en el corazón* (Spain in the Heart), a history of the Cuban international brigade during the Spanish Civil War. Not surprisingly, the film eschews nostalgia and stresses historical continuity (although it fails to note that revolutionary Cuba developed close economic ties with Franco's Spain). Of course, most of Cuba's Spanish Civil War vets were also veterans of the pre-1959 Cuban CP, an outfit which had opposed Fidel Castro until six months before the Triumph of the Revolution. Perhaps that's why it's Raúl—always a Communist—Castro and not brother Fidel who hands out the medals at the vets' reunion. As for those Cubans who fought in the Abraham Lincoln Brigade, they aren't mentioned at all.

Che hoy y siempre was greeted with warm applause, *Condenadme, no importa* got a standing ovation, *Aquí y en cualquier parte* rocked the house with rhythmic clapping. But the documentary hit of the festival was Estela Bravo's *Los Marielitos*—a film shot by a North American crew and edited in Havana—in which 11 Cubans who left the island during the mass exodus of 1980 compare their old lives with what they found in America (visualized mainly as Florida concentration camps and Lower East Side squalor). The subjects, naturally, are doozies. "In Cuba, I couldn't drink. In Cuba there is no freedom," one rumdum hiccups. Another rationalizes his flight as a perverse act of loyalty to Fidel. Everyone has a lot to complain about, from shitty health care to the American habit of smoking marijuana in the street. For the finale, the filmmakers produced a successful engineer who stands outside his Miami ranch house and admits that he's miserable.

Los Marielitos was telecast during the festival and Cubans often asked about it with pity and wonder. "Is it true that there are people sleeping in the streets of New York? And that you can get killed for money at 10 o'clock in the evening? Are rents really so high and for apartments such as those? Why are blacks not permitted in the same hospitals as whites? Are there that many people who have no jobs?"

Twenty-five years ago, less than three months after *los barbudos* entered Havana, the revolutionary Cuban regime enacted its first cultural reform, creating the *Instituto Cubano del Arte e Industria Cinematograficas*, ICAIC. Headed by Fidel's old college buddy, Alfredo (no relation to Che) Guevara, ICAIC appropriated cinemas and studios, taking charge of all Cuban film activity. Official mythology has it that, although Cuba has always been a movie-mad island, there was no Cuban cinema before the revolution—only ersatz Mexican musicals, badly made copies of Hollywood detective films, bogus Argentine melodramas, and sleazy pornography. Within 10 years, ICAIC films were famous all over the world.

First there was Santiago Alvarez—the director of the "Latin American Newsreel" series, producing one *noticiero* per week, a filmmaker who pulled together a Che Guevara obit less than 48 hours after the news of his death, and who once said, "Give me two photographs, a movieola, and some music, and I'll make you a film"—the greatest revolutionary documentary-maker since Dziga

Vertov. Then came Tomás Gutiérrez Alea's *Memories of Underdevelopment*, mixing Antonioni alienation with revolutionary pachanga, even as Julio García Espinosa's *The Adventures of Juan Quin Quin* and Manuel Octavio Gómez's *The First Charge of the Machete* conjoined formal innovation and revolutionary politics with a fervor unseen since the Soviet school of the '20s. And after the epic *Lucía* won a gold medal at the 1969 Moscow Film Festival, 26-year-old Humberto Solás was hailed as the new Eisenstein. (A recent poll of Cuban audiences listed *Potemkin, Gone with the Wind, Citizen Kane, The Gold Rush,* and *Modern Times* as the five most significant films of all time. *Lucía,* finishing 15th, was the highest ranked Cuban work.)

The late '60s were the halcyon days of the New Cuban Cinema, but Fidel's 1968 endorsement of the Warsaw Pact invasion of Czechoslovakia, the 1970 failure of the 10 million-ton sugar harvest, and the following year's First National Congress on Education and Culture—brought the directors down to earth. Documentaries were privileged over fiction films. There was a campaign against "foreign tendencies," "elitism," and homosexuals in cultural affairs. ICAIC continued to be run by the filmmakers themselves, but formal experimentation declined. Since then, although Cuban movie attendance has continued to rise and the Cuban film industry currently spends far more per feature than any other in Latin America, only two movies (the late Sara Gómez's *One Way or Another* and Pastor Vega's *Portrait of Teresa*) have made much impact on the international scene. But who knows what goes on in the heart of Havana? This is an anniversary year and all the heavies—Tomás Gutiérrez Alea, Humberto Solás, Santiago Alvarez, Pastor Vega, Manuel Octavio Gómez—are scheduled to premiere new films.

Immediate disappointment: Vega's *La Habanera*—said to concern the love life of a Cuban shrink—is not yet completed, while Alvarez's *Refugees from the Cave of the Dead*—his first fiction film, a docudrama of the Moncada raid—is so universally regarded as disastrous that, although Santiago is a member of the central committee, the film isn't even available to be screened in the festival market. Attention shifts to the premiere of Humberto Solás's *Amada,* and with good reason. Two years ago, Solás's mega-peso adaptation of the 19th century Cuban classic *Cecilia Valdés* consumed the lion's share of ICAIC's resources. Unveiled at Cannes, the film sank like a stone, then bombed with the home audience as well. Perhaps not coincidentally, ICAIC chief Alfredo Guevara was relieved of his post, shipped off to Switzerland as the new ambassador to UNESCO, and replaced at ICAIC by Julio García Espinosa, author of the famous manifesto "For an Imperfect Cinema."

Understandably defensive, Solás seems to have taken the most militant (that is to say, anti-European) aesthetic stance of all the directors who contributed statements to the current issue of *Cine Cubano.* His position makes sense once you see that his film totally contradicts it. Solás may be skating on thin ice; *Amada* turns out to be an elegantly mannered, Viscontian period piece detailing an unconsummated adulterous affair between two members of the fin-de-siècle Havana bourgeoisie. A vehicle really for the superb Eslinda Núñez (the domestic in *Memories of Underdevelopment* and the second "Lucia"), *Amada* was not generously received by the Cuban audience. In his postscreening remarks, Solás stressed his competence (pointing out that while *Cecilia* took 15 months to shoot, economical *Amada* was completed in a mere eight weeks) while gamely insisting on the film's political content—the frustrated love is "a reflection of the crisis in the fight for independence."

Nearly half of ICAIC's new documentaries are films with musical subjects, a bid, some think, to produce more foreign exchange. "Just as Hollywood directors must make the obligatory western," Julio García Espinosa has suggested, "Cuban filmmakers should be required to make a musical." Espinosa himself started a musical around 1978. Titled *Son o no son* (a pun on the name of a Cuban musical mode and Hamlet's "to be or not to be"), the film was evidently structured as a series of rehearsals for a musical revue at the Tropicana that never quite jells. *Son o no son* remains incomplete, however, and so the first director to accept the challenge is Manuel Octavio Gómez. Like Espinosa, Gómez has a long interest in popular culture as a vanguard form, and his *Patakín*—which takes its title from an African word for fable, its discreet crane shots and Jerome Robbins choreography from the Hollywood musicals of the 1950s, its strident colors and slangy, innuendo-ridden dialogue from Cuba's 19th century *Teatro Bufo*—transposes two figures out of Yoruba mythology to contemporary Cuba. Shangó, the thunder god, is here an irresistible lumpen layabout—when he shows up in his neighborhood, even octogenarians begin to rumba—while his nemesis, Ogun, is a staid model worker who drives the tractor on a collective farm.

With musical numbers more bossa nova than salsa, *Patakín* establishes a certain amiable innocence, abetted by a Tashlinesque sense of humor and some beach scenes that would hardly seem out of place in *How to Stuff a Wild Bikini*. The film pokes mild fun at the bureaucracy and frequently waxes reflexive. ("Aren't you paying attention to the picture?" characters ask each other when the plot grows convoluted.) But in addition to reclaiming a genre for Cuban filmmakers, *Patakín* makes a political point, being the most candid study of machismo of the several the festival offers. Although the virtuous Ogun defeats Shangó in a climactic boxing match—the finale has showgirls storming the ring with balloons and confetti for a mass cha-cha-cha—Shangó's appeal is never denied. "All men want to be Shangó," Ogun's lady friend tells him. "Not even you want to be Ogun."

Although the Cuban audience appears to adore *Patakín,* it's predictable that not all Oguns will find it so amusing. Indeed, it is the only Cuban premiere to get an afternoon rather than an evening slot. There is a streak of proletarian puritanism in the Cuban Revolution, and sure enough, *Patakín* is panned in the second-string CP daily, *Juventud Rebelde* (Rebel Youth). The music and dance are "inorganically inserted into the plot," the movie is filled with "forced jokes" and "stereotypical behavior." Making "insufficient use of expressive modes of cinema," it is an altogether disappointing effort from a director of Gómez's stature. That the critic takes *Patakín* to task on formal grounds—rather than engaging its ideological line—only underscores the movie's political content. But you can't truly appreciate *Patakín* until you've seen Tropicana.

Tropicana! *El cabaret más fabuloso del mundo,* located in an outdoor jungle garden! It's part of every package tour, and it's best seen with a group of American leftists. Imagine *las contradicciones*! Sexist? Of course—*y un poco* racist *también.* Tropicana! Formerly run by *yanqui* gangsters using George Raft as their front, the One and Only Tropicana is not simply *el paraíso de las estrellas*—the paradise of the stars—it's the Pasty World of Atlantis, the story of Cuba in song and dance *con mucho más* razzmatazz, it's *el teatro del* embarrassment *revolucionario*!

Feathered chandeliers floating overhead, showgirls in top hats and sequined bikinis strut down the aisles dodging the frozen-faced waitresses with nimble precision while flashing practiced smiles at bewildered *Vietnamitas.* The chanteuse on stage threatens to teach us how to love. The *espactáculo* begins. Omigod, is that capering bellhop actually wearing black face? *Compañera,* pass the rum. Is this number really a Yoruba ceremony celebrating the end of slavery—boys in silver lamé pants and Day-Glo doo-rags? Did the Taino Indians truly sing like Yma Sumac and cavort about like the June Taylor Dancers? And dig that wild and crazy Czechoslovakian at the next table. Will he make like Desi and call on Babaloo? Oh no! It's *caballero y dama* time. Lace mantillas, fluttering fans, lotsa *"mi corazón,"* castanets. *Más* rum *por favor.*

Tropicana! At once ridiculous and impressive, ultimately infectious. During the revolution, the July 26 movement planted bombs here. Now they treat the place like a national museum. (Ask a Cuban Communist what he thinks. Watch him laugh and tell you that when he was a *juventud rebelde* he saw Liberace make his grand entrance here riding on an *elefante.* Yes, and he was playing the piano.) With a maximum of *mucho* mass flouncing, the whole chorus appears in pink Flash Gordon jumpsuits singing "Never Again." The show's not over yet, folks; it's time for *La Habana Conga*! A multicolored waterfall is descending in the background. The palm trees are scintillating with red, blue, and silver lights. Dry-ice geysers are shooting up at our feet. Everyone is singing *Yo soy Tropicana*! ("What's this about orange juice?" a drunken gringo wants to know.)

The performers tell us they are a collective. They thank some visiting Rumanians, the Central American boxing champs, a Yugoslav trade delegation. They offer a fraternal hand to the Soviet people. You offer a fraternal hand to the nearest living creature and go off to dance *La Habana Conga* yourself.

COMPARED TO *PATAKÍN,* the new Gutiérrez Alea, *Hasta Cierto Punto* (To a Certain Point), is fairly predictable stuff. Although beautifully paced and edited, it's a small film that, as Alea himself observes, owes quite a bit in its mixture of drama and vérité to Sara Gómez's *One Way or Another.* A married, middle-aged dramatist, working on a script about the problems of women in the labor force, gets involved with a young *compañera* who works in the port, raising a number of not too startling questions about the relations between the sexes (as well as the classes). Still, it was satisfying to see the film win the grand prize. Everyone was relieved that one of the hometown boys had come through.

Few things are duller than film festival award ceremonies. The halls where they're held are often embarrassingly empty. The Cubans solve this problem by making invitations to a reception hosted by Fidel Castro contingent on attending the ceremonies—which are worse than most, since every ovation is a standing one of militant *solidaridad*. Afterwards, there's a long wait over at the Palace of the Revolution, but finally the doors open, you're on line, and there he is—large and graying with an unhealthy-looking ruddy complexion and deep wrinkles around his uncannily glowing eyes—*el último diablo,* the Cuban of Cubans in a spiffy olive green dress uniform. A quick hypnotized handshake and on to the best spread we've seen: lobster, shrimp, skewered chunks of barbecued chicken and pork, mounds of spicy cornmeal casserole, broiled red snapper, huge breads baked in the shapes of alligators. ("Now I know why they wouldn't let us bring cameras," someone cracks.)

Everybody is busy gorging themselves, washing the food down with 30-year-old rum—smooth as satin and straight to the cerebral cortex—when it suddenly becomes apparent that . . . He's in the room! It's Fidelmania! Forget Pete Seeger, the evening's other celeb and possibly the only man in Havana wearing a flannel shirt, Fidel is instantly besieged by a frantic mob of filmmakers desperately flacking their films. "Hey, Fidel! Did you see my movie? I'll get you a special screening, man!" Methodically making his way around the room, Fidel seems to have come alive working the crowd. Only five minutes before, people were criticizing the Cubans for using actresses to hand out the awards—so tacky, so macho. Now, it's as if Robert Redford had turned up at your neighborhood Pathmark. Reserved Brits clutch souvenir swizzle sticks and swear to treasure them forever. Seasoned feminists tremble like schoolgirls, stuff napkins in their mouths, and shriek, "He touched me!" Canny pol that he is, Fidel does have an eye for the ladies—patting their heads, kissing their cheeks, whispering in their ears.

Functioning on automatic pilot, I've blundered into an excellent field position just as Fidel comes around the bend. He spots the attractive *compañera* next to me, and as he rushes over to shake her hand for the third time, she tells him, "This guy has a question for you."

"Right," I say. "It's about *beisbol.*"

Beisbol. The entourage stops dead. Suddenly it's me and Fidel and the translator and the bodyguards and the *compañera* in the bizarrely world-historic eye of the storm. "Yes," I say. "I want to know why Cuban baseball uses the designated hitter."

The translator translates. Fidel considers the question and begins framing his reply. It's like a major policy statement. "The designated hitter," he says through the translator, "is part of the official international rules of baseball. As a member of the international community, Cuba, of course, must adhere to these rules . . ."

"Wait a minute," I hear myself say. This must be the 30-year-old rum talking. "The designated hitter isn't part of the official rules of baseball. Only one of the major leagues even uses it—the American League. Why should Cuba copy the American League?"

All around us Cubans are beginning to laugh. Did the *yanqui* catch Fidel? Clearly, the ball is still in my court, but I don't know what to say next. Pitcher is Fidel's position. Should I ask him how he likes giving up his turn at bat? (*Ordene!*) Or would that seem unduly provocative? Should I inquire how this specialization fits in with his conception of the New Socialist Man? Too theoretical. Cautiously, I decide to venture an opinion. "Speaking for myself, I think the designated hitter ruins the strategy of the game."

But now Fidel has formulated a line. Quickly he begins speaking through the interpreter. "That is regressive," he maintains, cocking his head earnestly. "We must not be afraid to change the existing rules. The rules of all games must be called into question." Now Fidel is beginning to cook. "For example," he says, "I think we should make new rules for basketball. I propose we have three kinds of basketball. One for people who are under five feet tall. Another for people who are five and a half feet tall. And a third for people who are over six feet tall." Fidel is watching me intently. "And that way," he concludes, "the Vietnamese will be able to win a basketball game!"

The Vietnamese! What is this, 1968? The Vietnamese won their basketball game 10 years ago! I jumped all over Fidel's first pitch, but this curve ball has me baffled. The Cubans laugh. I laugh. Fidel grins. He pumps my hand vigorously and the cult of personality moves on. I'm immediately surrounded by a minicult of Brits and Americans. What did he say? What did you say? What *is* a designated hitter, anyway? Some guy actually wants to set up an interview. *Mañana* for that, *compañero.*

Mañana, I'm on the plane wishing I'd spent more time at the beach and still wondering what that riff meant. In bringing up baseball was I reminding Fidel of Cuba's cultural links to the United States? And in invoking Vietnam was he alluding to the limitations of U.S. power? The Cuban identification with Vietnam is total. Was Fidel suggesting we judge Cuba on its own terms? And is that a novelty Americans can't bear?

Tokyo 1985

Originally published as "The Realm of the Senses" in *The Village Voice* (July 23, 1985).

THERE WAS AN international film festival in Tokyo's Shibuya district. But what *gaijin* had patience to sit still for it? The scene outside the theaters was hopelessly overstimulating, better than any theme park—the cleanest, most orderly urban chaos you can imagine. Twelve million people and the subway cars have upholstered seats. It's not uncommon to see groups of five-year-olds in school uniforms, traveling sans adult, standing under the glossy paper ads that flutter like banners from the subway car ceilings.

Japan, these days, exerts the same fascination for American businessmen and consumers that the Soviet Union held for American socialists 60 years ago: "I have seen the future and it works." But it's hard to see Tokyo (let alone Japan) as the future when its idiosyncratic past is still so present. Tokyo offers a white American all the comforts of home, plus the useful sensation of experiencing oneself as a racial minority, as well as the added pleasure of being in a non-Christian culture. Modern, affluent, and Other—you get the feeling this place is as foreign to the rest of Asia as it is to the West—Tokyo is both more familiar and more different than one might expect.

Kimonos may be only slightly less exotic here than on the Grand Concourse, but every *departo* (department store) is a video gallery, deploying banks of TVs with splendid insouciance, and each restaurant a museum, with plastic models of food displayed in the window. (Not just Japanese cuisine, either, but lo mein and lamb vindaloo, pizza and croissants, bacon and eggs and Kentucky Fried Chicken, not to mention those sinister-looking westernoid concoctions known as *yoshoku*.) Religion is where you find it: Visit any five-story temple of kiddy schlock, you'll see a dozen types of stuffed plush Godzillas and a cute li'l mechanical whatzit thoughtfully identified in English as "God Jesus Fortune-telling Robo."

Tokyo is notoriously a city without a center. Or rather, its "empty" center is ringed by a series of incredibly dense commercial-recreation-transportation nexuses following the path of the railway line that once encircled the city. Each nexus draws millions of commuters from beyond the city's old perimeter through its own feed of surface railroads and subways (owned, like everything else, by the *departos*). At the center of Shibuya stands the bronze statue of Hachiko, faithful Akita pup. Once upon a time, Hachi would escort his master to Shibuya station every morning and return each evening to meet his train. Then the master suffered a stroke. He never returned, but Hachi did—every evening for seven years. When Hachiko finally died, in 1935, he made the front page of every Tokyo newspaper. A collection was taken up to build a statue in his honor.

Only a bronze dog could withstand Shibuya today—it's about as tranquil as the 14th Street subway at rush hour. You wait for the light to change watching the human wave build at the opposite crossing. The multileveled Shibuya intersection—a fantastic web of highways, els, and pedestrian crosswalks threading their way through the enigmatic boxlike logos atop the skyscrapers, and sometimes the buildings themselves—is like a Day-Glo *Metropolis* or maybe Times Square as redesigned by Kenny Scharf. (One of the box logos even features Fred and Wilma Flintstone.) After four or five days of navigating this hallucinatory nabe and the consumer opulence of its all-powerful department stores, I have a dream in which my childhood housing project has been Tokyo'd into a garish, crowded, dazzling clutter.

Almost nobody jaywalks, but the tension is always there. Beat Takeshi, the

TV comic who had the title line in *Merry Christmas, Mr. Lawrence,* became famous telling Japanese that it's okay to cross against the light if everyone else does. Consensus is the magic word. In the context of this extraordinary socialization, the individualism celebrated in samurai films as disparate as Kurosawa's *Yojimbo* and the long-running Zatoichi series, or sociopath movies like Shohei Imamura's *Vengeance is Mine* and Mitsuo Yanagimachi's *A Farewell to the Land,* seems an even more potent fantasy. ("In Japan," says Yanagimachi, "individualism never finds a place.")

Even film criticism is supposedly governed by consensus: The first review(s) published set the line for all that follow, a situation that might strike some American critics as utopia itself.

CONSENSUS HELD Akira Kurosawa's *Ran,* which had its world premiere on the festival's opening afternoon, to be a masterpiece. Consensus included foreign as well as Japanese critics and was scarcely restricted to the experts. Released at 200 theaters, the film scampered off to a *Variety*-certified "socko start"—the largest day-one ever in Japan. Indeed, Kurosawa and *Ran* received the ultimate honor, a full-scale exhibit, easily eclipsing a concurrent one of French post-impressionist painting, on the top floor of the Tokyu department store. In the best Disney tradition, the impressive display of *Ran*'s costumes, storyboards, outtakes, and props segued into a miniboutique of souvenir *Ran* ashtrays, coffee mugs, and T-shirts, all designed by the director himself.

Although Kurosawa remained sequestered in his mountain retreat, one assumes he derived a certain grim satisfaction from this adulation. Like any Japanese who achieves international success, he had frequently been accused of pandering to foreign tastes. (Shohei Imamura, long considered quintessentially Japanese—and thus beyond the comprehension of *gaijin* audiences—suffered a similar fate once *The Ballad of Narayama* won the 1983 Cannes Film Festival's Golden Palm.) Moreover, Kurosawa, whose unaffectionate industry nickname is "The Emperor," had been trying to realize *Ran* for over a decade, making *Kagemusha* in the meantime as a sort of dry run. The film, a French co-production under the aegis of Serge Silberman, was to be the 75-year-old director's final statement.

Ran, which means chaos, is basically a Japanese *King Lear*—substituting sons for daughters and featuring a faded TV transvestite named Peter (who wowed the opening night reception by showing up in a floor-length, backless evening dress) in the role of the Fool. There's a sense in which the film is Kurosawa's *Tokyo Story*; it's filled with references to "this degraded age," and they don't only mean the 17th century. Deliberately nonempathetic (albeit occasionally sentimental), *Ran* is quieter and more controlled than *Kagemusha*. What's striking is how close to silent cinema it is, an impression Kurosawa fosters by brilliantly withholding the sound in one key battle sequence.

With its epic Eisensteinian compositions and mist-shrouded, color-coded armies, spectacularly flaming carnage, and juicy court intrigues, *Ran* holds its

160-minute length well. As Hidetora, the cruel but hapless lord betrayed by his sons, Tatsuya Nakadai is beetle-browed and glowering, made up beyond recognition. Nakadai looks sensational—there's a marvelous orange and gold painting of him outside the Shibuya theater where *Ran* has opened—and his mad scenes are unavoidably poignant, but he lacks the ferocious authority that Toshiro Mifune, estranged from Kurosawa, might have brought to the role.

Actually, the film is stolen by Mieko Harada, who plays Hidetora's scheming daughter-in-law Kaede. In makeup reminiscent of the Lady Macbeth equivalent in Kurosawa's previous Shakespeare adaptation, *Throne of Blood*, Kaede is the very spirit of *ran* amok, not to mention *Ran*'s arbitrary moral schema. Given her legitimate desire for revenge, she would be an Electra or Antigone in someone else's movie. *Ran,* however, is totally Kurosawa's. Grimly existential, its most powerful moment is the bleak, despairing ending. "Kurosawa has tried to make a Buddhist film," the distinguished critic Tadao Sato told me. "But, you know, he is not a Buddhist."

IF *RAN* JUSTIFIED the festival's ho-hum main section in itself, the structuring absence was Paul Schrader's *Mishima*—snubbed by the selection committee after much production publicity that it would close the festival as *Ran* opened it. If there is no Japanese consensus on Mishima the man, there was also no consensus as to why *Mishima* the film was turned down. Exegetes of this *Rashomon* story mainly noted the political connections of Mishima's widow, the menace of right-wing fanatics, a threatened plagiarism suit by Henry Scott Stokes, author of *The Life and Death of Yukio Mishima,* as well as the national tendency to make a "no" seem like "yes."

Verily, *Mishima* has come to seem a film without a country. Even Kurosawa got dragged into the controversy. Rumor had it that he's been pressured by *Mishima*'s makers to pull *Ran* in solidarity. Asked about this at an otherwise reverential press conference in the mountains, Kurosawa blandly replied that he too had heard this rumor—adding that he hadn't seen *Mishima* but assumed that if the film were worthwhile it surely would have been included. Meanwhile, the owner of the newly resurrected Daiei Studio (a company that switched from Zatoichi to supermarkets in the early '70s) used a press lunch announcing a $14 million epic set in scenic northwestern China to take personal credit for keeping *Mishima* out of the festival, proudly pronouncing it "unsuitable for Japanese minds."

While *The Burmese Harp*, Kon Ichikawa's superfluous remake of the script he directed to such splendid effect in 1956, rivaled *Mishima* as the festival's leading nonevent, the interest in the competitive "Young Cinema" section eclipsed everything else. Three Japanese corporations (CSK computer, Fuji Television, and Sega Enterprises) put up a $1.5 million prize with which to produce the winning director's next film. Entries included *Time Stands Still, Kiss of the Spider Woman, The Company of Wolves, Blood Simple, Old Enough,* and *1984,* which, appropriately enough, turned out to be the first film showing pubic hair ever exhibited in Japan. (Besides the Orwell adaption, nine other festival entries included scenes with full frontal nudity, and the festival had to issue an appeal to Japanese journalists to stop photographing the screen.)

Given the generosity of the prize, it seemed reasonable that the jury (David Puttnam, Shohei Imamura, Bernardo Bertolucci, and István Szabó, among others) would not only split the money but find some way to salute their hosts. Still, Shinji Somai, the 35-year-old director of the Japanese entry, *Typhoon Club*, nearly had a heart attack when his film was awarded first place and $750,000. *Time Stands Still*, the strongest film in competition, received $500,000, and *The Horse*, by Turkish director Ali Ozgenturk, was awarded $250,000.

Uneasily (if unsentimentally) pitched between black humor and nostalgia, *Typhoon Club* proved a Japanese cousin to *The Breakfast Club*, with the eponymous natural catastrophe (rather than bad behavior) serving to detain a select group of adolescents after school. From the opening scene—in which a group of rowdy girls, illegally swimming in the school pool at night, attempt to drown the nerd classmate spying on them—through the comic humiliation of a math teacher to the assorted incidents of rape, lesbianism, regression, and suicide triggered by the big storm, *Typhoon Club* exposes the strata of humiliation, rage, boredom, and violence that Japanese assure you exist just below the apparently tranquil surface of their family and educational institutions.

The film is obviously hyperbolic—but then so is the long-running animated TV series, *The Nuisance Planet Crowd*, which represents Japanese high school as the unending trial that a group of teenage aliens are forced to endure while on earth.

GIVEN THE FAR from subtle Japanese ambivalence toward *gaijin*, interplanetary or not, the real surprise of the *Mishima* affair is that the film's Japanophilic makers didn't predict it. For all its borrowings, Japanese culture is remarkably self-absorbed. American celebs and anonymous caucasoids may be a standard feature of Japanese TV commercials, but the content of the shows is overwhelmingly Japanese. This is the one place in the free world where *Dallas* flopped. Besides, everything the Japanese borrow they make indelibly their own.

Take TV. Tokyo has two educational channels and six commercial ones supplying a raucous assortment of variety shows, samurai dramas, quiz programs, skit comedies, sing-alongs, soap operas, cop shows, and aerobic dance shows complete with shrill English commands delivered by the woman identified, in English, as "our charming instructor." Baseball, another prime time fixture, dominates the news and more. (My trip coincided with a two-part made-for-TV movie on the life and hard times of home-run king Sadaharu Oh's mother.) It's all eminently watchable, but the cartoons and commercials are in a class by themselves. The former are particularly fond of robots—ranging from playful spheres and bionic felines to dwarf ninja and humanoid killing machines. Commercials thrive on anthropomorphic products, talking food, adorable tots, and silly special effects. You're astonished at just how juvenile they are, but that's the cult of cuteness that virtually rules Japan.

There's a sense in which Japan, land of the bonsai tree, is naturally cute, but you know you've arrived in the big town when you glom the highway sign "Welcome to Tokyo . . . Hello Kitty" or the flock of green tweety birds embellishing a skycraper Seiko clock. The women on TV or in print ads exude hardcore perk; the morning show weathergirl with spikey hair and one earring makes Martha Quinn seem like the Wicked Witch of the West. Everything is sweeter than candy; half the women you see in the street are dressed like boxes of Good and Plenty. The national color seems to be a pale nursery pink (far gentler than the fiery shade Diana Vreeland once called "the navy blue of India").

If Disneyland didn't exist the Japanese would have invented it. As it is, Disneyland Tokyo ("the Kingdom of Family Dreams") is an exact replica of the original—English signs and all. The insanely crowded Tsukuba Expo, 30-odd miles north of Tokyo, to which we're treated to a free trip, proves a comparable treasure trove of adorable corporate logos and cloying mystification. The Mitsubishi pavilion—whose slogan "Wonderful World, Beautiful People" might make even a mouseketeer gag—turned out to be a glorified Tunnel of Love ride through pablumatic representations of prehistoric and futuristic worlds. At Fujitsu, another highly touted pavilion (and, indeed, the only other one we're permitted to see), girls in metallic deely-bopper derbies vie for incredulity with braying dinosaur skeletons.

Actually, the trip to Tsukuba is less interesting for itself than as a crash course in being Japanese, or rather Japanese children (or rather, backward Japanese children). Half an hour is spent organizing us into groups and arranging said groups on specific buses. Halfway to Tsukuba we make a mandatory piss-stop. There will be no chance later to relieve ourselves, we're warned. Once at Tsukuba—"no individual movement," we're admonished. "You must stay together. Stick each other!" Each group of 12 is assigned four guides. Three of them spend the time counting their charges, while the fourth leads us on, waving a flag bearing the number of our group. As a reward, we get to experience ourselves on the JumboTRON, Sony's 14-story-high TV, described in *The Selected Guide to Expo '85* as being "to the electronic world what the pyramid is to Egypt."

Is this really the future? Or is Japan, as colleague Gerald Peary suggests, an alternate version of '50s America? The current Coke commercial has a '50s motif. Every Sunday afternoon, at the fringe of Yoyogi Park, cliques of kids in various '50s styles can be seen twisting away, putting the handful of inept breakdancers to shame.

THERE ARE, of course, some ways in which Tokyo is beyond au courant. There are TVs everywhere at Wave, the state of the art record store—all high-tech curved neon and chrome, as spiffy as a Columbus Avenue gelati palace and six stories tall. You can stay all day, listening to any number of 200 preselected hits or programming the music videos you can watch later that night on the television show that begins when some middle-aged square yells "Countdown U.S.A.!"

I never made it to Bar 69, a basement reggae club run by Japanese Rastafarians, but I did manage to find Tsubaki House (modestly termed "our paradise on earth"), a low-ceilinged disco located, Japanese-style, in a skyscraper and featuring Frank Chickens, a London-based female duo in *Liquid Sky* makeup, who chant a technopop blend of *enka,* reggae, and rap in a mixture of English and Japanese. As far as I was concerned, Frank Chickens established their credibility by converting a cheerfully trad drinking song into a chilling evocation of Hiroshima, before covering their eyes with mesh strainers to sing the theme from *Mothra.* In Britain, the duo had a top 10 hit, "We Are Ninja (Not Geisha)"; in Tokyo, the song was appreciated but its sentiments taken for granted. Abroad, Frank Chickens sing about the alienation of being Japanese, but they're hardly more at home here. Despite their evocation of such local subjects as earthquakes, movie star Ken Takakura, and the ultra cute-cult duo Pink Ladies, they're regarded as one more foreign import—just like most Japanese pop music.

After a while you're no longer surprised to hear the Sex Pistols serenading the "Bad Zone" at the Seibu department store (it is, after all, the part of the store devoted to "Young Ladies' Fashions"). *Departo* wonders never cease. Here's a counter filled with Gary Panter loose-leaf notebooks (pink or yellow, natch). There's a display of "treasured French film posters." The theaters atop the department stores are where you go to see avant-garde theater or the PIA festival of independent films.

It's there I catch *A Girl She Is 100%* (a wonderfully cynical and formally eccentric love story) and *Attack on a Bakery* (a shaggy dog story dealing with the peculiarities of Japanese politics), a pair of short movies by 28-year-old Naoto Yamakawa. The absence of subtitles made comprehension problematic; still, these are the only Japanese films I've seen even remotely to do with the seething Shibuya street scene outside.

AT THE MOMENT, there are three hot young directors in Japan—Yoshimitsu Morita, Kohei Oguri, and Mitsuo Yanagimachi—all of whom elude easy classification, particularly in Japan. "Their films are eccentric because of the struggle to get money," Tadao Sato carefully explains, adding, "Now only crazy people can make worthwhile films." That all have done their best work outside the industry was underscored by the failure of Morita's *Family Game* follow-up, a dismal youth film made for Toho.

Although Oguri's *Muddy River* may have been the best received Japanese film of the 1980s, the response to his second feature is severely mixed. Nothing if not ambitious, *For Kayako* addresses the legacy of Japan's imperial expansion by treating the prejudices suffered by the nation's 700,000 Korean residents. Although based on a novel by a Korean nisei, *For Kayako* never quite comes to grips with its subject. Ostentatiously understated and bizarrely abstract, the film boils down to a beautifully shot, numbingly repetitious series of confrontations. Oguri seems so consumed with his own empathy, he's forgotten everyone else's.

If *For Kayako* is a disappointment, however, the new Yanagimachi—*Himatsuri* (Fire Festival), the first film produced by the ubiquitous Seibu *departo*—is a triumph, as well as a current hit. Although as obliquely plotted and pictorial as *Kayako, Himatsuri* stages a far more frontal attack on audience sensibility. It's charged with vitality; Yanagimachi doesn't waste a setup. The film has a novelistic density, but, as abetted by Toru Takemitsu's moodily spare score, Yanagimachi's narrative style is pure cinema.

The 40-year-old director's previous *A Farewell to the Land,* shown in New York at the 1983 "New Directors" series, was the sprawling, elliptical fable of a young trucker's fatal overextension, as well as a rich panorama of modern Japan. *Himatsuri* treats the weakening of tradition in a similarly echt Japanese environment. The setting—a tiny fishing village nestled by wooded mountains in the extreme southwestern portion of the archipelago—is quintessential old Japan, the mythologically resonant spot where the first emperor landed, whose sanctity is threatened by a proposed tourist park. The film, however, is based on an actual incident: in this very village in 1980, a man killed his entire family and then committed suicide.

Pondering the riddle of this atrocity, *Himatsuri* attempts a kind of Shinto (as opposed to psycho-) analysis. Yanagimachi's protagonist, the lumberjack Tatsuo, is at once nature's mystic medium and its macho despoiler. "The mountain goddess is my girlfriend," is his hubristic boast. Although Tatsuo is wont to hunt as well as swim in sacred waters, he won't sell his land to the developers; according to Yanagimachi, Tatsuo "identifies so completely with nature he sacrifices himself to it." Another way of putting it would be that Tatsuo becomes possessed, the instrument of the gods' vengeance.

Given the Japanese obsession with their national identity, *nihonjinron* (the theory of Japanese-ness) has become something of a media industry. More than any of his contemporaries, Yanagimachi's films partake of this introspection. Yanagimachi, however, is hardly a man of consensus. Indeed, his ambivalent attitude toward modernization (and modernism), his search for an archaic (and male) Japanese essence, his apocalyptic sense of a lost harmony all suggest Yukio Mishima ("Mishima is always in my mind," Yanagimachi told me.)

But Yanagimachi's *nihonjinron* is rooted in Shinto rather than samurai ethics, nature rather than nation. *Himatsuri* already has an American distributor and an invitation to the New York Film Festival; when it opens here it will be the most Japanese Japanese film to be released here in years. If the universalist *Ran* demonstrates how much the Japanese are like everyone else, *Himatsuri* shows just how much they remain themselves.

Budapest 1986

Originally published as "Budapest's Business" in *Film Comment* (June 1986).

THE RICHNESS OF Hungary's film culture notwithstanding, the landscape itself produces chimeras and mirages. On one side of the Danube stands a wistful replica of Britain's House of Parliament, on the other a castle that never housed a king. These facades are less a Potemkin village to fool outsiders than the literalization of national longings and delusions: after 1920, Hungary remained a monarchy without a monarch; the regent of the now landlocked country was—what else?—an admiral. As the chanteuse sings in the hallucinatory opening sequence of the new Péter Gothár film, "Budapest is my Paris."

Thus, no less than the state-owned fast-food chain called (in English, yet) "City Grill," or the gentrification of the old Jewish quarter, and like the Szechuan restaurant which has materialized in the heart of the tourist district, or the pizza parlors that have mushroomed around town, the bland new hotel-convention center where this year's Hungarian Film Week was held supports the half-fiction of Budapest's "europeanization." Native filmmakers, however, are experts at peeling back the veneer to reveal the contradictions—if you can only decode them. Compared to 1985 when, led by *Colonel Redl*, co-productions and period pieces reigned supreme, the current crop of Hungarian films are nothing if not more specifically and topically Hungarian.

The great theme seemed to be coping with the nation's complicated mixed economy as it jolted through the Eighties. For 15 years, Hungarians have enjoyed the most developed consumer society in the Eastern bloc, and many films reflected the psychic cost of maintaining this standard of living; holding two or more jobs, backing into business, and having Hobbesian sex—nasty, brutish, and short. (Virtually every film featured at least one bout of hurried, joyless copulation—preferably standing up—in boutique dressing rooms or toilet stalls, against the walls of moving elevators, or the sides of trucks parked in the rain.) Even those movies in which the question of economic survival was eclipsed by more metaphysical issues exuded a defensive, ironic mixture of self-pity and pride, a morose sense that, as ingrown, marginal, and unique as Hungary is, there may be life elsewhere, but immigration is still desertion—in other words a particularly Hungarian form of Weltschmerz that belied the external trappings of Euro-urbanism.

György Szomjas's *The Wall Driller*—tapped to open the festival—told the sad, flashy tale of a factory worker ensconced in a depressing housing project who attempts to change his life. Purchasing a power drill, he turns entrepreneur, boring holes to order in his neighbor's walls. The metaphor is played for maximum raunchy innuendo, particularly once the wall driller gets mixed up with the prize member of a local prostitution ring staffed mainly by women on maternity leave. (Nothing if not topical, *The Wall Driller* followed by less than a year the sensational trial of a bevy of hookers who had plied their trade at a truckstop outside Szeged on the Yugoslav border.)

Even more fragmented and tricksy than Szomjas's previous film (which has been released in the U.S. as *Tight Quarters*), *The Wall Driller* holds the viewer firmly at arm's length, racking focus, changing filters, and interpolating bits of TV variety shows with impunity. Less delirious, Pál Schiffer's *Kovbojok* (*Cowboys*)—a four-hour documentary more appreciated by Hungarians than foreigners—depicts another sort of business failure. Here a group of five young, not particularly bright people come to grief attempting to make a profit by leasing cows from a less than cooperative state farm.

The most programmatic of the free enterprise tragedies, as well as the winner of the foreign critics' annual Gene Moskowitz award was Pál Erdöss' *Countdown*. A sequel of sorts to *The Princess* for which Erdöss was awarded the Camera d'Or at Cannes in 1983, *Countdown* follows the doomed career of the self-employed truckdriver who has married the protagonist of the earlier film. "Just like America!" the trucker exalts, having something like grossed a month's salary in his first day as an independent. The initial windfall is soon followed, however, by demands for kickbacks and cautionary beatings; finally the driver's back goes out under the strain of working 16 to 18 hours a day. Episodic and gritty, with domestic fight scenes for set pieces, *Countdown* is a respectable example of the post-Cassavetes pseudo-doc, but it's a movie one has the feeling of having seen a dozen times before, half of them in Hungary.

Despite Erdöss' hapless hero falling on his face, one kind of entrepreneur is evidently making a bundle these days. The proliferation of VCRs—the official estimate is over 100,000—has evidently spawned a booming, video black market. Even at the government "video kazzeták" stores, the 300 or so sanctioned tapes rent for seven or eight times the price of a movie ticket; meanwhile illegal operators reportedly earn ten times the average monthly wage supplying western video entertainments. Unlike Poland's Hungary's video underground seems fairly apolitical—unless you consider trafficking in porno and *Rambo* a threat to the social order. The forbidden has its own lure: official paranoia about the proliferation of *Gorky Park* tapes made this hitherto obscure spectacle of the KGB run amok, the hottest item on the black market.

FOR FOREIGN CRITICS, the most eagerly awaited and disappointing new film was Zsolt Kézdi-Kovács' *The Absentee*. Kézdi-Kovács' subtle, unsettling films mix defamiliarizing hyperrealism with a stringent lyrical streak, grounding suggestive metaphors in laconic observations of lower class disorder. A one-time assistant director to Miklós Jancsó and perhaps the strongest director of the "generation of 1956," Kézdi-Kovács hit his stride with *When Joseph Returns* (1975), the tenderly horrific contemplation of a rebellious young woman worker coping (badly) with her life in a worker's state, and *The Nice Neighbor* (1979), the most savage of housing shortage comedies. The director also received a measure of international recognition with the incest drama *Forbidden Relations* (1983), shown in competition at Cannes and later at the New York Film Festival. (Terming *Forbidden Relations* "a great love story," Dave Kehr recently observed in the *Chicago Reader* that the film "doesn't depend on identification—it may be the first film of its kind to deliberately forgo the old strategies and search for a fresh approach.")

Like *Forbidden Relations, The Absentee* is founded upon an eruption of the irrational. Abandoned by his French girlfriend, a young pilot (dourly played by Peter Berg of the émigré Squat Theater) commandeers a crop dusting plane and madly pursues her across the border where he crashes and is returned to Hungary. An overtly allegorical throwback to the somber kammerspiels of the early Seventies, *The Absentee* then explores the grounded pilot's tormented relation with a family that more or less stands for the Hungarian nation. His ex-wife is a terminally unstable alcoholic actress, his mother is a crass business operator, his sister a saintly true-believer.

Every performer in *Absentee* has a flaming subtext. As the alienated hero, Berg is the living emblem of a lost Hungarian avant-garde. Lili Monori, who plays his wife, is best known as the heroine of two previous Kézdi-Kovács films and several by Márta Mészáros. (A sensational actress, Monori is here close to self parody, worse than I've ever seen her.) The mother, Mari Töröcsik, is emblematic of Jancsó and the Sixties, while the sister, Vera Pap, played another sort of religious cultist as the anti-heroine of *Angi Vera*. Although Kézdi-Kovács retains his precise cinematography and unsentimental eye for locations, the film never finds its tone and soon grows as hysterically convoluted as mid-period Fassbinder.

More accessible and entertaining if no less schematic, *The Great Generation,* directed by Ferenc András from a script by Géza Bereményi, also deals with the return of a prodigal son. A prologue set in 1968 establishes György Cserhalmi as an opportunistic rogue who steals his friend's passport and leaves for America. After 17 years, the buddies meet in Budapest, their teenage children in tow. "America is America—bigger heap of junk with bigger roosters," Cserhalmi claims. The atmosphere of curdled nostalgia is reinforced by setting half the scenes in a Budapest disco called the Elvis Presley Club.

If *The Great Generation*'s ensuing drama of failed schemes and lost illusions would seem to have the makings of a local blockbuster, Péter Gothár's *Time,* on the other hand, proved an instant cause célèbre. Although no less drenched in Magyar Weltschmerz than *The Great Generation* or *The Absentee,* the film's manic profusion of sight gags and narrative switchbacks place it in a whole other category. Ostensibly the story of a 35-year-old worker who takes his family on vacation, *Time* continually segues in and out of other movies, not to mention TV commercials. Stumbling through the city, the hero encounters a variety of weird sexual scenes, emerges victorious from a Sergio Leone-style gunfight at his factory, and survives being hit by a bus.

Gothár's collaborator on the often hilarious script is novelist Péter Esterházy, a master of parody and pastiche whose postmodernist texts have yet to be translated into English. Albeit often visionary, the treatment needs a light directorial touch. Gothár's deliberate lack of couth—alternately suggesting such disparate wiseguys as Joe Dante, Peter Greenaway, and Raul Ruiz—reaches the point of diminishing returns; the film exhausts itself and loses its flow in the overall churning up of ideas. The vacation house is a lurid, haunted castle; the parks are full of punks and 18th century *huszars*. You get the picture: for those who expected *Time Stands Still* redux, the change in tone was a bit like *Revolver* after *Rubber Soul*. Too rich a stew for most foreigners, *Time* delighted the local audience with such delicacies as a Hungarian-speaking black dominatrix, an impersonation of the widely despised Stalin-era boss, Mátyás Rákosi, and probably the most gruesome-looking dildo east of the Duna.

THE DISCIPLES, written and directed by Géza Bereményi, might have been a better script for Gothár. The story of a stonefaced innocent (played by Károly Eperjes, the truckdriver in *Countdown*) up from the country to attend university in the capital, this evocation of the Thirties is no less ambitious than *Time*, nor any less a break with the Hungarian cinema of the Seventies and Eighties. Wandering through the fleshpots of a hilariously psychedelicized Budapest, Eperjes falls in with the degenerate Count Alex and then a gang of futuristic technocrats; the Felliniesque phantasmagoria is further complicated with flashfowards to a shabby housing tract in modern day Budapest, the fruit of scientific planning. *The Disciples* suffers from an overabundance of ideas, not to mention technique, but it is an auspicious debut for the most lavishly prolific Hungarian screenwriter of the past ten years.

Although *Time*, *The Wall Driller*, and *The Disciples*, as well as *Idiots May Apply*, the new film by Janos Xantos, makes you think they were directed by Ernie Kovacs if not the former Cardinal relief ace, Al "The Mad Hungarian" Hrabosky, their likely precursor is *Night Song of the Dog*, directed by Gábor Bódy in 1983. The closest thing to a midnight movie ever produced under the Warsaw Pact, this two-and-a-half-hour exercise in outrage and blasphemy, shot Lower East Side style by cinematographer Johanna Heer, conflated video, super-8, pseudo-porn, extraterrestrial voices, and punk bands in the service of a convoluted story of sex, Stalinism, and bogus religion.

The 39-year-old Bódy committed suicide in the fall of 1985 and his death cast a pall over the film week. Perhaps in tribute, *The Agitators*, a long-shelved item on which Bódy had been a major contributor, had its official premiere at the Film Museum. Directed by Deszö Magyar at the experimental Béla Balázs Studio in 1969, *The Agitators* was the only portrait of Hungary's short-lived 1919 Soviet Republic to be made on the occasion of its 50th anniversary. The script, by Magyar and Bódy, was taken from what was then a semi-proscribed novel by Ervin Sinkó, which described the young firebrands (including Georg Lukács and Béla Balázs) of the period; the cast seemed to include half the New Left superstars of late Sixties Budapest, among them the future lead-singer of the Hobo Blues Band, the future scriptwriter of *Mephisto*, and the future male stars of *The Great Generation* and *Time*. In one of the most outrageous touches, the son of Jószef Revai—Hungary's Stalin era minister of culture—plays his own father as a revolutionary youth. (After the film, the young Revai was tried for his "Maoism.")

Basically a barrage of talk (with vaguely folk rock interludes), *The Agita-*

tors is a kind of group psychodrama in which a gang of university leftists and would-be pop stars run around in leather caps and jackets making speeches about the Communist Party and the interests of the masses. Not only does Trotsky's name surface, there's a strong inference that class society still exists. Just to make sure the point is made, the film ends in a burst of belligerent ultra-leftism with the longhaired pop star atop a car roof, machine-gunning the crowd.

The Agitators, which was shot by Lajos Koltai, is one of the strongest evocations of the Sixties ever put on film—a fascinating artifact of the Hungarian New Left. Don't hold your breath, waiting to see it though. Money is so tight, one Hungarofilm official told me, that from now on they would only be able to subtitle "commercial" films: "There are," he solemnly pointed out, "limits to socialism." I dare say, but how does one define commercial? Or progress? A mixed economy should offer the best of both worlds. Hungarian filmmakers may one day learn that economic censorship can be as hard to get around as the political kind.

What's stranger than paradise? Or how we stopped worrying and learned to love the 'burbs

Originally published in *The Village Voice* (June 30, 1987).

For years we have been taught not to like things. Finally somebody said it was OK to like things. This was a great relief. It was getting hard to go around not liking everything.

—David Byrne, *True Stories* (the book)

WHO TAUGHT US not to like things? And who finally told us it was okay? Was it David Byrne? Andy Warhol? Ronald Reagan? (Was it . . . Satan?) Capping a trend that's been percolating for most of the decade, a new obsession with the strangeness—even the Otherness—of the American heartland characterizes a remarkable number of recent movies.

Call it Kitschy Kool or Americanarama, Jetsonism or the Hayseed Renaissance, the New Patriotism or Neo-Regional Backlash, Middle American Grotesque or Shopping Mall Chic, such disparate films as *Blue Velvet* and *Raising Arizona, Something Wild* and *True Stories, Making Mr. Right* and *Crimes of the Heart, Peggy Sue Got Married* and *Down By Law, Gates of Heaven, The Stepfather,* and *Sherman's March* are all transfixed—if not stupefied—by the American Way of Life. Coming in the wake of cult items as diverse as *Stranger Than Paradise, Blood Simple, Repo Man, UFOria, Static, The Atomic Café, Pee-Wee's Big Adventure,* and even *E.T.,* this trend has the force of a cultural upheaval.

The themes of these movies are as obsessive as their souvenir-stand iconography: the pathos of received ideas, the triumph of the ersatz, the wonder of bad taste, the dreamlike superimposition of the '50s over the '80s, the sense of Middle America as a kitsch theme park. That national "new morning" proclaimed by Ronald Reagan three years ago must be getting on toward high noon: *True Stories* celebrates small town American life with an exaggerated, shadowless clarity. Or maybe it's really later than we think. *Blue Velvet* defamiliarizes a similar landscape with the most sinister of twilights.

Are these films condescending or accepting? Do they reek of alienation or burble with self-love? Is there a new confidence in being American? Or a panicky realization that "America" is all we've got? Just what is it that makes the norms of American life seem so wonderfully exotic, if not downright bizarre? In retrospect, the key scene in recent America films occurs 20 minutes into *Stranger Than Paradise* when, interrogated by his greenhorn cousin, John Lurie launches into an impassioned defense of the TV dinner—a gag leaving the viewer to wonder if the Swanson's in question was not simply defrosted from the freezer but exhumed intact from a pharaoh's tomb.

Heineken?! Fuck that shit!! Pabst . . . Blue . . . Ribbon!!!
–Dennis Hopper, Blue Velvet

NATURAL PARADISE OR urban DMZ, the American landscape is the arena of moral forces. Whatever it may have become, this was once Europe's new Eden, its fabulous Second Chance, its verdant Blank Slate. The land itself signified "promise," and, in the absence of a classical tradition, a universal church, or a royal court, it was, for American artists, the source of transcendent value. Landscape painting is very much a 19th century phenomenon but, in the provincial first half of the 20th century, before New York wrested modern art away from Paris, virtually every indigenous movement was some sort of landscape art—the Ashcan group, Precisionism, Social Realism, Regionalism—while the strongest individuals, Edward Hopper and Georgia O'Keeffe, say, or Walker Evans, have all but left their names on specific vistas, Walt Disney-style.

It was Evans's protégé Robert Frank who burst like a bombshell on the photography world with the definitive vision of postwar America. First published in 1959 (complete with Jack Kerouac intro), *The Americans* plumbed the underside of the Eisenhower era: reveling in the seedy, the alienated, and the soulful, churning up image after image of hitherto invisible stuff and insisting on its intrinsic American-ness. It was Frank who invented Desolation Row—a new American landscape of two-lane blacktops and all-night diners with incandescent jukeboxes, bus depots and empty casinos, inhabited by a restless tribe of blurry drifters. Familiar enough now, Frank's elliptical, snapshot iconography was so radical in the late '50s he couldn't even get a New York gallery until his work was published in France.

Frank's debut preceded by two seasons the single most convulsive moment in American painting, the sudden rise and smashing victory of Pop Art. Static, anti-anecdotal, and monumental, Pop took consumer products and media icons—the very stuff that makes us American—and celebrated them as the demiurges of the new, triumphantly ersatz, non-European civilization. From Jasper Johns's bronze beer cans and Claes Oldenburg's fake fur Popsicles to Tom Wesselman's blatantly eroticized consumerscapes and Ed Ruscha's deadpan panorma of every building on the Sunset Strip, Pop created a new plastic pantheon. Pop's ideological avant-garde was the camp taste for the dated, extravagant detritus of American mass culture—the relics of our recent collective past. Cold War America had been doggedly earnest; by the mid '60s, Pop and Camp institutionalized irony, making any sort of ephemera reclaimable (and collectible). From there it was a simple step to the postmodern architects who advocated *Learning from Las Vegas* or the American Studies grad students who wrote dissertations on Johnny Carson.

The '60s brought the wholesale aestheticization of America. The more phenomenological wing of Pop and the more socially conscious branch of Minimalism saw interstate highways as something like cathedrals. Proto-Conceptualists Robert Smithson and Dan Graham wrote deadpan treatises on the monuments of Passaic or the aesthetics of suburban tract houses. (The '70s brought the even more neutral "new topographers," who photographed suburban backyards and, rather than the postcard or snapshot, privileged the real estate photograph as their preferred nonaesthetic form.) "I like to think about and look at those suburbs and those fringes, but at the same time, I'm not interested in living there. . . . It is the future—the Martian landscape" Smithson told Allan Kaprow in 1966, anticipating the gist of *More Songs About Buildings and Food* (and the validation of *Close Encounters of the Third Kind*) by about 10 years.

When it came to addressing this new American landscape, however, Hollywood was largely impervious. It's not just that the industry preferred such metaphoric substitutes as the Old West or Imperial Rome—it lacked the necessary distance. After all, the movies *were* the landscape. Still, in the halcyon days of the '50s, Frank Tashlin and Douglas Sirk, each in his own alienated way, were proto-Pop artists if not proto-Conceptualists (making films as interesting to think about as they are to watch). Both directors embraced American vulgarity in all its lurid, widescreen splendor, pushing what would some day be called "lifestyle" well past the point of sci-fi madness. Tashlin deployed such two-dimensional performers as Jayne Mansfield or Jerry Lewis as if to cast Sirk's most celebrated title, *Imitation of Life*. That one director made comedies and the other melodramas hardly mattered—both trafficked in Technicolor flesh-tones and laminated sheen, the flat, flaming, larger-than-life, all-American inauthenticity that European theorists Umberto Eco and Jean Baudrillard would call "hyperreality."

Other Hollywood examples were few and far between. There was George Axelrod's 1966 Tuesday Weld vehicle *Lord Love a Duck*. But just about everything else came from beyond the margins (Vernon Zimmerman's 1972 *The Unholy Rollers*, a drive-in paean to fast food, fast women, and fast skates), overseas (the Wisconsin sequences of Werner Herzog's 1977 *Stroszek*), or the regionalist fringe (George Kuchar's Bronx, John Waters's Baltimore, Les Blank's

Cajun country, James Benning's Midwest). There was also Robert Altman. But Alman's films reflected more a spasm of national self-hatred than an effusion of populist love. *Mosholu Holiday, Pink Flamingos,* and *11 × 14* were the exact opposite of *Nashville.* They treated industrial folk art with a sense of wonder and bemused affection—if not necessarily as the skeleton key to the American national character.

The true godfathers of Shopping Mall Chic are Errol Morris and Jonathan Demme, both of whom came out of left field in the mid-Carter years to meet heartland *meshugas* head-on—in part by dramatizing "true stories" of bizarre success and pathetic failure. The delicate sense of CB radio as a form of corn-fed astral projection made Demme's *Handle With Care* (1978) a critical favorite. But from his earliest days at American-International, the hallmark of Demme's career has been an appreciation for lower-class kitsch and the mass-produced, reified fantasy it embodies: theme restaurants and motels, while-u-wait wedding chapels and the accoutrements of an L.A.-style Christmas.

Based on the case of Melvin Dumar, mystery beneficiary of Howard Hughes's contested will, *Melvin and Howard* (1980) treats the contemporary West—Vegas, SoCal, Utah (with utopian intimations of Hawaii)—as a land of failed schemes and sweet disorder. The film is the real *Rocky,* Americans as feckless, media-blitzed dreamers and natural performers who think nothing of marrying each other twice, then spending their honeymoon playing nickel slots. Demme gives Frank's Desolation Row a benign shot of post-hippie oh wowism. (Who needs Nepal, check out the K-Mart.) A TV giveaway program—half *Gong Show,* half *Let's Make a Deal*—where Mary Steenburgen carries off the jackpot with her green sateen bellhop outfit and a slow tap to "Satisfaction" or the Christmas luau at the dingy bottling plant where Melvin hopes to become Milkman of the Month (and win a color TV) would have been nightmares of condescension in the hands of a lesser director.

While Demme is an affable fabulist, celebrating spongelike losers who soak up and exude an ambience that's as vivid and pungent as a Samarkand bazaar, Errol Morris observes the American dream with the unblinking cool of a NASA spaceprobe. *Blue Velvet* notwithstanding, Morris's 1978 *Gates of Heaven* is arguably the masterpiece of Americanarama, made nearly a decade before the trend coalesced. Certainly, for bottomline defamiliarizing weirdness, no film has ever surpassed this documentary account of two California pet cemeteries.

Mainly a succession of talking heads, *Gates of Heaven* constructs each frame as a sarcophagus all its own—the interviewees surrounded by totems ranging from *The Wall Street Journal* to a pair of bronzed baby shoes or a can of Coors, spilling their guts in a mélange of advertising clichés, talk show bromides, business school koans, and motivational slogans. Once the film moves to the Bubbling Well Pet Memorial Park (the proprietor assures bereaved clients that they will be reunited with their pets in the afterlife, while his own sons are buried alive in the family business), sentiment becomes even more awesomely reified: there are headstones carved with such devastating confessions as "I Knew Love—I Had This Dog."

Morris's conceptual rigor, combined with his blandly outré subject matter

and stark emphasis on his interviewee's iconic self-presentation, itself epitomizes the overall sense of alienation, displacement, and outlandish commodity
fetishism that characterizes Americanarama as a whole. That doesn't make his
films easy to take: There's very little distance between Morris and his subjects
and, even more than Demme, he's been a prophet without honor. Since *Gates of
Heaven,* he has completed only one film—the hour-long *Vernon, Florida* (1980),
a series of monologues featuring the more garrulous and eccentric citizens of the
eponymous panhandle backwater.

Here Morris approaches documentary ground zero: A turkey-hunting hipster, a worm farmer, a couple who once took a vacation in White Sands, New
Mexico, the crocks who hang out in front of Brock's Service Station, all become
as entrancing as the kinkiest Warhol superstar—and far more mysterious. At
one point, a local preacher delivers a sermon the word "therefore" that has the
effect of transforming language into a parade of empty, immanent signs—the
words rattle in our brains like the refuse of a cargo cult.

Ordinary fucking people, I hate 'em.

—Harry Dean Stanton, *Repo Man*

AMERIKITSCH HAS ANALOGUES in almost every field—the quizzical irony of
performance artist Mike Smith's "everyman," the hermetic solemnity of William Eggleston's Graceland photos, the prurient, candy-colored surfaces of
Frederick Barthelme's *New Yorker* stories, the adolescent hostility of California
hard-core or neo-underground comix like *Neat Stuff* and *Road Kill*—not to
mention a raft of book-length paeans: *Amazing America, Roadside America,*
Thomas Hine's *Populuxe,* a lavish celebration of American vernacular design
between the wars (Korean and Vietnam). But the most resonant manifestations
have appeared in the art world: Eric Fischl's suburban grotesques, Laurie
Simmons's staged photographs, the naked commodities of Group Material's
"Americana" installation at the '85 Whitney Biennial, Jeff Koons's vacuum-
sealed vacuum cleaners.

Koons, an artist who might have been invented by Frank Tashlin, anticipates the underglass look of *True Stories,* just as Eric Fischl's sense of transgres-
sive voyeurism parallels *Blue Velvet*'s, and the African fetish objects he tucks
into his haunted suburban interiors suggest *Something Wild.* ("America's not
Disneyland and we can't deny it any longer. Things smell, things have edges,
people get hurt," Fischl has remarked.) The Barbie-doll tourists of Laurie
Simmons's miniaturized make-believe world are first cousins to the carefully
outfitted, disillusioned Kewpies who inhabit Susan Seidelman's similarly stylized dollhouses. (*Making Mr. Right*'s pastel, Jetsonesque decor recalls Kenny
Scharf's self-proclaimed Jetsonism—although baroque artists like Scharf and
Pee-Wee Herman are more attuned to the tumult of '60s kitsch than to the
imperial detritus of the staid '50s.)

Postmodern as it is, Americanarama has its cliquish "ism" aspect. Demme
and Jarmusch have worked with David Byrne. Byrne and Susan Seidelman both

employed cameraman Ed Lachman and art director Barbara Ling. Robby Müller shot *Repo Man* and *Down By Law*. Tibor Kalman's M&Co did titles for *Something Wild* and *True Stories*. Seidelman, Jarmusch, and Joel Coen all attended film school at NYU. But that's not really the source of Kitschy Kool.

One could trace the attitude back to the CBGB of the mid '70s or the Club 57 of a few years later. Certainly, Talking Heads and the B-52s are avatars of Shopping Mall Chic, while Ann Magnuson's talent shows (Kenny Scharf dressing up as Bam-Bam Flintstone, John Sex lip-synching to "What's New Pussycat?") epitomize the vulgar postmodernism that underlies Americanarama. In each case, the performance is a costume drama, predicated on the recycling of mass cultural artifacts in new and inappropriate contexts—the elevation of television roulette to a form of automatic writing, a kind of free association raised to its most self-conscious level by SCTV.

The love of kitsch is itself camp. But, even more than camp, AmeriKitsch is governed by the regime of nostalgia—the sense that the present is secondhand, that nothing is new except the reshuffling of past styles—and a love for the ersatz (raised to a generic principle by *Making Mr. Right* and *True Stories*, which is *not* a documentary). Unlike, say, Marlene Dietrich, Fred Flintstone can't be a sacred monster. Nothing in the world of Americanarama has the authority of the sui generis. For while camp privileged the movies, AmeriKitsch is totally telecentric. The movies dazzled audiences with outsized archetypes, but TV is nature—only denatured. Television is our everyday environment, at once bleached out and tinnily intensified. Movies are events; TV is a continuum that, like the Blob, oozes out in all directions. Reruns notwithstanding, the tube presents an eternal now in which history is the history of style. (There's a wonderful intimation of this in *Something Wild*'s high school reunion, dubbed "'76 Revisited:" Resplendent in their red, white, and blue party hats, the former students cavort to the Feelies's version of "I'm a Believer" in front of a colossal American flag.)

Defining its viewer as both consumer and product, TV presents a miniaturized, ideologically constructed world—a dematerialized theme park—in which we all live and you are what you consume. If nothing is precisely authentic, everything is falsely familiar—at least a commodity (or the shadow of one). The characters in these TV-inflected movies live in a round of karmic desire by which their identity is defined, colonized, dissolved, and reconstructed by some external mechanism of production. Brand names and advertising slogans are their mantras. The conventions of the most conventional wisdom (get married, have a kid, grow old) motivate the protagonists of *True Stories*, *Peggy Sue Got Married*, *Raising Arizona*, *Blue Velvet*, *Making Mr. Right*, and *Sherman's March*. It's certainly funny—but are they having fun? Yet?

In a sense, TV has mass-produced Rimbaud's "I is Another," given it a new meaning and applied it to the consumer. As a spectator form, the tube has a built-in displacement, exemplified in the sitcom innovation of the laugh track: TV is what everyone else watches (just as public opinion is what everyone else thinks). That *True Stories*, *Raising Arizona*, and *Gates of Heaven* oscillate between smug put-on and enthusiastic condescension suggests precisely this ambivalence. One defense against tele-commodification is a bemused loathing for those *other* ordinary fucking people, constructed as they are by the absurd social codes, received languages, reified desires, and true stories of bourgeois America's "wild, wild life."

It's funny. You come to something new and everything looks the same.
                                        —Richard Edson, *Stranger Than Paradise*

IT'S BEEN SAID that artistic regionalism is the revolt of geography against history. What then is the particular ersatz regionalism of *Blue Velvet* and *Peggy Sue,* the Coen Brothers, Susan Seidelman, and David Byrne? Many of these filmmakers, and much of their audience, grew up in suburbia. AmeriKitsch, perhaps much of postmodernism itself, is the culture of suburban babyboomers. Neither as cozy as smalltown America, nor as heterogeneous as the city, the suburbs (like television) are nowhere in particular and everywhere at once. Could the region AmeriKitsch evokes be less a place than a time?

Attempts to revive the Summer of Love notwithstanding, the '50s remain our favorite theme park. The consensus is that the Eisenhower era was the last age of consensus. (Whether this is true or not hardly matters. As *American Graffiti* makes explicit, the '58–'62 period is fetishized because it was the last thing glimpsed before the escalating traumas of the '60s.) It's been years since the futuristic utopianism of the '60s was superseded by nostalgia. Just as *Populuxe* might have served as the recipe for *Making Mr. Right,* so Jarmusch recreates *The Americans* as a nostalgic pastorale. Indeed, nothing is more characteristic of Americanarama than the superimposition of the '50s over the '80s. The decade blur is explicit in *Peggy Sue,* blatant in *Blue Velvet,* implicit in *Something Wild* (as well as in the British *Absolute Beginners*), and latent in *True Stories*—not to mention the major theme of Ronald Reagan's presidency, *The Cosby Show,* and the programming philosophy of Pat Robertson's Christian Broadcast Network.

Nostalgia for the '50s is also present in the work of Steven Spielberg. But Spielberg differs from the practitioners of Americanarama in that his films (up until *The Color Purple*) followed the Godardian paradigm of movie quotation and genre appropriation; and more to the point, his suburbia is as apocalyptic as the Revelations of Saint John. A photo-realist appreciation for the nuances of tract-house life barely conceals the hysteria that underlies *Close Encounters* and *E.T.* (let alone *Poltergeist, Gremlins,* or *Back to the Future*). Lynch, Byrne, Seidelman, et al. try to construct families; for Spielberg, the Father's wish to flee the home is as absolute as Huck Finn's desire to light out for the territories— and a good deal more drastically regressive. Spielberg's is a desperate quest for rebirth.

Paradise, in Spielberg, is returning to the Mother Ship to be reunited with the radioactive embryos; paradise, in Byrne, is now. Still, something haunts *True Stories* et al., and Spielberg's paradoxical, inept attempt to portray absolute Otherness may furnish a clue to what it is. Gone is the ethnic chic of the '60s and '70s. The films I've been discussing are far whiter than the average television commercial—and the whites are strictly unhyphenated American. The burden of Otherness is shouldered by blacks, and it's illuminating to ponder their role. Whether cast as *Blue Velvet*'s blind seer or *True Stories's* voodoo priest, disguised as Jarmusch's nouveau White Negro or scattered over the landscape in *Something Wild,* this Other remains reproachful, unassimilated, establishing the margins of representation.

To me, what this suggests is the uneasy awareness that our suburban consensus is nothing but an idea. After all, Reaganism is a reaction against the '60s, but only in part. Much of what happened during that decade can be summed up in two phrases, which became common currency 20 years ago and have remained so ever since: the Media and the Third World. Not only did new actors tread upon the stage of history, but the nature of the stage was redefined. Americanarama, like Reaganism, embraces one and represses the other—setting the American subject in a media-amplified hall of mirrors. At best, the crypto Third World that populates *Something Wild* or *Down By Law* is a fugitive yearning for some other utopia—interracial, cross-cultural, class-effacing. The apparent impossibility of fully imagining this alternative is what accounts for the uncanny hermeticism, if not solipsism, of these films—and all Americanarama. *True Stories* idealizes the shopping malls in which it will presumably be shown.

We've come full circle: *True Stories* is as blandly positivist in its platitudes as *Nashville* was glibly negative. Here, the good life appears preserved, as it were, under glass—like one of the miniaturized, climate-controlled cities that Superman's nemesis Brainiac used to collect. Like our Great Communicator, the most pernicious Americanaramic films play let's pretend. They deny even the desperate denial that is the subject of *Gates of Heaven* or *Melvin and Howard.* Where America was the New Eden or the Golden Land, Americanarama is the game preserve of American hegemony, an island in a Third World sea—one nation, anesthetized, sealed in plastic, self-absorbed.

The last picture show

Originally published in *The Village Voice* (January 3, 1989), with excerpts from "Stars and Hype Forever," *The Village Voice* (January 29, 1985).

1. Who was that masked man?

Facts are stupid things.

—Ronald Reagan, 1988 Republican Convention

I N THE END, he told us the truth. Let's face it, facts *are* limited, tedious, stupid things. Facts affront the imagination. You don't have to tell Steven Spielberg that documentaries don't gross a hundred million bucks. Fantasies are box office—or were.

Jimmy Carter had promised never to lie to us—his mistake, even worse than walking home from his own inauguration. The upheavals of the past 25 years—the Bay of Pigs, the Kennedy assassinations, Vietnam, Watergate, the CIA revelations, our humiliation at the woggy hands of OPEC sheiks and Iranian mullahs, the black and sexual revolutions, the end of economic growth, the burden of history, the blah-blah-blahs—had surely blistered the paint and dulled the chrome on the American dream machine. Why should anyone want the facts? Shared fantasies are what hold a people together, provide their brightest symbols and most cherished assumptions.

And, with all due respect to George Bush's speechwriters, Ronald Reagan was the man who "lived the Dream." Departed warriors may dwell in Valhalla but Reagan was the first president to descend from our native heaven, Fantasy Central. He lived and loved in the utopia of mass entertainment; its heroes and villains, handkerchief scenes and happy endings, props and costumes, thrills and bromides. Trademarks and sell lines were his stock in trade. There's no need to rehearse the Reagan resume; suffice to say that he did everything from protect top secret "inertia projectors" and romance Shirley Temple to pitch in the majors and command a submarine, before settling down to become a TV personality and corporate spokesman.

In the sine qua non of American telepolitics, he was the best-trained candidate who ever lived. As lifelong media junkies, we were the best prepped audience he ever had. Even as Reagan changed the rules of the game, his will be one tough act to follow.

It is precisely because Reagan was himself a text that he became as much a master of intertextuality as any movie brat—quoting lines from *The State of the Union,* reliving scenes from *Wing and a Prayer.* Who can blame him for inadvertently calling his dog "Lassie" (reporters were watching) or telling Shimon Peres that his Culver City-based film corps had liberated a concentration camp or screening *Moscow Does Not Believe in Tears* before meeting Gorbachev (who was briefed to ask him about *Kings Row*). Even his post-assassination ripostes were quotations: "Honey, I forgot to duck," he told Nancy just as Jack Dempsey had quipped to his wife after losing to Gene Tunney in 1926. Faced with death, he thought of the epitaph on W. C. Fields's tombstone: "All in all, I'd rather be in Philadelphia." The Dream was all of a piece. Perhaps it is misleading to say that Reagan emerged from mass entertainment. Let us say he materialized—a magic bubble shimmering around him—like the good witch in *The Wizard of Oz.*

Ronald Reagan had been the mater of ceremonies for the televised opening of Disneyland in 1955. Twenty-five years later, in the tradition of Hugh Hefner, Walt Disney, and Howard Hughes—hell, in the tradition of America itself—Reagan created his own Magic Kingdom: an enchanted realm without poverty and racism, ozone depletion or dead dolphins. The Third World was a picturesque backdrop and your American Express card was always welcome. "Visiting Reaganland is very much like taking children to Disneyland, where they can deal with a New Orleans cut to their measure," wrote Gary Wills. "It is a safe past, with no sharp edges to stumble against." Mediated by the media, that past became a present—a perfect remake; Reagan led us not *Back to the Future* but rather backing into the future, eyes on some imaginary Golden Age.

These were the good old days, come around once more. It was as that poet of simulation, Jean Baudrillard, wrote of Peter Bogdanovich's early nostalgia film, *The Last Picture Show*: "You need only be sufficiently distracted, as I was, to see it as a 1950s original production: a good film of manners and the ambience of small town America, etc. A slight suspicion: it was a little too good, better adjusted, better than the others, without the sentimental, moral, and psychological tics of the films of that period. Astonishment at the discovery that it is a 1970s film, perfectly nostalgic, brand new, retouched, a hyperrealist restitution of that period." Like some supernatural suburban patriarch or benign TV impresario, Reagan conjured up the themes and creatures of the '50s—anticommunist paranoia, science fiction weaponry, conspicuous consumption—and let us experience them again as if in some spectacular sound and light show, as fantasy, as entertainment, at one step removed.

Because Reagain never left the Dreamtime, he truly understood the power of Rambo and Dirty Harry, the importance of watching network TV and being able to drop the name of Vanna White. The right stuff could move him to tears. He embodied the power of denial. He was our Teflon smile button. Facts *are* stupid things, and Reagan's conviction was such that it began to shape reality—as if in obedience to the drama of his narrative, the media began to fold back on itself. Beginning with John Hinckley's providential assassination attempt, Reagan's reign was a succession of tawdry spectaculars. Effacing popular memory of the 1982 recession, his first term brought *E.T.,* The Downing of KAL 007, The Conquest of Grenada, and the climactic road show "New Morning in America." Somewhat rockier, Reagan II included a few media events beyond administration control: Bitburg was quickly succeeded by *Rambo,* Bombing Qaddafi, and the Statue of Liberty Show; Iran-Contra subsumed by Ollie-mania (itself a debased remake of *Mr. Smith Goes to Washington*) and erased with the Moscow Summit.

If the theme of Reagan I was the menace of the Evil Empire, the theme of Reagan II, developed in collaboration with Mikhail Gorbachev, was *Friendly Persuasion,* if not *Butch Cassidy and the Sundance Kid*—the two movies that seemed most on the presidential mind during the ultimate summit. And then, from early 1983 on, there was the overarching dream of Star Wars—a fantasy so poignantly regressive and mind-boggling in its cost that it made the Pharaohs' tombs seem hovels for the homeless. Star Wars was the supreme metaphor: defense by mirrors, security through special effects. It was Reagan's visionary attempt to extend the magic bubble to include everyone—even, he would claim while debating Walter Mondale, those pesky Russians.

Four years ago, after an election in which only a few recalcitrant minorities seemed able to resist the spectacle of a 73-year-old ex-actor waxing nostalgic for God, neighborliness, the nuclear family, strong leadership, the work ethic, and Main Street, I wondered if Reagan was the greatest American who ever lived or

only the most American. Especially since—as everyone knew—he himself seldom attended church, rarely gave to charity, was divorced by his first wife,
communicated badly with his children (and indeed, everyone else if there was no
script), failed to control his own staff, kept banker's hours, hung out with a
passel of corrupt billionaires, and had fled the small town for the fleshpots of
California at the first opportunity.

It's been said that a great star resolves two conflicting images. Thus Marilyn
Monroe embodied sex and innocence, and Elvis Presley seemed simultaneously
black and white. John Wayne appeared at once brutal and chivalrous. Madonna
(like Shirley Temple before her) shows us hard work as constant play. But what
do you call a berouged creature of the consumer culture who endorses the old-
time Puritan religion as enthusiastically as he once promoted Chesterfields or
General Electric? Is there a term for a radical Social Darwinist who rejects the
Theory of Evolution? A president who smashes the New Deal coalition in the
name of Franklin Roosevelt? Bruce Springsteen registers as both Democrat and
Republican, but our Ronald incorporates so many contradictions we couldn't
even begin to list them.

2. One-eyed jacks

Democracy is no longer lived, but is increasingly represented.
>   —Timothy Lukes (after Guy Debord), "Televisual Democracy
>   and the Politics of Charisma"

American politics is the most refined of vicarious thrills. Our presidential
election is the World Series, the network sweeps, Oscar night, *Wheel of Fortune,*
Nintendo, and the Superbowl rolled, commercials and all, into one endless orgy
of navel-gazing and self-congratulation. The process creates a vortex of attention—the whole planet is watching the American electorate watch and define
itself in the fun-house mirror of public opinion. It's fun. It's us. It's America. We
should have known that Big Brother would arrive as a flag-waving Bozo the
Clown.

With the controlled spontaneity of Reaganmania, the 1984 campaign
played presidential politics as blockbuster entertainment—a parade of larger-
than-life symbols and titillating fantasies, snappy buzzwords and phantom
opponents. The most concrete analysis was delivered by one Dan Luch, a 28-
year-old engineer, described in *The New York Times* as "one of the young urban
professionals that the Democrats courted in the primaries with promises of new
ideas." Reagan, Luch explained in a kind of dreamlike free-association, is "a
man who, when he says something, sticks to his guns. It's a John Wayne type of
thing, you know, the Cavalry. . . . I have to say Mondale's just not as forceful. At
work the guys stick to Reagan primarily because they see the race as women
versus men, with Reagan standing for the values of the men." (But not just men:
It's more than appropriate that, in the weeks preceding Reagan's second inaugu-

ration, the nation's number one hit record was Madonna's "Like a Virgin"—at once prurient and puritanical, a song whose ideal video would present the singer dressed as the Statue of Liberty leading a motley chorus of yuppies and steelworkers, fundamentalists and bankers, all wearing smile buttons and brandishing big sticks, as she addresses her words toward a giant telescreen image of our President.)

We "wandered through the wilderness" and he made us "feel all shiny and new." It was too tacky to be true, too much fun to ignore. The spectacle was made to be televised and watched, if at all, with a willing suspension of disbelief, and then shaken off the morning after the election, the way a dogged rationalist might dismiss a puzzling dream or assert as meaningless the idiot sitcom that had only just before held him spellbound. It might work twice but not, perhaps, precisely the same way.

Thus, Reagan's first legacy was the 1988 campaign or rather, the 1988 metacampaign—a triumph of formalism in which the coverage (or spin) given the events easily overshadowed the events themselves. Now the media not only treated the campaign as a production, a succession of photo opportunities, a continually moving movie set, it also described it as such. But where was their star? Compared to him, the candidates were hopeless dwarfs and wimps. As virtually their first assignment both Bush and Dukakis—or rather their ectoplasmic forms—had to prove themselves "presidential." Both were Reagan disciples (as were key supporting players Jesse Jackson and Mikhail Gorbachev).

But, despite the shamelessly Reaganesque spectacle of the Democratic convention, Dukakis was a rank amateur. The Duke intentionally left his positions vague, put the emphasis on his personality, and sought parallels between himself and John F. Kennedy—not fully realizing that Reagan, with his cost-free strategy of national greatness, had coopted Kennedy long ago.

With this pathetic attempt at voodoo Reaganism, Dukakis was unable to define himself. "Bush must present a new master plan that will resolve the accumulated contradictions and keep the essence of Reaganism," Andrew Kopkind wrote in *The Nation* last August. No problem, dude. If it ain't broke . . . After an initial fake left, "Bush" ran a rerun of 1984, stressing the emotional issues of crime, drugs, gun control, abortion, the environment, and patriotism against a carefully selected succession of backdrops. A theme was determined, floated, and played until its legs gave out. First the pledge, then the furlough . . .

The 1984 campaign had been no less choreographed, but "Bush" was, of course, far cruder than the model. Trained by Reagan's '84 debate coach Roger Ailes, and working from a script, the docile vice-president managed to learn the John Wayne trick of speaking slowly and using his jaw to work key phrases, breaking a sentence if necessary to pause for applause. The endless repetition of toughness—"I am not going to let him get away with that"—ultimately gave "Bush" a patina of toughness. The continual Pavlovian deployment of the flag gave him the familiarity of a trademark. (Similarly, although Quayle was hopefully floated as a new Robert Redford, his main purpose was to make

"Bush" look paternal by comparison.) Meanwhile, his handlers assured sympathetic pundits that the candidate's bark was the worst of his soundbite. A man's gotta do what a man's gotta do—whatever it takes . . .

Could "Bush" fill Reagan's shoes as national symbolmaker? Could he be "the heart, the soul, the conscience of America"? The electorate recognized the script, but the man played good cop/bad cop so clumsily that his handlers finally decided to explain their strategy in the press. *The New York Times* dutifully reported that "Mr. Bush's image-makers—Mr. Ailes, Mr. Atwater and James A. Baker 3d, the campaign chairman—blended a Clint Eastwood image and dialogue with Mr. Bush's conventional Ivy League personality, producing a quiet guy with a steel core, willing to do and say what it takes to win the election. At the same time Peggy Noonan, Mr. Bush's speechwriter, analyzed his personality and wrote speeches playing to what she called the candidate's 'Gary Cooper' side—an appealing individualist, a man who may be occasionally bumbling and inarticulate."

As early as September 10 (or as late as four years after 1984 established the outer limits of teledemocratic hoopla), *The Washington Post* declared, "Bush Gaining in Battle of TV Images." Why not? He was merely recirculating the ones that had worked so well for his boss. By the time the *Times* had cautiously pronounced "The Medium is the Election," *Time* magazine featured not one, but two metacampaign covers: "Battle of the Handlers" and "1988, You're No 1960: Myth, Memory and the Politics of Personality." Of course, given *Time*'s credulous handling of 1984, this was something like the brain trying to look at the brain. Media self-analysis is now part of the act.

Accordingly, both the Republican and Democratic advertising strategies were given unprecedented formalist analysis. (Ironically, the Dukakis spot that attempted to go to the electronic interpersonal by attacking his opponent's packaging came in for the greatest criticism. Players play, commentators comment: show biz rules.) Thus Quayle was explained in terms of *The Candidate*, "Bush" ran against Dennis Hopper by boasting he helped to change America from a society that flocked to *Easy Rider* to one that exalted *Dirty Harry*, and Dukakis revealed more about himself than intended by praising *The Seduction of Joe Tynan*—a movie about the corruption of power in which liberal senator Alan Alda is undone by his extramarital affair with the charming labor lawyer Meryl Streep.

No wonder the first hero who popped into George Bush's mind was the subject of the movie *Stand and Deliver*. On the eve of the final debate, with Bush out campaigning alongside Chuck Norris (as he had, that week, appeared with tough guys Arnold Schwarzenegger, Tom Selleck, and Charlton Heston), the *Times*'s "Campaign Trail" turned to show biz in four out of four items: In the first, it was remarked that Lloyd Bentsen's "You're no Jack Kennedy" line had made him a "star." In the second, James Baker III was compared to Claude Rains in *Casablanca*. The third reiterated the vice-president's appropriation of the song "Don't Worry Be Happy," the last—a plant—had the "new" Dukakis emerging as "the Milton Berle of American politics."

Faux pas, that last one. Truly, Dukakis's discomfort in the Dreamworld never failed to astonish. His habitual expression was of Mr. Before in some antediluvian antacid commercial. Even so, one minute into the second debate, CNN newsman Bernard Shaw made the Duke a fantastic present—asking the governor if he would still oppose the death penalty if his wife, Kitty, were raped and murdered. Providentially, Shaw gave Dukakis the opportunity to play Charles Bronson in *Death Wish*. With one question he did more for Dukakis than any of his handlers. He created a scenario and offered the candidate an image. The Duke had only to live up to his nickname, to accept the role of a tough, little ethnic—imagine himself the liberal college professor savage enough (in his fantasies and ours) to go on a revengeful murder spree after his family is butchered—and be president.

The whole world was watching. Who was Dukakis, really? Or rather, who was Dukakis fakely? Could he be tough and tender, twinkly and bellicose, like our reigning poster boy and Great White Father? Dukakis's inability to distinguish his death wish from ours was as conclusive as Gary Hart's fatal attraction. For the first time, the networks and newsweeklies declared the utterly forgettable "Bush" the winner.

3. Happy trails

Politics is just like show business. You need a big opening. Then you coast for a while. Then you need a big finish.

–Ronald Reagan, 1966

For want of a scenario, George Bush won the privilege of playing Herbert Hoover to Reagan's Calvin Coolidge. As late as October 1986, polls showed that Reagan was considered the greatest president since FDR. But the drug was wearing off. The Daniloff swap, the Reykjavik confusion, the loss of the Senate, the Iran-Contra revelations, the partial erasure of *Rambo* by *Platoon* precipitated a 23 per cent drop in the President's approval rating, the steepest fall in modern times. Why then this tacit agreement to let him ride into the sunset, to have his happy ending—something that hasn't been granted a president in 28 years?

Just as Disneyland brought cartoons to life, Reaganland transformed America into its own ideal image—America as theme park and TV spectacular. Reaganland enables us to see and appreciate America as a symbolic representation. Where once we had the western, now there is only this. Reagan lives in Reaganland and sincerely believes in its values. We're the visitors who pretend to believe—so long as the Muzak is playing, the crowd control works, and the robots run.

There is a sense in which the Vietnam War was a massive public relations stunt, designed to convince the rest of the world of American might and resolve. Reaganism was a further refinement—predicated on the needs of a superpower to create images that will convince *itself* that it is the greatest power on earth. It is the power of positive thinking, the faith that allows Roger Rabbit to dash off a cliff and jog on thin air, and it worked, at least in the short run. The stock market crashes, yet the confidence game goes on. A biblical seven years of borrowing transform the United States from the world's leading creditor to the world's greatest debtor, and no one looks down.

As the 1988 campaign swung into its final stages, Reagan's popularity rose and voters were reported increasingly optimistic about the state of the nation. "He Isn't Running, but He's Winning," *The New York Times* noted the day after Dukakis self-destructed in the second debate. For lack of anything else, Reagan saw the election as a referendum on himself. Introduced at a Texas rodeo as "the grandest cowboy of them all," he told the crowd that "what you are really choosing is more than a slate of candidates, it's a vision of America, a dream we share." Reaganland is dead, long live Reaganland! Give Ron his Oscar!

Reagan isn't just our movie, we are his: "America, the movie." It's *Who Framed Roger Rabbit?* and we're Bob Hoskins in Toontown—real people wandering around a delirious mental landscape of special effects, feel-good fantasies, militarist spectacles, endless remakes. It's expensive—productive assets sold off to underwrite the personal consumption that keeps jobs intact, profits high, and the fantasy going—but who would have imagined that the spectacle of decay would be so mesmerizing? Pollution makes for the best sunsets. As America declines, its myth grows more potent, its self-absorption increasingly hypnotic.

Hooray for Hollywood. Live the Dream. Reagan reminded us that we are the movie the whole world watches. Is our industrial machine running on empty? Has the economy gone over a cliff? The Japanese will always need us to supply software for their VCRs.

Index